THE LAST FORTY YEARS can be called the 'age of development'. In its name, the South has struggled to catch up with the North, experts descended on villages near and far, and millions of people were turned into wage earners and consumers.

But 'development' has been much more than a socio-economic endeavour. It is a perception which models reality, a myth which comforts societies and a fantasy which unleashes passion. This book explores 'development' as a particular worldview.

In this pioneering collection, some of the world's most eminent critics of development review the key concepts of the development discourse in the post-war era. Each essay examines one concept from a historical and anthropological point of view and highlights its particular bias. Exposing their historical obsolescence and intellectual sterility, the authors call for a bidding farewell to the whole Eurocentric development idea. This is urgently needed, they argue, in order to liberate people's minds – in both North and South – for bold responses to the environmental and ethical challenges now confronting humanity.

These essays are an invitation to experts, grassroots movements and students of development to recognise the tainted glasses they put on whenever they participate in the development discourse. Each essay is followed by an annotated bibliography to encourage further studies in the cultural history of the development idea.

Also edited by Wolfgang Sachs:

GLOBAL ECOLOGY
A New Arena of Political Conflict

'In his seminal DEVELOPMENT DICTIONARY, Wolfgang Sachs and his colleagues convincingly showed that economic development was the problem rather than the solution. Now, in his equally seminal GLOBAL ECOLOGY, Sachs and his colleagues show us that it is only at the local grassroots level, rather than at the global level, that the sustainable society we are all talking about can be brought into being.'

– EDWARD GOLDSMITH, *THE ECOLOGIST*

THE DEVELOPMENT DICTIONARY

A Guide to Knowledge as Power

EDITED BY

WOLFGANG SACHS

Witwatersrand University Press

Johannesburg

Zed Books Ltd

London & New Jersey

The Development Dictionary was first published by
Zed Books Ltd, 7 Cynthia Street, London N1 9JF, UK,
and 165 First Avenue, Atlantic Highlands,
New Jersey 07716, USA, in 1992.

Third impression, 1993

This edition is published in southern Africa by
Witwatersrand University Press, P.O. Wits,
Johannesburg 2050, South Africa.

Cover designed by Andrew Corbett.
Typeset by EMS Photosetters, Thorpe Bay, Essex.
Printed and bound in the United Kingdom
by Biddles Ltd, Guildford and King's Lynn.

A catalogue record for this book is
available from the British Library

US CIP data is available from
the Library of Congress

ISBN 1 85649 043 2 Hb
ISBN 1 85649 044 0 Pb

In southern Africa
ISBN 1 86814 249 3

Contents

Introduction

Wolfgang Sachs

The last 40 years can be called the age of development. This epoch is coming to an end. The time is ripe to write its obituary.

Like a towering lighthouse guiding sailors towards the coast, 'development' stood as *the* idea which oriented emerging nations in their journey through post-war history. No matter whether democracies or dictatorships, the countries of the South proclaimed development as their primary aspiration, after they had been freed from colonial subordination. Four decades later, governments and citizens alike still have their eyes fixed on this light flashing just as far away as ever: every effort and every sacrifice is justified in reaching the goal, but the light keeps on receding into the dark.

The lighthouse of development was erected right after the Second World War. Following the breakdown of the European colonial powers, the United States found an opportunity to give worldwide dimensions to the mission their founding fathers had bequeathed to them: to be the 'beacon on the hill'. They launched the idea of development with a call to every nation to follow in their footsteps. Since then, the relations between North and South have been cast in this mould: 'development' provided the fundamental frame of reference for that mixture of generosity, bribery and oppression which has characterized the policies toward the South. For almost half a century, good neighbourliness on the planet was conceived in the light of 'development'.

Today, the lighthouse shows cracks and is starting to crumble. The idea of development stands like a ruin in the intellectual landscape. Delusion and disappointment, failures and crimes have been the steady companions of development and they tell a common story: it did not work. Moreover, the historical conditions which catapulted the idea into prominence have vanished: development has become outdated. But above all, the hopes and desires which made the idea fly, are now exhausted: development has grown obsolete.

Nevertheless, the ruin stands there and still dominates the scenery like a landmark. Though doubts are mounting and uneasiness is widely felt, development talk still pervades not only official declarations but even the language of grassroots movements. It is time to dismantle this mental structure. The authors of this book consciously bid farewell to the defunct idea in order to clear our minds for fresh discoveries.

Over the years, piles of technical reports have been accumulated which show that development does not work; stacks of political studies have proven that development is unjust. The authors of this book deal neither with development as technical performance nor with development as class conflict, but with development as a particular cast of mind. For development is much more than just a socio-economic endeavour; it is a perception which models reality, a myth which comforts societies, and a fantasy which unleashes passions. Perceptions, myths and fantasies, however, rise and fall independent of empirical results and rational conclusions; they appear and vanish, not because they are proven right or wrong, but rather because they are pregnant with promise or become irrelevant. This book offers a critical inventory of development credos, their history and implications, in order to expose in the harsh glare of sunlight their perceptual bias, their historical inadequacy, and their imaginative sterility. It calls for apostasy from the faith in development in order to liberate the imagination for bold responses to the challenges humanity is facing before the turn of the millennium.

We propose to call the age of development that particular historical period which began on 20 January, 1949, when Harry S. Truman for the first time declared, in his inauguration speech, the Southern hemisphere as 'under-developed areas'. The label stuck and subsequently provided the cognitive base for both arrogant interventionism from the North and pathetic self-pity in the South. However, what is born at a certain point in time, can die again at a later point; the age of development is on the decline because its four founding premises have been outdated by history.

First of all, it was a matter of course for Truman that the United States — along with other industrialized nations — were at the top of the social evolutionary scale. Today, this premise of superiority has been fully and finally shattered by the ecological predicament. Granted the US may still feel it is running ahead of the other countries, but it is clear now that the race is leading towards an abyss. For more than a century, technology carried the promise of redeeming the human condition from sweat, toil and tears. Today, especially in the rich countries, it is everbody's best kept secret that this hope is nothing other than a flight of fancy.

After all, with the fruits of industrialism still scarcely distributed, we now consume in one year what it took the earth a million years to store up. Furthermore, much of the glorious productivity is fed by the gigantic through-put of fossil energy; on the one side, the earth is being excavated and permanently scarred, while on the other a continuous rain of harmful substances drizzles down — or filters up into the atmosphere. If all countries 'successfully' followed the industrial example, five or six planets would be needed to serve as mines and waste dumps. It is thus obvious that the 'advanced' societies are no model; rather they are most likely to be seen in the end as an aberration in the course of history. The arrow of progress is broken and the future has lost its brightness: what it holds in store are more threats than promises. How can one believe in development, if the sense of orientation has withered away?

Secondly, Truman launched the idea of development in order to provide a comforting vision of a world order where the US would naturally rank first. The rising influence of the Soviet Union — the first country which had industrialized outside of capitalism — forced him to come up with a vision that would engage the loyalty of the decolonizing countries in order to sustain his struggle against communism. For over 40 years, development has been a weapon in the competition between political systems. Now that the East–West confrontation has come to a halt, Truman's project of global development is bound to lose ideological steam and to remain without political fuel. And as the world becomes polycentric, the scrapyard of history now awaits the category 'Third World' to be dumped, a category invented by the French in the early 1950s in order to designate the embattled territory between the two superpowers.

Nevertheless, new, albeit belated, calls for development may multiply, as the East–West division gets absorbed into the rich–poor division. In this light, however, the entire project fundamentally changes its character: prevention replaces progress as the objective of development; the redistribution of risk rather than the redistribution of wealth now dominates the international agenda. Development specialists shrug their shoulders about the long promised industrial paradise, but rush to ward off the flood of immigrants, to contain regional wars, to undercut illicit trade, and to contain environmental disasters. They are still busy identifying deficits and filling gaps, but Truman's promise of development has been turned upside down.

Thirdly, development has changed the face of the earth, but not in the way it had intended. Truman's project now appears as a blunder of planetary proportions. In 1960, the Northern countries were 20 times richer than the Southern, in 1980 46 times. Is it an exaggeration to say that the illusion of 'catching up' rivals on a world scale Montezuma's deadly illusion of receiving Cortez with open arms? Of course, most Southern countries stepped on the gas, but the North outpaced them by far. The reason is simple: in this kind of race, the rich countries will always move faster than the rest, for they are geared towards a continuous degradation of what they have to put forth: the most advanced technology. They are world champions in competitive obsolescence.

Social polarization prevails within countries as well; the stories about falling real income, misery and desperation are all too familiar. The campaign to turn traditional man into modern man has failed. The old ways have been smashed, the new ways are not viable. People are caught in the deadlock of development: the peasant who is dependent on buying seeds, yet finds no cash to do so; the mother who benefits neither from the care of her fellow women in the community nor from the assistance of a hospital; the clerk who had made it in the city, but is now laid off as a result of cost-cutting measures. They are all like refugees who have been rejected and have no place to go. Shunned by the 'advanced' sector and cut off from the old ways, they are expatriates in their own country; they are forced to get by in the no-man's-land between tradition and modernity.

Fourthly, suspicion grows that development was a misconceived enterprise from the beginning. Indeed, it is not the failure of development which has to be feared, but its success. What would a completely developed world look like? We don't know, but most certainly it would be both boring and fraught with danger. For development cannot be separated from the idea that all peoples of the planet are moving along one single track towards some state of maturity, exemplified by the nations 'running in front'. In this view, Tuaregs, Zapotecos or Rajasthanis are not seen as living diverse and non-comparable ways of human existence, but as somehow lacking in terms of what has been achieved by the advanced countries. Consequently, catching up was declared to be their historical task. From the start, development's hidden agenda was nothing else than the Westernization of the world.

The result has been a tremendous loss of diversity. The worldwide simplification of architecture, clothing, and daily objects assaults the eye; the accompanying eclipse of variegated languages, customs and gestures is already less visible; and the standardization of desires and dreams occurs deep down in the subconscious of societies. Market, state, and science have been the great universalizing powers; admen, experts and educators have relentlessly expanded their reign. Of course, as in Montezuma's time, conquerors have often been warmly welcomed, only to unveil their victory. The mental space in which people dream and act is largely occupied today by Western imagery. The vast furrows of cultural monoculture left behind are, as in all monocultures, both barren and dangerous. They have eliminated the innumerable varieties of being human and have turned the world into a place deprived of adventure and surprise; the 'Other' has vanished with development. Moreover, the spreading monoculture has eroded viable alternatives to the industrial, growth-oriented society and dangerously crippled humankind's capacity to meet an increasingly different future with creative responses. The last 40 years have considerably impoverished the potential for cultural evolution. It is only a slight exaggeration to say that whatever potential for cultural evolution remains is there in spite of development.

Four decades after Truman's invention of underdevelopment, the historical conditions which had given rise to the developmental perspective have largely disappeared. By now development has become an amoeba-like concept, shapeless but ineradicable. Its contours are so blurred that it denotes nothing — while it spreads everywhere because it connotes the best of intentions. The term is hailed by the IMF and the Vatican alike, by revolutionaries carrying their guns as well as field experts carrying their Samsonites. Though development has no content, it does possess one function: it allows any intervention to be sanctified in the name of a higher goal. Therefore even enemies feel united under the same banner. The term creates a common ground, a ground on which right and left, elites and grassroots fight their battles.

It is our intention, as the authors of this book, to clear out of the way this self-defeating development discourse. On the one hand, we hope to disable the development professional by tearing apart the conceptual foundations of his routines; on the other hand, we would like to challenge those involved in grassroots initiatives to clarify their perspectives by discarding the crippling development talk towards which they are now leaning. Our essays on the central concepts in the development discourse intend to expose some of the unconscious structures that set boundaries on the thinking of our epoch. We believe that any imaginative effort to conceive a post-developmental era will have to overcome these constraints.

The development discourse is made up of a web of key concepts. It is impossible to talk about development without referring to concepts such as poverty, production, the notion of the state, or equality. These concepts first rose to prominence during modern Western history and only then have they been projected on the rest of the world. Each of them crystallizes a set of tacit assumptions which reinforce the Occidental worldview. Development has so pervasively spread these assumptions that people everywhere have been caught up in a Western perception of reality. Knowledge, however, wields power by directing people's attention; it carves out and highlights a certain reality, casting into oblivion other ways of relating to the world around us. At a time when development has evidently failed as a socio-economic endeavour, it has become of paramount importance to liberate ourselves from its dominion over our minds. This book is an invitation to re-view the developmental model of reality and to recognize that we all wear not merely tinted, but tainted, glasses if we take part in the prevailing development discourse.

To facilitate this intellectual review, each chapter will dip into the archaeology of the key concept under examination and call attention to its ethnocentric and even violent nature. The chapters identify the shifting role each concept has played in the debate on development over the last 40 years. They demonstrate how each concept filters perception, highlighting certain aspects of reality while excluding others, and they show how this bias is rooted in particular civilizational attitudes adopted during the course of European history. Finally, each chapter attempts to open a window on to other, and different, ways of looking at the world and to get a glimpse of the riches and blessings which survive in non-Western cultures in spite of development. Each chapter will be of worth if, after reading it, experts and citizens alike have to blush, stutter or burst out laughing when they dare to mouth the old word.

This book, it must be said, is the fruit of friendship. Above all, it is our gift to one another. Over the years, all of us authors, in various contexts and associations, have been involved in a continuous conversation, spending days or weeks together chatting, cooking, travelling, studying and celebrating. We shared our uncertainties and championed our convictions; we lived through confusion and hit upon sudden insights; we challenged our idiosyncrasies and enjoyed inspiration. Slowly and sometimes inadvertently, a common frame of reference emerged and informed, in turn, our individual work. De-professionalized intellectuals, this is our experience, derive life from friendship and common commitment; otherwise, how could non-academic research be sustained? In our case, this would not have been possible without the personal and intellectual magnetism of Ivan Illich, in particular, who brought a number of us together and animated our thinking throughout the years. In the fall of 1988, sitting on the porch of Barbara Duden's wooden house at State College in Pennsylvania, we drew up the plan for this book after an intense week of debate interrupted by cutting onions and uncorking bottles.

I would like to thank Christoph Baker and Don Reneau for their help with translations. I gratefully acknowledge the institutional support of the Science, Technology and Society Programme at the Pennsylvania State University, where we convened several consultations, and of the Institute for Cultural Studies in Essen, Germany, where I carried out the editorial work.

Development

Gustavo Esteva

To say 'yes', to approve, to accept, the Brazilians say 'no' — *pois nao*. But no one gets confused. By culturally rooting their speech, by playing with the words to make them speak in their contexts, the Brazilians enrich their conversation.

In saying 'development', however, most people are now saying the opposite of what they want to convey. Everyone gets confused. By using uncritically such a loaded word, and one doomed to extinction, they are transforming its agony into a chronic condition. From the unburied corpse of development, every kind of pest has started to spread. The time has come to unveil the secret of development and see it in all its conceptual starkness.

The Invention of Underdevelopment

At the end of World War II, the United States was a formidable and incessant productive machine, unprecedented in history. It was indisputedly at the centre of the world. It was the master. All the institutions created in those years recognized that fact: even the United Nations Charter echoed the United States Constitution.

But the Americans wanted something more. They needed to make entirely explicit their new position in the world. And they wanted to consolidate that hegemony and make it permanent. For these purposes, they conceived a political campaign on a global scale that clearly bore their seal. They even conceived an appropriate emblem to identify the campaign. And they carefully chose the opportunity to launch both — January 20, 1949. That very day, the day on which President Truman took office, a new era was opened for the world — the era of development.

> We must embark [President Truman said] on a bold new program for making the benefits of our scientific advances and industrial progress available for the improvement and growth of underdeveloped areas.
>
> The old imperialism — exploitation for foreign profit — has no place in our plans. What we envisage is a program of development based on the concepts of democratic fair dealing.[1]

By using for the first time in such context the word, 'underdeveloped', Truman changed the meaning of development and created the emblem, a euphemism, used ever since to allude either discreetly or inadvertently to the era of American hegemony.

Never before had a word been universally accepted on the very day of its political coinage. A new perception of one's own self, and of the other, was suddenly created. Two hundred years of social construction of the historical-political meaning of the term, development, were successfully usurped and transmogrified. A political and philosophical proposition of Marx, packaged

American-style as a struggle against communism and at the service of the hegemonic design of the United States, succeeded in permeating both the popular and intellectual mind for the rest of the century.

Underdevelopment began, then, on January 20, 1949. On that day, two billion people became underdeveloped. In a real sense, from that time on, they ceased being what they were, in all their diversity, and were transmogrified into an inverted mirror of others' reality: a mirror that belittles them and sends them off to the end of the queue, a mirror that defines their identity, which is really that of a heterogeneous and diverse majority, simply in the terms of a homogenizing and narrow minority.

Truman was not the first to use the word. Wilfred Benson, a former member of the Secretariat of the International Labour Organization, was probably the person who invented it when he referred to the 'underdeveloped areas' while writing on the economic basis for peace in 1942.[2] But the expression found no further echo, neither with the public nor with the experts. Two years later, Rosenstein-Rodan continued to speak of 'economically backward areas'. Arthur Lewis, also in 1944, referred to the gap between the rich and the poor nations. Throughout the decade, the expression appeared occasionally in technical books or United Nations documents. But it only acquired relevance when Truman presented it as the emblem of his own policy. In this context, it took on an unsuspected colonizing virulence.

Since then, development has connoted at least one thing: to escape from the undignified condition called underdevelopment. When Nyerere proposed that development be the political mobilization of a people for attaining their own objectives, conscious as he was that it was madness to pursue the goals that others had set; when Rodolfo Stavenhagen proposes today ethnodevelopment or development with self-confidence, conscious that we need to 'look within' and 'search for one's own culture' instead of using borrowed and foreign views; when Jimoh Omo-Fadaka suggests a development from the bottom up, conscious that all strategies based on a top-down design have failed to reach their explicitly stated objectives; when Orlando Fals Borda and Anisur Rahman insist on participatory development, conscious of the exclusions made in the name of development; when Jun Nishikawa proposes an 'other' development for Japan, conscious that the current era is ending; when they and so many others qualify development and use the word with caveats and restrictions as if they were walking in a minefield, they do not seem to see the counter-productivity of their efforts. The minefield has already exploded.

In order for someone to conceive the possibility of escaping from a particular condition, it is necessary first to feel that one has fallen into that condition. For those who make up two-thirds of the world's population today, to think of development — of any kind of development — requires first the perception of themselves as underdeveloped, with the whole burden of connotations that this carries.

Today, for two-thirds of the peoples of the world, underdevelopment is a threat that has already been carried out; a life experience of subordination and of being led astray, of discrimination and subjugation. Given that precondition, the simple fact of associating with development one's own intention tends to annul the intention, to contradict it, to ensl e it. It impedes thinking of one's own objectives, as Nyerere wanted; it unde nes confidence in oneself and one's own culture, as Stavenhagen demands; it clamours for management from the top down, against which Jinoh rebelled; it converts participation into a manipulative trick to involve people in struggles for getting what the powerful want to impose on them, which was precisely what Fals Borda and Rahman wanted to avoid.

A Metaphor and its Contorted History

Development occupies the centre of an incredibly powerful semantic constellation. There is nothing in modern mentality comparable to it as a force guiding thought and behaviour. At the same time, very few words are as feeble, as fragile and as incapable of giving substance and meaning to thought and behaviour as this one.

In common parlance, development describes a process through which the potentialities of an object or organism are released, until it reaches its natural, complete, full-fledged form. Hence the metaphoric use of the term to explain the natural growth of plants and animals. Through this metaphor, it became possible to show the goal of development and, much later, its programme. The development or evolution of living beings, in biology, referred to the process through which organisms achieved their genetic potential: the natural form of the being pre-seen by the biologist. Development was frustrated whenever the plant or the animal failed to fulfil its genetic programme, or substituted for it another. In such cases of failure, its growth was not development but rather an anomaly: pathological, and even anti-natural behaviour. The study of these 'monsters' became critical for the formulation of the first biological theories.

It was between 1759 (Wolff) and 1859 (Darwin) that development evolved from a conception of transformation that moves toward the *appropriate* form of being to a conception of transformation that moves towards an *ever more perfect* form. During this period, evolution and development began to be used as interchangeable terms by scientists.

The transfer of the biological metaphor to the social sphere occurred in the last quarter of the 18th century. Justus Moser, the conservative founder of social history, from 1768 used the word *Entwicklung* to allude to the gradual process of social change. When he talked about the transformation of some political situations, he described them almost as natural processes. In 1774, Herder started to publish his interpretation of universal history, in which he presented global correlations by comparing the ages of life with social history. But he went beyond this comparison, applying to his elaborations the organological notion of development coined in the scientific discussions of his time. He frequently used the image of the germ to describe the development of organizational forms. By the end of the century, based on the biological scale of Bonnet, he tried to combine the theory of nature with the philosophy of history in an attempt to create a systematic and consistent unity. Historical development was the continuation of natural development, according to him; and both were just variants of the homogeneous development of the cosmos, created by God.

Towards 1800, *Entwicklung* began to appear as a reflexive verb. Self-development became fashionable. God, then, started to disappear in the popular conception of the universe. And a few decades later, all possibilities were opened to the human subject, author of his own development, emancipated from the divine design. Development became the central category of Marx's work: revealed as a historical process that unfolds with the same necessary character of natural laws. Both the Hegelian concept of history and the Darwinist concept of evolution were interwoven in development, reinforced with the scientific aura of Marx.

When the metaphor returned to the vernacular, it acquired a violent colonizing power, soon employed by the politicians. It converted history into a programme: a necessary and inevitable destiny. The industrial mode of production, which was no more than one, among many, forms of social life, became the definition of the terminal stage of a unilinear way of social evolution. This stage came to be seen as the natural culmination of the potentials already existing in neolithic man, as his logical evolution. Thus history was reformulated in Western terms.

The metaphor of development gave global hegemony to a purely Western genealogy of history, robbing peoples of different cultures of the opportunity to define the forms of their social life. The vernacular sequence (development is possible after envelopment) was inverted with the transfer. Scientific laws took the place of God in the enveloping function, defining the programme. Marx rescued a feasible initiative, based on the knowledge of those laws. Truman took over this perception, but transferred the role of prime mover — the *primum movens* condition — from the communists and the proletariat to the experts and to capital (thus, ironically, following the precedents set by Lenin and Stalin).

The debris of metaphors used throughout the 18th century began to become part of ordinary language in the 19th century, with the word 'development', accumulating in it a whole variety of connotations. This overload of meanings ended up dissolving its precise significance.

The *Encyclopedia of All Systems of Teaching and Education* was published in Germany in 1860. Its entry on 'development' indicated that 'this concept is applied to almost all that man has and knows.' The word, said Eucken in 1878, 'has become almost useless for science, except in certain areas.'

Between 1875 and 1900 there were published, in English, books whose titles alluded to the *development* of the Athenian constitution, the English novel, the transportation system in the United States, marriage, parenting and so on. Some authors preferred 'evolution' in the title of their books studying the thermometer or the idea of God. Others preferred 'growth' in the title, but even they used development in the text as the principal operative term.[3]

By the beginning of the 20th century, a new use of the term became widespread. 'Urban development' has stood, since then, for a specific manner of reformulation of urban surroundings, based on the bulldozer and the massive, homogeneous industrial production of urban spaces and specialized installations. But this specific use, an anticipation of Trumanism, did not succeed in establishing the generalized image that is now associated with the word.

In the third decade of the century, the association between development and colonialism, established a century ago, acquired a different meaning. When the British government transformed its Law of Development of the Colonies into the Law of Development *and Welfare* of the Colonies in 1939, this reflected the profound economic and political mutation produced in less than a decade. To give the philosophy of the colonial protectorate a positive meaning, the British argued for the need to guarantee the natives minimum levels of nutrition, health and education.[4] A 'dual mandate' started to be sketched: the conqueror should be capable of economically developing the conquered region and at the same time accepting the responsibility of caring for the well-being of the natives. After the identification of the level of civilization with the level of production, the dual mandate collapsed into one: development.[5]

Throughout the century, the meanings associated with urban development and colonial development concurred with many others to transform the word 'development', step by step, into one with contours that are about as precise as those of an amoeba. It is now a mere algorithm whose significance depends on the context in which it is employed. It may allude to a housing project, to the logical sequence of a thought, to the awakening of a child's mind, to a chess game or to the budding of a teenager's breasts. But even though it lacks, on its own, any precise denotation, it is firmly seated in popular and intellectual perception. And it always appears as an evocation of a net of significances in which the person who uses it is irremediably trapped.

Development cannot delink itself from the words with which it was formed — growth, evolution, maturation. Just the same, those who now use the word cannot free themselves from a web of meanings that impart a specific blindness to their language, thought and action. No matter the context in which it is used, or the precise connotation that the person using it wants to give it, the expression becomes qualified and coloured by meanings perhaps unwanted. The word always implies a favourable change, a step from the simple to the complex, from the inferior to the superior, from worse to better. The word indicates that one is doing well because one is advancing in the sense of a necessary, ineluctable, universal law and toward a desirable goal. The word retains to this day the meaning given to it a century ago by the creator of ecology, Haeckel: 'Development is, from this moment on, the magic word with which we will solve all the mysteries that surround us or, at least, that which will guide us toward their solution.'

But for two-thirds of the people on earth, this positive meaning of the word 'development' — profoundly rooted after two centuries of its social construction — is a reminder of *what they are not*. It is a reminder of an undesirable, undignified condition. To escape from it, they need to be enslaved to others' experiences and dreams.

Colonizing Anti-Colonialism

In the grandiose design of Truman's speech, there was no room for technical or theoretical precision. The emblem defines a programme conscious of Mao's arrival, looking for evolution as an antidote for revolution (in the Herder tradition) while simultaneously adopting the revolutionary impetus with which Marx endowed the word. The Truman design sometimes uses development in the transitive sense of the British colonial administrators, in order to clearly establish the hierarchy of initiatives that it promotes. But it can also pass without difficulty to the intransitive use of the term, in the finest Hegelian tradition.

As it was taken for granted that underdevelopment itself was out there, that it was something real, 'explanations' of the phenomenon began to appear. An intense search for its material and historical causes immediately started. Some, like Hirschman, gave no importance to the gestation period. Others, on the contrary, made this aspect the central element of their elaborations and described in painstaking detail colonial exploitation in all its variations and the processes of primitive accumulation of capital. Pragmatic attention also began to be given to the internal or external factors that seemed to be the current cause of underdevelopment: terms of trade, unequal exchange, dependency, protectionism, imperfections of the market, corruption, lack of democracy or entrepreneurship . . .

In Latin America, the Peace Corps, the Point Four Program, the War on Poverty, and the Alliance for Progress contributed to root the notion of underdevelopment into popular perception and to deepen the disability created by such perception. But none of those campaigns are comparable to what was achieved, in the same sense, by Latin American dependency theorists and other leftist intellectuals dedicated to criticizing all and every one of the development strategies that the North Americans successively put into fashion.

For them, as for many others, Truman simply had substituted a new word for what had already been there: backwardness or poverty. According to them, the 'backward' or 'poor' countries were in that condition due to past lootings in the process of colonization and the continued raping by capitalist exploitation at the national and international level: underdevelopment was the creation of development. By adopting in an uncritical manner the view to which they meant to be opposed, their efficient criticism of the ambiguity and hypocrisy of the Western promoters of development gave a virulent character to the colonizing force of the metaphor. (How to ignore, Marx said once, 'the indubitable fact that India is bound to the English yoke precisely by an Indian army supported by India?').

The very discussion of the origin or current causes of underdevelopment illustrates to what extent it is admitted to be something real, concrete, quantifiable and identifiable: a phenomenon whose origin and modalities can be the subject of investigation. The word defines a perception. This becomes, in turn, an object, a fact. No one seems to doubt that the concept does not allude to real phenomena. They do not realize that it is a comparative adjective whose base of support is the assumption, very Western but unacceptable and undemonstrable, of the oneness, homogeneity and linear evolution of the world. It displays a falsification of reality produced through dismembering the totality of interconnected processes that make up the world's reality and, in its place, it substitutes one of its fragments, isolated from the rest, as a general point of reference.[6]

Conceptual Inflation

Development, which had suffered the most dramatic and grotesque metamorphosis of its history in Truman's hands, was impoverished even more in the hands of its first promoters, who reduced it to *economic growth*. For these men, development consisted simply of growth in the income per person in economically underdeveloped areas. It was the goal proposed by Lewis in 1944 and insinuated by the United Nations Charter in 1947.

Lewis' 1955 dictum 'First it should be noted that our subject matter is growth, and not distribution',[7] reflects the mainstream emphasis on economic growth which permeated the whole field of development thinking. Paul Baran, by far the most influential development economist among the leftists, wrote in 1957 on the political economy of *growth* and defined growth *or* development as the increase in the per capita production of material goods.[8] Walter Rostow, who had a very impressive impact on institutional thinking and the public, presented his 'non-communist manifesto' in 1960 as a description of the stages of economic growth, assuming that this single variable can characterize a whole society.[9] Both of them were, of course, dealing with a lot more than short-sighted economic growth, but their emphasis reflected the spirit of the times . . . and the crux of the matter.[10]

Such an orientation was neither an underestimation of the social consequences of rapid economic growth nor neglect of social realities. The first *Report on the World Social Situation*, published in 1952, aroused unusual interest both inside and outside United Nations institutions. The Report concentrated on the description of 'existing social conditions' and only incidentally dealt with programmes to improve them. But the proponents of such programmes found in it inspiration and support for their concern with immediate measures for the relief of poverty. Like many others, they were trying to develop in the 'underdeveloped' countries the basic social services and the 'caring professions' found in the advanced countries. These pragmatic concerns, as well as early theoretical insights going beyond the dogmatic vision of economic quantifiers, were, however, overshadowed by the general obsession with all-out industrialization and GNP growth which dominated the 1950s. Optimism prevailed; according to statistical indices and official reports, both the social situation and social programmes of these countries were continually improving. Such progress, following conventional wisdom, was but the natural consequence of rapid GNP growth.

The endemic controversy between the economic quantifiers and the social service specialists was not eliminated by such evolution. The *Reports* on the social situation, prepared periodically by the UN, tangentially documented it. The expression 'social development', slowly introduced in the *Reports*, appeared without definition, as a vague counterpart for 'economic development' and as a substitute for the static notion of the 'social situation'. The 'social' and the 'economic' were perceived as distinct realities. The idea of a kind of 'balance' between these 'aspects' became first a desideratum and later the object of systematic examination. The Economic and Social Council of the United Nations (Ecosoc) in 1962 recommended the integration of both aspects of development. That same year, the *Proposals for Action* of the First UN Development Decade (1960–70) established that:

> The problem of the underdeveloped countries is not just growth, but development. . . . Development is growth plus change, [it added]. Change, in turn, is social and cultural as well as economic, and qualitative as well as quantitative. . . . The key concept must be improved quality of people's life.[11]

The creation of the United Nations Research Institute for Social Development (Unrisd), in 1963, was in itself an illustration of the concerns of the period. Another Ecosoc resolution, in 1966, recognized the interdependence of economic and social factors and the need for harmonizing economic and social planning.

In spite of this gradual change, throughout the First UN Development Decade development continued to be perceived as a definable path of economic growth passing through various stages, and 'integration' was the watchword linking the social aspect to the economic aspect. In the 1960s, as Unrisd acknowledged later, social development 'was seen partly as a precondition for economic growth and partly as a moral justification for it and the sacrifices it implied'.[12]

At the end of the decade, however, many factors contributed to dampen the optimism about economic growth: the shortcomings of current policies and processes were more conspicuous than at the beginning of the decade; the attributes demanding integration had widened; and it became clear that rapid growth had been accompanied by increasing inequalities. By then, the economists were more inclined to acknowledge social aspects as 'social obstacles'. Standard evidence permeated the official bodies:

> The fact that development either leaves behind, or in some ways even creates, large areas of poverty, stagnation, marginality and actual exclusion from social and economic progress is too obvious and too urgent to be overlooked.[13]

Conceptually, there was a generalized revolt against the straitjacket of economic definitions of development, constraining its goals to more or less irrelevant quantitative indicators. The question was clearly posed in 1970 by Robert S. McNamara, president of the World Bank. After recognizing that a high rate of growth did not bring satisfactory progress in development during the First Decade, he insisted that the 1970s should see more than gross measures of economic growth.[14] But the 'dethronement of GNP', as this crusade was then called, did not go very far: no international or academic consensus around any other definition was possible.

While the First Decade considered the social and economic aspects of development separately, the Second Decade involved merging the two. A new paradigm had to be formulated, that of integration, after recognizing the necessary interaction of physical resources, technical processes, economic aspects and social change. The International Development Strategy, proclaimed on 24 October 1970 called for a *global* strategy, based on joint and concentrated action in all spheres of economic and social life. The turning point, however, was not in the Strategy but in an almost simultaneous UN resolution establishing a project for the identification of a *unified approach* to development and planning, 'which would fully integrate the economic and social components in the formulation of policies and programmes'. This would include components designed:

(a) To leave no sector of the population outside the scope of change and development;

(b) To effect structural change which favours national development and to activate all sectors of the population to participate in the development process;

(c) To aim at social equity, including the achievement of an equitable distribution of income and wealth in the nation;

(d) to give high priority to the development of human potentials . . . the provision of employment opportunities and meeting the needs of children.[15]

The quest for a unified approach to development analysis and planning thus began which looked simultaneously for cross-sectoral and spatial, or regional, integration and for 'participative development'. As a UN endeavour, it was a very short-lived and frustrating project. Its results were both controversial and disappointing. Its critique of prevailing ideas and methods of economic development encountered considerable resistance. And its failure to produce simple universal remedies doomed it to rapid extinction. But the project incubated most of the ideas and slogans and animated the development debate during the years that followed.

The Second Decade, which started with this concern for a unified approach, evolved in fact in the opposite direction: dispersion. 'Major problems', like environment, population, hunger, women, habitat or employment, were successively brought to the forefront. Every 'problem' followed for a time an independent career, concentrating both public and institutional attention. Later, the complex relation of each 'problem' with all the others was demonstrated and the pertinent exercise of unification started, with one of the 'problems' at the centre of the process. The key candidates for unification were constantly in dispute, arising from the old controversy over priorities and the day-to-day disputes among bureaucratic bodies for survival and allocation of resources.

The quest for a unifying principle continued on different terrain. In 1974 the Declaration of Cocoyoc emphasized that the purpose of development 'should not be to develop things, but to develop man'. 'Any process of growth,' it added, 'that does not lead to the fulfilment [of basic needs] — or, even worse, disrupts them — is a travesty of the idea of development.' The Declaration also emphasized the need for diversity and 'for pursuing many different roads to development', as well as the goal of self-reliance and the requirement of 'fundamental economic, social and political changes'.[16] Some of these ideas were expanded in the proposals of the Dag Hammarskjold Foundation, which suggested, in 1975, *another development*,[17] and specially in the search for *human-centred development*. Following Johan Galtung, for whom development has to be 'the development of a people', the experts judged that man should have a greater influence in the development process and that this should be, as Unesco insisted, *integrated development*: 'a total, multi-relational process that includes all aspects of the life of a collectivity, of its relations with the outside world and of its own consciousness'.[18]

In 1975, the Seventh Special Session of the United Nations General Assembly asked for an approach more effective than that of the International Development Strategy (adopted in 1970) for achieving social objectives of development. The Conference on Employment, Income Distribution and Social Progress, organized by the ILO in June 1976, offered an answer: the *Basic Needs Approach*, 'aiming at the achievement of a certain specific minimum standard of living before the end of the century'.[19]

One of the documents supporting the Approach explicitly recognized that development would not eliminate hunger and misery, and that, on the contrary, it would surely worsen the levels of 'absolute poverty' of a fifth, and probably of two-fifths, of the population. The Approach proposed the idea of dealing directly with the task of coping with those needs, instead of expecting their satisfaction as a result of the process of development. For two or three years the proposal became fashionable. The World Bank found it particularly attractive since it appeared as the natural sequel to its experiments with 'target groups', which it had started in 1973 when its development strategy was concentrated on the rural poor and small farmers. The Approach was also promoted by many governments and the experts. It possessed the virtue of offering 'universal applicability', while being at the same time relative enough to be 'country specific'. In 1976, the satisfaction of the basic needs of each country's population defined the first and central portion of the Programme of Action of the Tripartite World Conference on Employment, Income Distribution and Social Progress and the International Division of Labour.

The experts of Unesco, for their part, promoted the concept of *endogenous development*. For some time, this conception won more acceptance than all the others. It seemed clearly heretical, openly contradicting the conventional wisdom. Emerging from a rigorous critique of the hypothesis of development 'in stages' (Rostow), the thesis of endogenous development rejected the necessity or possibility — let alone suitability — of mechanically imitating industrial societies. Instead, it proposed taking due account of the particularities of each nation. Little acknowledged, however, was the fact that this sensible consideration leads to a dead-end in the very theory and practice of development, that it contains a contradiction in terms. If the impulse is truly endogenous, that is, if the initiatives really come out of the diverse cultures and their different systems of values, nothing would lead us to believe that from these would necessarily arise development — no matter how it is defined — or even an impulse leading in that direction. If properly followed, this conception leads to the dissolution of the very notion of development, after realizing the impossibility of imposing a single cultural model on the whole world — as a conference of Unesco experts pertinently recognized in 1978.

The next decade, the 1980s, was called 'the lost decade for development'. In spite of the fireworks of the four Asian Tigers, pessimism prevailed. The 'adjustment process' meant for many countries abandoning or dismantling, in the name of development, most of the previous achievements. By 1985, a post-development age seemed to be in the offing.[20]

The 1990s, by contrast, have given birth to a new development ethos. This follows two clearly distinguishable lines. In the North, it calls for *redevelopment*, i.e. to develop again what was maldeveloped or is now obsolete. In the United States and the Soviet Union, in Spain as in Switzerland, Austria, Poland or Britain, public attention is drawn by the speed and the conditions under which what was previously developed (socialized medicine, nuclear plants, steel production, pre-microchip manufacturing, polluting factories or poisonous pesticides) may be destroyed, dismantled, exported or substituted.

In the South, redevelopment also requires dismantling what was left by the 'adjustment process' of the '80s, in order to make room for the leftovers from the North (atomic waste, obsolete or polluting manufacturing plants, unsellable or prohibited commodities . . .) and for the *maquiladoras*, those fragmented and temporary pseudo-factories that the North will keep in operation during the transitional period. The obsession with competitiveness, for fear of being left out of the race, compels acceptance of the destruction of whole sections of what was 'developed' over the last 30 years. Sacrificed on the altar of redevelopment, these will instead be inserted in transnational designs consistent with world market demand.

In the South, however, the emphasis of redevelopment will not be on such ventures, existing in the form of technological and socio-political enclaves. Rather, redevelopment implies the economic colonization of the so-called informal sector. In the name of modernization and under the banner of the war on poverty — pitting as always the waged against the poor, not a war against poverty itself — redeveloping the South involves launching the last and definitive assault against organized resistance to development and the economy.

Conceptually and politically, redevelopment is now taking the shape of *sustainable development*, for 'our common future', as prescribed by the Brundtland Commission. Or else, it is being actively promoted as green and democratic redevelopment, for those assuming that the struggle against communism, the leitmotiv of Truman's speech, is over. But in its mainstream interpretation, sustainable development has been explicitly conceived as a strategy for sustaining 'development', not for supporting the flourishing and enduring of an infinitely diverse natural and social life.

The current decade has also given birth to a new bureaucratic exercise to give development another lease of life. The United Nations Development Programme (UNDP) published in 1990 the first *Human Development Report*.[21]

This clearly follows in the steps of the economic quantifiers, while paying appropriate consideration to Unrisd's efforts for measurement and analysis of socio-economic development and to the tradition of the *Reports* on the world social situation.

Following this new Report, 'human development' is rendered a process and a level of achievement. As a process, it is 'the enlargement of relevant human choices'. As a level of achievement, it is 'the internationally compared extent to which, in given societies, those relevant choices are actually attained'. The authors of the Report found very expedient ways to overcome the traditional challenges of quantification and international comparisons, as well as the conceptual puzzles of their endeavour. Human development is presented by them through an 'internationally comparative level of deprivation', which determines how far from the most successful national case are the other countries. The most ambitious goal of the Report is to produce a Human Development Index, 'synthesizing, along a numerical scale, the global level of Human Development in 130 countries'. The method: combining life expectancy deprivation, adult literacy deprivation and real GNP per capita deprivation. The Report also includes analysis of the social conditions existing in these countries for the period 1960–88, after gathering the data for a wide collection of variables and a series of projections, presenting 'viable social targets' to be achieved by the year 2000.

Adopting the yardstick of GNP per capita in real dollar terms is not without courage! The authors of the Report thought that expectancy of a long life, together with full literacy, are not enough to give a human being reasonable room for choice if he is at the same time deprived of access to resources for the satisfaction of his material needs. But measuring the latter is plagued with difficulties; the Report acknowledged them and opted for a simple solution — a technical refinement of the good old, universal yardstick, GNP.

Expanding the Reign of Scarcity

During the 19th century, but in fact starting much earlier in Europe, the social construction of development was married to a political design: excising from society and culture an autonomous sphere, the economic sphere, and installing it at the centre of politics and ethics. That brutal and violent transformation, first completed in Europe, was always associated with colonial domination in the rest of the world. Economization and colonization were synonymous. What Truman succeeded in doing was freeing the economic sphere from the negative connotations it had accumulated for two centuries, delinking development from colonialism. No more of the 'old imperialism', said Truman. In retrospect, it is possible to see that the emphasis on economic growth of the first post-Truman developers was neither a detour nor a mistaken interpretation of the Truman proposal: rather, it was the expression of its very essence.

As a conceptual construction, economics strives to subordinate to its rule and to subsume under its logic every other form of social interaction in every society it invades. As a political design, adopted by some as their own, economic history is a story of conquest and domination. Far from being the idyllic evolution pictured by the founding fathers of economics, the emergence of economic society is a story of violence and destruction often adopting a genocidal character. Little wonder, resistance appeared everywhere.

Establishing economic value requires the disvaluing of all other forms of social existence.[22] Disvalue transmogrifies skills into lacks, commons into resources, men and women into commodified labour, tradition into burden, wisdom into ignorance, autonomy into dependency. It transmogrifies people's autonomous activities embodying wants, skills, hopes and interactions with one another, and with the environment, into needs whose satisfaction requires the mediation of the market.

The helpless individual, whose survival now becomes necessarily dependent on the market, was not the invention of the economists; neither was he born with Adam and Eve, as they contend. He was a historical creation. He was created by the economic project redesigning mankind. The transmogrification of autonomous men and women into disvalued 'economic man' was in fact the precondition for the emergence of economic society, a condition that must be constantly renewed, reconfirmed and deepened for economic rule to continue. Disvalue is the secret of economic value, and it cannot be created except with violence and in the face of continuous resistance.

Economics recognizes no limits to its application. This contention is predicated on the assumption that no society is free from the 'economic problem', as economists call their definition of social reality. At the same time, they proudly acknowledge that their discipline, as a science, was an invention. They love to trace its roots back to antiquity, using Aristotle and his worries about value as a case in point. But they see those ancient insights as mere initial intimations heralding the advent of the patron saints of the science, those who discovered economy in the 18th century.

Economists, of course, did not invent the new patterns of behaviour emerging with economic society through the creation of the modern market. But the founding fathers of the discipline were able to codify their observations in a form that fitted well with the ambitions of the emerging interests: they offered a 'scientific' foundation to the political design of the new dominant class. When that form was 'received' as truth by the public and absorbed into common language, it was able to transform popular perceptions from within by changing the meaning of previously existing words and assumptions.

The founding fathers of economics saw in *scarcity* the keystone for their theoretical construction. The finding marked the discipline forever. The whole construction of economics stands on the premise of scarcity, postulated as a universal condition of social life. Economists were even able to transform the finding into a popular prejudice, a self-evident truism for everyone. 'Common sense' is now so immersed in the economic way of thinking that no facts of life contradicting it seems enough to provoke critical reflection on its character.

Scarcity connotes shortage, rarity, restriction, want, insufficiency, even frugality. Since all these connotations alluding to conditions appearing everywhere and at all times are now mixed up with the economic denotations of the word, as a *terminus technicus*, the popular prejudice about the universality of economics, with its premise of scarcity, is constantly reinforced.

Little understood is the fact that the 'law of scarcity' formulated by economists and now appearing in every textbook does not allude directly to the common situations denoted by the word. The sudden shortage of fresh air during a fire is not scarcity of air in the economic sense. Neither is the self-imposed frugality of a monk, the insufficiency of stamina in a boxer, the rarity of a flower, or the last reserves of wheat mentioned by Pharaoh in what is the first known historical reference to hunger.

The 'law of scarcity' was construed by economists to denote the technical assumption that man's wants are great, not to say infinite, whereas his means are limited though improvable. The assumption implies choices over the allocation of means (resources). This 'fact' defines the 'economic problem' *par excellence*, whose 'solution' is proposed by economists through the market or the plan. Popular perception, especially in the Northern parts of the world, even shares this technical meaning of the word scarcity, assuming it to be a self-evident truism. But it is precisely the universality of this assumption that is no longer tenable.

A few years before Truman's speech, just at the end of the War, Karl Polanyi published *The Great Transformation*.[23] Convinced that economic determinism was a 19th century phenomenon, that the market system violently distorted our views of man and society, and that these distorted views were proving one of the main obstacles to the solution of the problems of our civilization,[24] Polanyi carefully documented the economic history of Europe as the history of the creation of the economy as an autonomous sphere, disjoined from the rest of the society. He showed that the national market did not appear as the gradual and spontaneous emancipation of the economic sphere from governmental control, but quite the opposite: the market was the result of a conscious and often violent intervention by government. In the years that followed, Polanyi laid down the foundations for comparative economic history.

After him, many others have followed this road, retracing economic history as merely one chapter in the history of ideas. Louis Dumont, among others, has shown that the discovery of the economy through the invention of economics was, in fact, a process of the social construction of ideas and concepts.[25] The economic 'laws' of the classical economists were but deductive inventions which transformed the newly observed patterns of social behaviour, adopted with the emergence of economic society, into universal axioms designed to carry on a new political project. The assumption of the previous existence of economic 'laws' or 'facts', construed by economists, is untenable when confronted with what we know now about ancient societies and cultures, and even with what we can still see in some parts of the world.

Marshall Sahlins and Pierre Clastres, among others, have given detailed and well documented accounts of cultures in which non-economic assumptions govern lives and which reject the assumption of scarcity whenever it appears among them.[26] Men and women seen today on the margins of the economic world, the so-called marginals, find support in that tradition as they continue to challenge economic assumptions both in theory and in practice. All over the world, descriptions of a whole new set of experiences of those peoples are trying to find a place in the shelves of the libraries, but they do not fit in well with any of the social classifications tainted by the economists' lenses.

New Commons

Struggling to limit the economic sphere is not, for the common man at the margins or the majority of people on earth, a mechanical reaction to the economic invasion of their lives. They are not Luddites. Rather they see their resistance as a creative reconstitution of the basic forms of social interaction, in order to liberate themselves from their economic chains. They have thus created, in their neighbourhoods, villages and *barrios*, new commons which allow them to live on their own terms.

In these new commons, there are forms of social interaction that have appeared only in the post-war era. Still the people in these new spaces are the heirs of a diversified collection of commons, communities and even whole cultures destroyed by the industrial, economic form of social interaction. After the extinction of their subsistence regimes, they tried to adopt various patterns of accommodation to the industrial form. The failure of both industrial society and the remnants of traditional forms of interaction to effect this accommodation was the precondition of the social inventions whose consolidation and flourishing has been further stimulated by the so-called crisis of development.

For people on the margins, disengaging from the economic logic of the market or the plan has become the very condition for survival. They are forced to confine their economic interaction — for some, very frequent and intense — to realms outside the spaces where they organize their own modes of living. Those spaces were their last refuge during the development era. After experiencing what survival means in economic society, they are now counting the blessings they find in such refuges, while working actively to regenerate them.

By equating education with diplomas, following the economic definition of learning, they lacked teachers and schools. Now, after re-embedding learning in culture, they have the affluence of constantly enriching their knowledge with a little help from friends bringing to them experiences and remedies from outside their tradition.

After equating health with dependence on medical services, they lacked doctors, health centres, hospitals, drugs. Now, after recognizing health again as the autonomous ability to cope with the environment, they are regenerating their own healing capability, benefiting from the traditional wisdom of their healers and from the richness of the curative capacity of their environments. This, too, with a little help from their friends, when something beyond their reach or their traditional realm requires external help.

After equating eating with the technical activities of production and consumption, linked to the mediation of the market or the state, they lacked income and suffered scarcity of food. Now, they are regenerating and enriching their relationships with themselves and with the environment, nourishing again both their lives and their lands. And they are usually coping well with the shortages still affecting them — as a consequence of the time and effort required to remedy the damage done by development or their temporary inability to escape from the damaging economic interactions they still have to maintain. It is not easy, for example, to step out of commercial crops or give up the addiction to credit or industrial inputs; but intercropping helps regenerate both land and culture, in time providing an improvement in nutrition.

Peasants and grassroots groups in the cities are now sharing with people forced to leave the economic centre the ten thousand tricks they have learned to limit the economy, to mock the economic creed, or to refunctionalize and reformulate modern technology. The 'crisis' of the 1980s removed from the payroll people already educated in dependency on incomes and the market, people lacking the social setting enabling them to survive by themselves. Now the margins are coping with the difficult task of relocating these people. The process poses great challenges and tensions for everyone, but it also offers a creative opportunity for regeneration, once they discover how mutually supportive they can be for one another.

The basic logic of human interactions inside the new commons prevents scarcity from appearing in them. People do not assume unlimited ends, since their ends are no more than the other side of their means, their direct expression. If their means are limited, as they are, their ends cannot be unlimited. Within the new commons, needs are defined with verbs that describe activities embodying wants, skills and interactions with others and with the environment. Needs are not separated into different 'spheres' of reality: lacks or expectations on one side, and satisfiers on the other, reunited through the market or the plan.

One of the most interesting facets of the ongoing regeneration in the new commons being created by ordinary men and women is precisely the recovery of their own definition of needs, dismantled by development in perception or in practice. By strengthening forms of interaction embedded in the social fabric and by breaking the economic principle of the exchange of equivalents, they are recovering their autonomous ways of living. By reinstalling or regenerating forms of trade operating outside the rules of the market or the plan, they are both enriching their daily lives and limiting the impact and scope of the commercial operations they still have to maintain, and also reducing the commodification of their time and the fruits of their effort.

The leading actor of the economy, economic man, finds no feasible answers for coping with the 'crisis' of development, and frequently reacts with desolation, exhaustion, even desperation. He constantly falls for the political game of demands and promises, or the economic game of carpetbagging the present for the future, hopes for expectations. In contrast, the leading actor of the new commons, the common man, dissolves or prevents scarcity in his imaginative efforts to cope with his predicament. He looks for no more than free spaces or limited support for his initiatives. He can mix them in political coalitions increasingly capable of reorienting policies and changing political styles. Supported by recent experiences, the new awareness emerging from the margins can awaken others, broadening those coalitions towards the critical point in which an inversion of the economic dominance begins to be feasible.

The economy of economists is nothing but a set of rules by which modern societies are governed. Men and societies are not economic, even after having created institutions and forms of interaction of an economic nature, even after having instituted the economy. And those economic rules are derived from the chronic scarcity of modern society. Rather than being the iron law of every human society, scarcity is a historical accident: it had a beginning and can have an end. The time has come for its end. Now is the time of the margins, of the common man.

In spite of the economy, common men on the margins have been able to keep alive another logic, another set of rules. In contrast with the economy, this logic is embedded in the social fabric. The time has come to confine the economy to its proper place: a marginal one. As the margins have done.

The Call

This essay is an invitation to celebrate and a call for political action.

It celebrates the appearance of new commons, creatively opened by common men and women after the failure of the developers' strategies to transform traditional men and women into economic men. These new commons are living proof of the ability and ingenuity of common people to react with sociological imagination, following their own path, within hostile environments.

This essay is also a plea. It pleads, first of all, for political controls to protect those new commons and to offer common men a more favourable social context for their activities and innovations. Such political controls can be implemented only after public awareness of the limits of development has become firmly rooted in society. Even those still convinced that development goals are pertinent ideals for the so-called underdeveloped should honestly recognize the present structural impossibilities for the universal materialization of such goals. The cynicism of those who, knowing such limits, continue to proclaim the myth, should be publicly exposed.

This essay requests public witness and invites public debate on the post-economic events now appearing everywhere, in order to limit the economic damage and give room for new forms of social life. It challenges the social imagination to conceive political controls that allow for the flourishing of post-economic initiatives.

This essay also pleads for research and public discussion of the issues that give content to citizens' coalitions for implementing political controls on the economic sphere, while re-embedding economic activities in the social fabric. It pleads for a new, dignified, public appraisal of the views now emerging as rumours among common men, defining limits to the economy while trying to renew politics at the grassroots level.

The new commons, created by common men, are heralding an era which ends privilege and licence. This essay celebrates the adventure of common men.

Development has evaporated. The metaphor opened up a field of knowledge and for a while gave scientists something to believe in. After some decades, it is clear that this field of knowledge is a mined, unexplorable land. Neither in nature nor in society does there exist an evolution that imposes transformation towards 'ever more perfect forms' as a law. Reality is open to surprise. Modern man has failed in his effort to be god.

To root oneself in the present demands an image of the future. It is not possible to act here and now, in the present, without having an image of the next instant, of the other, of a certain temporal horizon. That image of the future offers guidance, encouragement, orientation, hope. In exchange for culturally established images, built by concrete men and women in their local spaces, in exchange for concrete myths, truly real, modern man was offered an illusory expectation, implicit in the connotation of development and its semantic network: growth, evolution, maturation, modernization. He was also offered an image of the future that is a mere continuation of the past: that is development, a conservative, if not reactionary, myth.

It is now time to recover a sense of reality. It is time to recover serenity. Crutches, like those offered by science, are not necessary when it is possible to walk with one's own feet, on one's own path, in order to dream one's own dreams. Not the borrowed ones of development.

Notes

1. Harry S. Truman, Inaugural Address, January 20, 1949, in *Documents on American Foreign Relations*, Connecticut: Princeton University Press, 1967.

2. Wilfred Benson, 'The Economic Advancement of Underdeveloped Areas', in *The Economic Basis of Peace*, London: National Peace Council, 1942.

3. Peggy Rosenthal, *Words and Values: Some Leading Words and Where They Lead Us*, Oxford: Oxford University Press, 1984.

4. W. K. Hancock, quoted in H. W. Arendt, 'Economic Development: A Semantic History', in *Economic Development and Cultural Change*, Vol. 26, April 1981.

5. Wolfgang Sachs, 'The Archaeology of the Development Idea' *Interculture*, Vol. 23, No. 4, Fall 1990.

6. Eric Wolf, *Europe and the People Without History*, Berkeley: University of California Press, 1982.

7. W. Arthur Lewis, *The Theory of Economic Growth*, Homewood, Ill.: Richard D. Irwin, 1955.

8. Paul N. Baran, *The Political Economy of Growth*, New York: Monthly Review Press, 1957.

9. Walter W. Rostow, *The Stages of Economic Growth: A Non-Communist Manifesto*, Cambridge: Cambridge University Press, 1960.

10. Baran assumed that economic development always implied a profound transformation of the economic, social and political structures of the society, of the dominant organizations of production, distribution and consumption. But he equated both growth and development to the increase in the production per capita of material goods. Rostow recognized that modern history cannot be reduced to the limited and arbitrary classifications of stages of economic growth, but he found that such generalization may be the key for confronting the current challenges.

11. United Nations, *The UN Development Decade: Proposals for Action*, New York: UN, 1962.

12. UNRISD, *An Approach to Development Research*, Geneva: UNRISD, 1979.

13. United Nations, 'Report of the 1969 Meeting of Experts on Social Policy and Planning', in *International Social Development Review*, No. 3, 1971.

14. Robert S. McNamara, 'The True Dimension of the Task', in *International Developmen Review*, 1970, Vol. 1.

15. UNRISD, *The Quest for a Unified Approach to Development*, Geneva: UNRISD, 1980

16. The Cocoyoc Declaration was adopted by the participants in a UNEP–UNCTAC Symposium on the Pattern of Resource Use, Environment and Development, in Cocoyoc Mexico, October 1974.

17. Dag Hammarskjold Foundation, 'What Now? Another Development', a special issue o *Development Dialogue*, Uppsala: the Foundation, 1975.

18. Unesco, *Plan à moyen terme (1977–1982)*, Document 19 c'4, 1977.

19. ILO, *Employment, Growth and Basic Needs*, Geneva: ILO, 1976.

20. Gilbert Rist, *Toward Post-Development Age*, Geneva: Fondation Christophe Eckenstein 1990.

21. UNDP *Human Development Report*, directed by Mahbub ul Haq and a team of UNDF experts, New York: Oxford University Press, 1990.

22. Ivan Illich. 'El desvalor y la creación social del desecho', *Tecno-política*, Doc. 87–03.

23. Karl Polanyi, *The Great Transformation*. New York: Rinehart and Co., 1944.

24. Karl Polanyi, 'On belief in economic determinism', *Sociological Review*, Vol. xxxix Section One, 1947.

25. Louis Dumont, *From Mandeville to Marx: The Genesis and Triumph of Economi Ideology*, Chicago: University of Chicago Press, 1977.

26. Marshall Sahlins, *Stone Age Economics*, New York: Aldine, 1972 and Pierr Clastres, *La société contre l'état*, Paris: Les Editions de Minuit, 1974.

Bibliography

For the history and foundations of economic thinking, and development concepts anc theories, great dictionaries are very helpful: *OED*, of course, but also the *Great Sovie Encyclopedia*, and the German and French classic dictionaries.

Among the bibliographies, I find especially useful: Jorge García-Bouza, *A Basic Need Analytical Bibliography*, Paris: OECD Development Centre, 1980; Guy Gran, *An Annotate Guide to Global Development*, Pittsburgh: University of Pittsburgh, 1987; Elsa Assidon et al. *Economie et Sociologie du Tiers-Monde: Un guide bibliographique et documentaire*, Paris Editions L'Harmattan, 1981; Charles W. Bergquist, *Alternative Approaches to the Problem o, Development: A Selected and Annotated Bibliography*, Durham: Carolina Academic Press 1979; Guy Caire 'Bibliographie analytique et critique' in Jacques Austruy, *Le Scandale dt Developpement*, Paris: Editions Marcel Riviere, 1965. Also the selection of Gerald Meier (se below).

A. N. Agarwala and S. P. Singh, *Economics of Underdevelopment*, New York: Oxfor University Press, 1963, is a collection of 'classic' articles and essays, representing th intellectual perception in the 1950s. Those of Colin Clark, Paul Baran, Hla Myint, Arthu Lewis, Rosenstein-Rodan and H. W. Singer seem particularly interesting.

Conventional wisdom may be best traced in I. Alechina, *Contribution du systeme des Nation Unies a l'elaboration de nouvelles conceptions theoriques du developpement*, Ulan-Bator Unesco, 1980; Gerald Meier, *Leading Issues in Economic Development*, Oxford: Oxfor University Press, 1984, which includes very good bibliographical selections; Paul Isenman e al., *Poverty and Human Development: A World Bank Publication*, New York: Oxford Universit Press, 1980; and *Le developpement: ideologies et pratiques*, Paris: Orstom, 1983; as well as in th not so conventional UNRISD, *The Quest for a Unified Approach to Development*, Geneva UNRISD, 1980.

The post-Truman classics are still useful: Raúl Prebisch, 'The Economic Development c Latin America and its Principal Problems', in *Economic Bulletin for Latin America*, Vol. 7

1950; Bert F. Hoselitz, *The Progress of Underdeveloped Areas*, Chicago: University of Chicago Press, 1951; W. Arthur Lewis, *The Theory of Economic Growth*, London: Allen and Unwin, 1955; Paul Baran, *The Political Economy of Growth*, New York: Monthly Review Press, 1957; Gunnar Myrdal, *Economic Theory and Under-developed Regions*, London: Duckworth, 1957; Albert O. Hirschman, *Strategy of Economic Development*, New Haven: Yale University Press, 1958; Raymond Barre, *Le developpement economique: Analyse et politique*, Paris: ISEA, 1958; and W. W. Rostow, *The Stages of Economic Growth: A Non-Communist Manifesto*, Cambridge: Cambridge University Press, 1960.

For the debate on limits to growth, see Willem L. Otmans, ed., *On Growth: The Crisis of Exploding Population and Resource Depletion*, Utrecht: A. W. Bruna, 1973; H. V. Hodson, *The Diseconomics of Growth*, New York: Ballantine Books, 1972; Joseph Hodara and Iván Restrepo, *¿Tiene límites el crecimiento?* Mexico: Editorial El Manual Moderno, 1977; and Fred Hirsch, *Social Limits to Growth*, Cambridge: Harvard University Press, 1980.

For radical critiques: Ivan Illich, *Celebration of Awareness*, London: Calder & Boyars, 1971, and *Toward a History of Needs*, New York: Pantheon Books, 1977; Jacques Attali et al., *Le mythe du developpement*, Paris: Editions du Seuil, 1977; Gilbert Rist et al., *Il y était une fois le développement . . .*, Lausanne: Edition d'en bas, 1986; Serge Latouche, *Faut-il refuser le developpement?* Paris: PUF, 1985; T. Verhelst, *No Life Without Roots*, London: Zed Books, 1989; and Robert Vachon et al., *Alternatives au Developpement*, Montreal: Centre Interculturel Monchanin, 1988. With 'Development: Metaphor, Myth, Threat' in *Development*, 1985:3. I suggested that the future of development studies was to be found in archaeology (to explore the ruins left by development), and my 'Regenerating People's Space' in *Alternatives*, Vol. 12, 1987, pp. 125–52, highlighted social praxis after the demise of development.

For the conceptual history of development, in addition to the dictionaries, see H. W. Arendt, *The Rise and Fall of Economic Growth: A Study in Contemporary Thought*, Chicago and London: University of Chicago Press, 1978, and 'Economic Development: A Semantic History' in *Economic Development and Cultural Change*, Vol. 26, April 1981; Lord Robbins, *The Theory of Economic Development in the History of Economic Thought*, London: Macmillan St Martin's Press, 1968; G. Canguilhem et al., *Du developpement a l'evolution*, Paris: PUF, 1962; Teodor Shanin, *Late Marx and the Russian Road: Marx and 'The Peripheries of Capitalism'*, New York: Monthly Review Press, 1983; Albert Hirschman, 'The Rise and Decline of Development Economics' in *Essays in Trespassing*, Cambridge: 1981; Arturo Escobar, *Power and Visibility: The Invention and Management of Development in the Third World*, Berkeley: Ph.D. dissertation, 1987; Franz Hinkelammert, *Ideologías del desarrollo dialética de la historia*, Buenos Aires: Paidós, 1970; Enrique E. Sánchez Ruiz, *Requiem por la modernizacion: perspectivas cambiantes en estudios del desarrollo*, México: Universidad de Guadalajara, 1986; Magnus Blomstrom and Bjorn Hettne, *Development Theory in Transition*, London: Zed Books, 1984; and Wolfgang Sachs, 'The Archaeology of the Development Idea', *Interculture*, Vol. 23, No. 4, Fall 1990.

Environment

Wolfgang Sachs

Neil Armstrong's journey to the moon brought us under the spell of a new image — not of the moon but of the earth. Looking back from the Apollo spaceship on to distant earth, Armstrong shot these pictures which now adorn the cover of almost every report about the future of the planet — a small and fragile ball, shining blue against the dark of outer space, delicately covered by clouds, oceans, greenery and soils. Never before had the planet been visible to the human eye in its full shape; it was space photography which imparted a new reality to the planet by turning it into an object lying right there before our eyes. In its beauty and vulnerability, the floating globe arouses wonder and awe. For the first time it has become possible to speak of *our* planet.

But the possessive noun reveals at the same time a deep ambivalence. On the one hand, 'our' can imply participation and highlight man's dependence on an encompassing reality. On the other hand, it can imply ownership and emphasize man's vocation to master and to run this common property. Consequently, the image of 'our' planet conveys a contradictory message; it can either call for moderation or for megalomania.

The same ambivalence characterizes the career of the concept 'environment'. While it was originally advanced to put development politics under indictment, it is now raised like a banner to announce a new era of development. Indeed, after 'ignorance' and 'poverty' in previous decades, 'survival of the planet' is likely to become that well publicized emergency of the 1990s, in whose name a new frenzy of development will be unleashed. Significantly, the report of the World Commission on Environment and Development (Brundtland Report), after having evoked the image of the planet floating in space, concludes the opening paragraph by stating: 'This new reality, from which there is no escape, must be recognized — *and managed*.'[1]

Setting the Stage for the Brundtland Report

For better or worse, the vicissitudes of the international development debate follow closely the rise and fall of political sensibilities within the Northern countries. Unfettered enthusiasm for economic growth in 1945 reflected the West's desire to restart the economic machine after a devastating war, the emphasis on manpower planning echoed American fears after the shock of Sputnik in 1957, the discovery of basic needs was stimulated by President Johnson's domestic war on poverty in the 1960s, and so, too, for the concern about worldwide inequality. What development means depends on how the rich nations feel. 'Environment' is no exception to this rule.

The UN Conference on the Human Environment held in Stockholm in June 1972, the occasion on which the 'environment' arrived on the international agenda, was first proposed by Sweden, which was worred about acid rain, pollution in the Baltic, and the levels of pesticides and heavy metals in fish and birds. What could be called massive accidental internationalization cast its shadow before it: industrial wastes escape national sovereignty, they don't show up at customs posts or travel with passports. Countries discovered that they were not self-contained units, but contingent on actions taken by others. Thus a new category of problems, the 'global issues', emerged. The Stockholm Conference was the prelude to a series of large UN meetings throughout the 1970s (on population, food, human settlements, water, desertification, science and technology, renewable energy) that set out to alter the post-war perception of an open global space where many nations can individually strive to maximize economic growth. Instead a different view began to be promoted: from now on, the concept of an inter-related world system, which is seen as operating under a number of common constraints, took hold.

The cognitive furniture for this shift was provided by a particular school of thought that had gained prominence in interpreting the significance of pollution and man-made disasters. In the US during the 1960s, environmental issues forced their way into public consciousness: Los Angeles smog and the slow death of Lake Erie, oil spills and the planned flooding of the Grand Canyon led to articles on the environment in the *New York Times* skyrocketing from about 150 in 1960 to about 1,700 to 1970. Local incidents, which were increasingly seen as adding up to a larger picture, were put into a global perspective by scientists who borrowed their conceptual framework from ecosystems theory in order to interpret the predicament of a world rushing towards industrialization. Infinite growth, they maintained, is based on self-delusion, because the world is a closed space, finite and of limited carrying capacity. Perceiving global space as a system whose stability rests on the equilibrium of its components, like population, technology, resources (including food) and environment, they foresaw — echoing Malthus' early challenge to the assumption of inevitable progress — an imminent disruption of the balance between population growth (exacerbated by technology) on the one hand, and resources and environment on the other. Besides Ehrlich's *Population Bomb*[2] or *The Ecologist*'s 'Blueprint for Survival',[3] it was especially the Club of Rome's *Limits to Growth*[4] which made it seem natural to imagine the future of the globe as the result of the interaction of quantitative growth curves operating in five dimensions.

The global ecosystems approach was not without competitors; but both the biocentric and the humanist perspectives were foreign to the perceptions of the international development elite. Attributing absolute value to nature for its own sake, as environmentalists in the tradition of Thoreau, Emerson and Muir did, would have barred the way to continuing, albeit in a more sophisticated and flexible manner, the exploitation of nature. And recognizing the offences against nature as just another sign of the supremacy of technological expansion over people and their lives, as humanist authors like Mumford or Schumacher suggest, would go against the grain of development aspirations and could hardly please the guardians of the growth machine. In fact, only an interpretation which magnified rather than undermined their managerial responsibilities could raise their spirits, even in spite of dim prospects. It was the global ecosystems approach which perfectly suited their vantage point at the summits of international organizations for it proposed the global society as the unit of analysis and put the Third World, by denouncing population growth, at the centre of attention. Moreover, the model rendered intelligible what would otherwise have appeared as a messy situation by removing resource conflicts from any particular local or political context. The language of aggregate data series suggests a clearcut picture, abstract figures lend themselves to playing with scenarios, and a presumed mechanical causality among the various components creates the illusion that global strategies can be effective. And even if the ideal of growth crumbled, there was, for those who felt themselves in charge of running the world, still some objective to fall comfortably back on: stability.

However, there was still a long way to go until, in 1987, the Brundtland Report could finally announce the marriage between the craving for development and concern for the environment. As the adamant rejection of all 'no-growth' positions, in particular by Third World governments at the Stockholm Conference demonstrated, the compulsion to drive up the GNP had turned many into cheerful enemies of nature. It was only in the course of the 1970s, under the additional impact of the oil crisis, that it began to dawn on governments that continued growth not only depended on capital formation or skilled manpower but also on the long-term availability of natural resources. Worried first of all about the conservation of inputs for future growth, development planners gradually adopted what had been a strand of thought as far back as the introduction of forest management in Germany around 1800 and the American Progressive movement after 1900: that — in the words of Gifford Pinchot, the steward of Theodore Roosevelt's conservation programme — 'conservation means the greatest good for the greatest number for the longest time.' Tomorrow's growth was seen to be under the threat of nature's revenge. Consequently it was time to extend the attention span of planning and to call for the 'efficient management of natural resources' as part of the development package: 'We have in the past been concerned about the impacts of economic growth upon the environment. We are now forced,' concludes the Brundtland Report, 'to concern ourselves with the impacts of ecological stress — degradation of soils, water regimes, atmosphere, and forests — upon our economic prospects.'[5]

Another roadblock on the way to wedding 'environment' to 'development' had been an ossified vision of growth. The decades of smoke-stack industrialization had left the impression that growth was to be invariably linked to squandering ever more resources. Under the influence of the appropriate technology movement, however, this univocal notion of development began to crumble and give way to an awareness of the availability of technological choices. It was, after all, in Stockholm that NGOs (Non-Governmental Organizations) had gathered for the first time to stage a counter-conference which called for alternative paths in development. Later on, initiatives like the Declaration of Cocoyoc and 'What Now?' of the Dag Hammarskjöld Foundation helped to — perhaps unwittingly — challenge the assumption of an invariable technological process and to pluralize the roads to growth. Out of this awareness of technological flexibility grew, towards the end of the '70s, a new perception of the ecological predicament: the 'limits to growth' are no longer seen as an insurmountable barrier blocking the surge of growth, but as discrete obstacles forcing the flow to take a different route. Soft-path studies in areas from energy to health-care proliferated and charted new riverbeds for the wrongly headed stream.

Finally, environmentalism was regarded as inimical to the alleviation of poverty throughout the 1970s. The claim to be able to abolish poverty, however, has been — and still is — the single most important pretension of the development ideology, in particular after its enthronement as the official No. 1 priority after Robert McNamara's World Bank speech at Nairobi in 1973. Poverty was long regarded as unrelated to environmental degradation, which was attributed to the impact of industrial man; the world's poor entered the equation only as future claimants to an industrial lifestyle. But with spreading deforestation and desertification all over the world, the poor were quickly identified as agents of destruction and became the targets of campaigns to promote 'environmental consciousness'. Once blaming the victim had entered the professional consensus, the old recipe could also be offered for meeting the new disaster: since growth was supposed to remove poverty, the environment could only be protected through a new era of growth. As the Brundtland Report puts it: 'Poverty reduces people's capacity to use resources in a sustainable manner; it intensifies pressure on the environment. . . . A necessary but not sufficient condition for the elimination of absolute poverty is a relatively rapid rise in per capita incomes in the Third World'.[6] The way was thus cleared for the marriage between 'environment' and 'development': the newcomer could be welcomed to the old-established family.

'No development without sustainability; no sustainability without development' is the formula which establishes the newly formed bond. 'Development' emerges rejuvenated from this liaison, the ailing concept gaining another lease on life. This is nothing less than the repeat of a proven ruse: every time in the last 30 years when the destructive effects of development were recognized, the concept was stretched in such a way as to include both injury and therapy. For example, when it became obvious, around 1970, that the pursuit of development actually intensified poverty, the notion of 'equitable development' was invented so as to reconcile the irreconcilable: the creation of poverty with the abolition of poverty. In the same vein, the Brundtland Report incorporated concern for the environment into the concept of development by erecting 'sustainable development' as the conceptual roof for both violating and healing the environment.

Certainly, the new era requires development experts to widen their attention span and to monitor water and soils, air and energy utilization. But development remains what it always comes down to, an array of interventions for boosting the GNP: 'given expected population growth, a five- to ten-fold increase in world industrial output can be anticipated by the time world population stabilizes sometime in the next century'.[7] Brundtland thus ends up suggesting further growth, but not any longer, as in the old days of development, in order to achieve the happiness of the greatest number, but to contain the environmental disaster for the generations to come. The threat to the planet's survival looms large. Has there ever been a better pretence for intrusion? New areas of intervention open up, nature becomes a domain of politics, and a new breed of technocrats feels the vocation to steer growth along the edge of the abyss.

A Successful Ambivalence

Ecology is both computer modelling and political action, scientific discipline as well as all-embracing worldview. The concept joins two different worlds. On the one side, protest movements all over the globe wage their battles for the conservation of nature, appealing to evidence allegedly offered by that scientific discipline which studies the relationships between organisms and their environment. On the other side, academic ecologists have seen with bewilderment how their hypotheses have both become a reservoir for political slogans and been elevated to principles for some post-industrial philosophy. The liaison between protest and science can hardly be called a happy one. While the researchers have resented being called on to testify against the rationality of science and its benefits for humankind, activists have, ironically enough, adopted theorems like the 'balance of nature' or the 'priority of the whole over its parts' at a moment when they had already been abandoned by the discipline.

However, without recourse to science, the ecology movement would probably have remained a bunch of nature freaks and never acquired the power of a historical force. One secret of its success lies precisely in its hybrid character. As a movement highly suspicious of science and technical rationality, it plays anew the counter-melody which has accompanied the history of modernity ever since romanticism. But as a science-based movement, it is capable of questioning the foundations of modernity and contesting its logic in the very name of science. In fact, the ecology movement seems to be the first anti-modernist movement attempting to justify its claims with the enemy's own means. It resorts not only to the arts (like the romantics), to organicism (like the conservatives), to the glory of nature (like preservationists), or to a transcendental creed (like fundamentalists), although all these themes are present, but it bases its challenge on ecosystems theory which integrates physics, chemistry and biology. This unique achievement, however, cuts both ways: the science of *ecology* gives rise to a scientific anti-modernism which has succeeded largely in disrupting the dominant discourse, yet the *science* of ecology opens the way for the technocratic recuperation of the protest. It is this ambivalence of ecology which, on the epistemological level, is responsible for the success as well as the failure of the movement.

While its roots go back to 18th century natural history, ecology was successful in becoming a full-fledged discipline — with university chairs, scholarly journals and professional associations — only during the first two decades of this century. It inherited from its precursors in the 19th century a predilection for looking at the world of plants (and later animals) in terms of geographically distributed ensembles. The tundra in Canada is evidently different from the rainforest in Amazonia. Consequently, pre-ecology organized its perception of nature, following the core themes of romanticism, around the axiom that place constitutes community. From an emphasis on the impact of climatic and physical circumstances on communities, the attention shifted, around the turn of the century, to the processes within these communities. The competitive/co-operative relations between organisms in a given environment and, under the influence of Darwinism, their adaptive change through time ('succession') emerged as the new discipline's field of study. Impressed by the mutual dependency of species in biotic communities, the ecologists began to wonder just how real these units were. Is a given ensemble only the sum of individual organisms or does it express a higher identity? Up to the Second World War, the latter conception was clearly dominant: plant/animal societies were seen as super-organisms that evolve actively, adapting to the environment. In opting for organicism — the postulate that the whole is superior to its parts and an entity in its own right — the ecologists were able firmly to constitute the object of their science.

This anti-reductionist attitude was doomed after the War when, across disciplines, mechanistic conceptions of science again prevailed. Ecology was ripe for a restructuration along the lines of positivist methodology; like any other science, it was supposed to produce causal hypotheses which are empirically testable and prognostically relevant. The search for general laws, however, implies concentrating attention on a minimum of elements which are common to the overwhelming variety of settings. The appreciation of a particular place with a particular community loses importance. Moreover, these elements and their relationships have to be measurable; the quantitative analysis of mass, volume, temperature and the like replaced the qualitative interpretation of an ensemble's unity and order. Following physics, at that time the lead science, ecologists identified energy as the common denominator that links animals and plants with the non-living environment. Generally, the calorie became the unit of measurement for it permitted description of both the organic and the inorganic worlds as two aspects of the same reality — the flow of energy.

Biology in this way was reduced to energetics. But the holistic tradition of ecology did not wither away. It reappeared in a new language: 'system' replaced the concept of 'living community', and 'homoeostasis' the idea of evolution towards a 'climax'. The concept of system integrates an originally anti-modern notion, the 'whole' or the 'organism', into scientific discourse. It allows one to insist on the priority of the whole without vitalist overtones, while it acknowledges an autonomous role for the parts without, however, relinquishing the idea of a supra-individual reality. This is accomplished by interpreting the meaning of wholeness as 'homoeostasis' and the relations between the parts and the whole, in the tradition of mechanical engineering, as 'self-regulatory feedback mechanism' steadily maintaining that homeostasis. It was the concept of ecosystem that thus combined the organicist heritage with scientific reductionism. And it is this concept of ecosystem that gave to the ecology movement a quasi-spiritual dimension and scientific credibility at the same time.

Since the 1960s, ecology has left the biology departments of universities and migrated into every man's consciousness. The scientific term has turned into a worldview. And as worldview, it carries the promise of reuniting what has been fragmented, of healing what has been torn apart, in short of caring for the whole. The numerous wounds inflicted by modern, goal-specific institutions have provoked a renewed desire for wholeness, and that desire has found a suitable language in the science of ecology. The conceptual switch that connected the biology circuit with that of society at large was the notion of ecosystem. In retrospect, this comes as no surprise, since the concept is well equipped to serve this function: in scope, as well as in scale, it has an enormous power of inclusion. It unites not only plants and animals — as already the notion of 'living community' did — but also includes within its purview the non-living world on the one hand, and the world of humans on the other. Thus, any ontological difference between what once had been called the mineral kingdom, the plant and animal kingdoms, and the kingdom of man vanishes: the concept's scope is universal. Likewise, 'ecosystems' come in many sizes, big and small, nesting like babouschka dolls, each within the next, from the microscopic to the planetary level. The concept is free-ranging in scale. Omnipresent, as eco-systems appear to be, they are consequently hailed as the keys to understanding order in the world. More so, as they appear to be all-essential for the continuance of the webs of life, they call for nothing less than care and reverence. A remarkable career, indeed — a technical term that been blown into the realms of the metaphysical. For many environmentalists now, ecology seems to reveal the moral order of being by uncovering simultaneously the *verum*, *bonum*, and *pulchrum* of reality: it suggests not only the truth, but also a moral imperative and even aesthetic perfection.

On the other hand, however, ecosystems theory, based on cybernetics as the science of engineering feedback mechanisms, represents anything but a break with the ominous Western tradition of increasing control over nature. How can a theory of regulation be separated from an interest in manipulation? After all, systems theory aims at control of the second order; it strives for controlling (self-)control. As is obvious, the metaphor underlying systems thinking is the self-governing machine, i.e. a machine capable of adjusting its performance to changing conditions according to pre-set rules. Whatever the object being observed, be it a factory, a family or a lake, attention focuses on the regulating mechanisms by which the system in question responds to changes in its environment. Once identified, the way is open to condition these mechanisms so as to alter the responsiveness of the system. Today, however, the responsiveness of nature has been strained to the uttermost under the pressures of modern man. Looking at nature in terms of self-regulating systems therefore, implies either the intention to gauge nature's overload capacity or the aim of adjusting her feedback mechanisms through human intervention Both strategies amount to completing Bacon's vision of dominating nature albeit with the added pretension of manipulating her revenge. In this way ecosystem technology turns finally against ecology as worldview. A movement which bade farewell to modernity ends up welcoming her, in new guise through the backdoor.

Survival as a New *Raison d'état*

In history, many reasons have been put forward to justify state power and its claim on citizens. Classical objectives like law and order or welfare through redistribution have been invoked time and again, and, more recently, development has become the goal in the name of which many Third World governments sacrifice the vital interests of half of their populations. Today, 'survival of the planet' is well on its way to becoming the wholesale justification for a new wave of state interventions in people's lives all over the world.

The World Bank, for instance, sees a gleam of hope for itself again, after its reputation has been badly shaken by devastating criticism from environmentalists: 'I anticipate,' declared its Senior Vice-President David Hopper in 1988, 'that over the course of the next year, the Bank will be addressing the full range of environmental needs of its partner nations, needs that will run from the technical to the institutional, from the micro-details of project design to the macro-requirements of formulating, implementing and enforcing environmental policies.'[8] The voices of protest, after finally penetrating the air-conditioned offices in Washington, have called forth a rather self-defeating answer: the very demands to halt World Bank activities have provoked — their expansion!

While environmentalists have put the spotlight on the numerous vulnerabilities of nature, governments as a result discover a new conflict-ridden area in need of political governance and regulation. This time, not peace between persons is at stake, but the orderly relations between man and nature. To mediate in this conflict, the state assumes the task of gathering evidence on the state of nature and the effects of man, of enacting norms and laws to direct behaviour, and enforcing compliance with the new rules. On the one hand, the continuance of nature's capacity to render services, e.g. clean air and water or a reliable climate, has to be closely watched. On the other, society's innumerable actions have to kept under sufficient control in order to direct the exploitation of nature into tolerable channels. To carry out these formidable objectives, the state has to install the necessary institutions like monitoring systems, regulatory mechanisms and executive agencies. A new class of professionals is required to perform these tasks, while ecoscience is supposed to provide the epistemology of intervention. In short, the experts who used to look after economic growth now claim to be presiding over survival itself.

However, as is well-known, many rural communities in the Third World do not need to wait until specialists from hastily founded research institutes on sustainable agriculture swarm out to deliver their recipes against, say, soil erosion. Provision for the coming generations has been part of their tribal and peasant practices since time immemorial. What is more, the new centrally designed schemes for the 'management of environmental resources' threaten to collide with their locally based knowledge about conservation.

For example, the Indian Chipko movement has made the courage and wisdom of those women who protected the trees with their bodies against the chainsaws of the loggers a symbol of local resistance acclaimed far beyond the confines of India. Yet their success has had its price: forest managers moved in and claimed responsibility for the trees. All of a sudden the conflict took on a different colour: the hard-nosed woodcutters had given way to soft-spoken experts. They brought along surveys, showed around diagrams, pointed out growth curves, and argued over optimal felling rates. Planting schemes along with wood-processing industries were proposed, and attempts made to lure the villagers into becoming small timber producers. Those who had defended the trees to protect their means of subsistence and to bear witness to the interconnectedness of life, saw themselves unexpectedly bombarded with research findings and the abstract categories of resource economics. And throughout this new assault on them, the 'national interest' in 'balanced resource development' was invoked. It mattered little in the face of these alien priorities what significance the forest had for the villagers who lived there, or what species of tree would be most suitable for the people's sustenance. An ecology that aimed at the management of scarce natural resources clashed with an ecology that wished to preserve the local commons. In this way, national resource planning can lead to, albeit with novel means, a continuation of the war against subsistence.

Though the resource experts arrived in the name of protecting nature, their image of nature profoundly contradicts the image of nature held by the villagers. Nature, when she becomes the object of politics and planning, turns into 'environment'. It is misleading to use the two concepts interchangeably for it impedes the recognition of 'environment' as a particular construction of 'nature' specific to our epoch. Contrary to its connotations we are currently being socialized into accepting, there has rarely been a concept that represented nature in a form more abstract, passive, and void of qualities than 'environment'. Squirrels on the ground are as much a part of the environment as water in aquifers, gases in the atmosphere, marshes along the coast or even high-rise buildings in inner cities. Sticking the label 'environment' on the natural world makes all concrete qualities fade away; even more, it makes nature appear passive and lifeless, merely waiting to be acted upon. This is obviously a far cry from, for instance, the Indian villager's conception of Prakriti, the active and productive power which permeates every stone or tree, fruit or animal, and sustains them along with the human world. Prakriti grants the blessings of nature as a gift; she has consequently to be honoured and wooed.[9]

Cultures that see nature as a living being tend to carefully circumscribe the range of human intervention, because a hostile response is to be expected when a critical threshold has been passed. 'Environment' has nothing in common with this view; through the modernist eyes of such a concept, the limits imposed by nature appear merely as physical constraints on human survival. To call traditional economies 'ecological', is often to neglect that basic difference in approach.

Towards a Global Ecocracy?

In the late 1980s, concern about depleting resources and worldwide pollution reached the commanding heights of international politics. Multilateral agencies now distribute biomass converters and design forestry programmes. Economic summits quarrel about carbon dioxide emissions. And scientists launch satellites into orbit in order to check on the planet's health. But the discourse which is rising to prominence has taken on a fundamentally biased orientation: it calls for extended management, but disregards intelligent self-limitation. As the dangers mount, new products, procedures and programmes are invented to stave off the threatening effects of industrialism and keep the system afloat. Capital, bureaucracy and science — the venerable trinity of Western modernization — declare themselves indispensable in the new crisis and promise to prevent the worst through better engineering, integrated planning, and more sophisticated models. However, fuel-efficient machines, environmental risk assessment analyses, the close monitoring of natural processes and the like, well-intended as they may be, have two assumptions in common: first, that society will always be driven to test nature to her limits, and second, that the exploitation of nature should neither be maximized nor minimized, but ought to be optimized. As the 1987 report of the World Resources Institute states programmatically on its first page: 'The human race relies on the environment and therefore must manage it wisely.' Clearly, the word 'therefore' is the crux of the matter; it is relevant only if the competitive dynamic of the industrial system is taken for granted. Otherwise, the environment would not be in danger and could be left without management. Calls for securing the survival of the planet are often, upon closer inspection, nothing else than calls for the survival of the industrial system.

Capital-, bureaucracy-, and science-intensive solutions to environmental decline, in addition, are not without social costs. The Promethean task of keeping the global industrial machine running at ever increasing speed, and safeguarding at the same time the bisophere of the planet, will require a quantum leap in surveillance and regulation. How else should the myriads of decisions, from the individual to the national and the global levels, be brought into line? It is of secondary importance whether the streamlining of industrialism will be achieved, if at all, through market incentives, strict legislation, remedial programmes, sophisticated spying or outright prohibitions. What matters is that all these strategies call for more centralism, in particular for a stronger state. Since eco-crats rarely call in question the industrial model of living in order to reduce the burden on nature, they are left with the necessity of synchronizing the innumerable activities of society with all the skill, foresight and tools of advancing technology they can muster — a prospect which could have inspired Orwell to another novel. The real historical challenge, therefore, must be addressed in something other than ecocratic terms: how is it possible to build ecological societies with less government and less professional dominance?

The eco-cratic discourse which is about to unfold in the 1990s starts from the conceptual marriage of 'environment' and 'development', finds its cognitive base in eco-systems theory, and aims at new levels of administrative monitoring and control. Unwilling to reconsider the logic of competitive productivism which is at the root of the planet's ecological plight, it reduces ecology to a set of managerial strategies aiming at resource efficiency and risk management. It treats as a technical problem what in fact amounts to no less than a civilizational impasse — namely, that the level of productive performance already achieved turns out to be not viable in the North, let alone for the rest of the globe. With the rise of eco-cracy, however, the fundamental debate that is needed on issues of public morality — like how society should live, or what how much and in what way it should produce and consume — falls into oblivion. Instead, Western aspirations are implicitly taken for granted, and not only in the West but worldwide, and societies which choose not to put all their energy into production and deliberately accept a lower throughput of commodities become unthinkable. What falls by the wayside are efforts to elucidate the much broader range of futures open to societies which limit their levels of material output in order to cherish whatever ideals emerge from their cultural heritages. The ecocratic perception remains blind to diversity outside the economic society of the West.

References

1. World Commission on Environment and Development, *Our Common Future*, Oxford: Oxford University Press 1987, p. 1. Author's italics.

2. P. Ehrlich, *The Population Bomb*, New York: Ballantine Books, 1968.

3. 'Blueprint for Survival', *The Ecologist*, Vol. 2, 1972, pp. 1–43.

4. D. H. Meadows et al., *The Limits to Growth*, New York: Basic Books, 1972.

5. World Commission on Environment and Development, op. cit., p. 5.

6. Op. cit., pp. 49–50.

7. Op. cit., p. 15.

8. D. Hopper, 'The World Bank's Challenge: Balancing Economic Need With Environmental Protection'. Seventh Annual World Conservation Lecture, 3 March, 1988.

9. V. Shiva, *Staying Alive: Women, Ecology and Development*, London: Zed Books, 198? p. 219.

Bibliography

'Environment' finally moved to the centre stage of the international debate with the report of the World Commission on Environment and Development, *Our Common Future*, Oxford: Oxford University Press, 1987. Various lines of the history leading up to that conceptual innovation are highlighted in A. Biswas & M. Biswas, 'Environment and Sustainable Development in the Third World: A Review of the Past Decade', *Third World Quarterly*, Vol. 4, 1982, pp. 479–91; J. McCormick, 'The Origins of the World Conservation Strategy', *Environmental Review*, Vol. 10, 1986, pp. 177–87; F. Sandbach, 'The Rise and Fall of the Limits to Growth Debate', *Social Studies of Science*, Vol. 8, 1978, pp. 495–520; and H. J. Harborth, *Dauerhafte Entwicklung: Zur Entstehung eines neuen ökologischen Konzepts*, Wissenschaftszentrum Berlin, 1989. M. Redclift, *Sustainable Development: Exploring the Contradictions*, London: Methuen, 1987, offers a more systematic treatment.

D. Worster, *Nature's Economy: A History of Ecological Ideas*, San Francisco: Sierra Club, 1977, is a masterly introduction to the history of ecology, the science which gave its name to the political movement. Its oscillations between romanticism and scientism is traced by L. Trepl, *Geschichte der Ökologie*, Frankfurt: Athenäum, 1987; and P. Acot, *Histoire de l'ecologie*, Paris: Presses Universitaires de France, 1988, shows its rise to an all-inclusive mode of explanation. How close the links between the hopes of social engineering and the formation of the eco-system concept were, is elaborated by P. Taylor, 'Technocratic Optimism: H. T. Odum, and the Partial Transformation of Ecological Metaphor after World War II', *Journal of the History of Biology*, Vol. 21, 1988, pp. 213–44; while Ch. Kwa, 'Representations of Nature Mediating Between Ecology and Science Policy: The Case of the International Biological Programme', *Social Studies of Science*, Vol. 17, 1987, pp. 413–42, calls attention to the affinity between perceptions in the political sphere and systemic versions of biology.

For representations of nature different from environment, which motivate present-day movements, see V. Shiva, *Staying Alive: Women, Ecology and Development*, London: Zed Books, 1989. P. Richards, *Indigenous Agricultural Revolution: Ecology and Food Production in West Africa*, London: Hutchinson, 1985, points out the wisdom of traditional knowledge systems. The history of the concept of nature has been extensively reviewed by C. Glacken, *Traces on the Rhodian Shore: Nature and Culture in Western Thought*, Berkeley: University of California Press, 1967; while J. B. Callicott (ed.) has assembled a number of authors who examine the role of nature in some non-Western traditions: *Nature in Asian Traditions of Thought*, State University of New York Press, 1989.

Access to the cultural anthropology of nature can be found in the entries 'nature', 'mountains', 'trees', 'metals' etc. of M. Eliade (ed.) *The Encyclopedia of Religions*, New York: Macmillan, 1987. Y.-F. Tuan shows us systematically how many different ways the environment, across history and cultures, figured in human imagination: *Topophilia: A Study of Environmental Perceptions and Values*, Englewood Cliffs: Prentice-Hall, 1974. Regarding the discontinuities in European history, C. Merchant, *The Death of Nature: Women, Ecology and the Scientific Revolution*, San Francisco: Harper and Row, 1980, recounts the major rupture in Western attitudes, while her most recent book, *Ecological Revolutions: Nature, Gender, and Science in New England*, Chapel Hill: University of North Carolina Press 1989, documents how the ways of knowing nature have changed from the native Indian to the colonialist and industrialist modes, focusing on the evidence from a limited geographical area.

The rising eco-cratic discourse can be best examined in the special issue of the *Scientific American*, Vol. 261, September 1989, with the title 'Managing Planet Earth'. For another example, much in the same vein, see M. Rambler (ed.), *Global Ecology: Towards A Science of the Biosphere*, New York: Academic Press, 1989. I have called attention ('The Gospel of Global Efficiency: On Worldwatch and Other Reports on the State of the World'. *IFDA Dossier*, No. 68, Nov./Dec. 1988) to hidden assumptions in L. Brown et al's yearly message (*The State of the World*, New York: Norton, 1984 and subsequent years). In contrast, I learned a lot about the deeper civilizational issues which are at stake in the present debate through J. Bandyopadhyay and V. Shiva, 'Political Economy of Ecology Movements', in *IFDA Dossier*, No. 71, May/June 1989; and B. McKibben, *The End of Nature*, New York: Random House, 1989. As a reference tool for the literature on ethics and the environment. I found the annotated bibliography of D. E. Davis *Ecophilosophy: A Field Guide to the Literature*, San Pedro: Miles, 1989, very helpful.

Equality

C. Douglas Lummis

Unlike some of the words examined in this book, equality is no neologism. Nor is it a word that can be declared wholly toxic and expelled from our political vocabulary. But in the modern era, and particularly in the context of the development discourse, it has taken on certain toxic meanings. This, in fact, is its specific danger: the vagueness of the word places its present toxic meanings under the protection of the dignity of its older uses. The purpose of this essay is to disentangle this confusion.

Fairness and Sameness

In the various notions of equality, it is possible to distinguish two families of meaning. In the first, equality indicates a kind of justice or fair treatment. In the second, equality indicates sameness or homogeneity. In some contexts the two meanings may overlap or converge, but they are different. To treat people justly may require treating them differently; on the other hand, to treat them as if they were the same is not necessarily to treat them justly. Moreover, the two meanings are different in kind. Equality as justice is a value statement concerning how people ought to be treated; it refers to relations between persons. Equality as sameness, however, is an allegation of fact; it postulates common characteristics in people. A value statement may be derived from it. However, if equality as sameness is asserted as a value, it may turn out to allege not a fact that is, but a fact that ought to be created. When this notion becomes attached to power, the consequences can be frightening.

The manner in which these concepts divide and intertwine can be illuminated by looking at their classical origins. Already the most primitive notion of justice, vengeance, aims at a kind of equality ('getting even' as we say today). The ancient expression 'an eye for an eye and a tooth for a tooth' is written as an equation, as is the gentler 'do unto others as you would have others do unto you'. Equality is present in any notion that people ought to come under the same set of rules, or that a judge ought to give the same consideration to the claims of both parties in a dispute.

The insight that there is an inner connnection between the political notion of justice and the physical or mathematical notion of equality is very ancient. The Roman goddess Iustitia was traditionally depicted carrying scales, as were the Greek goddesses Themis and Dike. Aristotle saw the two as so inseparable that he even argued that the word *dikast* (one who judges) must be linguistically connected to the word *dichast* (one who bisects). (*Nicomachean Ethics*, 1132a)

Consequently, the Greek *isos* which was the dominant concept by which to judge conditions in the *polis*, comes to mean both physical/mathematical equality and fairness. It enabled the comparison of persons, notwithstanding their otherwise incommensurable differences, by isolating and weighing one aspect, e.g. their rights, status, or merit. Likewise, the Latin *aequalitas* and *aequus*, from which the English word 'equality' derives, could mean either equality in amount, or political equality or fairness.

In contrast to *isos*, however, the other Greek word, *homoios*, emphasizes likeness in kind and not proportion in relationship. Rather than 'equality', it is better translated as 'like, resembling . . .'. In political discourse it is not used as a substitute for *isos*, but rather to suggest harmony or likemindedness. But not always. Aristotle also uses it in his definition of envy — the pain men feel 'at the sight of good fortune . . . of those like (*homoios*) themselves.' (*Rhet.*, 1378b).[1]

In Greek political discourse, this distinction was kept clear. When Pericles made his famous boast in the Funeral Oration that Athens' laws offer equal justice to all, it was for the purpose of making the point that this did not prevent the citizens from cultivating their differences. (*Thucydides*, Bk II, XXXVII) *Isos* was a characteristic of justice, not of people. For Aristotle, the application of equal justice to unequal people was a complex business. In the case of distributive justice, *isos* meant distribution of equal shares to equals, and unequal shares to unequals. Distribution had to be equal to merit, but the problem was deciding which sort of merit mattered: 'democrats make the criterion free birth; those of oligarchical sympathies wealth, or in other cases birth; upholders of aristocracy virtue.' (*Nicomachean Ethics*, 1131a) In the case of corrective justice, *isos* became the capacity of the judge to *ignore* the differences between the parties: 'For it makes no difference whether a good man has defrauded a bad man, or a bad a good one . . . the law looks only at the nature of the damage, treating the parties as equal. (*Nicomachean Ethics*, 1132a) Equality here becomes a kind of scientific method, a hypothetical holding of other things to be equal in order to isolate and identify the factor under investigation. Perhaps a useful metaphor for how *isos*, the abstract principle of equality, fits into the irregular material world is the isobar, the line on weather maps which joins points of equal barometric pressure, which is never straight.

None of this means, however, that the Greeks saw no injustice in a wide gap between rich and poor. If we take as the first step towards the establishment of Greek democracy Solon's reforms in the constitution of Athens, it is worth remembering that the first of these reforms was when he 'made the people free both at that time and for the future by prohibiting loans secured on the person . . . and enacted cancellations of debts both private and public'. (Aristotle, *The Athenian Constitution*, VI 1) In Western history, therefore, debt relief is as old as politics. The Athenians did not call this equality, however, but the shaking off of burdens. At the same time, perfect economic equality was not beyond their political imagination. Aristotle recorded (and opposed) a proposal by Phaleas of Chalcedon for an ideal *polis* based on equality of property. (*Politics*, 1266 a,b)

From Alexander to Lincoln

In none of these notions is there an idea of equality as a universal principle joining all people in the world. According to one view, the first step in this direction can be precisely identified:

> The day — one of the critical moments of history — when, at a banquet at Opis, Alexander prayed for a union of hearts (*homonoia*) and a joint commonwealth of Macedonians and Persians.[2]

One may doubt whether the idea appeared so suddenly, but it is significant that tradition has it coming first from the lips of the Conqueror: it fits well with his project of tearing people away from their local loyalties and homogenizing them into a vast empire. It was in the context of the world which Alexander built that the Stoics developed 'the idea of universality, a worldwide humanity in which all are endowed with a common human nature'.[3] Later the Romans adopted this Stoic philosophy as appropriate for their rule over the multitude of peoples in their empire.

The other decisive moment in the formulation of the idea of universal equality was when the early Christians made their fateful decision to carry their new religion to the Gentiles. Peter's 'I perceive that God is no respecter of persons' (*Acts* 10:34) was uttered at the moment he realized that Cornelius, a Roman centurion, had become a true Christian. This idea, which has since had momentous consequences for Europe and for the world, is fraught with ambiguity. On the one hand, especially when spoken by Peter, it suggests respect for all humans simply by virtue of their being human, as when he says to the kneeling Cornelius, 'Stand up: I myself am a man' (*Acts* 10:26), and in his 'God hath shewed me that I should not call any man common or unclean.' (Acts 10:28) At the same time it can suggest the opposite, that people, beneath their superficial diversity, are equal first of all in their wretchedness, and can become worthy of respect only by *becoming* the same, that is, by becoming Christians. In Paul, this negative sense dominates:

> What then, are we better than they? No, in no wise: for we have before proved to Jews and Gentiles that they are all under sin. (*Romans* 3:9)

> Now we know, that what things soever the law saith, it saith to them who are under the law; that every mouth may be stopped, and all the world may become guilty before God. (*Romans* 3:19)

One wonders whether Peter, instead of asking the centurion to stand, ought to have fallen down himself.

During the European Middle Ages the expression 'an equal' was commonly used to mean one of the same social class, in terms of the feudal class system. It was through this usage that the English word 'peer', which originally meant an equal, came to mean a member of the British aristocracy. The notion of universal equality existed as a theological idea. The claim that Christian morality was universal meant that all people were equal before it: high and low would be judged equally on the Day of Judgement. The principle of equality under the law remained a powerful tradition, if not in the sense that all were treated equally by the law, at least in the sense that all, rulers and ruled alike, were equally under the law, and ought to be equally required to obey it. Equality as opposition to class society was an undying tradition among the common people, appearing sometimes as a practical force in rebellions such as the English Peasants' Rebellion of 1381 (which gave us the famous slogan, 'When Adam delved and Eve span/Who was then the gentleman?'). Social equality may have been believed to be an ideal inappropriate to this world of sinners, but it was not an idea unfathomable to the medieval mind.

The idea of equality reappears as a major historical force in the context of the English revolution of the 17th Century. In pamphlet after pamphlet, Levellers and Diggers argued for equality on the basis that 'God is no respecter of persons'. (The phrasing, incidentally, is that of the King James translation, which had only just become available in 1611). But there was a wide difference of opinion as to how to apply this ambiguous assertion to the world. It was variously used to argue for equality under the law, equal right to vote (for men, or for men of property), abolition of the monarchy and peerage, equal right to preach the gospel (equality of conscience), and equal right to land. Beneath this, deeper struggles were going on. Did equality mean that all are clean, or all unclean? Did it mean all are equal in dignity, or in abject powerlessness under the Almighty? Did it mean that people should be respected in their differences, or are the same, or can be made the same?

Two of the most notable definitions of equality appearing in this period illustrate how differently the notion can be interpreted. The first is that of Colonel Rainsborough, the Leveller. In the debate held in the revolutionary New Model Army at Putney in 1647, Rainsborough argued for government by consent, saying: 'I think that the poorest he in England hath a life to live as the greatest he.'[4] The greatness of this definition lies, first of all, in the fact that it grounds equality neither in religion nor in an abstract principle, but in the human condition. People are not equal because they are so regarded by God, nor are they equal only in contrast to the vast gap that separates them from God. And they are not equal because natural law so decrees. Rather, they are equal in that they confront the same existential task: they must live a life. Moreover this notion liberates equality from its mathematical overtones: the fact of having a life to live does not lend itself easily to exact calculation. It sets aside the question of merit or ability. Whatever one's station or powers, one must stand up. And it contains no idea that people are or ought to be homogeneous. It is important to keep in mind, however, that the Levellers were defeated in the English Revolution.

The second definition from this time is that of Thomas Hobbes, the philosopher. In *De Cive* (1642), and later in *Leviathan* (1651), Hobbes argued that people are equal, that is, alike, in their utter inability to live their lives except insofar as they submit themselves totally to the All-Powerful Sovereign. People differ slightly in wit and strength, but not enough to matter:

For if we look on men full-grown, and consider how brittle the frame of our human body is, which perishing, all its strength, vigour and wisdom itself perishes with it, and how easy a matter it is, even for the weakest man to kill the strongest, there is no reason why any man, trusting to his own strength, should conceive himself made by nature above others. They are equals who can do equal things one against the other; but they who can do the greatest things, namely kill, can do equal things. All men therefore among themselves are by nature equal.[5]

For Hobbes, equality is first of all not a characteristic of justice, but of people. People are the same in that they can never by their own strength decisively get the better of each other; they are equal in their 'brittleness'. This put them, as Aristotle discerned, in a constant state of envy, and therefore fear, of one another. If all equally stand up, the result is war of each against all. To secure the minimum conditions for living of life, therefore, all must equally fall down. The social contract, in which each man ('man' is the right word here; women were not held to be able to sign the social contract) abrogates his natural right, establishes in a much firmer fashion than Alexander ever could a concord of uprooted individuals, now equal in the sense that their differences are nothing compared to the vast gap that separates them from the Almighty Sovereign:

> As in the presence of the master, the servants are equal, and without any honour at all; so are the subjects in the presence of the sovereign. And though they shine some more, some less, when they are out of his sight; yet in his presence, they shine no more than the stars in the presence of the sun.[6]

The notion of equality as justice has ramified into many forms since then. It has been used to attack the pretensions of class (as the poet Burns: 'Gie fools their silks, and knaves their wine/ A man's a man for a' that.'). It has been used to attack repression. It has been used to evoke human respect; in this century it has been the slogan with which to attack racial, ethnic and sexual discrimination. The idea that inequality of wealth is unjust is behind the centuries of workers' struggles (in the Putney Debates of 1647 the landowners stated clearly that they would not give the vote to the landless because they feared they would use their political power to equalize property; that fear has continued through the whole history of capitalism ever since). And the notions of equal rights and equality under the law remain at the centre of our conceptions of law and citizenship.

On the other hand, the homogenizing notion of equality has also been a powerful force. Hobbes' image of people as alike as grains of sand, or atoms, who can create value only as constituent parts of the great machine of the state, has operated actually to make people that way. And as the European idea of civil society gradually evolved from that of a polity to that of an economy, the picture of its standardized constituent part evolved from that of the citizen to that of the economic man. People came to be seen as equal (alike) in their natural propensity to truck, barter and exchange.

Tocqueville believed that there was an inevitable historical trend toward homogenizing equality, and that the vanguard in this respect was the United States. He also believed that this trend was a threat to freedom, and his classic study, *Democracy in America*, was aimed at studying that threat and searching for ways of countering it. In that work he used the word 'democracy' as a virtual synonym for 'equality', by which he meant 'equality of condition' or 'uniformity'. He saw US society as made up of isolated and homogeneous individuals cut off from the past and unable to make permanent ties either with the land or with each other. We can understand what he meant by democracy (equality) from his description of what he believed to be its limiting case:

> In the Western settlements we may behold democracy arrived at its utmost limits. In these states, founded offhand and as it were by chance, the inhabitants are but of yesterday. Scarcely known to one another, the nearest neighbors are ignorant of each other's history. . . . The new states of the West are inhabited, but society has no existence among them.[7]

He did not know that this condition would soon be duplicated in the industrial city. He invented the term 'individualism' to describe the peculiar (and, he believed, mistaken) belief of Americans that they could each live without depending on others, and he noted how this very illusion, paradoxically, contributed to the unprecedented homogeneity of American custom and opinion.

Tocqueville made clear that the atomization of society into uniform individuals did not mean a tendency toward economic equality:

> I know of no country, indeed, where the love of money has taken a stronger hold on the affections of men and where a profounder contempt is expressed for the theory of the permanent equality of property.[8]

On the contrary, the process of uprooting people from the soil, from the past, and from each other — a process one could also think of as the historical disembedding of economic man — released competitive energies which Tocqueville found awesome. The American people, he said:

> Like all great peoples, has but one thought, and presses forward to the acquisition of riches, the single end of its labours, with a perseverance and a scorn of life which one would call heroic, if that word were properly used of anything but the strivings of virtue.[9]

It was in the context of this 19th Century America that equality was once again redefined, this time as 'equality of opportunity'. For equality of opportunity only makes sense in a society organized as a competitive game, in which there are winners and losers. What is equal is not the people, but the rules of the game. In this sense it is a kind of economization of equality under the law. The difference is that the object of the game is precisely to produce inequality. The idea is that the division of society is fair if it takes place under fair rules. Equality of opportunity can thus be seen as a device for legitimizing economic inequality. And indeed it was only after the property owners in the industrial countries felt confident that equality of opportunity had replaced levelling as the dominant definition of equality, that they began granting the right to vote to the propertyless classes.

Equality of opportunity does have some homogenizing effect. To accept equality of opportunity is to accept the game, and to accept the game is to accept the identity of player. In this way, equality of opportunity incorporates some elements from the traditional meanings of equality and eliminates others, producing a remarkable paradox, a system which generates homogeneity and economic inequality, and pronounces the consequence just.

The Politics of Catching Up

We may now turn to the question of the form equality has taken in the context of the post-war ideology of world economic development. This may be divided into two parts, the equality that economic development promises and the equality it actually produces. What it promises is equal justice (which it defines as economic equality) and what it produces is homogeneity (while maintaining and intensifying economic inequality). How does this happen?

The essence of economic development equality is contained in the phrase, 'catching up', or 'narrowing the gap'. For example, in the Declaration on the Establishment of a New International Economic Order, adopted by the United Nations on May 1, 1974, it was announced that the NIEO:

> shall correct inequalitites and redress existing injustices, making it possible to eliminate the widening gap between the developed and the developing countries and ensure steadily accelerating economic development.[10]

The idea that a difference in wealth between countries could be described as inequality, in the sense of injustice, would have been unintelligible a few hundred years ago. The accusation of injustice cannot traditionally be made against inequalities between systems, but only within a system. The fact that the idea is intelligible today is evidence of the degree to which we accept that the world has been organized into a single economic system. Just as universal equality, which made no sense in the age of the Greek *polis*, subsequently made sense in the world conquered by Rome, so today it makes sense in a world conquered by a global capitalist economy.

A second novel idea is that economic equality can be achieved, or at least inequality reduced, by 'steadily accelerating economic development'. When the capitalist system was confined mainly to the US and Europe, it was always understood that its free operation produced inequality, and that reduction of inequality could be achieved only by *political* activity such as organizing unions, fighting for labour governments and welfare policies. The idea, that now the world economy has become capitalist it can generate equality through its own 'development', is remarkable.

Of course, the NIEO was itself a political action. It hoped to use the new political power of Third World countries to force changes in the world economic system and set it in a different direction. But if the direction is to be changed by politics, it remains the case that equality is supposed to be achieved by economics; the purpose of the political changes is to release the 'developing countries to concentrate all (*sic*) their resources for the cause of development'.[11]

A third novelty is the idea that development can lead to international eocnomic equality in levels of affluence, 'ultimate prosperity' as Harry Truman put it in his 1949 speech announcing the Point Four Program. Thus the NIEO Declaration offers the hope that 'the prevailing disparities in the world may be banished and prosperity secured for all'.[12] Put so baldly, the idea is startling, but at the same time it has become quite familiar to us. In polite development discourse there is never talk of levelling down, only of levelling up. That's what 'catching up' means.

Like equality of opportunity, the idea of world development equality presupposes that everyone in the world is or ought to be playing the same game. For the peoples of the world to play the development game, they must first be made over into players. In the early, optimistic days of development theory, the modernization theorists were frank about how deep into culture and personality this homogenization had to penetrate:

> Part of the process of modernization involves the learning of new skills and the acceptance of new ideas about the nature of the world and of human relations. Another part of the process entails the acceptance of new values and the changing of preferences. A still deeper dimension of the process calls for a fundamental change in motivations and in the direction in which it is felt that human energies can properly be directed. [13]

To 'mobilize' (i.e. to conscript) peoples and cultures into the world economic system would require the same disembedding of economic man, the same uprooting, as occurred in the migrations to the US or in the land enclosure movement in England. Only this time, the scale is awesome. The whole teeming multiplicity of the world's cultures, developed (in the older sense of the word) through the labour and imagination of all of human history, is now to be placed under a single standard of value, and all which do not fit that standard are to be discarded with the most damning judgement the utilitarian can make — useless:

> The political public, unattached to any standards of judgement other than those provided by ethnicity, locality, party or passion . . . will be useless to the political culture of a modern society. [14]

Following their own local standards of judgement, the peoples of the world had had in times past their own notions of prosperity (often involving moderation as one of the means for achieving it) and of economic justice (often with mechanisms of redistribution for reducing inequality). Now all this is disvalued by the Western modernizer as so much waste ('useless' in Edward Shils' words); all the treasure trove of diverse human cultures redefined as the wretched and pitiable condition of 'underdevelopment'.

Development promises economic equality for the distant future; what it does now, after more than 40 years, is produce devastating inequality.

The Empty Call for Global Equality

Some might judge the sacrifice worth making, if only the promise is kept. Therefore it is worth mentioning some of the reasons why it never can be.

First, consider the statistics. According to the World Bank's 1988 *World Development Report*, the per capita GNP for what they call Industrial Market Economies (i.e. the 20 richest capitalist countries) was $12,960 in 1986, with an annual average growth rate (1965–86) of 2.3%. A simple calculation gives a yearly increase in per capita income of $298.08. The per capita GNP for the poorest 33 countries in the same year was $270, with a growth rate of 3.1%. The same calculation gives an annual increase in income of only $8.37. Little wonder that the gap between North and South is getting wider year by year. Of course if the poor countries maintain a growth rate higher than the rich countries for a very long time, theoretically they can eventually catch up. But how long would that take? Supposing the growth rates in the *World Development Report* remained unchanged, we can calculate that the poor countries would achieve the 1986 income level of the rich countries in 127 years' time. They would catch up with the rich countries in half a millennium, 497 years to be precise. The world average per capita income at that time would be $1,049 billion! Even if we assume the impossible, a sustained growth rate for all the poor countries of 5%, they would still only catch up in 149 years' time, at an average per capita income of just under $400,000 per year. In fact, the growth rate for these countries, excluding India and China, is only 0.5%. Clearly they will catch up never.

These figures should help us avoid being unnecessarily surprised when we hear that, after all the efforts that have gone into 'development', the gap between the rich and poor countries continues to widen at an accelerating pace. Part of the reason, if economists such as A. G. Frank, Samir Amin and Immanuel Wallerstein are correct, is that the world is not a collection of separate national economies, as depicted in the World Bank Report, but a single economic system that operates to transfer wealth from the poor to the rich countries. A big part of the 'economic development', i.e. the wealth, of the rich countries *is* wealth imported from the poor countries. The world economic system *generates* inequality and it *runs on* inequality. Just as the internal combustion engine is propelled by the difference in pressure above and below the piston, the world economy is propelled by the difference between rich and poor.

If any doubt remains about catching up, we can refer to the authority of the former president of the World Bank, Robert McNamara, who in his celebrated speech to the Bank's Board of Governors in 1973 said that for the rich to oppose development is 'shortsighted, of course, for in the long term they, as well as the poor, can benefit.'[15] We can be sure that any development that makes the poor a little better off will make the rich a lot better off.

Some supporters of development argue that this is only true of a certain kind of development, and that there is another kind — alternative development, authentic development, pro-people development, or the like — that can bring equality and prosperity to all the world. If this means that a different political and economic world structure could bring an end to oppression and starvation and establish international peace and justice, then this certainly describes a hope that must never be abandoned. But if it means that there is some process of economic development that could establish economic equality between countries at a level of what is understood today as prosperity, that is altogether another matter.

It has been estimated, for example, that for the present world population to live at the per capita energy consumption level of the city of Los Angeles would require five planets. The precise figure may be dubious, but the general point remains indisputable. Leaving aside that even the fabulously high energy consumption level of LA has not produced economic equality, or eliminated poverty, in that city, the earth can barely sustain the minority in the rich countries living at those consumption levels today. The myth that it is possible is, of course, functional. It distracts people's attention from the real inequality generated by the world economy; it also legitimizes the vast development industry and keeps many good-hearted people in it. But the fact remains that in this or any other economic system, the consumption levels of today's rich, if extended at all, would consume the world.

Finally, it is simply not in the nature of 'rich' that everyone can share it. What, after all, is 'rich'? The *Oxford English Dictionary* tells us that before it became an economic word, 'rich' had a political meaning. It comes from the Latin *rex*, 'king', and its oldest English definition, now obsolete, was 'powerful, mighty, exalted, noble, great'. Another obsolete form of the word is 'riche', which meant 'a kingdom, realm, royal domain'. Originally to be rich meant to have power of the sort a king has, that is, power over other people. It meant the kind of power you can only have when other people do not: where there are no subjects, there is no king. Only later was the word specialized to mean the particular kind of power you have over people by having more money than they do. Being rich, in essence, does not mean controlling wealth, but controlling people through wealth. The value of money is, after all, not some magical property, but lies in what we call its purchasing power.[16] The point was made incisively a century ago by John Ruskin:

> I observe that men of business rarely know the meaning of the word 'rich'. At least, if they know, they do not in their reasonings allow for the fact, that it is a relative word, implying its opposite 'poor' as positively as the word 'north' implies the word 'south'. Men nearly always speak and write as if riches were absolute, and it were possible, by following certain scientific precepts, for everybody to be rich. Whereas riches are a power like that of electricity, acting only through the inequalities or negations of itself. The force of the guinea in your pocket depends wholly on the default of a guinea in your neighbour's pocket. If he did not want it, it would be of no use to you; the degree of the power it possesses depends accurately upon the need or desire he has for it — and the art of making yourself rich is therefore equally and necessarily the art of keeping your neighbour poor.[17]

The division into rich and poor, then, is not simply a consequence of a particular economic structure; it is an axiom inherent in the phenomenon of rich. It is fraud to hold up the image of the world's rich as a condition available to all. Yet this is what the economic development mythology of 'catching up' does. It pretends to offer to *all*, a form of affluence that presupposes the relative poverty of *some*. It idealizes the lives of people who do less than their share of the world's productive work (because others do more), who consume more than their share of the world's goods (because others consume less), and whose lives are made pleasant by an army of servants (directly or indirectly employed) and workers. If the economy is arranged as a pyramid, it is understandable that everyone might want to stand on top. But there is no way that it can be arranged.

This *a priori* inequality is also inherent in contemporary consumption. As we were taught a century ago by Thorstein Veblen, much of the consumption which we associate with affluence is 'conspicuous consumption', the specific pleasure of which is that there are others who cannot afford it. Nor is conspicuous consumption limited to the rich: establishing a mental association between a product and upper-class life styles is how non-essential goods are sold to the poor, as every advertising agency knows. Nor is conspicuous consumption unknown in poor countries: the implantation of the desire for it is a big part of what modernizationists have touted as 'the revolution of rising expectations'. By implanting in people the desire for elite status, and by convicing them that bits and pieces of that status are infused in various consumer goods, the salesmen hope to keep the development squirrel mill turning for ever. Veblen's words take on an added significance in an age when we know that endless growth can only mean ecocatastrophe:

> If . . . the incentive to accumulation were the want of subsistence or of physical comfort, then the aggregate economic wants of a community might conceivably be satisfied at some point . . . ; but since the struggle is substantially a race for reputability on the basis of an invidious comparison, no approach to a definitive attainment is possible.[18]

It is by a relentless logic, then, that the former socialist societies aspiring to achieve US standards of living break apart into new class structures in the process. The US (i.e. US well-to-do) standard of living has class built into it. It is, as US slang accurately tells us, 'classy'.

Development equality — catching up with the rich through economic activity — is thus a notion that goes against both common sense and economic science; it is a physical impossibility (assuming the Earth is the only planet we have) and a logical contradiction. At the same time it operates, in fact, to establish new forms of inequality. Placing the world under a single standard of measurement, it destroys the possibility of what might be called 'the effective equality of incommeasurables'. For if it could be recognized that different cultures really have their own standards of value, which cannot be subsumed into one another or rank-ordered on some supra-cultural scale, it would make sense to give each equal respect and equal voice. The contrary notion, and the one that prevails today, that all the world's cultures can be measured against a single 'standard of living' measure (which implies the standardization of all living) renders all those cultures commeasurable, and hence unequal. It dispossesses the world's peoples of their own indigenous notions of prosperity. And it helps in the practical recruiting and organizing of more and more people into the global economic system as the world's 'poor' corresponding to its 'rich', whose poverty makes the rich people's richness, whose economic powerlessness generates their economic power, whose humiliation generates their pride, and whose dependency generates their autonomy. Catch-up equality is the myth behind which the organization and rationalization of inequality is the reality.

Common Wealth

Rich, of course, is not the only form of wealth. There are other forms that can be shared in common. But these forms of wealth are more political than economic. The expression 'commonwealth' is, after all, a translation into English of the Latin *res publica*, public thing, i.e. republic. Common wealth is not something achieved by economic development but by the political ordering of a community. This idea is known to most of the world's societies, and is not unknown even in the most fiercely competitive capitalist societies. Common wealth may find its physical expression in such things as public roads, bridges, libraries, parks, schools, churches, temples, or works of art that enrich the lives of all. It may take the form of 'commons', shared agricultural land, forests or fisheries. It may take the form of ceremonies, feast days, festivals, dances, and other public entertainments celebrated in common. On the whole, communities which choose to put their main emphasis on their commonwealth, and its co-operative use, will also be likely to nurture a taste for private moderation.

Placing all the world under a single yardstick, so that all forms of community life but one are disvalued as underdeveloped, unequal and wretched, has made us sociologically blind. By eliminating this stupefying category from our minds, we should be able to look at the world afresh and see not just two possibilities — development or its absence — but a multiplicity of actual and possible ways of ordering communities. Rediscovering the values in these diverse communities does not mean discovering a value in being poor, but discovering that many of the things that have been called 'poor' were actually different forms of prosperity. 'Prosper' (Latin *pro spere*) originally meant 'according to hope'. How and when a people prospers depends on what it hopes, and prosperity becomes a strictly economic term only when we abandon or destroy all hopes but the economic one.

If wealth is economic surplus, different communities may make different choices as to what forms that surplus is to take. Surplus can take the form of private consumption or of public works. It can take the form of reducing work time and creating the maximum leisure for art, learning, festivals or ceremonies. These are not economic inevitabilities but political choices, if by political we mean the fundamental decision-making in a community as to how its goods are distributed. If the rule of just distribution is to give each his or her due, we need to understand that there are in the world communities which have organized themselves as to give the land its due, the sea its due, the forest its due, the fish, birds and animals their due. These communities which have organized themselves so as to give the land its due, the extremities of poverty, actually maintained in this way a vast 'surplus' and shared a common wealth. A marriage of the ancient idea of *commonwealth* with our presently emerging (or re-emerging) understanding of *environment* could give birth to a promising new notion of what 'wealth' really is.

None of this means that inequality is not a problem in the world today. It is, but it is problem of *isos*, not of *homoios*. It is a problem that calls for justice, not for the integration and homogenization of all the world's peoples into a single world economic and cultural system. Inequality is not, in short, an economic problem. Strictly speaking, economics has no vocabulary for describing inequality as a problem, but only as a fact: 'justice' is not a term in economic science. If inequality is a problem, it is a political problem. Its solution is not a matter of development, but of the shaking off of burdens.

Finally, the above analysis also enables us to locate the problem of inequality socially. The *problem* of the problem of inequality lies not in poverty, but in excess. 'The problem of the world's poor,' defined more accurately, turns out to be 'the problem of the world's rich'. This means that the solution to that problem is not a massive change in the culture of poverty so as to place it on the path of development, but a massive change in the culture of superfluity in order to place it on the path of counterdevelopment. It does not call for a new value system forcing the world's majority to feel shame at their traditionally moderate consumption habits, but for a new value system forcing the world's rich to see the shame and vulgarity of their overconsumption habits, and the double vulgarity of standing on other people's shoulders to achieve those consumption habits. Again we may turn for wisdom to Aristotle, who said:

> The greatest crimes are committed not for the sake of necessities, but for the sake of superfluities. Men do not become tyrants in order to avoid exposure to the cold. (*Politics* 1267a)

References

1. I thank Reginald Luÿf and Hans Achterhuis for pointing out the significance of this passage to me.
2. W. W. Tarn, *Hellenistic Civilization* (1927), quoted in George H. Sabine, *A History of Political Theory*, New York: Henry Holt, 1937, p. 141.
3. Ibid., p. 143.
4. 'The Putney Debates' in David Wootton, ed., *Divine Right and Democracy*, Harmondsworth: Penguin Books, 1986, p. 286.
5. Thomas Hobbes, *Man and Citizen* edited by Bernard Gert, Glouster, Mass.: Peter Smith, 1978, p. 114.
6. Thomas Hobbes, *Leviathan*, edited by Michael Oakeshott, p. 141.
7. Alexis de Tocqueville, *Democracy in America*, edited by Phillips Bradley, New York: Vintage Books, 1960, pp. 53–4.
8. Ibid., p. 53.
9. Alexis de Tocqueville, 'A Fortnight in the Wilds,' in *Journey to America*, edited by J. P. Mayer, New York: Doubleday, 1971, p. 364.
10. Declaration on the Establishment of a New International Economic Order, General Assembly Resolution 3201 (S-VI), Preamble.
11. Ibid., 4.(r).
12. Ibid., 4.(b).
13. Lucian W. Pye, 'Communications and Motivations for Modernization' in Pye, ed., *Communications and Political Development*, Princeton, N. J.: Princeton University Press, 1963, p. 149.
14. Edward Shils, 'Demagogues and Cadres in the Political Development of the New States,' in Pye, op. cit., p. 64.
15. Robert S. McNamara, Address to the Board of Governors, World Bank, Nairobi, Kenya, 24 September 1973.

16. It is worth making the point that many 'economic' terms orginally had non-economic meanings indicating naked power relations which are now hidden in the 'free contract' mythology of market economics. As the *OED* makes clear, 'purchase' (from the Latin, *pro captiare*, to chase, hunt, capture) originally meant in English 'seizing or taking forcibly or with violence; pillage, plunder, robbery, capture,' 'Finance' meant 'a payment for release from captivity or punishment'. And 'pay' comes from the Latin *pacere*, to appease, pacify, reduce to peace.

17. John Ruskin, *Unto This Last*, Lincoln, Nebraska: University of Nebraska Press, 1967 (original edn., 1860), p. 30.

18. Thorstein Veblen, *The Theory of the Leisure Class*, Mentor, 1953, p. 39.

Bibliography

Probably the first affirmation of political equality in the West is that found in Pericles' Funeral Oration in Thucydides (*The Peloponnesian War*, Crawley, tr., with intro. by John H. Finley, Jr., New York: Modern Library, 1951). It is often forgotten that the statement appears in the context of the tale of how equality-in-hubris brought disaster to the Athenians. Plato (*The Republic*: New York: 1968: I recommend the Allan Bloom translation, though not necessarily his interpretive essay) builds his ideal *polis* on the presupposition of radical inequality, and satirizes democracy which extends equality even to animals. Serious philosophical discourse on equality begins with Aristotle (*Politics*, London and Cambridge: Loeb Classical Library, 1932, book II; *Nicomachean Ethics*, London and Cambridge: Loeb Classical Library, 1926, Book V).

Christopher Hill (in many works, notably *The World Turned Upside Down*, Penguin, 1972) presents a vivid picture of the struggle for liberty and equality in the English Revolution, from a position generally sympathetic to the Diggers. It's hard to believe he wasn't there. A good and easily available collection of documents from the time, including key portions of the Putney Debates, has been edited by David Wootton (*Divine Right and Democracy*, Penguin, 1986). Driven to a state of radical fear by these matters, Thomas Hobbes (*Leviathan*, Michael Oakeshott, ed., intro. by Richard S. Peters, New York and London: Collier, 1962) developed the classic model showing how equality-as-sameness leads inexorably to absolute inequality in power. The great theorist of the Glorious Revolution of 1688 (in which the chief revolutionary act was to install a legitimate monarchy) was John Locke (*Two Treatises of Government*, ed. with intro. by Peter Laslett, London: Cambridge University Press, 1963) who in a masterstroke of liberal legerdemain placed revolutionary equality into a box and pulled out the English bourgeoisie.

One of the most impassioned assaults on inequality ever made is Jean Jacques Rousseau ('A Discourse on the Origin of Inequality' in *The Social Contract and Discourses*, tr. with intro. by G. D. H. Cole, New York and London: Everyman, 1950). It is equalled in power, if not erudition, by the famous speech by the organizer of *la conspiration des equaux*, Graccus Babeuf (*The Defence of Graccus Babeuf Before the High Court of Vendome*, New York: Schocken, 1972). In what is as much an attack on Rousseau's misogyny as on the failure of the French Revolution to include women in its ideal of equality, Mary Wollstonecraft (*A Vindication of the Rights of Woman*, Carol H. Poston, ed., New York and London: Norton, 1975) laid the first groundwork for the idea of equal rights for women. Written in the same period, Robert Burns' great anti-class poem 'A Man's a Man for A' That' is still worth reading or singing on any public occasion.

John Ruskin's brilliant analysis of 'rich' and 'poor' (*Unto This Last*, Lincoln, Nebraska: University of Nebraska Press, 1967) fizzles out with its weak conclusion that the rich should treat the poor better. On the other hand, his disciple William Morris (*News from Nowhere*, in G. D. H. Cole, ed., *William Morris*, London: Nonesuch Press, 1948) produced what is perhaps the only utopia to succeed in depicting equality and diversity together.

The historian Henry Adams gave us a novel (*Democracy*, New York: New American

Library, 1961 [orig. 1880]) that reveals the fierce desire for inequality at the heart of US democracy. Alexis de Tocqueville's portrayal of the intellectual, cultural and spiritual costs of equality-as-sameness in US society (*Democracy in America*, in two volumes, New York: Schocken, 1961) remains unsurpassed. The classic work on conspicuous consumption, written in a conspicuous rhetorical style, is that of Thorstein Veblen (*The Theory of the Leisure Class*, New York: Mentor, 1953). Two fine essays providing a map through contemporary discussions of equality have been written by John H. Schaar ('Some Ways of Thinking About Equality' and 'Equality of Opportunity and Beyond', both in Schaar, *Legitimacy and the Modern State*, New Brunswick and London: Transaction, 1981).

A key document on the notion that development should produce international economic equality is the Declaration of the Establishment of a New International Economic Order (UN General Assembly Declaration 3201 [S-VI]). On the impossibility of this under the present world economic system, see Andre Gunder Frank (*Latin America: Underdevelopment or Revolution*, New York: Montly Review Press, 1969), Samir Amin (*Unequal Development*, New York: Monthly Review Press), Immanuel Wallerstein, ed. (*World Inequality*, Montreal: Black Rose Books, 1975).

Much has been written on the disfigurement of the human spirit wrought by, and necessary to sustain, human inequality. I shall limit myself to recommending only the following two: Dorothy Dinnerstein (*The Mermaid and the Minotaur*, New York: Harper, 1976) and Frantz Fanon (*The Wretched of the Earth*, Constance Farrington, ed., New York: Grove, 1966).

Helping

Marianne Gronemeyer

The times in which helping still helped, certainly in the form of 'development assistance' as we shall see, are irrevocably past. The very notion of help has become enfeebled and robbed of public confidence in its saving power. These days help can usually only be accepted if accompanied with threats; and whoever is threatened with it had better be on their guard. Already more than a hundred years ago, after he had withdrawn into the woods to live for a while outside the turmoil of the world, Henry David Thoreau wrote:

> If I knew for a certainty that a man was coming to my house with the conscious design of doing me good, I should run for my life . . . for fear that I should get some of his good done to me.[1]

Help as a threat, as the precursor of danger? What a paradox!

The yoking together of help and threat is contrary to common sense, however, only because, despite manifold historical instances to the contrary, the welcome ring of the idea of helping has survived in the consciousness of ordinary people. Help thus appears to them as innocent as ever, although it has long since changed its colours and become an instrument of the perfect — that is, elegant — exercise of power. The defining characteristic of elegant power is that it is unrecognizable, concealed, supremely inconspicuous. Power is truly elegant when, captivated by the delusion of freedom, those subject to it stubbornly deny its existence. 'Help', as will be shown, is very similar. It is a means of keeping the bit in the mouths of subordinates without letting them feel the power that is guiding them. In short, elegant power does not force, it does not resort either to the cudgel or to chains; it helps. Imperceptibly the state monopoly on violence transforms itself, along the path of increasing inconspicuousness, into a state monopoly on solicitude, whereby it becomes, not less powerful, but more comprehensively powerful.

Now, if help has become hypocritical, distorted to the point of unrecognizability, what should be its actual meaning? What advantageous euphony in the word has been inherited?

The positive image of help that is firmly seated in people's heads originates in old stories — the good Samaritan binding up the wounds of the man who fell victim to robbers; or the legend of St Martin sharing his coat with a beggar. Naturally, or perhaps strangely, such stories — despite the modern disfiguration of the very idea of help — still appear today, stories in which, often at great cost, the life of some unknown person in danger is saved.

Common to all of these stories is their characterization of help as unconditional — given without regard to the person in need, the situation, the probability of success, or even the possibility of injury to the person offering aid. *Misericordia*, the 'rueful sympathy' that comes from the heart,[2] pity in the face of the need of another, is what simply prompts the act of helping. The helper is literally overwhelmed by the sight of need. The help provided in these circumstances is — like the compassion itself — much more an event than a deliberate act; it is 'an experience that occasionally flashes out'.[3] It is the anomalous, momentary instance — spontaneous, unplanned.

Modern help has transgressed all the components of this traditional conception of help. Far from being unconditional, modern assistance is frankly calculating. It is much more likely to be guided by a careful calculation of one's own advantage than by a concerned consideration for the other's need.

Nor is help any longer, in fact, help to someone in need; rather it is assistance in overcoming some kind of deficit. The obvious affliction, the cry for help of a person in need, is rarely any longer the occasion for help. Help is much more often the indispensable, compulsory consequence of a need for help that has been diagnosed from without. Whether someone needs help is no longer decided by the cry, but by some external standard of normality. The person who cries out for help is thereby robbed of his or her autonomy as a crier. Even the appropriateness of a cry for help is determined according to this standard of normality.

That help might be furnished without first thinking carefully about the person in need hardly exists any more in the modern peson's mind, such is the extent to which help has been transformed into an instrument through which one can impose upon others the obligation of good conduct. Help as a means to discipline has a long tradition. Whoever desires help is 'voluntarily' made subject to the watchful gaze of the helper. This gaze has nowadays assumed the place of the compassionate.

And finally, it is no longer true that help is the unpredictable, anomalous instance. Instead it has become institutionalized and professionalized. It is neither an event nor an act; it is a strategy. Help should no longer be left to chance. The idea of help, now, is charged with the aura of justification. A universal claim to help is derived from the right to equality, as is an all-encompassing obligation to help. Nowadays the idea and practice of help have become boundless in their expansionist drive. Their blessings have made their way into the most distant corners of the world, and no sector of social or individual life is any longer proof against the diagnosis of a need for help.

In the area of development aid, the perversion of the idea of help has gone to particular extremes. Even the highly expensive installation of what amounts to the machinery for genocide on foreign terrain — which is ruinous economically, politically and morally for the recipient countries — is now called aid: military aid. And recently it has even been possible to subsume the convenient dumping of contaminated, highly poisonous industrial waste under the general rubric of economic help. The 'good' garbage remains at home in local authority dumps and recycling centres: the 'bad' garbage, on the other hand, is shipped to the Third World to be incinerated or stored there.

Even what is called rural development or food aid, in reality, holds out the prospect of an apocalypse of hunger. It prepares the way for the global domination of a handful of giant corporations wielding their control through seed grain. For 'seed grain is the first link in the nutrition chain. Whoever controls seed grain controls food supplies and thereby the world.'[4]

However obviously fraudulent use of the word 'help' to describe development aid may be, the word continues to be taken as the gospel truth, not least by those upon whom the fraud is committed. The concept of help appears to have forfeited scarcely any of its moral self-justification. Its suggestive power remains unbroken. Evidently the mere gesture of giving is sufficient these days for it to be characterized as help — irrespective of the intention of the giver, the type of gift, or its usefulness to the recipient. The metamorphosis from a colonialism that 'takes' to one that supposedly 'gives' has been completed under the protection of this euphonious word, help.

How, then, did help become what it predominantly is today, an instrument for the sophisticated exercise of power? How did help become so thoroughly modern? What follows recalls a few of the key stages in this modernization of the idea of help.

Medieval Alms Giving

It is easier for a camel to pass through the eye of a needle than for a rich man to enter the kingdom of heaven. This is the unsettling admonition under the threat of which the medieval system of alms giving came into being. From this bleak point of view, to be in need of help applies not to the recipient of gifts, but to the giver, for it is the salvation of his soul that is at stake. Since poverty is taken to be pleasing to God, the poor in this respect are already taken care of. In the poor,

> One saw the image of Christ himself. . . . The rulers and feudal lords customarily maintained a large number of beggars in their courts, gave them money and food and lodging. Great significance was (also) lent to the maintenance of beggars and persons in need in the cloisters. In Cluny, for example, in some years as many as 17,000 of the poor were nourished.[5]

It was not, however, the compassionate gaze upon beggars that stimulated the readiness to give, but the fearful contemplation of the future of one's own soul. The existence of the poor offered a welcome opportunity for taking care of the salvation of one's soul, without having to become poor in order to do so. Subsequently, in the course of secularization, there was a decline in fear for the soul. And with the rapid growth in the number of beggars, the latter lost their popularity, a process that was accompanied by a fall in the readiness of the powerful to give alms.

> Beggars from distant provinces appeared in the fields and streets of the town of Troyes in 1573, starving, clothed in rags and covered with fleas and vermin. The rich citizens of the town soon began to fear 'sedition' by these miserable wretches and 'in order to make them leave, the rich men and the governors of the aforesaid town of Troyes were assembled to find the expedient to remedy it. The resolution of this council was that they must be put outside the town, without being told why, and after the distribution to each one of his bread and a piece of silver, they would be made to leave the town by the aforesaid gate which would be closed on the last one and it

would be indicated to them over the town walls that they go to God and find
their livelihood elsewhere, and that they should not return to the aforesaid
Troyes before the new grain from the next harvest. This was done. After the
gift, the dismayed poor were driven from the town of Troyes.[6]

From then on it was downhill all the way for beggars, until they were eventually
declared actual enemies of the state:

> In the 16th century a beggar was taken care of and fed before he was sent
> away. At the beginning of the 17th century, his head was shaved. Later he
> was flogged; and toward the end of the century repression resorted to its
> ultimate means and made him a convict.[7]

But before things had gone so far, the intercessory energies of the Church
concentrated on the administration of heavenly wages, not so much the just
distribution of earthly goods. Social assistance was more of a secondary
undertaking. No wonder, then, that there was no question of planned,
organized help for there existed no criteria of need for the giving of alms.
Consequently, there was no distinction, which would later become so
indispensable, made between those *unable* to work and those who were
unwilling. The receipt of alms was neither bound up with humiliating
procedures nor in any way made the cause of discrimination. The help given
was also not educational in relation to the recipient; rather whatever
educational purposes of improvement were connected with help applied much
more to the givers.

Help was, however, already established as an economic category in one
sense. It was subject to a well conceived cost-benefit analysis and owed its
existence to the benefits which it resulted in — for the giver. Moreover it was
still not the poor themselves who had to pay the bill. The maxim *do ut des* did
not yet apply; rather the idea of 'God's reward'. And it was the *soul* not *profit*,
that was at stake.

Help Overseas

In the 16th century the impulse to help turned to the conquered territories
overseas in reaction to the indescribable atrocities committed by the
conquistadors against the inhabitants of the Caribbean. To be sure, the natives
had first to be raised by papal pronouncement to a status appropriate to
salvation, that is, they had to be made *capable of being helped*.

Pope Paul III (1534–49), in his bull *Sublimis Deus*, took a position opposed to
the claim that the Indians were not human beings. This followed Bartolomé de
las Casas who had already made himself an unflinching and passionate
advocate of the Indians in 1514. The new papal position was that, in His glory,
God had given to man the capacity to reach the pinnacle of being. 'All people
are capable of receiving the gospel.' Only the archenemy of the human race —
Satan himself — had led people to believe that the Indians were animals

> created to do our bidding, since they were incapable of comprehending the
> Catholic faith. We . . . nevertheless say that the Indians are truly people, and

not only capable of comprehending our faith, but . . . also urgently desiring to do so. . . . Thus do we declare that the Indians are under no circumstances to be robbed of their freedom and their goods.[8]

To save the Indians, there had to be constituted a *single humanity* bound together through its filial relation to God. From the acknowledgment of their status as human, and only from that, stemmed both the Indians' right to the Christian message as well as the duty of the Church to Christianize them. At the same time the Indians were still in the stage of humanity's infancy and had to be brought up by education to the level that now prevailed (in Europe). Bernhardino von Sahagun, a Franciscan missionary to the Indians, put it very clearly: the missionary must regard himself as a doctor, and the alien culture as a kind of disease that has to be cured.[9]

Even if the papal decree on the enslavement of the Indians bore no great results in practical terms, the argument did add a number of elements to the repertoire of meanings surrounding the idea of help, which then stood in good stead for later secularization: (1) The *global dimension* of the right to receive, and duty to provide, help — an effort no longer applied only to the poor on one's own threshold or the beggars before the cloister door. (2) The *utopian content* — hopes of ultimate redemption were attached to the notion of help. And (3) the *idea of improvement* — only through help is the recipient raised to the level of true humanity. This implies a view of the cultural and spiritual superiority of the giver. Help still applies to the salvation of souls, but now not to the souls of the givers, but the souls of the recipients. But, at least, exploitation itself had not yet been — as it was in effect to become eventually — declared to be help.

Making the Poor Fit for Work

In the 18th and 19th centuries, with the beginning of the industrial revolution, production — strictly speaking, the mass production of goods on the basis of the division of labour — became the new myth. Inherent in it lies the promise that there will finally be enough for all. Simultaneously with this myth of production arose the myth of the machine. Thus began the long history of the subordination of people to the machines people themselves have made. The human being has to become fit for the machine — an idea which makes necessary a complete change in the fundamental conception of man. Henceforth he is conceived as *homo laborans*; he can realize his nature as a human being only through work. What is appropriate to his nature, and is therefore virtuous, is taken from the requirements of mechanical production. The new catalogue of virtues is dictated by the operating laws of the machine, as exemplified by that most perfect of machines, the clock — discipline, accuracy, order, diligence, neatness, stamina and punctuality.

The first generation of wage labourers was very far from agreeing to the veneration of production. In view of their lamentable situation, they were profoundly sceptical about the promises based on production. They put up a tenacious resistance to their training in factory discipline and their physical and psychological subordination to the pounding rhythms of the machine. They had to be forced into the yoke of labour with draconian penalties and corporal punishment.

> In Lancaster, as in other industrial cities, a steam whistle would blow at five in the morning to wrest people from their sleep. If that proved insufficient, employers would hire 'knockers up', men who went from flat to flat 'rapping on bedroom windows with long poles'. Some of the knockers up even pulled strings 'dangling from a window and attached to the worker's toe'.[10]

Churches and schools undertook the task of implanting in the workers the seeds of the virtues demanded by the machine:

> A wise and skilled Christian should bring his matters into such order that every ordinary duty should know his place, and all should be . . . as the parts of a clock or other engine, which must be all conjunct and each right placed. [And] the schoolroom is supposed to be a training ground for the 'habit of industry', in which the children at the earliest possible age are 'habituated, not to say naturalized, to labour and fatigue'.[11]

Beggars, vagabonds and the unemployed were regarded from this perspective as anti-social elements and shunners of work. Poverty was interpreted as the refusal to work. Begging, as a result, prompted diligent pursuit by the police, and prisons and workhouses were built to see that no one escaped his fated labour. Thus did the perception of need also undergo a transformation. It no longer called up pity, but provoked mistrust and surveillance. Alms in these circumstances, it was argued, could only worsen the situation. For that reason, from now on the strategies that were proposed against poverty amounted to a mix between discipline and remedial education.

Helping the poor no longer appeared as a gesture of charity, but in the form of social regimentation. The first commandment for helping the poor was that any help rendered must remain clearly below the level of a factory wage, even if that meant dropping it to an inhumane minimum. Despite its severity, helping the poor cloaked itself with the self-righteousness of philanthropy and believed itself fully justified in making use of the concept of help. After all, does it not act on human nature and thereby contribute to the general welfare? Certainly, with this change, help was fundamentally secularized. It no longer applied to the salvation of souls, but to the training of the body and the breaking of the will; in short, to the modelling of an extremely this worldly system of work.

Help became completely the subject matter of educational strategies. The productive person was of a crude make, as if in the raw state, so long as his obedience to the required virtues of labour had to be maintained by external compulsion. Of course, identifying help with an apparatus of compulsion was ruinous to the whole idea of helping, and destructive of social harmony. Only when the laws of production had been written into the worker, when they had entered into his very being, could the transformation be counted as completed. The enhancement of production had to correspond with the impulse to self-enhancement. Efficiency must become a need and acceleration a cherished value. Only once this was imprinted on human minds did labour become truly available to employers.

Mass misery existed, to be sure, on a level that now exceeded the Church's capacity to care for the poor, and so help had to be gradually transformed into a bourgeois system. Helping the poor became a complicated balancing act between the exaction of strict discipline on the one side and the granting of concessions, to check revolutionary tendencies, on the other. This interplay of forces could only be severely disrupted by the Church's care of the poor, which still bore traces of the old idea of *misericordia* and the commandant to love thy neighbour. Help had to become as efficient and rational as factory labour itself. That required its bureaucratic organization. Therefore, it became increasingly the obligation of the state. This meant that the spontaneous readiness to help deteriorates into being only a marginal phenomenon, just as does the habitual, self-evident practice of giving help. Instead it is replaced by the newly institutionalized duty of the state, and increasingly by the codified right to help by means of which citizens can assert their claims.

Reaching for Worldwide Simultaneity

Modern help has learned its historical lesson. It has absorbed into its conception of help all the deformations accumulated by the end of the Second World War. It has learned to be calculating. Self-interest is how the decisive factor in the provision of help which — to rid itself of the ugly flavour of exploitation — is termed 'enlightened and constructive'.[12] It has inherited universalism from the idea of the Christian mission and accepted the challenge of encompassing the whole world. It has understood its fantastic qualification as an *instrument of training* and prescribed to itself the demands for labour discipline and productive diligence, which, naturally, are to be worldwide as well. And finally, it has thrown off the ballast of compassion and accepted the necessity of being efficient and supportive of the state.

And yet the modern, up-to-date conception of help is more than the sum of its historically developed meanings. Its essential impulse nowadays is to overcome a deficit, *the* important deficit to be precise. It conducts a struggle against backwardness. It wants to achieve a worldwide simultaneity. It wants to make up for the 'delay of reason' (in H. Blumenberg's phrase) all over the world. Help is now 'the mobilization of the will to break with the past'.[13]

Modernized help can only be understood as help rendered to the process of modernization. Modern help is the self-help of modernity. And what is modernity's fundamental impulse? For it, indeed, constitutes the deepest drive of the world encompassing idea of help. The cultural historian, E. Friedell, ventures to try and mark the date of modernity's advent precisely: 'The year of the conception of the modern person is the year 1348, the year of the Black Death.' Modernity, therefore for him, begins with a severe illness of European humanity.[14]

Confronted with mortality on such a mass scale, Petrarch (1304–74) describes death for the first time in European intellectual history as a *life-denying* principle threatening the dignity of humanity. At the same time death was discovered to be a natural phenomenon, an immutable force of nature.[15]

Death ceases to be seen as a divine penalty and instead is declared to be a human scandal, one fit to be regarded as an outrage. As a natural phenomenon it is included in the essentially modern programme of mastering nature. Modernity's idea of progress is, in part, a rebellion against humanity's humiliating state of subjection to death, a declaration of war on the fundamental insecurity of human existence which seems to be directed by chance or capricious fate. Pre-modern consciousness, in contrast, had been deeply pervaded by the experience 'that things always turn out differently than one thinks'.

> Modernity has unhinged the old ecology of human power and impotence. Inspired by an epoch-making mix of optimism and aggression, it has posed the prospect of the creation of a world in which things turn out as one expects because one can do whatever one wants.[16]

Opposition to death has in the meantime — as long as death cannot be actually overcome — two thrusts: it must make life *more secure* and it must make it *faster*. More secure in order to free it from chance; faster in order to make optimal use of our biologically limited lifespan. The gigantic endeavours that result are tellingly characterized by P. Sloterdijk as a 'general mobilization'. His choice of a metaphor from the world of preparations for war is deliberate. The modern person places him or herself under an uncompromising optimization imperative. No one is allowed to rest until everything that is has been improved. i.e. No one is ever allowed to rest. For everything that has been improved is good only for a fleeting historical moment. Afterwards it is once again overdue for being surpassed.

Improvement in the service of security means increasing the degree of predictability, planning, manageability, understandability and homogeneity. In the service of acceleration, it means increasing the mobility of people, materials and social relations. Progress is only conceivable as 'those motions . . . that lead to a higher capacity for motion'.[17]

The idea of development is enthusiastic about this gigantic project of standardization. 'The main cause of fear,' as Descartes wrote, 'is surprise.' Being secure means to be secure against surprises. Security demands exclusion of the unforeseeable. This understanding of security involves establishing the same degree of familiarity and knowledge the world over. And in order to produce a worldwide homogeneity, one has to undertake the eradication of all that is foreign. 'The best surprise is no surprise,' according to the advertising slogan of an international American hotel chain. The idea of development promises that one will be able to feel at home everywhere in the world. The unalterable precondition of homogeneity is worldwide simultaneity. Everything backward, everything that has not yet been drawn into the whirlpool of the 'general mobilization' of modernity represents resistance to it and must therefore be brought into the present in order to become fit for the future. And what is not matched to the time will be relegated to a place in the museum or a reserve. This relegation is made with all the conscientiousness requisite to historical responsibility and the diligence of the collector.

And for the standard by which the tasks of development are set, it must be the world's most advanced organization and the most fast-paced lifestyle; in short, the model of life in the highly developed industrial nations. Modern help is help to flee. It offers the possibility — at least it claims to do so — of slipping off the shackles of one's native culture and falling into line with the thoroughly organized bustle of the unitary world culture.

SOS is the old signal of an emergency at sea: Save Our Souls. The seamen in need summon others to save them and they issue their call by referring to the fact that their souls are in danger. If one takes the idea of an emergency call literally and turns it on its head, then the abbreviation SOS is also applicable to modern help. The emergency call of those in danger has become the call to battle of the helpers. Help turns into the act of saving oneself. The object being saved is not the soul, but that which is soulless — SOS: Save Our *Standards*. Help is extended for the sake of the achievements of one's own (Western) civilization. It serves to confirm and secure the standards of a normality raised to the level of a worldwide validity. It is at the same time a runway for new high altitude flights of fancy on which the standards valid a moment ago are constantly being left behind as the obsolete fashion of the past. Help signifies, for those who 'need' it, the long haul still be be covered before arrival in the brave new world of modernization. Not salvation from emergency, but a promise of the future is its leitmotif.

Without people's scandalized consciousness in the face of death at the beginning of the modern period, however, and without the resulting 'general mobilization' (the idea of development) and the subsequent elevation of this project into a moral necessity, the most recent manifestation of help as worldwide aid for development would not have been plausible.

Aid and the Elegance of Power

It was only a matter of time before the onward movement of modernization would spring the bounds of the highly mobilized, productively unshackled Western industrial countries to discover an intolerable obstruction to its further movement in the sluggish stagnation of the backward 'Third World' countries. The arguments of both left and right in favour of development aid presuppose that this movement has to expand without hindrance. They only differ from one another on how the integration of the retarding rest of the world into the universal movement can be accomplished on terms that are economically efficient or morally acceptable. As the Pearson Report put it: 'the acceleration of history, which is largely the result . . . of modern technology, has changed the whole concept of national interest. . . . We must show a common concern for the common problems of all peoples.' The acceleration of history, taken as an established fact, makes it necessary to think of the world's population as a 'world community' and the planet as a 'global village'.[18] Not the other way around: it is humanity that must be constituted as a 'world community' in order to give free reign to the acceleration of 'progress'.

In 1949, President Truman postulated the obligation of the United States to offer financial and economic aid beyond its borders as a contribution of the Free World to global stability and orderly political development. Truman's speech concluded a momentous process of reconceptualization, the guiding coordinates of which were marked by two *development plans*: the Morgenthau Plan, which both Roosevelt and Churchill favoured in 1944, and the Marshall Plan, which was put into effect in 1948. The Morgenthau Plan foresaw the complete reverse development of a dangerous industrial nation into an agrarian state. Defeated Germany was to be demilitarized after the war and comprehensively dismantled industrially. For only a short historical moment, to be sure, could the desire for punishment — directed against the nation that had set the world on fire — dominate the political calculus. Punishment is conceivable from the perspective of modernity only as enforced retardation — being detached from the general movement onward and upward. Within three years of the decision in favour of the Morgenthau Plan, the idea of help had triumphed over the thought of revenge. A Germany pushed back into the past and slowed down would have been disadvantageous in the extreme to the American movement for progress. It is fruitless to speculate as to what would have become of Germany had the Morgenthau Plan prevailed. In truth, this anti-modern proposal had no realistic chance of being implemented. The tracks of history had long since been switched to run in another direction. Integration into the West was the motto for Germany from then on, and this integration was conceivable only as an industrial mobilization, and subsequently a military mobilization as well.

Turning to the Marshall Plan (the European Recovery Programme), it must be regarded as a political master stroke that its designers succeeded in presenting it to the American population and to the recipient countries as a generous offer to *help*. Its high reputation has hardly worn thin to this day. In particular, in the western part of Germany, where the Plan was received as a visible expression of reconciliation with the victors, it was eagerly misunderstood. In reality, the package of measures was the prototype of all future development help. In it, help is conceived for the first time as pure self-help, though it nevertheless remained a *public gesture of giving*. World politics had never before been so elegant. The boundaries between giving and taking were blurred to the point of unrecognizability. There were two benefits stemming from this 'help': economic–material and political–legitimizing. On the one hand, the aid helped the stagnating American economy which was reorienting itself to peacetime production. Only a recovered industrial Europe could create sufficient demand for goods made in the USA. On the other hand, the aid programme confirmed America in the role of the leading nation of the 'Free World'.

Truman's speech thus expressed, although still only with reference to Western Europe, the three-fold nature of the motives for transnational help, which later, at the beginning of the First Development Decade, would also guide international development aid to the Third World. Help is offered for reasons of the helper's own *national security*, for the purposes of maintaining its own *prosperity*, and for the sake of *moral obligation*, to convey to others the good that has come to a nation in the course of history. This last motive is especially liable to cause confusion. There is to be recognized in it both national modesty as well as gratefulness for a benevolent historical fate. By virtue of having so benefited, however, it assserts, self-confidently and without doubt, that it is superior to precisely this historical configuration. All three motives are then bundled together in the overarching task of the 'Free World' (more accurately, the 'Free West') to create a 'bulwark against communism'. Henceforth, help is help against communism — until its collapse 40 years later in Eastern Europe in 1989 and the Soviet Union in 1991.

At the beginning of the First Development Decade in 1960, the moral appeal to his own nation's willingness to help was presented with great verve by the American President, J. F. Kennedy, in two major addresses to Congress (1961 and 1963).[19] Down to the very choice of words, the two Kennedy speeches are characterized by confidence and a revolutionary dynamic, determined and prepared to assume the role of the leading nation of the 'Free World' in the post-colonial era, and in the full consciousness of how weighty is the burden of responsibility:

> Looking toward the ultimate day, when all nations can be self-reliant and when foreign aid will no longer be needed . . . (with the) eyes of the American people, who are fully aware of their obligations to the sick, the poor, and the hungry, wherever they may live . . . as leaders of the Free World.[20]

This corresponds to 'the deep American urge to extend a generous hand to those working toward a better life for themselves and their children.'

Behind President Kennedy's moral appeal to the American people to accept this last great historical exertion, there is concealed the self-consolation (and self-assurance), which, in one form or another, every epoch pervaded with a belief in progress has needed — the tendency of the present to conceive of itself as the penultimate stage of history, to fancy itself in a kind of positive final time in which only the last breakthrough remains before the harvest of history can be gathered into humanity's granary. The confidence with which an epoch fantasizes itself into the universal inheritance and final configuration of history is what protects it against the unbearable consciousness of the 'lostness of the present in time' (H. Blumenberg). The diagnosis of the 'end of history' — as an American State Department official put it in 1990 after the collapse of the bureaucratic socialist regimes in Eastern Europe — is offered up against the vexing experience of being always a mere transitional stage in a higher course of progress, whose beneficiaries will be those who come later. It serves the purpose of self-defence against an exaggerated sense of generational envy. At the same time, the sense of immediate expectancy aroused is a powerful historical impulse which has lent the idea of progress new force and compelled it to further acceleration whenever spirits have begun to flag.

The Ambiguity of Self-Help and Sharing

Compared to this euphoria, the non-governmental organizations supplying help, in particular the religious welfare agencies and grassroots groups, have maintained a critical scepticism from the very beginning. But let us not forget that they raise no opposition to the idea of development itself, but merely reject the insinuation that the global responsibility for development can be had for the low cost of pursuing the national self-interest of the donor nations.

The changing discussion of international aid inside the Church is a good example. Ever since the end of the Second World War, it has been essentially characterized by two tendencies. First, a widening of the range of the Church's responsibility, both geographical as well as substantive and institutional. And second, a continual displacement of the very idea of help. Help appears more and more as a conceptually unsuitable means of promoting development. In short, help does not help.

The programmatic statements of international ecumenical conferences of the 1960s illustrate the following, very important transitions: away from the model of inter-church help (in devastated post-war Europe) to the idea of *service* to the comprehensive world community; (New Delhi, 1961): away from service to *social action*; away from personal piety to a concern with the problem of *justice*; away from the particular institution to the worldwide *ecumenical* plane; away from inside to beyond the walls of the Church; an opening to the world of societies; a movement beyond mere help to the *transformation of structures and overcoming of the status quo*. 'Only a Christianity that is fully conscious of its social responsibility can be adequate to a dynamic, changing society.' (Geneva, 1965) 'The great and constantly growing undertaking upon which we have entered does not permit us to live from hand to mouth . . . [We] must . . . *test, plan, and develop a kind of strategy*.'[21]

Doubtless these considerations are based in an ethic other than the merely strategic. In agreement with the protest movements of these years that were critical of capitalism, and in opposition to the misuse of foreign aid for purposes of power politics, help from the international Christian Church becomes politicized.

After the founding of the German church aid agency, Misereor in 1958, the talk was originally exclusively of person-to-person relationships and personal repudiation ('Those who have been driving a Volkswagen and can now permit themselves a Mercedes remain with the Volkswagen' and 'those who have money for four weeks of vacation might satisfy themselves with three.') As a goal, they set their sights on a victory over hunger and leprosy — not yet on poverty and underdevelopment. In a critical self-limitation, the church's welfare organization was obliged to stick by its instruments of government to the task of 'summoning to the works of charity' and to leave to the world concern for a just distribution of land, the creation of sufficient jobs, and the containment of Bolshevism. Even explicitly missionary motives were repudiated. The point was professedly 'simply . . . the confirmation of Christian compassion. For this reason everyone should receive assistance, without regard to faith and whatever the prospects for success.'[22]

The concept of help, however, became increasingly tricky: 'The ecumenical deaconry could no longer limit itself to help for victims, but had to find a way to contribute to overcoming the causes of human and social need.'[23] A critical consideration of development help requires one to understand the nature of need. That means — what enlightenment has always meant since the days of Copernicus — that one has to learn to distrust fundamentally the appearance of things. Need ceased being what it had appeared to be in the founding years of the aid agencies, namely need pure and simple, which could be subject to help. Need ceased to be something monolithic, cast in a common mould. Instead it came to be seen as a complex system of countless, mutually reinforcing obstacles to development. Theorists tirelessly construed 'vicious circles of poverty', in which the chess moves of power politics on the part of the rich countries find just as much place as the structural weaknesses of the countries of the Third World — ranging from the terms of trade to the population explosion and from the illiteracy of the impoverished population to the inadequacies of the infrastructure. From this perspective, everything that stands in the way of industrial production is a contributing cause of need.

To the extent that concrete human need disappears under the analytic gaze and necessarily gives way to an abstract system of powerful negative factors, the help or aid enterprise itself looks hopelessly backward, inadequate to confront the overwhelming facts at issue, too apolitical, almost irrational, criminally naive. Help proves itself to be counterproductive for the development venture, for, by taking need at face value, it affirms the delusory context that surrounds it.

But it is not only because it is abused for the purposes of power politics that help has fallen into disrepute. It ought to be much more discredited because of its quasi-feudal character, because of the power differential that it is itself responsible for establishing. The ecumenical movement's discussion of aid right up to the 1980s revolved around the 'problem of giving and receiving'.[24] What was meant here was the relation of superiority and inferiority that help creates; the shame of the receiver and arrogance of the giver. This tactfulness, however generous-hearted it might at first glance appear, has something astonishing about it. If we stick to the scenario of the person who innocently suffers need and to whom help is to be given, it is by no means obvious why help discriminates against that person. Nor does the act of helping in itself establish a power differential between the two. The person who is saved, naturally, owes their saviour thanks, but in no case submission. Help supplied does not always establish a paternalistic relationship, and it certainly does not occur when it is unconditional assistance given in an emergency.

The embarrassment surrounding foreign aid, which makes it so difficult to spare the receiver shame, comes from the fact that it is *development* help. Only under this rubric is help not help in need, but help in the overcoming of a deficit. Between these two types of help there exists an unbridgeable difference. To understand it, one has to have considered the equally profound distinction between need and neediness.

The person suffering need experiences it as an intolerable deviation from normality. The sufferer alone decides when the deviation has reached such a degree that a cry of help is called for. Normal life is both the standard of the experience of need as well as of the extent of the help required. Help is supposed to allow the sufferer to reapproach normality. In short, the sufferer of need, however miserable that person may be, is the master of his or her need. Help is an *act of restoration*.

The needy person, on the other hand, is not the master of his or her neediness. The latter is much more the result of a comparison with a foreign normality, which is effectively declared to be obligatory. One becomes needy on account of a diagnosis — *I* decide when *you* are needy. Help allotted to a needy person is a *transformative intervention*.

Development help inherited the missionary idea, with its accursed crusade to win converts and mania for redemption. The message of salvation has been secularized compared to the missionary era, but that is precisely the reason why the condition of 'not yet partaking' appears in the shaming form of a deficit. However emphatically cultural particularity and historically evolved multiplicity, may be discussed, the modern missionary idea still declares that a shortfall of civilization must be remedied, an incorrect historical development corrected, an excessively slow pace accelerated. Even the self-criticism of development aid manoeuvres itself into a paradoxical situation. It regards its opposite numbers in the Third World as comprehensively needy, backward according to valid standards of normality, and subject to an essential catching up process. And at the same time it broods tormentedly over the arrogance of the rich nations, makes propaganda for the idea of the fundamental equality of foreign cultures, shows its willingness to engage in dialogue, and condemns tutelary and dependency relations and cultural imperialism.

The only help which, examined critically, did not prove disreputable or counterproductive, and which seemed to point a way out of the dilemma, was *help for self-help*. This perspective became the guiding principle for the development policy of non-state welfare organizations. In offering training for self-help, help apparently rediscovers its innocence. For this is help that renders itself superfluous within an appropriate time period and the dependency it establishes is allegedly a transitional stage with a tendency to dissolve of itself.

Help for self-help, however, still does not reject the idea that the entire world is in need of development; that, this way or that, it must join the industrial way of life. Help for self-help still remains development help and must necessarily, therefore, still transform all self-sufficient, subsistence forms of existence by introducing them to 'progress'. As development help, it must first of all destroy what it professes to save — the capacity of a community to shape and maintain its way of life by its own forces. It is a more elegant form of intervention, undoubtedly, and with considerably greater moral legitimacy. But the moral impulse within it continues to find its field of operation in the 'development-needy countries', and to allow the native and international policy of plunder to continue on in its unenlightened course. In this light, the sole helpful intervention would be to confront and resist the cynical wielders of power and the profiteers in one's own home country. Help for self-help is only a half-hearted improvement on the idea of development help because it exclusively mistrusts help, and not development itself.

In the most recent phase of the Church's discourse on development policy, the guiding principle of help for self-help is being replaced by the concepts of one world and mutual sharing. What this brings into relief is much less a radical redistribution of wealth than 'relationships within the totality, . . . participation and mutuality'. It attacks the superiority complex of Western civilization created by economic efficiency and promotes the vindication of other cultures.

Every culture in the 'one world' is simultaneously giving and receiving. The point is to recognize the equality of all cultures and make mutual learning possible within a cultural dialogue. Mutuality is supposed to be drawn out of the fixed roles of giving and taking.

Once again, the idea is based on a peculiarly grandiose notion of culture: 'Every particular culture realizes a limited number of human possibilities . . . [and], on the other hand, stifles others, which, then, are able to be developed in other cultures.'[25] What then is more obvious for transcending the limitations in a large-scale cultural project encompassing the entire world than bringing together into a whole the parts conceived as fragments of human possibilities? But in a reversal of the systems theory principle that the whole is more than the sum of its parts, this approach holds, in regard to cultural multiplicity, that the contradictory parts are more than the comprehensive whole, or, in other words, that the whole is the false (Theodor Adorno).

Herbert Achternbusch summarizes it:

> World (and 'one world') is an imperial concept. Where I live has meanwhile become the world. Earlier Bavaria was here. Now the world reigns. Bavaria, like the Congo or Canada, has been subjugated to the world, is ruled by the world. . . . The more the world rules, the more will the world be annihilated, will we, who inhabit this piece of the earth, be annihilated. . . . The imperial law of the world is understanding. Every point in this world must be understood by every other point. As a consequence, every point in the world must be equivalent to every other point. Thus is understanding confused with equality and equality with justice. But how is it that it is unjust if I cannot make myself understandable to someone else? Is it the oppressed or the dominated who want to make themselves understood? Naturally, it is the oppressor and the dominator. It is domination that must be understandable.[26]

To be a deacon (in Christian terms) involves being prepared to validate one's calling by service to life; it is claimed to be an 'option for life'. But even this formulation remains on the well trodden path. If one really opts for life, the discussion must return to the origin of the breakthrough into modernity. With that the doom of the development idea truly begins because it cannot supply the foundation for its own renunciation. E. M. Cioran complains that he finds himself on an earth

> where our mania for salvation makes life unbreathable. . . . Everyone is trying to remedy everyone's life . . . the sidewalks and hospitals of the world overflow with reformers. The longing to become a source of *events* affects each man like a mental disorder or a desired malediction. Society — an inferno of saviours! What Diogenes was looking for with his lantern was *an indifferent man.*[27]

References

1. Henry David Thoreau, *Walden*, in *The Portable Thoreau*, edited by C. Bode, New York: Penguin Books, 1977, p. 328.

2. Georges Kleine, *Lateinisch-Deutsches Handwörterbuch*, Leipzig: 1869, Sp. 497.

3. R. Safranski, *Schopenhauer und Die Wilden Jahre der Philosophie*, Munich: 1988, p. 349.

4. P. R. Mooney, 'Saatgut — Die Geschichte von den Herren der Erde. Über die Macht der Konzerne,' in D. Cwienk (ed.), *Konsum* Graz: 1987, p. 194.

5. A. J. Gurjewitsch, *Das Weltbild des mittelalterlichen Menschen*, Munich: 1980, p. 277.

6. F. Braudel, *Capitalism and Material Life 1400-1800*, New York: Harper & Row, 1967, p. 40.

7. Ibid., p. 72.

8. M. Erdheim, 'Anthropologische Modelle des 16. Jahrhunderts,' in K.-H. Kohl (ed.), *Mythen der Neuen Welt*, Fröhlich und Kaufmann, 1982, p. 61.

9. Ibid., p. 63.

10. Jeremy Rifkin, *Time Wars*, New York: A Touchstone Book, 1989, p. 106.

11. Ibid., pp. 111–12.

12. L. B. Pearson, *Partners in Development: Report of the Commission on International Development*, New York and London, p. 9.

13. Ibid., p. 7.

14. A. Legner (ed.), *Die Parler und der schöne Stil, 1350-1400*, Cologne: Ein Handbuch zur Ausstellung des Schnütigen-Museums, 1978, p. 73.

15. Ibid.

16. P. Sloterdijk, *Eurotaoismus: Zur Kritik der politischen Kinetik*, Frankfurt: 1989, p. 21ff.

17. Ibid., p. 37.

18. L. B. Pearson, op. cit., pp. 8–9.

19. J. F. Kennedy, 'Foreign Aid, 1961' and 'Foreign Aid, 1963', in R. A. Goldwin (ed.), *Why Foreign Aid?*, Chicago: 1963, p. 1ff and p. 13ff.

20. Ibid., pp. 5, 132.

21. K. Kinnamon, 'Konsultation über "Verständnis von Diakonie heute," 1982. Geschichtlicher Überblick,' in K. Raiser (ed.), *Ökumenische Diakonie, eine Option für das Leben (Beiheft zur Ökumen. Rundschau, 57)*, Frankfurt am Main: 1988, p. 14ff. And Philip Potter, *Die Geschichte des ökumenischen Austauschs*, ibid., p. 60ff.

22. J. Kardinal Frings, 'Abenteur im Heiligen Geist: Rede vor der Vollversammlung der deutschen Bischöfe in Fulda, August 15–21, 1958' in Bischöfliche Kommission für Misereor, ed., *Misereor - Zeichen der Hoffnung*, Munich: 1976, pp. 20, 23, and 32.

23. K. Raiser, 'Einleitung', in Raiser (ed.), *Ökumenische Diakonie*, op. cit., p. 9.

24. Philip Potter, op. cit., p. 62.

25. K. Galling (ed.), *Die Religion in Geschichte und Gegenwart*, Tübingen: 1960, Vol. IV, 'Kultur', col. 94.

26. H. Achternbusch, *Die Olympiasieger*, Frankfurt am Main: 1982, p. 11.

27. E. M. Cioran, *A Short History of Decay*, trans. by Richard Howard, New York: The Viking Press, 1975, pp. 4–5.

Bibliography

Arguments against development aid can be raised on several levels. Most easily available are critical evaluations of aid projects. B. Erler, *Tödliche Hilfe*, Freiburg: Dreisam, 1985, recounts the failure of numerous projects, even if they have been set up with local participation. Drawing also on her earlier work, T. Hayter, *Exploited Earth: Britain's Aid and the Environment*, London: Earthscan, 1989, surveys the political context of aid and particularly examines its effects on tropical forests. R. Gronemeyer, *Hirten und Helfer*, Giessen: Focus,

1988, bids a sad farewell to nomadic ways of life which have been devastatingly affected by aid. With regard to the discussion within the development establishment, see for instance R. Cassen, *Does Aid Work? Report to an International Task Force*, Oxford: Oxford University Press, 1986. A debunking insight into how development agencies work is offered by G. Hancock, *Lords of Poverty*, London: 1989, while R. Mooney, *Seeds of the Earth: A Private or Public Resource?*, London: International Coalition for Development Action, 1979, exposes the criminal practices of agribusiness.

Unfortunately, an intellectual history of the idea of international aid, to my knowledge, remains still to be written. It would have to take off from a history of helping in Europe. Changing European policies towards the poor are traced in B. Geremek, *La pietà e la forca: Storia della miseria e della carità in Europa*, Roma: Laterza, 1986, while Ch. Sachsse & F. Tennstedt, *Geschichte der Armenfürsorge in Deutschland*, Stuttgart: 1980, outline the change in the institutional framework of assistance, focusing in particular on aid as education.

In the development context, aid has meant help for the purpose of modernization. It implied nothing less than drawing all peoples worldwide into a simultaneous reality and exposing them to the waves of global acceleration. I was stimulated to this way of thinking about modernity by P. Sloterdijk, *Eurotaoismus: Zur Kritik der politischen Kinetik*, Frankfurt: Suhrkamp, 1989; the wide-ranging reflections of H. Blumenberg, *Lebenszeit und Weltzeit*, Frankfurt: Suhrkamp, 1986; and the essay of J. Rifkin, *Time Wars*, New York: Holt, 1987, on modern civilization's concept of time. An early attack (1956), lucid but little known, on the global diffusion of the industrial revolution and the corruption of cultures in the face of consumer gadgets was launched by G. Anders, *Die Antiquiertheit des Menschen*, 2 vols., München: Beck, 1980.

I owe the insight about how modern experience, since the time of the plague, was shaped by the negation of death to E. Friedell, *Die Kulturgeschichte der Neuzeit*, Vol. 1, München: 1976 (originally 1926). How efforts at modernization can be read as attempts to achieve security in a world without afterlife, can be inferred from J. Delumeau, *La peur en occident*, Paris: Fayard, 1978. Security implies refusal of the Other as well. This is analysed in B. Waldenfels, *Der Stachel des Fremden*, Frankfurt: Suhrkamp, 1990.

Market

Gérald Berthoud

It is widely accepted that with the 1980s we entered the era of the New Right or the conservative revolution. In this new era, the market is not considered merely as a technical device for the allocation of goods and services, but rather as the only possible way to regulate society. This economic ideology is more than a little reminiscent of the dominant worldview at the end of the 18th century, with its emphasis on the virtues of '*doux commerce*'. Undeniably, our time is characterized by a deep belief in the powers of the market to solve the world's development problems.

In the West, there is a broad consensus that market capitalism — by which I mean the generalized use of commodities — is indissolubly linked with democracy and, as such, the best possible system for the whole of humanity. In Eastern Europe and the Soviet Union, the total failure of central planning as the sole regulatory device is viewed by many as the final victory of liberal capitalism. Market principles are quite explicitly contrasted with the totalitarian experience, and considered as the only way to escape insufferable bureaucracy and to guarantee a minimally decent material life for all.

As for the South, it also is swept up by this general ideological movement. Most countries have no choice; they are forced to increase their integration within and dependence on the international market economy in one way or another. In numerous cases, the impact of the market on the whole of social life leads to dramatic consequences, clearly illustrated by the policy of structural adjustment. But, seemingly irresistibly, the market still appears the only possible path to development despite innumerable difficulties and setbacks. Indeed, it is argued quite matter of factly that 'if one wants to improve the material condition of people, especially of the poor, one will do well to opt for capitalism.'[1]

In the minds of a growing number of decision-makers, it has become increasingly self-evident that the market should no longer be viewed as an institution which must be regulated by external social forces, but, on the contrary, that it should be used to regulate society as a whole. Market thus becomes the leading principle for guiding individual and collective action.

With the present tendency to impose market mechanisms and principles on a global scale, development is held to be possible only for those who are ready to rid themselves entirely of their traditions, and devote themselves to making economic profit, at the expense of the whole gamut of social and moral obligations. Too often a radical choice is imposed between individual freedom and collective solidarity. Such seems, today, the price to pay if one wishes to walk the long path of development.

More than in the past four decades, development now means integration into the national and international capitalist markets, and this integration in turn becomes the minimal condition for a region or country to be considered 'developed'. Following this market logic, relations at the private and collective levels must be mutually useful. If one side has nothing tangible to offer, the other has no reason at all to pursue the unbalanced relationship. For traditional morality, this position would be regarded as self-interested, even cynical; in the contemporary spirit of utilitarianism, it appears normal.

A growing number of Third World countries are no longer in a position to engage in utilitarian exchanges with rich countries. Development through the market is then a selective process: only those areas which promise economic growth are considered. For the huge majority, struggling to obtain the strict necessities of life, consumption remains far beyond their means.

Guided by this ideological conformism, the market appears as an implicit assumption in virtually all development theory and policy. A confused amalgam of ideas, it has become a magical term hypnotically repeated throughout the world, a catchword. Clearly, this ideological conviction is a necessary condition for the imposition of a market economy but it is not sufficient. Very often, ideological violence is expressed in the cold logic of political power. Thus, to quote an American official, 'we must also counter, both in the UN and within the framework of the North–South dialogue, any discussion of global problems which questions the validity of the free market and of free enterprise in countries of the Third World.'[2]

This normative representation of social regulation is increasingly reinforced by technological innovations in key sectors like information, telecommunications and biogenetics. The clearest result of this process is market dynamism, giving the impression that commoditization has no limits whatsoever. 'Can *everything* be bought and sold?' is a moral question which has been progressively emptied of all meaning. Faith in unlimited expansion follows from the close connection made between technoscience and the market. The former, with its conquest of new social spaces unthinkable not long ago, is seen as irresistible. Under pressure from the ideological success of technology, there is little chance of any effective general acceptance of ethical limits to market expansion. We are all subject to the compelling idea that everything that can be made must be made, and then sold. Our universe appears unshakeably structured by the omnipotence of technoscientific truth and the laws of the market.

The middle-class ideal of our time is to establish a fully competitive society, composed of individuals for whom freedom of choice is the only way to express independence from their natural and social environment. But one unavoidable question remains: is not our reductive view — of supposedly independent individuals as the universal future for mankind — ultimately self-deceptive; and are we not thereby misleading the entire world as well as ourselves?

The Rise of Global Neo-Liberalism

Since its beginnings some 40 years ago, development policy has necessarily been defined within the omnipresent conflict between East and West for global dominance. Two models of development were imposed by these historical circumstances: on the one side, market capitalism; on the other side, socialism, with centralized planning as its key regulatory mechanism. Here for obvious reasons (the total collapse of so-called socialism) only capitalism and its free market ideal need be considered.

For the last three or four decades, economic growth has been regarded in different ways, from the extremely critical perspectives of the New Left radicals in the 1960s to the dogmatic approbation of the 1980s New Right ideologues. So far, however, the negative views of a minority of thinkers have not posed a threat to the dominance of the orthodox credo. The idea of growth is essential to our modern way of viewing human life. Economic expansion based on constant technical innovation is widely thought of as the only way to solve the world's problems. Growth, beyond its immediate economic meaning, is a core cultural complex of ideas and beliefs which organizes the whole of modern life. It is simultaneously a universal truth and the only possible normative means of concerning the good society. As such, development implies, explicitly or implicitly, that the Western way of life is the only means to guarantee human happiness.

At the individual level, economic growth finds its expression in the continual search for material well-being, this quest itself having been elevated to the status of a fundamental requirement of human nature. In the 1950s, a relative consensus among political and economic leaders in the North, as in the South, took hold to the effect that economic well-being should be considered an end in itself for the whole of humanity. In other words, material well-being tends to be seen not as a culture-bound ideal but, on the contrary, as a universal value. All peoples throughout the world are thought to have the right to a comfortable standard of living. Within this ideological context, the developed Western nation-states have a collective duty or moral obligation to aid those countries which lie outside the universe of economic growth.

However, to attain the two combined objectives of global growth and individual well-being throughout the world implies the removal of various obstacles and submission to a number of drastic conditions. At root, what must be created is universal middle-class culture. Development, beyond the obvious need to produce ever more goods and services, is a process through which must emerge a new kind of human being and corresponding institutions. What must be universalized through development is a cultural complex centred around the notion that human life, if it is to be fully lived, cannot be constrained by limits of any kind.

To produce such a result in traditional societies, for whom the supposedly primordial principle of boundless expansion in the technological and economic domains is generally alien, presupposes overcoming symbolic and moral 'obstacles', that is, ridding these societies of various inhibiting ideas and practices such as myths, ceremonies, rituals, mutual aid, networks of solidarity, and the like. Three decades ago, these stringent conditions necessary to development had already been violently set forth:

Economic development of an underdeveloped people by themselves is not compatible with the maintenance of their traditional customs and mores. A break with the latter is a prerequisite to economic progress. What is needed is a revolution in the totality of social, cultural and religious institutions and habits, and thus in their psychological attitude, their philosophy and way of life. What is, therefore, required amounts in reality to social disorganization. Unhappiness and discontentment in the sense of wanting more than is obtainable at any moment is to be generated. The suffering and dislocation that may be caused in the process may be objectionable, but it appears to be the price that has to be paid for economic development; the condition of economic progress.[3]

From its beginnings, the goal of development has remained constant. What has changed is the means to achieving such an extension of market economics or private sector capitalism. Roughly speaking, development has been promoted by two institutions, the state and the market, indissolubly linked by the project of modernity. From as early as the 1950s up through the end of the 1970s, there was a wide consensus that the state should exercise the Benthamite function of realizing the greatest happiness for the greatest number. However, even as a welfare agency the state does not work against the market. Rather, it is a complementary institutional device which promotes the extension of the market. Through the state, as the theory goes, one creates, maintains and regulates markets for economic growth, the results of which should be distributed as fairly as possible throughout society. Growth with redistribution is clearly the model's ideal of social justice. Needless to say, such a process has totally failed in the South.

Since the 1980s, a remarkable shift, ideological but also operational to a degree, has taken place. The market itself is increasingly viewed as the only means to promote development. Within this neo-liberal framework, economic growth as such — without any redistribution at all — should allow us to solve the dramatic problem of poverty throughout the world without the smallest contribution imposed upon the rich. Efficiency is preferred to social justice as a means to an end, but also, sometimes, as an end in itself, as is well illustrated by the attempts of the IMF and the World Bank to impose liberalism on a worldwide scale through the process of structural adjustment. Their explicit objective is to inculcate solely economic motivations in the rich as well as in the poor.

The impact of this policy shift on aid is quite obvious. Increasingly, the very idea of aid is called into question, with the debate over whether aid promotes or retards development already well under way. Among arguments for the drastic limitation of aid, it is frequently declared that nothing is free, that people must learn to become self-supporting. The seductive power of the market is so powerful today that aid is no longer viewed as a normal policy. With the failure of the centralized planning model and the rise of the new market mentality, aid is quite explicitly defined in purely utilitarian terms. On this premise, a number of countries which are devoid of assets are at best condemned to the fringes of the development process.

In spite of their obvious differences, what should be noted for our purposes is that both models of development (whether based on the active intervention of the state in the market or on the dynamics of the market alone) produce self-interested individuals, reputedly liberated from all moral or social obligation. A world of opulence, a global society of total freedom — these are the illusory promises of development conceived as the expansion throughout the world of technological and economic modernity. Development is presented as the only and indisputable way out of an 'inhuman' universe of shortages and constraints. Needless to say, liberty and prosperity can be expected only through incessant work. Opulence, thus, does not mean the effective enjoyment of wealth, but rather the never-ending quest for 'something more' and 'something new'.

Paradoxically, perhaps, the actual obstacles to solving the world's most acute problems are less the cultural traditions of a large number of peoples than our own ingrained belief that the boundless progress which results from technology and the market can somehow liberate us from nature and society.

Market: A Place and a Principle

The market may appear today as so commonplace a term that to question its origin, its meaning, or its functions is a fundamentally meaningless enterprise. More than an institution, the market is viewed as a constitutive component of the human condition. Adam Smith's famous statement about 'the propensity in human nature to truck, barter and exchange one thing for another' expresses still today the widely accepted notion of the natural origins of the market principle.

If, however, we persist in our endeavour to understand something about the institution of the market, its transformation through time and the development of the associated concept, with its various meanings, we had better skip over economic science properly speaking. Three terms — supply, demand and price — are economics' basic tools for specifying what the market is doing, but not what it is. This refusal to examine the origins and nature of markets is clearly expressed with Gary Becker, a well-known proponent of the universal validity of economic logic, who states that: 'the economic approach is a comprehensive one that is applicable to all human behaviour.' For Becker such an approach is made up, as a matter of course, of 'the combined assumptions of maximizing behavior, market equilibrium, and stable preferences'.[4]

What about social sciences like sociology, anthropology and history? Unfortunately, following the generally accepted theoretical division of labour among disciplines, the market as an object of reflection has until recently been outside the realm of sociology. In anthropology, although several works, beginning with Malinowski and Mauss, have raised important questions about the nature of economic phenomena, there is nothing like a comparative theory of the market. Historians, tending to emphasize description over theory, most often simply rely on the orthodox notion of the universality of the market principle, as is well exemplified by the impressive work of Fernand Braudel. As a rule, in these three related disciplines the homogenizing effects of a generalized economic approach are obvious. Only with a small number of scholars, and more particularly with the outstanding work of Karl Polanyi, is the market seen as something more than a mere given.

In rejecting the ahistorical definition of market posited by economics, we are confronted with a clear distinction between the market as public place and the market as principle for regulating social relations. At first sight, no link at all seems conceivable between these two senses of market, except perhaps a chronology. Are we thus constrained to choose between the notion of a great divide between place and principle, and the idea of a substantive continuity from the former to the latter?

The market as place is a bounded, situated phenomenon, clearly differentiated from ordinary life. Numerous cases, both historical and ethnographic, could illustrate the extreme cultural and social variety of these formal characteristics. Very often the marketplace lies at a distance from the inhabited area, and functions as a neutral meeting space. Elsewhere, as for instance in Ancient Greece with the *agora*, the market is no longer a marginal area, but the merchant, as the intermediary of market exchanges, is thought to practise a debased activity.

What kinds of interactions do we find within the confines of the marketplace? For what purposes and with what motives do individuals act? Ideally, the individual is totally free to act in his own interests; no explicit limits are imposed. Such behaviour would be dangerously uncontrollable in everyday social practice. Hence, individuals in the marketplace are no longer seen as social beings with particular rights and duties. They are liberated from a deep feeling of belonging to a community. Furthermore, they may not bring their potential conflicts with them. To express this in a positive way, individuals must be able to initiate utilitarian exchange with anyone they choose. In this idealized scheme, the marketplace is composed of an aggregate of strangers willing to exchange with each other for their mutual advantage.

In fact, the marketplace is a much more complex locus, in which different kinds of social interactions take place. However, as a general rule, within any marketplace there is effective competitive behaviour between and among sellers and buyers, at least in an adumbrated form. In a sense, the main aspects of the market principle are already present within the marketplace. In other words, the marketplace contains the market principle in both senses of the verb 'contain': the market principle is found within the marketplace, but also held by it within specific limits.

Let us cite very briefly one example. Within Hausa society in Nigeria and Niger, one of the important traditional institutions is the marketplace (*kasuwa*). Within this well-defined area, located outside the village or town, buying and selling of goods takes place through various monetary devices. The people gathered in such a place come from various ethnic origins, and thus most of them are strangers involved in anonymous relations. The price of transacted objects is settled through the competitive mechanism of supply and demand. Personal relationships, though not totally absent, are therefore quite subordinated.

Sellers, professional or not, and buyers, no matter what their social position, must be free to go to the marketplace. And if people are periodically freed from cultural constraints, the same is true for the objects themselves. Indeed, as commodities, they are deprived of any symbolic or spiritual significance.

People become pure individuals just as commodities are pure things. Ideally speaking, anonymity is the rule and the precondition to becoming a liberated individual.[5]

This example (and there are many others possible) is meant to illustrate our main issue: how and why human societies have passed from a limited expression of the market principle to its generalization. The market in modern society has been fundamentally transformed from a particular to a universal phenomenon. To be sure, comparing the market as place and as abstract principle through time and space, in order to point out simultaneously identities and differences, is far from a simple task. Such a comparison raises a great number of questions. Here, I will be only able to address a few of them.

To being with, is the market in its most encompassing meaning a spontaneous natural order, as Friedrich Hayek argued? Is the market self-generating, even within a hostile institutional context? Or rather, according to the antithetical position of Karl Polanyi, is the market principle or the price-making market — the expression of the autonomy of the economic sphere — artificially produced? To accept this position would mean accepting the absence of any necessary connection between the market as a place and as a principle. Would it not be better to avoid both of these antagonistic interpretations, interpretations which, in their extremism, suggest the influence of the passions, either love or hatred?

Is it acceptable, intellectually and normatively, to conceive of a supposedly natural economic order based on the fundamental determinant of self-interest? Such a widespread view is the easiest but also the most superficial way to understand the validity and the legitimacy of a *sui generis*, self-regulating market.

In the opposite view, the determinative emphasis is shifted from the supposition of rational human nature to institutional relativity. Self-regulating markets are produced only under specific historical and cultural circumstances. Such is our modern singularity, according to Polanyi, for whom the price-making market is 'unnatural' and 'exceptional'. It is not the result of a long, natural process which transformed isolated and regulated markets.

While from the point of view adopted here Hayek's unconditionally pro-market position is highly debatable, the static Polanyian opposition to it must also be reconsidered. If the marketplace and the self-regulating market are operationally or even institutionally opposed, then they would seem to be two quite different phenomena. But if market-like behaviour develops within the very strictly defined limits of a marketplace, then neither a great divide nor an absolute continuity between the particular place and the generalized principle is conceivable.

Note that the artificiality posited by Polanyi is still applicable under the assumption of universal market elements. What is 'unnatural' and 'exceptional' is the project of an economic order autonomous of society at large. Once the elements constitutive of the market principle are no longer confined within the well-defined space and time of the marketplace, a radical change takes place. For reasons of space, only a few hints as to the nature of such a change are possible here.

During the 16th century in Europe, and more particularly in Holland and England, there was already active pressure to deregulate the different markets of mercantile capitalism. However, it is commonly acknowledged that the end of the 18th century, or even the early 19th century, is the moment when the price-making market system transformed both products and factors of production into commodities.

By way of simplification, a linear evolution in three steps can be outlined. Each of these steps is ordered in historical, but not necessarily linear, succession. The second step, for example, is not a direct and necessary product of the first. It is therefore more appropriate to speak of a sequential model. First, there are those societies in which the market principle is strictly limited to the space and time of the marketplace, or is more or less actualized only in peripheral exchange. Second are those societies in which purely economic activities, without explicit limits, are institutionally possible. However, people involved in commercial activities belong to one of the lowest categories or groups of society, or are foreigners, tolerated but deprived of social status. Ancient Greece, dynastic China, and the European Middle Ages are classic examples of this second stage. Finally, in a third stage of economic modernity, all attempts to limit the market become unacceptable. The whole of society is somehow viewed through the integrative force of the market.

The Middle-Class Filter

The idea of the market, as a principle of social regulation and as a mode of socialization, is historically and logically connected with the middle classes. In middle-class mentality, 'civilized' human beings correspond to those human beings who are convinced that the 'desire of wealth' is a natural and universal motivation. To fully understand this highly valued objective, it is necessary to form a more complex and systematic representation of what are believed to be the determinants of human action. J. S. Mill, one the most important thinkers of the 19th century, has given us one of the most explicit portraits.

For Mill, the 'desire for wealth' is confronted with two 'antagonizing principles' or two 'perpetual counter-motives' which are 'aversion to labour' and 'desire of the present enjoyment of costly indulgences'.[6] In Mill's scheme, the natural environment with its limited resources is a formidable obstacle to the practice of indolence and the immediate enjoyment of life. The outside world thus imposes the virtue of labour and the individual security of private ownership against these two 'counter-motives'. Such are the fundamental requirements to 'better our condition', in the words of Adam Smith. Quite clearly, this means that to be properly human one must transform oneself, must dominate the destructive part of one's nature. Only through hard work can man hope to achieve his true essence.

Within this middle-class worldview, the acquisitive quality of man must be viewed according to two well defined categories of traditional thought, the simplified dichotomies between rich and poor, and between property owners and labourers. These distinctions, even if they are a highly abstracted view of the complexity of social situations, are a way to make clear the conditions for successful market behaviour.

Let us follow the argument of Adam Smith, whose ideas are today widely shared by various representatives of the neo-liberal and new economics schools of thought. For Smith, the rich are defined by their 'avarice and ambition', whereas the poor are characterized by 'the hatred of labour and the love of present ease and enjoyment'.[7] According to him, the rich and the poor are the objects of opposing social evaluations. There is a 'disposition to admire, and almost to worship, the rich and the powerful, and to despise or, at least, to neglect persons of poor and mean condition'.[8]

Following this argument, the truth about human society is restricted to the logic of individual interests, fully expressed in free, voluntary and intentional exchange, institutionally organized and regulated by the market. Within this social space, viewed from this middle-class perspective, persons and things are to be somehow 'desocialized' or liberated from all imposed relations. What is transferred is wealth, viewed socially as pure means. The market, as an inextricable network of utilitarian exchanges, is thus frequently conceived as a device which liberates persons and things from what is quite diffusely defined as the imperialism of culture.

What lies behind such a belief is the idea of a whole society based on fungible qualities. This is particularly obvious with the general principles of exchangeability, equivalence or liquidity. Commodity exchange presents all the characteristics of a social abstraction objectified through the concept of price. Market relations are thus reduced to numerical values; with the price mechanism, the market appears to be composed of strangers connected only at the level of appearances, with all signs of friendship, loyalty or affection put aside.

There is a long tradition in Western thought which insists that social relations should not rest on such personal sentiments. For instance, in an essay entitled 'Deux paradoxes de l'amitié et de l'avarice' written at the end of the 16th century, friendship is viewed as an unreasonable passion, a 'great cause of division and discontent', whereas the search for wealth is highly praised as a 'moral virtue' and a 'civic responsibility'.[9] Four hundred years later, the same position reappears with Hayek's Great Society, radically opposed to any form of community. Relationships take place between abstract men, with neither passion nor sentiment. Therefore, 'one should keep what the poor neighbours would surely need, and use it to meet the anonymous demands of thousands of strangers.'[10]

The middle-class conception of society is that of an idealized market system. In reality, of course, market exchange is not a founding principle of social life, but a practice based on a number of institutional prerequisites. The market is not simply the realm of purely voluntary transfers by free individuals, that is, the pure aggregate of maximizing agents. However, this quite immediate and superficial way of viewing the general process of commodity exchange remains a highly persuasive ideology.

At first sight, we are given the impression that the great superiority of the market, as compared to interpersonal exchanges like the gift cycle, is that it, in a sense, externalizes individual social motivations, objectifying them through money. An internal part of the self is thus crystallized into a monetary object which constitutes, paradoxically perhaps, a polyvalent medium for all kinds of interchangeable relationships.

More globally, the price-making market as an encompassing social institution is a mediating collective artefact linking so-called free individuals through alienable things. Market exchange is, to use an evocative formula, a mode of communication designed to keep the other at arm's length. Certainly, gift exchange, contrary to what is too often stated, is also a mediating device which unites and separates at the same time. But with the market, the element of mediation is so obvious that individuals may have the impression that they are independent. More and more, the conjunctive forces of market and technology increase the distance among men, and between them and nature.

But the relative independence experienced by individuals through abstract and rationalized relationships does not mean the absence of constraining effects created by the social whole. Let us consider here only price. Beyond immediate perceptions, price is, in objectified form, a main component of the social totality. It significantly and unavoidably marks everybody's behaviour. Money, for example, is not simply a commodity: to this purely economic dimension must be added two others, one political, and one social. The two sides of any coin symbolize on the one, economic value and, on the other, political power. But such a double determination is not sufficient. The phenomenon of money, and more widely the market system, implies a reference to something internalized within each person. A diffuse feeling of social membership through common values, a single language and set of moral obligations, largely shared confidence, habits and even forms of hierarchy — all of these form the prerequisites of the market.

Market: A Transformative Power

To conceive of the market system as a man-made institution rather than as a self-creating, self-perpetuating order is a way of recognizing that the market is controlled by various traditional political, social and moral constraints, and reinforced by a number of political and cultural innovations. In other words, the existence and expansion of the market is dependent on institutions and cultural values. At the same time, however, the market tends to dominate the whole social context, the effects of this dominance varying according to concrete socio-cultural situations.

In today's environment, however, the tendency is, to the contrary, to grant the market transformative power. As such, it is one of the main challenges to the contemporary world. In various parts of the Third World, this transformation is purely disruptive. The market is viewed as an inevitable force, and it therefore becomes increasingly difficult to limit its expansion.

The twin forces of constant technical innovation and commodity exchange are basic pre-conditions for our modern ideal of manipulation and mastery of the human, social and natural domains. Both *homo faber* and *homo oeconomicus* become universal models. Efficiency and wealth are thus sought as ends in themselves. The subversive process, which is the potential transformation of everything into products, and then into commodities, is generally viewed as a necessary requirement for the 'good life'.

As stated above, it would be a serious error to believe that the long historical process from the physical marketplace to the ideal market as self-regulating process is a simple, spontaneous development. On the contrary, a radical change of values was necessary to move us from the limited and controlled expression of the market principle found in numerous historical and cultural situations, to the present, with our more or less general acceptance of the boundless extension of the market.

Let us state such a change in an exaggerated opposition. Previously, the full expression of one's individuality was generally possible within a well defined economic sphere which maintained necessary social cohesion against the market's destructive potentiality. With modernity for the first time, the whole of humanity, under the continuing pressure of the Western world, attempts unrestrainedly to organize social life on the basis of voluntary actions of individuals whose values are — or are supposed to be — dominantly, if not exclusively, utilitarian. Increasingly, it is becoming an imperative of mere existence to judge human action as good or bad not in and of itself, but by its results. Of course, various utilitarian moral philosophers have been repeating such a rule of conduct for two or even three centuries.

With this mandatory, individualist quest for material pleasure, not only have the products of labour taken the universal form of commodities, but human beings themselves, even outside the labour market, as well as natural components, are transformed into commodities through biotechnological innovation. Social relations are thus increasingly viewed as relations among private owners, buying and selling all manner of commodities among themselves.

More broadly, with the market as the exclusive mode of social distribution, the all-powerful technosciences are taken as givens which cannot be subject to question. They are considered our only path to worldly happiness. 'It works' comes the reply to any critical interrogation. With this pragmatist ethos in the ascendency, any search for the values founding our individual and collective choices is considered sterile, metaphysical speculation.

Technosciences and the market have become simply self-evident. According to the contemporary utilitarian credo, they accomplish the most desirable objective of our human condition, that is, to produce and distribute material prosperity for the greatest possible number. The process of commoditization which transforms all spheres of social life is at work throughout the world, with varying effects. We see here the extent to which development, as a policy and a practice, is a forceful attempt to implant new ways of thinking and acting which follow the rules of the market. At the level of localized projects, however, development still appears under the guise of apparent neutrality provided by its technical and productive characteristics.

Of course, from the situation of self-support at subsistence levels to direct insertion in the international market, there is a long and uncertain process of development. In various parts of the world, beginning immediately with the colonial era, the explicit objective was to impose practices like 'forced labour' or taxes, the necessary pre-conditions for introducing the 'natives' to market relationships such as 'free labour' and the voluntary sale of one's product for money. 'The tax ... promotes the circulation of currency with its attendant benefits to trade', proclaimed the *Instructions to political officers* for the English colonial programme in Africa.[11]

Development, from colonial times to the present day, is thus fundamentally the imposition, in one form or another, of a new institutional framework with its concomitant values as the prerequisites for the dynamism of the market. For the greater part of the world's population, development is the destruction of ethnic identities and solidarity networks in order to promote the legitimacy of self-interest as a fundamental human motivation. Very often, development means the possibility for a small minority to make large profits at the expense of the majority. With money as a supreme value, life counts less. The social imperative is quite obviously to get money by any available means.

The more individuals and groups are 'developed', the more they struggle for material advantages. Rural areas, particularly so-called backward ones, are to a certain, albeit declining, degree protected against this disintegrating modernity, as well as against the increased criminality it engenders. But, in difficult economic situations, traders endeavour, very often with success, to produce generalized scarcities of basic products by temporarily withdrawing from the market. Such profit-oriented practices endanger the very lives of many people. Imported displays of luxury goods become indicators of material success, and for the poor a mandatory but inaccessible model of the only real way to live.

Schematically, three categories of people result from such forced development. First, a small class of ultra-rich, who can accumulate much wealth while spending ostentatiously. Secondly, a varying number of people in an intermediary position. They represent the middle classes, those who balance production and consumption. Finally, there are the poor, excluded from the sharing of wealth, and preoccupied by problems of mere survival.

Development tends to produce shortages for a great number of people as the condition of excess for a small minority. It is also a kind of expropriation of multiple social relations in order to bring everybody into market conformity. Too often taken as equivalent to economic growth, development should more appropriately be viewed as a form of generalized violence. Of course, for those who view accumulation of wealth as the natural tendency for the whole of humanity, development is just a push in the right direction of aiding human nature to fulfil itself.

Contrary to this ideology of the 'natural identity of interests', development must be conceived as an 'artificial identification of interests' resulting from all kinds of disruptive constraints, to borrow Halévy's well-known phrase from his seminal work *The Growth of Philosophic Radicalism*, published in the first years of this century.[12] Paradoxically, to understand fully the phenomenon of development requires a radical questioning of ourselves. The true problem of our time is fundamentally our own Western or modernist cultural universe, based on the limitless expansion of technosciences and the market.

On Being Human

Confined as we are within a triumphant market ideology, it may appear incongruous even to raise the question of the limits of the market. More than ever, the world is confronted today with an alternative — should the market be contained by society or, on the contrary, should it be allowed to regulate the total social whole?

According to orthodox history, right from the days of the early marketplace to the present era of the price-setting principle, there has been or should have been a progressive evolution from a strictly limited market to a limitless one. If such a position is taken for granted, then market behaviour is obviously the universal path to true humanity. But how ought one to evaluate this market definition of what it is to be human?

A market definition of humanity is based on a few specific assumptions about motivation and cultural values. Being human is thought to be motivated by a constant search for material well-being, a desire to have more and more objects at one's disposal. This materialist assumption was already well expressed by Adam Smith when he spoke of 'bettering our condition'. Such an idea has been, and still is, considered a universal value somehow transcending all the particulars of culture and society.

The validity of this so-called universal value is based on the widely held representation of a constitutive contradiction in the human condition. The infinite wants of man are categorically opposed to the scarce resources of nature. Human beings are never satisfied, whatever their level of material abundance. In this worldview, humanity, constrained by its very nature to live in a finite universe, strives to have ever more effective control over nature and society. The great capitalist epic is the story of man's emancipation from this original destitution. According to such a 'tale', once upon a time there were human beings deprived of everything and consumed by innumerable wants and desires.

For the greatest part of its existence, humanity has been confined within a limited natural environment. However, with the Industrial Revolution's full development in the 19th century, the fantastic promise that one could free the whole of humanity from its primordial condition began to spread throughout the world. Only market capitalism was deemed capable of radically transforming traditional societies, and thus successfully leading humanity from poverty to unlimited wealth. The heroes of this epic are, of course, the middle classes.

To believe in such a tale, one must accept as an absolute truth the structural imbalance between wants and available resources. This is obviously a *sine qua non* for maintaining the 'desire of wealth'. In other words, to be human is to strive to escape from constraints, both natural and social, to become an independent individual. Of course, such an independence is not absolute; it must be qualified. Being human means being independent through the use of limitless technological innovation and a boundless market. Consequently, one is free and may act voluntarily, but only in order to increase exchanges. Within these combined technological and market imperatives, the individual is left to devote himself to his own self-interest unfettered.

Once more, Adam Smith expresses very clearly what we should consider as 'true humanity' and the 'good society' to be. For him, although he thinks that 'mutual love' and 'affection' could make society more 'happy' and 'agreeable', he is nevertheless convinced that: 'Society may subsist among different men, as among different merchants, from a sense of its utility . . .; and though no man in it should owe any obligation, or be bound in gratitude to any other, it may still be upheld by a mercenary exchange of good offices according to an agreed valuation.'[13]

To be human is thus simply to participate in market exchanges. For Adam Smith, as is well known, this 'propensity' is common to all men and is what differentiates them from animals. This is why the poor, more particularly beggars, guilty of laziness, are not really human, and as such are despised, whereas the rich are admired.

The common denominator of this omnipotent market ideology, the yardstick of measurement for both things and persons, is quite obviously price, both in its direct and metaphorical senses. Human beings not only have a price; they must be calculating subjects who know exactly on what criteria their worth is being evaluated.

To be human is thus to be able to exercise one's individual rights to accumulate goods within a culturally recognized competitive context. Note that this market modernity is the result of a symbolic and ethical reversal — economic logic is projected on to the social whole, to the point where it encompasses the very totality of which it is a part. In contrast to the situation in traditional societies, where those who were fully involved in market exchange had relatively low social status, today, according to Adam Smith and his numerous followers, we should all behave like 'merchants' if we really want to achieve our objectives as human beings. The market tends to become the only mode of social communication, even between those who are intimately connected. Within this universe of generalized commodities, it becomes logical that individuals increasingly become strangers to one another. Even for those who are culturally and socially close, the market mentality maintains a distance between them as individuals, almost as if close and distant relationships had become indistinguishable.

Georg Simmel's famous work, *The Philosophy of Money*, describes this transformation particularly well. For Simmel:

> Modern man's relationship to his environment usually develops in such a way that he becomes more removed from the groups closest to him in order to come closer to those more remote from him. The growing dissolution of family ties; the feeling of unbearable closeness when confined to the most initimate group, in which loyalty is often just as tragic as liberation; the increasing emphasis upon individuality which cuts itself off most sharply from the immediate environment. . . . The overall picture that this presents surely signifies a growing distance in genuine inner relationships and a declining distance in more external ones.[14]

Once human beings have been defined by the principle of utility, the virtues of development can no longer be called into question. If it is an imperative that every individual must accumulate ever more profit, it becomes relatively easy to define what is a backward country. Development, though it very often brings poverty for the majority, is consequently viewed as the only way to get out of the 'inhuman' state of 'want'. One might ask how we can elevate limitless well-being to the position of ultimate universal value when in the West itself grave problems, such as the ecological threat and the constitutive injustice of our social organization, are endangering the whole world.

Within the dominant market mentality, we can be but partially human at best. We stand on the verge of renouncing an essential part of our humanity. To build a society made up ideally of utilitarian exchanges between individuals and groups looking out for their own interests is to produce, in Marcuse's words, a 'one-dimensional man' in search of wealth as an end in itself.

Within a more humanist, moral and philosophical framework, this reductive view of human beings could be transcended. Human beings would be viewed as persons, following Kant's categorical imperative, and not simply as pure individuals. Of course, this principle of humanity is not absent from our Western traditions and from our present values, but it is largely subordinated to the principle of utility, according to which true human life is completely confined within the universe of things. With the principle of humanity on the contrary, being human would mean, according to Castoriadis, being an autonomous subject with a capacity for self-limitation. In an abstract sense, this autonomous subject is quite distinct from the independent individual subject to the heteronomous effects of technology and the market.

Our modernity, this radical project to create a new man and a new society, implies a difficult combination and constant tension between the two antagonistic principles of utility and humanity. Are we so confident that this secularizing project gives us the key to distinguishing, in the individual, social and cultural domains what is true and false, good and evil? Can a society be built and maintained only on the basis of universalist values such as these? Surely the valuing of human relations in itself, as the very foundation of any society, is what is missing. Indeed, this is precisely what is destroyed in the name of development.

Modernity cannot take into account the social dimension of man. Even for the individual strongly marked by modernity's imperatives, to learn to be human is possible only within a specific social context. To be human is to be at one and the same time an (economic) individual, a (psychological) person and a (social) being. This third dimension may be defined as the principle of community, emphasizing the inescapably particularistic aspect of the human condition. Values like solidarity, generosity, brotherhood and the like are all traditional. They contribute strongly to establishing and maintaining social cohesion, and to making our lives meaningful. They are values without which no society is viable, as has been pointed out by Durkheim and the members of the French sociological school who refer to the 'non-contractual element in contract'.

The insistence here is obviously on social relations as such. This brings us necessarily to the work of Mauss, and his famous essay *The Gift*. According to

Mauss, the gift is a condensed institution implying three social obligations: the obligation to give, to receive and to reciprocate. As such, gift exchange creates a fundamentally inclusive social relationship. Thus, by speaking of the 'atmosphere of the gift, where obligation and liberty intermingle', Mauss sees this institution as 'a considerable part of our morality and of our lives themselves'. Insisting on 'the egoism of our contemporaries and the individualism of our laws', he invites us to 'return to archaic society and to elements in it'. This has nothing to do with a utopian vision of mankind's future. Such a return would simply counterbalance the dominant principle of utility and its market manifestations. But more fundamentally, according to Mauss, 'the morality of the exchange-through-gift' is 'eternal', as it is 'the very principle of normal social life'.[15] These are the conditions on which every society should, in some respect, be built.

Even in a society in which the market principle is becoming the generalized guide to social interaction, a whole universe of interpersonal relationships remains a basic mode of social existence. Kinship and friendship networks are obvious examples of such a principle of community. This principle should be actualized more generally as a constitutive part of a wide variety of social links, even when the economic dimension is quite effective. No sustainable society is possible when nobody owes anything to anybody else.

It is scarcely necessary to say that the very existence of these conditions of a viable social system is dangerously threatened by the full modernist imposition of current economic and political institutions. With the combined effects of the state and the market, a number of intermediary forms of socialization are so weakened as no longer to fulfil any meaningful function. When social obligations like solidarity, generosity or mutual aid are replaced by administrative measures provided by the state, the self-interested individual is set free to act fully within the market sphere. Political redistribution is then made possible through the mediation of money. In a way, the state recreates in different form what has been destroyed in the process of modernization.

The ideal we presently diffuse throughout the world in the name of development is manifestly the model of an unbalanced society in which a limited and limiting norm of the independent individual is equated with 'the human'. A 'good society' is thus made up of individuals related by way of technology and the market. For us in the West, and increasingly for all others, this technological and market dependence is becoming the only way to conceive of freedom. To be free is to devote oneself to consumption; even people themselves are reduced to consumer goods.

The universalization through development of this mode of being human is simultaneously the destruction of various forms of sociality which should be taken today as prerequisites for a balanced social organization. Any viable alternative to our current market developmentalism should be based on a drastic reconsideration of our cultural values. Traditionally, in all societies, trading and technological activities were both strictly regulated and subjected to symbolic constraints. With development, all of these religious and spiritual limits are progressively removed. The end result, as is well demonstrated by contemporary Western societies, is a hypertrophic economic order, a subordinated political domain, and an indefinable social sphere of only residual significance. Individual freedom, this cardinal value of our cultural system, thus involves the boundless use of all manner of resources, and as such it presents a fundamental threat to our ecology, even our very survival.

To date, the project for the total 'liberation' of man has all the appearances of an ineluctable movement, imposed by the two closely connected forces of technological and market utopianism. Within such a context, how are we to preserve what is properly human in each of us when our modes of action and our ways of thinking are subject to these powerful constraints? How are we to avoid becoming individually and collectively the instruments and the victims of systems of our own construction, systems which we have taken as the expression of our own aspirations?

What is at stake in this generalized process of artificialism and individualism is the loss of our capacity for self-limitation, that distinctive quality of humanity, alone capable of taking a certain distance and reflecting on its plight.

References

1. P. L. Berger, *The Capitalist Revolution: Fifty Propositions About Prosperity, Equality, and Liberty*, New York: Basic Books, 1986, p. 48.

2. 'Full Text of the Kirkpatrick Plan', Congressional Record, The Senate, 11 May 1984.

3. J. L. Sadie, 'The Social Anthropology of Economic Underdevelopment', *The Economic Journal*, No. 70, 1960, p. 302.

4. G. Becker, *The Economic Approach to Human Behavior*, Chicago: University of Chicago Press, 1976, p. 8 and p. 5.

5. See G. Nicolas, *Dynamique sociale et appréhension du monde au sein d'une société hausa*, Paris: Institut d'ethnologie, 1975, pp. 166–70.

6. See M. Blaug, *The Methodology of Economics*, Cambridge: Cambridge University Press, 1980, p. 60.

7. A. Smith, *An Inquiry into the Nature and Causes of the Wealth of Nations*, Oxford: Clarendon Press, 1976, p. 709 (first published in 1776).

8. A. Smith, *The Theory of Moral Sentiments*, Oxford: Clarendon Press, 1976, p. 61 (first published in 1759).

9. L. Rothkrug, *Opposition to Louis XIV: The Political and Social Origins of the French Enlightenment*, Princeton: Princeton University Press, 1965, pp. 301–2.

10. See Ph. Nemo, *La société de droit selon F. A. Hayek*, Paris: P.U.F., 1988, p. 298.

11. Lord Lugard, *Political Memoranda*, Revision of instructions to political officers on subjects chiefly political and administrative, 1913–1918, London: Frank Cass, 1970, pp. 205–6.

12. See E. Halévy, *The Growth of Philosophic Radicalism* (abridged edition), London: Faber & Faber, 1972.

13. A. Smith, *The Theory of Moral Sentiments*, op. cit., p. 86.

14. G. Simmel, *The Philosophy of Money*, London: Routledge & Kegan Paul, 1978, p. 476 (first published in German in 1907).

15. M. Mauss, *The Gift: The Form and Reason for Exchange in Archaic Societies*, London: Routledge, 1990, pp. 65, 69, 70 (first published in French in 1924).

Bibliography

Both the work of K. Polanyi and the contributions of a number of scholars, particularly among the Austrian school, are indispensible guides to the main issues in the theoretical debate on the idea and the reality of the market. With Polanyi, the self-regulating market is created by the state in the 19th century. A discontinuity is thus obvious between such a price-making market and all other forms of exchange, including the regulated market and marketplaces. These views are developed in three works: *The Great Transformation*, Boston: Beacon, 1957 — first edition 1944; *Trade and Market in the Early Empires*, Glencoe, Illinois: The Free Press, 1957, edited with C. M. Arensberg and H. W. Pearson; and *The Livelihood of Man*, (New York: Academic Press, 1977. For L. von Mises *Human Action*, New Haven: Yale University Press, 1949, third revised edition in 1966, and F. A. Hayek, *Law, Legislation and Liberty*, 3 vol., London: Routledge and Kegan Paul, 1982, two well-known representatives of the Austrian school, the free market is a spontaneous order, and, as such, is the natural outcome of a long evolutionary process based on self-interested human nature.

P. Rosanvallon, *Le liberalisme economique*, Paris: Le Seuil, 1989, offers a comprehensive view of the history of the idea of the market as a principle of social regulation in classical social thought. A. Hirschman, *The Passions and the Interest: Political Arguments for Capitalism before its Triumph*, Princeton: Princeton University Press, 1977, elegantly traces the hopes behind the rise of the market principle, while J. Appleby, *Economic Thought and Ideology in Seventeenth Century England*, Princeton: Princeton University Press, 1978, gives an account of the intellectual debate which mirrored the clash between the values of the ancient moral economy and the values of the nascent liberal economy. How especially free trade was the puzzling issue which brought forth the formulation of new principles, is shown by W. Barber, *British Economic Thought and India 1600–1858: A Study in the History of Development Economics*, Oxford: Clarendon, 1975.

For a wide variety of empirical data on the manifold phenomena of the market through time and space, consult F. Braudel, *The Wheels of Commerce*, New York: Harper & Row, 1982, and P. Bohannan & G. Dalton, *Markets in Africa: Eight Subsistence Economies in Transition*, Evanston: Northwestern University Press, 1962. C. Geertz, 'Suq: The Bazaar Economy in Sefrou', in C. Geertz et al., *Meaning and Order in Moroccan Society*, Cambridge: Cambridge University Press, 1979, provides a detailed anthropological account of a particular pre-modern market.

Ideologically, the market society is composed of independent individuals who are contractually linked, as exemplified in the work of Adam Smith. Today such a view is quite widespread. See, for instance, J. M. Buchanan, *Liberty, Market and State: Political Economy in the 1980s*, Brighton: Wheatsheaf Books, 1986, and A. H. Shand, *Free Market Morality: The Political Economy of the Austrian School*, London: Routledge, 1990, G. Dworkin et al., *Markets and Morals*, New York: J. Wiley, 1977, discuss various issues concerning ethics and market behaviour, while R. Heilbronner, *Behind the Veil of Economics*, Cambridge: Cambridge University Press, 1988, exposes the hidden assumptions of the market mentality.

Needs

Ivan Illich

No matter where you travel, the landscape is recognizable. All over the world it is cluttered with cooling towers and parking lots, agribusiness and megacities. But now that development is ending — earth was the wrong planet for this kind of construction — the growth projects are rapidly turning into ruins, into junk, among which we must learn to live. Twenty years ago, the consequences of the worship of growth already appeared 'counter-intuitive'. Today, *Time* magazine publicizes them with apocalyptic cover stories. And no one knows how to live with these frightening new Horsemen of the Apocalypse, many more than four of them — a changing climate, genetic depletion, pollution, the breakdown of various immunities, rising sea levels and millions of fugitives. Even to address these issues, one is caught in the impossible dilemma of fostering either panic or cynicism. But even more difficult than to survive with these environmental changes is the horror of living with the habits of needing which four decades of development have established. The needs that the rain dance of development kindled not only justified the despoliation and poisoning of the earth; they also acted on deeper level. They transmogrified human nature. They reshaped the mind and senses of *homo sapiens* into those of *homo miserabilis*. 'Basic needs' may be the most insidious legacy left behind by development.

The transformation occurred over a couple of centuries. During this time the root certainty was change, sometimes called progress, sometimes development, sometimes growth. In this secular process, men claimed to have discovered 'resources' in culture and nature — in what had been their commons — and turned them into economic values. The historian of scarcity relates the story. Like churned cream which suddenly congeals into butter, *homo miserabilis* recently appeared, almost overnight, from a mutation of *homo economicus*, the protagonist of scarcity. The post-World War II generation witnessed this change of state in human nature from common to *needy* man. Half of all individuals born on the earth as *homo* are of this new kind.

Archaeological estimates place the total number of adult individuals belonging to *homo sapiens* who have ever lived at no more than five billion. They lived between the time the Early Stone Age hunting scenes of Lascaux were painted and the year Picasso shocked the world with the horror of Guernica. They made up ten thousand generations and lived in thousands of different lifestyles speaking innumerable distinct tongues. They were snow men and cattle breeders, Romans and Moguls, sailors and nomads. Each mode of living framed the one condition of being human in a different way: around the hoe, the spindle, wood, bronze or iron tools. But in each instance, to be human meant communal submission to the rule of necessity in this particular place, at this particular time. Each culture translated this rule of necessity into a different idiom. And each view of necessity was expressed in a different way — whether it was to bury the dead or to exorcize fears. This enormous variety of cultures bears witness to the plasticity of desire and longing which is tasted so differently in each individual and society. Fancy drove Tongans on their outriggers across thousands of miles of ocean. It drove Toltecs from Mexico to build temple outposts in Wisconsin, Muslims from Outer Mongolia to visit the Ka'aba and Scots the Holy Land. But in spite of all the forms of anguish and awe, terror and ecstasy, the unknown following death, nothing indicates that the ancestral half of humanity experienced anything like what we take for granted under the designation of need.

The second and larger part of humanity was born in the epoch that I can remember, after Guernica, 1936. Most people who are now adults are addicted to electric power, synthetic clothing, junk food and travel. They do live longer; but if we are to believe the osteo-palaeontologists who rummage through cemeteries to study bones, the second half of humanity contains a large proportion of people who are malnourished and physically impaired. And most of these five billion currently alive accept unquestioningly their human condition as one of dependence on goods and services, a dependence which they call need. In just one generation, needy man — *homo miserabilis* — has become the norm.

The historical movement of the West, under the flag of evolution/progress/ growth/development, discovered and then prescribed *needs*. In this process, we can observe a transition from man, the bungling toiler, to man, the needy addict. I divide this essay into two parts. In the first I gather together some observations on the phenomenology of needs, and in the second I trace the history of *homo miserabilis* as it is reflected by the term 'needs' in the context of the official discourse on development started by President Harry Truman.

Neither Necessities Nor Desires

It is difficult to speak convincingly about the historicity of needs. The existence of specifiable and measurable human needs has become so natural that we are prepared to attribute the need for oxygen to certain bacteria, while at the same time we reserve a condescending smile for Albert the Great who spoke about the desire of a heavy stone to fall downwards until it reaches the centre of the Earth.

The human condition has come to be defined by the needs common to its members. For the new generation, the needs that are common to men and women, yellow and white — rather than common dignity or common redemption in Christ or some other god — are the hallmark and manifestation of common humanity. With unscrupulous benevolence, needs are imputed to others. The new morality based on the imputation of basic needs has been far more successful in winning universal allegiance than its historical predecessor, the imputation of a catholic need for eternal salvation. As a result, needs have become the worldwide foundation of common social certainties that relegate inherited cultural and religious assumptions about human limitation to the realm of so-called personal values that, at best, deserve tolerant respect. The spread of needs that modern development has wrought will not be stemmed by the end of the development discourse.

It is easier to junk the inefficiently air-conditioned skyscrapers of San Juan de Puerto Rico than it is to extinguish the yearning for an artificial climate. And once this yearning has become a need, the discovery of comfort on an island exposed to the trade winds will become very difficult. The right to full employment will long have been exposed as an impossible pursuit, before women's need for full-time jobs will have been deconstructed. Twenty years after the public recognition that medical ministrations are marginal to a nation's health, the costs of unhealthy professional medicine continue to outpace those of a healthy life style. It will be much easier to gain a UN consensus that the development epoch has come to an end, that it is time to delink the pursuit of peace and justice from the organized satisfaction of needs, than it will be to find acceptance for the idea that needs are a social habit acquired in the 20th century and a habit that needs to be kicked in the next.

For people shaped by the moral climate of the last 50 years, questions about the notional status of needs sound offensive to the hungry, destructive of the one common base for morality we have and, in addition, pointless. These people need to be reminded that the social reconstruction of *homo sapiens* (the wise or tasteful human) into *needy man* has transformed the status of necessity. From being part and parcel of the human condition, necessity was turned into an enemy or an evil.

The development decades can be understood as the epoch during which, at immense cost, a worldwide ceremony has been celebrated to ritualize the end of necessity. Schools, Hospitals, Airports, Correctional and Mental Institutions, the Media can be understood as networks of temples built to hallow the deconstruction of necessities and the reconstruction of desires into needs. Well into the industrial age, for most people living in subsistence cultures, life was still predicated on the recognition of limits that just could not be transgressed. Life was bounded within the realm of immutable necessities. The soil yielded only known crops; the trip to the market took three days; the son could infer from the father what his future would be. For 'need' meant of necessity 'as needs must be'. Such needs, meaning necessities, had to be endured.

Each culture was the social *gestalt* assumed by the acceptance of needs at one place, in one particular generation. Each was the historical expression of a unique celebration of life within an art of suffering that made it possible to celebrate necessities. What mediated between desire and suffering differed from culture to culture. It could be good or bad stars — or just plain luck; ancestral blessings and curses — or personal karma; witchcraft and evil spirits — or providence. In a moral economy of subsistence, the existence of desires is taken as much for granted as the certainty that they could not be stilled.

When needs occur in the modern development discourse, however, they are neither necessities nor desires. Development is the word for a promise — for a guarantee proffered to break the rule of necessity, using the new powers of science, technology and politics. Under the influence of this promise, desires also changed their status. The hope to accomplish the good has been replaced by the expectation that needs will be defined and satisfied. Emphatically, expectations refer to a different 'not yet' than hopes. Hope springs from the necessity that fosters desire. Hope orients toward the unpredictable, the unexpected, the surprising. Expectations spring from needs fostered by the promise of development. They orient toward claims, entitlements and demands. Hope appeals to the arbitrariness of a personal other, be he human or divine. Expectations build on the functioning of impersonal systems that will deliver nutrition, health care, education, security and more. Hope faces the unpredictable, expectation the probable.

Hopes mutate into expectations. Desires mutate into claims when necessities fade in the light of development. When this happens, hope and desire appear as irrational hangovers from a dark age. The human phenomenon has ceased to be defined by the art of suffering necessity; now it is understood as the measure of imputed lacks which translate into needs.

This translation, for most of the world's people, has happened during the last 30 years. Needs have only very recently become a universal experience, and only just now, have people come to speak of their needs for shelter, education, love and personal intimacy. Today it has become almost impossible to deny the existence of needs. Under the tacit assumption of development, a heart bypass is no longer seen as a wanton desire or a fancy demand of the rich. Within the context of an obstinate rebellion against necessity, the stranger has become the catalyst who amalgamates desire and transgression into the felt reality of a need. Paradoxically, this reality acquires its absolute legitimacy only when the needs I experience are attributed to strangers, even when it is obvious that for the majority of them they just cannot be met. Need, then, stands for the normal condition of *homo miserabilis*. It stands for something that is definitely beyond the majority's reach. To see how this impasse was reached, it is instructive to trace the stages through which the notion of needs was related to economic and social development during the last few decades.

'Needs' in the Development Discourse

The political pursuit of development brought needs into the Western political discourse. In his Inaugural Address of 1949, US President Harry Truman sounded altogether credible when he advocated the need for US intervention in foreign nations to bring about 'industrial progress' in order 'to raise the standard of living' in the 'underdeveloped areas' of the world. He did not mention revolution. His aim was to 'lighten the burden of the poor', and this could be accomplished by producing 'more food, more clothing, more materials for housing and more mechanical power'. He and his advisers saw 'greater production as the key to prosperity and peace'.[1] He spoke in terms of legitimate aspirations, not about needs. Indeed Truman was very far from imputing to people everywhere a catholic set of defined needs which demand satisfaction that development must bring.

When Truman spoke, poverty — in terms of a market economy — was still the common lot of the overwhelming majority in the world. Surprisingly, a few nations appeared to have overcome this fate, thereby stimulating the desire in others to do the same. Truman's common sense led him to believe that a universal law of progress was applicable, not only to isolated individuals or groups, but also to humanity at large through national economies. Thus he used the term 'underdeveloped' for collective social entities, and spoke of the need to create 'an economic base' capable of meeting 'the expectations which the modern world has aroused' in people all over the planet.[2]

Twelve years later, Americans heard that: 'People in huts and in villages of half the globe struggle to break the bonds of mass misery. . . . We pledge to help them to help themselves. . . . We pledge this, not because we seek their votes, but because it is the right thing.'[3] Thus spoke John F. Kennedy in his Inaugural Address in 1961. Where Truman had noticed awakening expectations, Kennedy perceived people's secular struggle against an evil reality. Besides meeting new expectations, development therefore had to destroy inherited bonds. His statement symbolized an emerging consensus in the US that most people are needy, these needs give them rights, these rights translate into entitlements for care, and therefore impose duties on the rich and the powerful.

According to Kennedy, these needs are not just economic in nature. The 'poor' nations 'have recognized the need for an intensive program for self-help', a need 'for social progress which is an indispensable condition for growth, not a substitute for economic development. . . . Without social development the great majority of the people remain in poverty, while the privileged few reap the benefits of rising abundance.'[4]

One year after Castro's rise to power, Kennedy promised more than mere economic or technical help; he solemnly pledged political intervention — 'help in a peaceful revolution of hope'. Further, he went on to adopt fully the prevailing conventional rhetoric of political economy. He had to agree with Khrushchev who told him in Vienna: 'The continuing revolutionary process in various countries is the status quo, and anyone who tries to halt that process not only is altering the status quo but is an aggressor.'[5] So Kennedy stressed 'the shocking and urgent conditions' and the need for an 'alliance for social progress.' For Truman, it was the modern world 'which arouses new aspirations', and he focused on the need 'to lighten the burden of their poverty'. Kennedy believed that half the world 'lives in the bonds of misery' with a sense of injustice 'which breeds political and social unrest'. In the perspective of the 1960s White House, poverty ceased to be fate; it had become an operational concept — the result of unjust social and economic conditions, the lack of modern education, the prevalence of inadequate and backward technology. Poverty was now viewed as a plague, something amenable to therapy, a problem to be solved.

In 1962, the United Nations began to operationalize poverty. The Secretary General referred to 'those people who live below an acceptable minimum standard'. He gave credence to two notions: humanity could now be split into those above and those below a measurable standard; and a new kind of bureaucracy was called for to establish criteria of what is acceptable — and what is not. The first instrument that was created to establish this standard was called the GNP. This device, which was first publicly used in the late 1940s, is a surprising mental eggbeater that compounds all goods and all services produced by all people and defines the resulting omelette as the gross value of a nation. This gross national hotchpotch strains from reality all and only those characteristics that economists can digest. By the late '70s, it was obvious that, under the aegis of development, most people become poorer as GNP grows.

In 1973 the President of the World Bank declared that: 'Progress measured by a single measuring rod, the GNP, has contributed significantly to exacerbate the inequalities of income distribution.' For this reason, McNamara declared that the central objective of development policies should be 'the attack on absolute poverty' which resulted from economic growth and which affected '40% of the nearly two billion individuals living in the developing nations'. According to him, this side-effect of development is 'so extreme that it degrades the lives of individuals below minimal norms of human decency'.[6] He established a brains trust within the World Bank which began to translate these 'norms of human decency' into technical measurements of disembedded, specific needs that could be expressed in monetary terms. Reference to 'needs' became the method by which, henceforth, social scientists and bureaucrats could distinguish between mere growth and true development.

As long as poverty had been a synonym for the human condition, it was understood as a pervasive feature in the social landscape of every culture. Primarily and above all, it referred to the precarious conditions within which most people survived most of the time. Poverty was a general concept for a specific cultural interpretation of the necessity to live within very narrow limits, defined differently for each place and time. It was the name for a unique and ecologically sustainable style of coping with historically given, rather than technically construed, necessity, the 'need' to face the unavoidable, not a lack. Poverty, in Christian Europe at least, was recognized as the inevitable destiny of the powerless. It denotes the ontological situation of all those who 'need to die . . . but not yet'. Certainly, neither power, nor wealth, nor poverty were related to the productivity of groups or people.

This necessity to accept fate, kismet, providence, the will of God had been eroded with the spread of Enlightenment. During the earlier 20th century it lost much of its legitimacy as progress became the name for the technological and political revolt against all ideologies that recognize the rule of necessity. Already in the epoch of steam, the engineer had become the symbol of the liberator, a messiah who would lead humanity to conquer nature. By the early 20th century, society itself had become the subject of manipulative engineering. But it was only the social translation of progress into professionally guided development which made the rebellion against necessity a programmed infection. Nothing shows this more clearly than the identification of charity with the technical sponsorship of progress, as reflected in the social Encyclicals of Pope Paul VI. This Pope was deeply devoted to St. Francis of Assisi — the spouse of Lady of Poverty. And yet, he instructed his faithful on the duty to increase productivity and to assist others in their development.

> Individual nations must raise the level of the quantity and the quality of production to give the life of all their citizens truly human dignity, and give assistance to the common development of the human race.[7]
>
> The complete development of the individual must be joined with that of the human race and must be accomplished by mutual effort.[8]

In sentences of this kind, religious leaders of all denominations, shades and political allegiance have given their blessing to the revolt against the human condition. Paul VI is remarkable because, in a way, he took the lead on the left. In this encyclical the Pope, however, still speaks in the language of the 1950s. As with Truman, poverty for him still represented a kind of common floor: a condition from which progress starts.

By 1970 poverty in public parlance had acquired a new connotation — that of an economic threshold. And this changed its nature for modern humans. Poverty became a measure of a person's lack in terms of 'needed' goods, and even more in 'needed services'. By defining the poor as those who lack what money could buy for them to make them 'fully human', poverty, in New York City as well as in Ethiopia, became an abstract universal measure of underconsumption.[9] Those who survive in spite of indexed underconsumption were thereby placed into a new, sub-human category, and perceived as victims of a double bind. Their *de facto* subsistence became almost inexplicable in economic terminology, while their actual subsistence activities came to be labelled as sub-human, if they were not frankly viewed as inhuman and indecent.

Politicians incorporated the poverty line into their platforms and economists began to explore the theoretical significance of this inelastic threshold. In economic theory it is improper to speak of (economic) wants below an income level where demands have become substantially incommensurable. People who have lost their subsistence outside the cash economy, and who under these conditions have only occasional and minimal access to cash, lack the power to behave according to economic rationality; they cannot, for example, afford to trade food for shelter or for clothing or tools. They are neither members of the economy, nor are they capable of living, feeling and acting as they did before they lost the support of a moral economy of subsistence. The new category of economic cripples, thus defined, may in fact survive, but they do not fully partake of the characteristics of *homo economicus*. They exist — all over the world — but they are marginal, not just to the national economy but to modern humanity itself, since the latter, from the time of Mandeville, has been defined in terms of the ability to make choices under the assumption of scarcity. Unlike their ancestors, they do have urgent economic needs, and unlike legitimate participants in the modern economy — no matter how poor — any choice between alternative satisfactions, which is implied in the concept of economic need, is ruled out for them.

No wonder that 'population characteristics' began to figure in the development calculus. Populations ceased to be the exogenous object for whom development could be planned. Instead they came to figure as endogenous variables alongside capital and natural resources. While, at the beginning of the 1950s, the problem of developing countries was viewed essentially as a problem of productive wealth, by the end of that decade it became widely acknowledged that the crucial factor was not production, but rather the capacity to produce which is inherent in people.[10] People thus became legitimate ingredients of economic growth. It was then no longer necessary to distinguish economic and social development, since development — as distinct from a growth in GNP — automatically had to include both.

Insufficiently qualified or capitalized people were increasingly mentioned as a burden or brake on development. This third evolutionary step, which integrates the people factor into the economic growth calculus, has a history which throws light on the semantics of the word, needs.

In the mid-1950s, economists under the influence of W. Arthur Lewis had begun to argue that certain components of medical and educational services should not be understood as personal consumption because they were necessary prerequisites of economic development.[11] The great differences in the results of similar development policies in countries at the same levels of monetary income, could not be explained without paying attention to the investments made in human beings. The quality and distribution of training, physical well-being, social discipline and participation came to be called 'the residual factor'. Independent of the amount of capital and labour available, economic development seemed to hinge on these social qualifications of people in terms of their relevance for the economy. Economic progress by the mid-1960s was conditioned by the ability to instil in large population groups the need for 'manpower qualifications'. Education, public health, public information and personnel management were prominently discussed as so many sectors of 'manpower planning'. Leaders of popular movements who promoted 'conscientization' from Trivandrum to Brazil, in effect, supported the same idea — until people change and recognize their needs, they cannot contribute to the growth of productive forces.

This euphoria did not last. During the 1970s, two empirical observations qualified the concept of human capital[12] that had been developed in the 1960s. On the one hand, the assumption that the value of education or medical services is directly reflected in manpower qualifications lost much of its credibility. No proof could be found that investment in schools or clinics was causally connected with the appearance of more productive people. On the other hand, the labour theory of value lost its meaning, even in the weak sense in which it had entered mainstream economics. It became obvious that, irrespective of available manpower qualifications, the modernized sector could not be made sufficiently labour-intensive to provide enough jobs to justify the economically necessary redistribution of income implied by social service expenditure. And no conceivable employment-oriented development strategy could create the paid work which would employ the most disadvantaged third of the population in any but the most exceptional of the developing nations. As a result, planners during the 1980s transposed the development melody to a fourth key. Under various designations, they undertook the economic colonization of the informal sector. Let people who have become conscious of their needs fend for themselves in satisfying them.

New stress was put on incentives for activities that would keep people busy in the black market, in the barter economy, or self-supporting in the 'traditional sector'. Above all, shadow work became quantitatively more important, not just in practice, but also in policy. By shadow work I mean that the performance of unpaid activities that, in a market-intensive society, are necessary to transform purchased commodities into consumable goods. Finally, self-help activities, which in the 1960s smacked of second best, became a favourite growth sector of planners and organizers during the 80s. This is the context within which the resuscitation of the discourse on needs must be interpreted.

Under the Mask of Compassion

Development can be visualized as a process by which people are lifted out of their traditional cultural commons. In this transition, cultural bonds are dissolved, even though culture can continue to tinge development in superficial ways — one need only observe rural people recently transplanted to the megacities of the Third World. Development can be imagined as a blast of wind that blows people off their feet, out of their familiar space, and places them on an artificial platform, a new structure of living. In order to survive on this exposed and raised foundation, people are compelled to achieve new minimum levels of consumption, for example, in formal education, public health measures, frequency in the use of transportation and rental housing. The overall process is usually couched in the language of engineering — the creation of infrastructures, the building and co-ordination of systems, various growth stages, social escalators. Even rural development is discussed in this urban language.

Under the heavy weight of the new structures, the cultural bedrock of poverty cannot remain intact; it cracks. People are forced to live on a fragile crust, below which something entirely new and inhuman lurks. In *traditional* poverty, people could rely on finding a cultural hammock. And there was always the ground level to depend on, as a squatter or beggar. This side of the grave, no one could sink below ground. Hell was a real pit, but it was for those who had not shared with the poor in this life, to be suffered after death. This no longer holds. Modernized drop-outs are neither beggars nor bums. They are victimized by the needs attributed to them by some 'poverty pimp'.[13] They have fallen through the poverty line, and each passing year diminishes their chances of ever rising again above the line to satisfy the needs they now attribute to themselves.

Welfare is not a cultural hammock. It is an unprecedented mediation of scarce resources through agents who not only define what need is, and certify where it exists, but also closely supervise its remedy — with or without the needy's approval. Social insurance is not reliance on community support in case of disaster. Rather, it is one of the ultimate forms of political control in a society in which protection against future risks is valued higher than access to present satisfaction or joy. Needs, discussed as criteria for development strategies, clearly have nothing to do with either traditional necessities or desires, as I suggested above. And yet, during the second and third 'development decades', people by the million have learned to experience their poverty in terms of unmet operationalized needs.

Paradoxically, 'needs' became a most powerful emblem in spite of the fact that, for the mainstream economist, 'need' is a non-word. Economic theory does not acknowledge that there are such things as needs. Further, economics can say much that is useful about wants, preferences and demands. But 'need' is a moral, psychological or physical imperative which brooks no compromise or adjustment — or (economic) analysis.

Most economists, up to the present day, declare themselves incompetent to include needs in their analysis, and prefer to leave the needs discussion to philosophers or politicians. On the other hand, a growing number of economists, critical of conventional development theory and practice, place in 'basic needs' the foundation for what came to be called 'the new economic order'.[14] They find in needs the term for non-negotiable, mutually incommensurable requirements of human nature. Powerfully, they root economic theory in the ontological status of being human. They argue that, unless basic needs are provided for by the economy, economic preferences, choices and wants just cannot be effectively formulated. Their new world order is built on the foundations of a humanity whose basic needs have been met, thanks to a new kind of economy that recognizes their existence.

But before the concept of needs could be incorporated in an economic argument, it had to be defined and classified. For this undertaking, Abraham Maslow's theory of a needs hierarchy somewhat belatedly became very influential. Indeed, physical safety, affection, esteem and, ultimately, self-realization needs underlie most current discussion as the key categories. Unlike wants which, since Hobbes, are considered as equal to each other — 'since they are simply what people want' — needs are consistently discussed as fitting into a hierarchy which has an objective and normative status. They are generally spoken about as realities to be disinterestedly studied by needs experts. Some of the new economists go so far as to make of this needs hierarchy the cornerstone of a new ethic. For example, Erich Fromm believed that 'the sane society' is an arrangement that

> corresponds to the needs of man, not necessarily to what he feels to be his needs (because even the most pathological aims can be felt subjectively as that which the person wants most) but to what his needs are objectively, as they can be ascertained by the study of man.[15]

Up to now, the most complete critical study of the needs discourse and its implications has been made by Marianne Gronemeyer.[16] She argues that needs, in the current sense, are a new way of formulating the assumption of universal scarcity. Following her argument, it becomes likely that the public credibility of economic assumptions, which is already wavering, can survive only if a new economics reconstructs itself on the assumption of definable 'basic needs'. Further, Gronemeyer shows that needs, defined in terms of ostensibly scientific criteria, permit a redefinition of human nature according to the convenience and interests of the professionals who administer and serve these needs. An economy based on wants — whether it be for therapy, education or transportation — now inevitably leads to socially intolerable levels of polarization. By contrast, an economy based on needs — including their identification by experts and well managed satisfaction — can provide unprecedented legitimacy for the use of this science in the service of the social control of 'needy' man.

Needs, as a term and as an idea, occupy a place within current mental topology that did not exist in the constellation of meanings of previous epochs. During the Second Development Decade, the notion of needs began to shine like a supernova in the semantic sky. As Gronemeyer has argued, insistence on basic needs has now defined the human phenomenon itself as divisible — the needs discourse implies that you can become either more or less human. It is as normative and double-edged a tool as some powerful drug. By defining our common humanity by common needs, we reduce the individual to a mere profile of his needs.

From Needs to Requirements

Just as the Enlightenment's idea of progress prepared the ground for what was almost certain to happen anyway, the management of social change in the name of development has prepared the political environment for the redefinition of the human condition in terms of cybernetics — as an open system that optimizes the maintenance of the provisional immunity of individuals reduced to sub-systems. And just as needs became an important emblem which allowed managers to provide a philanthropic rationale for the destruction of cultures, so, now, needs are being replaced by the new emblem of 'basic requirements' under which the new goal, 'survival of the earth' can be justified.

In the 1970s, experts presented themselves as servants who helped the poor become conscious of their true needs, as a Big Brother to assist them in the formulation of their claims. This dream of bleeding hearts and blue-eyed do-gooders can today be easily dismissed as the nonsense of an age already past. 'Needs', in a vastly more interdependent, complex, polluted and crowded world, can no longer be identified and quantified, except through intense teamwork and scrutiny by systems specialists. And in *this* new world, the needs discourse becomes the pre-eminent device for reducing people to individual units with input *requirements*.

When this occurs, *homo economicus* is rapidly recognized as an obsolete myth — the planet can no longer afford this wasteful luxury — and replaced by *homo systematicus*. The needs of this latter invention metamorphose from economic wants into system requirements, these being determined by an exclusivist professional hegemony brooking no deviation whatsoever. The fact that many people today already recognize their systemic requirements principally argues the power of professional prestige and pedagogy, and the final loss of personal autonomy. The process began originally with the loss of the commons and now appears complete as people are turned into abstract elements of a mathematical stasis. The latest conceptualization of these abstract elements has been reached recently through the reinterpretation of the common man, who is now seen as a fragile and only provisionally functioning immune system always on the brink of breakdown. The literature of this development accurately mirrors the esoteric character of its conceptualization. The condition of post-modern man and his universe has become, according to this view, so complex that only the most highly specialized experts can function as the priesthood capable of understanding and defining 'needs' today.

Thus, the human phenomenon is no longer defined by what we *are*, what we face, what we can take, what we dream; nor even by the modern myth that we can produce ourselves out of scarcity; but by the measure of what we lack and, therefore, need. And this measure, determined by systems theory thinking, implies a radically new conception of nature and law, and prescribes a politics more concerned with the provision of professionally defined requirements (needs) for survival, than with personal claims to freedom which would foster autonomous coping.

We are on the threshold of a still unnoticed transition from a political consciousness based on progress, growth and development — rooted in the dreams of the Enlightenment — to a new, yet unnamed consciousness defined by controls which ensure a 'sustainable system' of needs satisfaction. Development is dead, yes. But the well-meaning experts who propagate needs are now busily at work reconceptualizing their discovery, and in the process redefining humanity yet again. The citizen is being redefined as a cyborg. The former individual, who as a member of a 'population' has become a 'case', is now modelled in the image of an immune system that can provisionally be kept functioning if it is kept in balance by appropriate management.

Thirty years ago 'needs' was one of a dozen concepts out of which a global worldview was shaped. The term, like 'population', 'development', 'poverty' or 'planning', belongs to one category of words which I consider to be surreptitious neologisms — old words whose predominant current meaning is new while those who use them still have the impression of saying what has always been said. Within the development discourse, the word and the concept of 'need' became increasingly attractive. It became the most appropriate term to designate the moral relations between strangers in a dreamt of world made up of well-fare states. Such a world has lost credibility in the matrix of a new world now conceived as a system. When the term, needs, is now used within this new context, it 'functions' as a euphemism for the management of citizens who have been reconceptualized as subsystems within a population.

References

1. H. S. Truman, Inaugural Address, January 20, 1949.
2. H. S. Truman, Message to Congress on Point Four, June 24, 1949.
3. J. F. Kennedy, Inaugural Address, January 20, 1961.
4. J. F. Kennedy, Special Message to Congress Requesting Appropriations for the Inter-American Fund for Social Progress and for Reconstruction in Chile, March 14, 1961.
5. Quoted in R. Nixon, *1999: Victory Without War*, London: Sidgwick, 1988, p. 48.
6. R. S. McNamara, Address to the Board of Governors, World Bank, Nairobi, September 24, 1973.
7. Pope Paul VI, 'On Promoting the Development of Peoples', Encyclical Letter, Rome, March 26, 1967, p. 20.
8. Ibid., pp. 18–19.
9. According to the *New Oxford English Dictionary*, the concept 'poverty line' seems to have been coined in 1901 by the chocolate-producing Quaker philanthropist and friend of Lloyd George, B. S. Rowntree. The synonym 'poverty level' has been adopted more recently, in 1976.

10. *The United Nations Development Decade: Proposals for Action*, New York: UN Department of Economic and Social Affairs, 1962.

11. See R. Findlay, 'On W. Arthur Lewis' Contribution to Economics', in *Journal of Economics*, 1(1982), pp. 62–76.

12. The concept is defined in its full brutality by S. Rosen, 'Human Capital: A Survey of Empirical Research', in R. Ehrenburg, *Handbook of Labour Economics*, Vol. 1, Greenwich: Jai Press, 1972.

13. The expressions 'poverty pimp' and 'povertician' were coined during Edward Koch's campaign for Mayor of New York in 1988.

14. For example, M. Lutz and K. Lux, *Humanistic Economics: The New Challenge*, New York: The Bootstrap Press, 1988.

15. E. Fromm, 'The Psychology of Normalcy', in *Dissent*, 1(1954), p. 43.

16. M. Gronemeyer, *Die Macht der Bedürfnisse*, Reinbek: Rowohlt, 1988.

Bibliography

Murray's original *Oxford English Dictionary* in 1892 divides the article on the noun 'need' into two parts only: (a) the necessity to do something, and (b) the imperial demand to have something. Through the centuries, to 'have need to' meant to be under an inescapable necessity of doing or obtaining something. The *OED* gives first evidence of a third meaning, (c) a state of physiological or psychological want that motivates behaviour towards its satisfaction, in 1929. It is only then that 'need' can refer to a want or claim to something. A similar shift, albeit much earlier, in German has been noted by J.B. Müller, 'Bedürfnis', in O. Brunner, W. Conze & R. Koselleck (eds.), *Geschichtliche Grundbegriffe*, Stuttgart: Klett, 1972, Vol. 1, pp. 440–89. The book by P. Springborg, *The Problem of Human Needs and the Critique of Civilization*, London: Allen and Unwin, 1981, seems to be the only monographic attempt at retracing the perception of the analogues of 'need' in Western thought from the Greeks to the present.

Discussions about true or false needs, basic needs, or social versus individual needs usually pay no attention to the commodity-intensity of society. They are therefore irrelevant to the argument advanced above. W. Leiss, *The Limits to Satisfaction: An Essay on the Problem of Needs and Commodities*, Toronto: Toronto University Press, 1976, explored the genesis of needs in the transformation of desire into demand for commodities. A persuasive statement about the descent of man from the kingdom of preference into the bondage of needs was made by D. Baybrooke, 'Let Needs Diminish That Preferences May Prosper', in N. Resher (ed.), *Studies in Moral Philosophy*, Oxford: Blackwell, 1968. In a similar vein, I have published a number of essays, in particular *Towards A History of Needs*, New York: Pantheon, 1978.

The sudden resuscitation of discussion of needs in the 1960s was a reaction against the value-neutral approach of orthodox social science. It was first initiated by C. W. Mills and G. Myrdal in political economy, and taken up by A. Maslow and E. Fromm from the point of view of psychological anthropology. All four authors give central importance to the position of the young Marx, a heritage which has been thoroughly analysed by A. Heller, *The Theory of Needs in Marx*, London: Allison and Busby, 1976. Due to that tradition, maybe, the term 'basic needs' can be made to sound like a humanist invention when it is used within the development discourse. P. Streeten, *Development Perspectives*, London: Macmillan, 1981, and J. Galtung, 'The Basic Needs Approach', in K. Lederer et al. (eds.), *Human Needs: A Contribution to the Current Debate*, Königstein: Athenaeum, 1980, pp. 55–128, were authoritative voices, and B. Wisner, *Power and Need in Africa*, London: Earthscan, 1988, shows the deep ambivalence of 'strategies' carried out under that slogan. However, it seems impossible to speak about 'basic needs' without implying the commodity-orientation of human nature. This has been forcefully argued by M. Gronemeyer, *Die Macht der Bedürfnisse*, Reinbek: Rowohlt, 1988. M. Ignatieff, *The Needs of Strangers*, London: Chatto, 1984, has brilliantly pointed out how need is a term to designate moral relations between people who are strangers.

To understand how needs are being recast today as requirements to fit into the mental construct of systems thinking, insights can be gained from J. D. Bolter, *Turing's Man: Western Culture in the Computer Age*, Chapel Hill: University of North Carolina Press, 1984, and M. Berman, *Coming To Our Senses: Body and Spirit in the Hidden History of the West*, New York: Simon & Schuster, 1989. Equally, W. R. Arney & B. Bergen, *Medicine and the Management of Living*, Chicago: University of Chicago Press, 1984, and D. Haraway, 'The Biopolitics of Post-modern Bodies: Determinations of Self in Immune System Discourse', in *Differences*, 1(1989), pp. 3–43, provide instruments which can be used for analysing the medicalization of the planet.

The subtle and asymmetrical power relationship implicit in the concept of needs was clearly perceived by S. de Beauvoir in *The Second Sex*, New York: Bantam Books, 1952: 'In the relation of master to slave the master does not make a point of the need that he has for the other; he has in his grasp the power of satisfying the need through his own action. Whereas the slave, in his dependent condition, his hopes and his fears, is quite conscious of the need he has for the master. Even if the need were, at the bottom, equally urgent for both, it always works in the favour of the oppressor and against the oppressed.'

One World

Wolfgang Sachs

At present, roughly 5,100 languages are spoken around the globe. Just under 99 per cent of them are native to Asia and Africa, the Pacific and the American continents, while a mere 1 per cent find their homes in Europe. In Nigeria, for instance, more than 400 languages have been counted; in India 1,682; and even Central America, tiny as it is geographically, boasts 260.[1] A great number of these languages cling to remote places. They hide out in isolated mountain valleys, far-off islands and inaccessible deserts. Others govern entire continents and connect different peoples into a larger universe. Taken together, a multitude of linguistic worlds, large and small, covers the globe like a patchwork quilt. Yet many indicators suggest that, within a generation or two, not many more than 100 of these languages will survive.

Languages are dying out every bit as quickly as species. While, in the latter case, plants and animals disappear from the history of nature never to be seen again, with the demise of languages, entire cultures are vanishing from the history of civilization, never to be lived again. For each tongue contains its own way of perceiving man and nature, experiencing joy and sorrow, and finding meaning in the flow of events. To pray or to love, to dream or to reason, evokes different things when done in Farsi, German or Zapotec. Just as certain plants and animals are responsible for the maintenance of large ecosystems, so languages often carry subtle cultures through time. Once species disappear, ecosystems break down; once languages die out, cultures falter.

Along with languages, entire conceptions of what it means to be human have evaporated during the development decades since 1950. And yet, the death of languages is only the most dramatic signal of the worldwide evaporation of cultures. Transistor radios and 'Dallas', agricultural advisers and nurses, the regime of the clock and the laws of the market have triggered an unprecedented transformation. It is, after all, scarcely an accident that Europe, the home of literacy as well as the nation-state, has only 1 per cent of all languages left. Whichever way one looks at it, the homogenization of the world is in full swing. A global monoculture spreads like an oil slick over the entire planet.

Forty years of 'development', fashioned on the model of 'one world', have gone by. The upshot of it all, if appearances do not deceive, is a looming vision of horror — modern man all alone for ever in the world. Ideas such as 'world society', 'unified world market', or even 'global responsibility' have in the past stimulated noble minds, and are again bandied about today, albeit with a tone of much more moral pathos than even a few years ago. But their innocence in an age of cultural evaporation is now tarnished.

One Mankind

There is a brass plate at the Fairmont Hotel on Union Square, San Francisco, to remind the passing visitor that it was here, on 4 May 1945, that a global hope was initialled. In Room 210, delegates from 46 countries agreed on the text of the United Nations Charter. Hitler's Germany was finally defeated and time was running out for Japan. The Charter promulgated those principles which were designed to usher in a new era of peace. No wars any more and no national egoisms. What counted was international understanding and the unity of mankind! After devastating conflicts, the Charter held out the prospect of universal peace, echoing the pledge of the League of Nations in 1919, but pointing far beyond a mere security system.

The Charter, in fact, conceptualized peace not just as the non-violent regulation of conflicts, but as the result of a global leap forward. Violence breaks out when progress is blocked. That was the conclusion the victorious powers drew from the past experience of economic depression and ensuing totalitarianism. Consequently, in the Preamble to the Charter, the United Nations solemnly announced the determination 'to promote social progress and better standards of life in larger freedom . . . and to employ international machinery for the promotion of the economic and social advancement of all peoples'.[2] The delegates in Room 210 were not timid in their vision. In their eyes, Austrians and Australians, Zulus as well as Zapotecos, shared in the same aspiration for 'social progress and better standards of life in larger freedom'. The histories of the world were seen as converging into one history, having one direction, and the UN was seen as a motor propelling less advanced countries to move ahead. The project to banish violence and war from the face of the earth was clearly linked to the vision of mankind marching forward and upward along the road of progress. Mankind, progress and peace have been the conceptual cornerstones for erecting the sprawling edifice of UN organizations. The idea that both mankind and peace realize themselves through progess/development is the expectation built into their structure. The UN's mission hinges on faith in progress.

The United Nations Charter appeals to ideas which had taken shape during the European Enlightenment. At the time of Voltaire, the all-embracing, unifying power of Christianity had faded and given way to 'humanity' as the dominant collective concept. Ever since the apostle Paul had shattered the validity of worldly distinctions in the face of God's gift of salvation, it had become thinkable to conceive of all humans as standing on the same plane. The Enlightenment secularized this heritage and turned it into a humanist creed. Neither class nor sex, neither religion nor race count before human nature, as they didn't count before God. Thus the universality of the Sonship of God was recast as the universality of human dignity. From then on, 'humanity' became the common denominator uniting all peoples, causing differences in skin colour, beliefs and social customs to decline in significance.

But 'mankind', for the Enlightenment, was not just an empirical concept meaning the inhabitants of the globe; it had a time arrow built in. 'Mankind', in effect, was something yet to come, a task to be realized as man moves along the path of progress, successively shedding the ties of authority and superstition until autonomy and reason would reign. In the perspective of the Enlightenment, neither social roots nor religious commitments mattered much. The utopian intention aimed at a world of individuals who follow only the voice of reason. In that sense, the utopia of mankind was populated by men disembedded from their stories of the past, disconnected from the context of their places, and detached from the bonds of their communities, and united instead under the rule of science, market and the state. Hume as well as Kant saw humanity as something to be attained by spreading the universal values of civilization and drawing ever more people into the course of progress. Mankind was to be the result of becoming modern. The Enlightenment's idea of unity cannot be separated from the assumption that history moves towards the rule of universal reason. It was one of those ideas, typical of that period, which were pregnant with an infinite future.

However, the rise of humanity by no means obliterated the image of the Other in European thought. Just as Christians had their heathens, philosophers of the Enlightenment had their savages. Both figures embodied the negation of what the respective societies held as their self-images. Heathens were those outside the Kingdom of God, while savages lived outside the kingdom of civilization. But there was one crucial difference. Whereas for Christendom heathens populated geographically remote areas, for the Enlightenment savages inhabited an infant stage of history. Europe of the Enlightenment no longer felt separated from the Other spatially, but chronologically. As a matter of fact, the existence of strange peoples like the Iroquois, Asante or Bengali at the borders of (European) civilization contradicted the very idea of one mankind. But the contradiction was resolved by interpreting the multiplicity of cultures in space as a succession of stages in time. So the 'savage' was defined as one who would grow up and enter the stage of civilization. The 'savage', though he lived now, was assigned the status of a child in the biography of mankind, a child which was not yet fully mature, and was in need of guidance by a strong father.

In the Preamble to the UN Declaration, the quest for peace was closely linked to the hope for advancement of peoples around the globe. Towards the end of the 18th century the traditional notion that peace would be the fruit of justice had lost ground. It gave way to the expectation that peace would be the result of mankind reunited under the achievements of civilization. Reason and freedom would overcome prejudice and narrow-mindedness, and the age of harmony would dawn. Peace, progress and humanity were for the Enlightenment nothing less than the different faces of an eschatological future to come. The belief that mankind could be improved upon has driven political action from Voltaire right through to our own time.

The philosophy underlying the UN Declaration makes little sense without the view of history as the royal road to progress upon which all peoples converge. The conception of achieving 'one world' by stimulating progress everywhere betrays the evolutionary bias. It inevitably calls for absorbing the differences in the world into an ahistorical and delocalized universalism of European origin. The unity of the world is realized through its Westernization. By the mid 20th century the term 'underdeveloped' had taken the place of 'savages'. Economic performance had replaced reason as the measure of man. However, the arrangement of concepts remains the same — the world society has to be achieved through the improvement of the backward. And indissolubly linking the hope for peace to this world-shaking endeavour leads to a tragic dilemma — the pursuit of peace implies the annihilation of diversity, while seeking diversity implies the outburst of violence. The dilemma is unlikely to be resolved without delinking peace from progress and progress from peace.

One Market

Today it seems almost strange, but the founding fathers of the United Nations, as well as the architects of international development policy, were inspired by the vision that the globalization of market relationships would be the guarantee of peace in the world. Prosperity, so the argument went, derives from exchange, exchange creates mutual interests, and mutual interests inhibit aggression. Instead of violence, the spirit of commerce was to reign on all sides. Instead of firepower, productive strength would be decisive in the competition between nations. The unity of the world, it was thought, could only be based on a far-reaching and closely interconnected network of economic relations. And where goods were in circulation, weapons would fall silent.

With a naivete hardly distinguishable from deception, the prophets of development polished up a utopia envisioned as long ago as the 18th century, as if time had stopped and neither capitalism nor imperialism had ever appeared on the scene. After Montesquieu, the Enlightenment had discovered commerce as a means of refining crude manners. In this view, trade would spread rational calculation and cold self-interest, precisely those attitudes which make the passion for war or the whims of tyrants appear self-destructive. Trade creates dependence and dependence tames. This is the logic which runs from Montesquieu through the UN down to the present-day integration of Eastern Europe and the USSR since the collapse of bureaucratic socialism there following the upheavals of 1989. And indeed, as the European Community and the Pax Americana after World War Two suggest, economic dominions have largely replaced military dominions. The conquest of foreign territories by bellicose states has given way to the conquest of foreign markets by profit-seeking industries. Global order, after World War Two, was conceived in terms of a unified world market.

One of the most highly praised virtues of the world market is increased interdependence. The network of interests created is supposed to knit the nations together, for better or worse. From that perspective, the Pearson Report exhorted the industrialized nations in 1969:

> There is also the appeal of enlightened and constructive self-interest. . . . The fullest possible utilization of all the world's resources, human and physical, which can be brought about only by international co-operation, helps not only those countries now economically weak, but also those strong and wealthy.[3]

Ten years later, this trust in the unifying power of mutual interest was reiterated in the Brandt Report:

> Whoever wants a bigger slice of an international economic cake cannot
> seriously want it to become smaller. Developing countries cannot ignore the
> economic health of industrialized countries.[4]

But the ideology of mutual interests could not hide its major fallacy for long —
the playing out of these interests takes place under unequal terms. The
economists' doctrine of comparative advantage had it that the general
well-being would increase if each nation specialized in doing things at which
nature and history had made it most proficient — raw sugar from Costa Rica,
for example, in exchange for pharmaceuticals from Holland. But the flaw in
this reasoning is that, in the long run, the country which sells the more
complex products will grow stronger and stronger, because it will be able to
internalize the spin-off effects of sophisticated production. Pharmaceuticals
stimulate research and a host of technologies, while sugar cane doesn't! The
alleged mutual interest in free trade ends up cumulatively strengthening the one
and progressively weakening the other. And when the richer country comes up
with high tech innovations that render the products of the weaker country
obsolete, as with natural sugar being replaced by bio-engineered substitutes,
then mutual interest withers away to the point where the weaker country
becomes superfluous.

Apart from its built-in tendencies to discrimination and inequality, however,
the obsession with the market as the medium of unification for the whole world
is rapidly pushing all countries into a tight spot. The world market, once
brandished as a weapon against despotism, has itself turned into a closet
dictator under whose dominion both rich and poor countries tremble. The fear
of falling behind in international competition has seized governments North
and South, East and West. Not to lose ground in the economic arena has
become an obsession which dominates politics down to the local level. This
overruling imperative drives developing countries further into self-exploitation,
for the sake of boosting exports, and industrial countries further into the
wasteful and destructive mania of accelerated production, for the sake of
protecting their markets.

What is overrun in this hurly-burly is the space for a policy of self-
determination. The categorical imperative of world market competition
repeatedly thwarts attempts to organize societies creatively and differently.
Mobilizing for competition means streamlining a country; diversity becomes
an obstacle to be removed. Some countries cannot keep up without sacrificing
even more of their land for agricultural exports, others cannot afford to drop
out of the high tech race. There is scarcely a country left today that seems able to
control its own destiny. In this respect the differences between countries are
only relative: the United States enjoys more scope than India, but itself feels
under intense pressure from Japan. For winners and losers alike, the
constraints of the global market have become a nightmare.

One Planet

Since the late 1960s, another image of 'one world' has edged its way into contemporary consciousness — the globe in its physical finiteness. We share in 'humanity', we are connected by the 'world market', but we are condemned to one destiny because we are inhabitants of one planet. This is the message conveyed by the first photograph of the 'one world', taken from outer space, which has irresistibly emerged as the icon of our age. The photo shows the planet suspended in the vastness of the universe and impresses on everybody the fact that the earth is one body. Against the darkness of infinity, the circular earth offers itself as an abode, a bounded place. The sensation of being on and inside it strikes the onlooker almost instantly. The unity of the world is now documented. It can be seen everywhere. It jumps out at you from book covers, T-shirts and commercials. In the age of TV, photographs are our eyewitnesses. For the first time in history, the planet is revealed in its solitude. From now on, 'one world' means physical unity; it means 'one earth'. The unity of mankind is no longer an Enlightenment fancy or a commercial act but a biophysical fact.

However, this physical interconnectedness stands in relief against the background of proliferating dangers. From creeping desertification to impending climatic disaster, alarm signals multiply. The biosphere is under attack and threatens to cave in. Local acts such as driving a car or clearing a forest add up, when multiplied, to global imbalances. They turn beneficial cycles into vicious ones that undermine the reliability of nature. In the face of incalculable debacles, concerned voices call for a global political coherence which would match the biophysical interconnections. 'The Earth is one but the world is not. We all depend on one biosphere for sustaining our lives.' After having intoned this leitmotif, the Brundtland Report spells out the fateful new meaning of unity:

> Today the scale of our interventions in nature is increasing and the physical effects of our decisions spill across national frontiers. The growth in economic interaction between nations amplifies the wider consequences of national decisions. Economics and ecology bind us in ever-tightening networks. Today, many regions face risks of irreversible damage to the human environment that threatens the basis for human progress.[5]

The Brundtland Report, the leading document on development policy in the late 1980s, takes unity for granted, but a unity which is now the result of a threat.

Things have come a long way since the promulgation of the UN Charter — from the moral hope of a mankind united by reason and progress to the economic notion of countries weaving themselves together through commercial ties, and finally, to the spectre of unity in global self-destruction. What used to be conceived of as a historical endeavour — to accomplish the unity of mankind — now reveals itself as a menacing fate. Instead of hopeful appeals, sombre warnings provide the accompaniment. The slogan 'one world or no world' captures this experience. Seen in this light, humanity resembles a group of individuals thrown together by chance, each dependent on the others for his own survival. No one can rock the boat without causing all of us to be united — in our collective destruction. Living on earth, the ancient formula, appears to have taken on a new meaning. There are no terrestrial wanderers any more longing for the eternal kingdom, but only passengers clinging fearfully to their vessel as it splits apart. Talk about unity has ceased to hold out promises and instead has taken on a grim connotation. As already foreshadowed by the Bomb, unity in our age has become something which may be finally consummated in catastrophe.

Amidst the wailing sirens of the rescue operations undertaken in the name of some lifeboat ethics, the pressure on peoples and countries to conform to an emergency discipline will be high. As soon as worldwide strategies are launched to prevent the boat from capsizing, things like political autonomy or cultural diversity will appear as the luxuries of yesteryear. In the face of the overriding imperative to 'secure the survival of the planet', autonomy easily becomes an anti-social value, and diversity turns into an obstacle to collective action. Can one imagine a more powerful motive for forcing the world into line than that of saving the planet? Eco-colonialism constitutes a new danger for the tapestry of cultures on the globe.

It is perfectly conceivable that, in the face of mounting pressure on land, water, forests and the atmosphere, global measures will have to be taken to trim down the intake from nature as well as the output of waste worldwide. Satellites are already prepared to monitor the consumption of resources on the planet, computer models are being devised to simulate what happens when, and a new generation of experts is in the making to survey and synchronize the manifold gestures of society. It is not the engineer, building bridges or power grids, who will be the protagonist of this new epoch, as in the old days of development, but the systems analyst.

NASA, for example, has already got its own ideas about the 'one earth':

> The goal of Earth system science is to obtain a scientific understanding of the entire Earth system on a global scale by describing how its component parts and their interactions have evolved, how they function and how they may be expected to continue to evolve on all timescales. The challenge is . . . to develop the capability to predict those changes that will occur in the next decade to century both naturally and in response to human activity.[6]

The oneness of the earth is understood according to this paradigm in system categories, its unity as the interaction of component parts, and the historical task as keeping the vital processes from destabilizing irretrievably. What links the peoples of the world together is not the rule of civilization any more or the interplay of demand and supply, but their shared dependence on biophysical life-support systems. The metaphor of spaceship earth captures nicely the gist of this thinking. Consequently, unity is not to be pursued any longer through the spread of progress or the stimulation of productivity, but through securing the necessary system requirements.

But efforts to curb soil erosion, control emissions, regulate water consumption or save biodiversity, although done with the best of intentions, will put people's daily activities under a new kind of scrutiny. Neither collecting firewood nor opening spray cans are any longer innocent activities, and how you heat your home and the food you eat become matters of global relevance. In such a perspective, the world is perceived as a single homogeneous space, this time not constituted by reason or the fluctuation of prices, but by geophysiological macro-cycles.

The consequences, however, are not likely to differ from the effects already observed in the wake of the rise of reason and the market to world dominance — namely the slow evaporation of customs and cultures. The current changes in development language from 'people' to 'populations', 'needs' to 'requirements', and 'welfare' to 'survival' are indicative of a growing negligence towards cultures in favour of mere existence. Whatever has survived the rise of industrialism, is now in danger of being drawn into the maelstrom of its fall.

But recognizing the pitfalls of global eco-management does not solve the dilemma which will stay with us in the decades to come. Both alternatives — to think in categories of one world as well as not to think in such categories — are equally self-destructive. On the one hand, it is sacrilege in our age of cultural evaporation to apprehend the globe as a united, highly integrated world. On the other hand, a vision of the globe as a multitude of different and only loosely connected worlds cannot dispense with the idea of ecumenism in the face of lurking violence and the devastation of nature. Not surprisingly, calls for global consciousness abound. Given that local events can affect the conditions of life in remote places, these calls aim at bringing into congruence the range of our responsibility with the range of our effects. However, and here lies the dilemma, the urge for global responsibility tends to drive out the devil with Beelzebub — universalism is being invoked for salvation from the present predicament, while universalism was precisely the original sin by which the predicament was provoked.

Space Against Place

For centuries, universalism has been at war with diversity. Science, state and market have dominated this campaign, while an innumerable variety of communities with their languages, customs and cosmologies, though they have sometimes struck back and reinvigorated themselves through resistance, have been the losers. It has been an unequal clash. Not only did the protagonists often fight with unequal arms when the universalist powers employed guns and dollars but, more importantly, they were unequal in their cognitive might.

Science, state and market are based on a system of knowledge about man, society and nature that claims validity everywhere and for everybody. As a knowledge which has successfully shed all vestiges of its particular origin, place and context, it belongs nowhere and can therefore penetrate everywhere. In a certain sense, mechanistic causality, bureaucratic rationality and the law of supply and demand are rules which are cleansed of any commitment to a particular society or culture. It is because they are disembedded from broader contexts of order and meaning that they are so powerful in remodelling any social reality according to their limited but specific logic. As a consequence, they are capable of unsettling all kinds of different cultures, each one locked in its own imagination. Since these cultures are connected to particular places with their own particular peoples, memories and cosmologies, they are vulnerable to a mental style which is not linked to any place, but rests instead on the concept of space. One way to grasp the fundamental difference between universalism and localism is to focus on the dichotomy of space and place. Universalist aspirations are generally space-centred, while localist worldviews are mainly place-centred. This distinction illuminates both the rise of universalism in the past, and the tension between universalism and diversity in the present.

In mediaeval times, when a person talked about the entire 'world', he did not evoke in his listeners the image of the planet with its many inhabitants, but instead the image of an earth overarched by several spheres or heavens in permanent revolution. The tiny earth was at the centre, yet not central. Most of the attention was concentrated on the relations between the chance-governed terrestrial realm and the immutable, eternal realm of the heavens. The mediaeval cosmos took shape around a vertical axis which linked a hierarchy of strata of different qualities. Man's view was directed upwards to grasp the vaulting architecture of the cosmos, as if attracted by the soaring arches and spires of a gothic cathedral. Though this 'world' was immense, it was nevertheless finite and had a definite shape — to look up to the heavens was like looking up to a high vault.

In early modern times, the concept of a stratified and bounded cosmos was gradually abolished in favour of a universe infinitely extended in space. The vertical axis was tilted over and laid out on a horizontal plane; what mattered now was no longer the view upwards, but the view into the distance. As the vertical dimension faltered, so the idea of qualitative differences between lower and upper layers of reality also faded away and was replaced by the conception of a homogeneous reality which could only be ordered through measurable differences in geometrical fashion. It is the horizontal plane which now dominates the imagination. The world is not seen any more as marked by boundaries and upward-rising, but as limitless and extending in circles of ever greater distance. As a result, not upward–downward movements, but geographical movements to destinations close and far, hold people's attention. 'World' now evokes the surface of the globe and not the height of the cosmos.

In other words, the abolition of the stratified cosmos has made possible the rise of 'space' to its prominent position in modern consciousness. And the rise of a space-centred perception has made it possible to conceive of 'one world'. In this perception, the world is on one level, stretching out as a two-dimensional plane where each point equals any other point; what distinguishes them is only their geometrical position. The purest case of a space-centred perception can obviously be found in cartography. On maps, the world is flattened out and places are defined by their locations in the grid of longitudinal and latitudinal lines.

However, nobody is capable of living only in 'space'; everyone lives also in 'place'. This is because being human means, all attempts to the contrary notwithstanding, to be in a physical body, and the body is necessarily tied to a place. Human experience, for that reason, evolves in specific local places. Some points in space, as a result, are always more important to people than others, since they have been the scenes of individual and collective imagination and action. Having a memory, relating to others, participating in a larger story, calls for involvement, requires presence. This presence, naturally, is lived out in particular physical settings like piazzas or streets, mountains or seashores. And these locations are in turn imbued with experience past and present. They become places of density and depth. Therefore, certain places have a special 'thickness' for certain people. It is there that the ancestors walked the earth and the relevant memories are at home. It is there that one is tied into a web of social bonds and where one recognizes and is recognized by others. And it is there that people share a particular vantage point and that language, habits and outlook combine to constitute a particular style of being in the world. Consequently, thinking in terms of places means to work on the assumption that a place is not just the intersection of two lines on a map, but a concentration of meaningful human activity which gives it a distinct quality, a distinct aura.

Ever since the temples of Tenochtitlan were destroyed in Mexico and a Spanish cathedral built out of their stones, European colonialism has been busy ravaging place-centred cultures and imposing on them space-centred values. In ever new waves and on all five continents, the colonialists have been terribly inventive in robbing peoples of their gods, their institutions and their natural treasures. The establishment of universities in New Spain, the introduction of British law in India, the blackmailing of North American Indians into the fur trade, these were all instances in the history of spreading science, state and market throughout the world.

The period of development after the Second World War fits into that history. Viewed with the space-trained eyes of the West, numerous cultures appeared as backward, deficient and meaningless. The globe looked like a vast homogeneous space, waiting to be organized by universally applicable programmes and technologies. And the developmentalists did not hesitate. They went about transferring the Western model of society to countries of a great variety of cultures.

But place-centred perceptions are far from gone. On the contrary, the more universalism prevails, the more particularism thrives. Indeed, throughout the last centuries, the advance of space-centred perceptions has been both successful and unsuccessful. On the one side, universalism has gained the upper hand, but on the other, place-bound aspirations have affirmed themselves over and over again. Innumerable revolts against colonialism expressed the will of the particular to survive. Independence movements launched indigenous claims.

A similar picture has prevailed in recent decades during the development era. Nationalist demands, ethnic strife, tribal tensions abound. And not to forget: the failure of a universalist development is in large part due to people's tenacious adherence to the old ways proper to their respective places. To be sure, localist conceptions do not remain the same. They are reformulated, altered and newly invented in a continuous vortex of dialogue and antagonism.

Equally, universalist conceptions, though advancing powerfully, are constantly watered down, curtailed and adapted, to the perennial dismay of Western do-gooders. And repeatedly, from the Orientalist movement in the early 19th century to alternative travellers in our own days, dissident elites, deeply steeped in a space-intensive worldview, discover place-bound traditions and turn them into weapons against the European civilization.

Cosmopolitan Localism

Today, more than ever, universalism is under siege. To be sure, the victorious march of science, state and market has not come to a stop, but the enthusiasm of the onlookers is flagging. Few still believe that order and peace will dawn at the end of the march. The centuries-old movement of carrying the torch of reason and progress to the furthest corners of the earth is tapering off. To the degree that it continues, it is carried out more from inertia than from missionary conviction.

Utopias crystallize longings that arise from frustration with the state of society. The ambition to create larger and larger unified spaces — from nation-states to regional integration and world government — has been fuelled by frustration with chauvinism and violence. Yet that concern retreats into the background as the opposite frustration spreads — the disappointment with a world that has fallen prey to homogenization. All of a sudden, the customary association of differences with violence vanishes; differences are now something to be cherished and cultivated. Indeed, the fear that modern man will encounter nobody else but himself on the globe is about to revolutionize contemporary perceptions. The pursuit of space-centred unity is turning into the search for place-centred diversity. After all, it is only from places that variety crops up, because it is in places that people weave the present into their particular thread of history. Thus, native languages are beginning to be revaluated, traditional knowledge systems rediscovered, and local economies revitalized. And, as the popularity of the prefix 're-' indicates, the unconventional is today often launched under the guise of a renaissance. The disquieting anticipation of a world fully illuminated by the neon light of modern rationality motivates the search for the darker zones, where the special, the strange, the surprising lives. A world without the Other would be a world of stagnation. For, in culture as well as in nature, diversity holds the potential for innovation and opens the way for creative, non-linear solutions. And with these misgivings growing, the tide changes. The globe is not any longer imagined as a homogeneous space where contrasts ought to be levelled out, but as a discontinuous space where differences flourish in a multiplicity of places.

Moreover, the vision of a world integrated under the rule of reason and welfare was carried by a view of history which today is rapidly becoming ripe for the museum. The unity of mankind was a project of the future, made possible by the expectation that human action would keep the course of history always on an upward road. Progress was the guarantee of unity. In the space-centred perception, the differences on the globe would fall into oblivion because they were outshone by the bright light of progress; it was in relation to that promise that they didn't matter any more. But clearly enough, if our present experience shortly before the end of the 20th century can be wrapped up in one formula, it is precisely this: that the belief in progress has crumbled, the arrow of time is broken. The future doesn't hold much promise any more; it has become a repository of fears rather than of hopes.

At this juncture, therefore, it is wide of the mark to think that the coherence of the world could be achieved by pushing ahead along a common path towards some distant promised future. Instead, coexistence has to be sought in the context of the present. Thinking unity within the horizon of the present is much more demanding for all the players involved, since the attainment of a peaceful world would then be on today's agenda and could not be postponed to a far future.

Three ideals emerge for conceiving a politics which could shoulder the responsibility of acting for a diverse but coherent world — regeneration, unilateral self-restraint and the dialogue of civilizations. Regeneration takes into account that the royal road of development has vanished since there is no longer any ideal of progress to indicate a common direction. Regeneration calls instead for actualizing the particular image of a good society which is present in each culture. As for unilateral self-restraint, this can take the place of the ideal of interdependent growth. It implies instead that each country puts its own house in order in such a way that no economic or environmental burden is pushed on to others which would constrain them in choosing their own path. And, finally, a dialogue of civilizations is imperative as the search for peaceful and sustainable coexistence puts the challenge of self-examination before each culture. A simultaneous process of confrontation and synthesis can lead to coherence, while avoiding the pitfalls of homogeneity.

Though universalism has exhausted its utopian energies, any new localism will have a window on to the world at large. The opposite of the dominion of universal rules is not egoism, but a higher capacity for self-observation. People are seldom residents of only one mental space. They have the ability to change their point of view and to look with the other's eye at themselves. In fact, people often hold multiple loyalties at one and the same time. In many instances they combine rootedness in a place with affiliation to a larger community. An inhabitant of mediaeval Cologne knew how to be a member of the Christian Church; a villager in Rajasthan was aware of Bharat, Mother India; and Croatian peasants as well as the citizens of Cracow were part of the Habsburg empire.

In a similar vein, the one world may be thought of in terms of a meta-nation instead of in terms of a super-nation. It constitutes the horizon within which places live out their density and depth. In this perspective, 'one world' is not a design for more global planning, but an ever present regulative idea for local action. Cosmopolitan localism seeks to amplify the richness of a place while keeping in mind the rights of a multi-faceted world. It cherishes a particular place, yet at the same time knows about the relativity of all places. It results from a broken globalism as well as a broken localism. Maybe Tzvetan Todorov wanted to illustrate such an attitude when he used a phrase of the 12th century Hugh of St. Victor: 'The man who finds his country sweet is only a raw beginner; the man for whom each country is as his own is already strong; but only the man for whom the whole world is like a foreign country is perfect'.[7]

References

1. U. Pörksen, *Plastikwörter: Die Sprache einer internationalen Diktatur*, Stuttgart: Klett-Cotta, 1988, p. 15.
2. *Preamble to the Charter of the United Nations*, New York: UN Office of Public Information, 1968.
3. L. Pearson, *Partners in Development*, New York: Praeger, 1969, p. 9.
4. W. Brandt, *North–South: A Programme for Survival*, Cambridge, Mass.: MIT Press, 1980, p. 21.
5. World Commission on Environment and Development, *Our Common Future*, Oxford: Oxford University Press, 1987, p. 27.
6. Quoted in M. Finger, *Today's Trend: Global Is Beautiful*, Ms., 1989.
7. T. Todorov, *The Conquest of America*, New York: Harper & Row, 1984, p. 250.

Bibliography

The idea of 'mankind' figures prominently in the Charter of the United Nations, New York: UN Office of Public Information, 1968; the notion of 'one world' in L. Pearson, *Partners in Development: Report of the Commission on International Development*, New York: Praeger, 1969; and W. Brandt, *North–South: A Programme for Survival: Report of the Independent Commission on International Development Issues*, Cambridge: MIT Press, 1980; and the concept of 'one earth' in B. Ward & R. Dubos, *Only One Earth: The Care and Maintenance of A Small Planet*, New York: Norton, 1972, and the World Commission on Environment and Development, *Our Common Future*, Oxford: Oxford University Press, 1987.

A very elaborate commentary on the UN Charter is offered by J. Cot & A. Pellet, *La Charte des Nations Unies*, Economica: Paris, 1985. H. Jacobson, *Networks of Independence: International Organizations and the Global Political System*, New York: Knopf, 1984, gives an overview of the emergence of international organizations, while P. de Senarclens, *La crise des Nations Unies*, Paris: Presses Universitaires de France, 1988, provides a conceptually oriented history of the UN.

Regarding the history of the idea of 'mankind', I found particularly useful H. C. Baldry, *The Unity of Mankind in Greek Thought*, Cambridge: Cambridge University Press, 1965, and, for the 17th century, W. Philipp, 'Das Bild der Menschheit im 17. Jahrhundert des Barock' in *Studium Generale*, 14, 1961, pp. 721–42. An excellent analysis of the semantic formation of 'peace' and 'mankind' during and after the Enlightenment is available with the articles 'Friede' and 'Menschheit' in O. Brunner & W. Conze, (edited by R. Koselleck), *Geschichtliche Grundbegriffe: Historisches Lexikon zur politisch-sozialen Sprache in Deutschland*, Stuttgart: Klett-Cotta, 1975, Vols. 2 and 3. Very instructive on the position of the Other in different cosmologies is M. Harbsmeier, 'On Travel Accounts and Cosmological Strategies: Some Models in Comparative Xenology' in *Ethnos*, 48, 1983, pp. 273–312. For the early association of the market with peace, see A. Hirschmann, *The Passions and the Interests: Political Arguments for Capitalism Before its Triumph*, Princeton: Princeton University Press, 1977, and for the secular substitution of economic for military competition, R. Rosecrance, *The Rise of the Trading State: Commerce and Conquest in the Modern World*, New York: Basic Books, 1986.

To understand the transition from 'place' to 'space', I have benefited from M. Eliade & L. Sullivan, 'Center of the World' in M. Eliade (ed.) *The Encyclopedia of Religions*, New York: Macmillan, 1987, vol. 3 pp. 166–71; from Y.-F. Tuan, *Topophilia: A Study of Environmental Perception, Attitudes, and Values*, Englewood Cliffs, N.J.: Prentice-Hall, 1974; and C. S.

Lewis's article on the concept of 'world' in *Studies in Words*, Cambridge: Cambridge University Press, 1960.

Those who want to have a clearer sense about the 'internationalism' of the electronic media may look at M. Ignatieff, 'Is Nothing Sacred? The Ethics of Television' in *Daedalus*, 114, 1985, pp. 57–78; and J. Meyrowitz, *No Sense of Place: The Impact of Electronic Media on Social Behavior*, New York: Oxford University Press, 1985.

Furthermore, I found R. Panikkar, 'Is the Notion of Human Rights a Western Concept?' in *Interculture*, 17, Jan.–March 1984, pp. 28–47, a penetrating reflection on universalism, and I liked the dense presentation of the pitfalls of Westernization in S. Latouche, *L'occidentalisation du monde*, Paris: La Decouverte, 1989. T. Todorov, *La conquête de l'Amérique*, Paris: le Seuil, 1982, and E. Morin, *Penser l'Europe*, Paris: Gallimard, 1987, have given me many insights into how to think of a world of multiple unity.

Participation

Majid Rahnema

Modern jargon uses stereotype words like children use Lego toy pieces. Like Lego pieces, the words fit arbitrarily together and support the most fanciful constructions. They have no content, but do serve a function. As these words are separate from any context, they are ideal for manipulative purposes. 'Participation' belongs to this category of words.

For the *Oxford English Dictionary*, participation is 'the action or fact of partaking, having or forming a part of'. In that sense, participation could be either transitive or intransitive; either moral, amoral or immoral; either forced or free; either manipulative or spontaneous.

Transitive forms of participation are, by definition, oriented towards a specific goal or target. By contrast, in its intransitive forms, the subject lives the partaking process without any predefined purpose. While one is listening, loving, creating, or fully living one's life, one partakes without necessarily seeking to achieve a particular objective.

Participation acquires a moral aspect, according to the ethically defined nature of the goals it pursues. It is generally associated with moral or desirable goals and, as such, given a positive connotation. It seldom comes to mind that the act of partaking may apply to evil or malicious purposes.

From a third perspective, and perhaps with the same positive connotations generally associated with the word, participation tends to be perceived as a free exercise. This perception neither conforms to the meaning of the word, nor the way in which it is translated into practice. For, more often than not, people are asked or dragged into partaking in operations of no interest to them, in the very name of participation. Neither the pyramids, nor the many contemporary mass demonstrations in favour of repressive regimes, have represented free acts of participation.

This leads us, finally, to distinguish between manipulated, or teleguided, forms of participation, and spontaneous ones. In the former, the participants do not feel they are being forced into doing something, but are actually led to take actions which are inspired or directed by centres outside their control.

Considering these various forms of participation, it is almost a tautology to state that all societies, in particular vernacular or traditional ones, are participant. This is, however, questioned by many a developer and modern thinker. Amongst them, Daniel Lerner, a prominent spokesman of the development ideology, emphatically states that 'traditional society is non-participant', while 'modern society is'.[1] In order to better understand the basic changes which have occurred in our perception of the concept during the present economic age, that statement should be coupled with the following, belonging to the same current of thought: 'A nation's level of political participation co-varies with its level of economic development.'[2]

Human Software

The words 'participation' and 'participatory' appeared for the first time in the development jargon during the late 1950s. The social activists and field workers who had joined the development bandwagon in the hope that they could help the oppressed 'unfold, like a flower from a bud',[3] had come up against a reality which was totally different from their earlier expectations. This led them to attribute most of the failures of development projects to the fact that the populations concerned were kept out of all the processes related to their design, formulation and implementation. In their great majority, they started to advocate the end of 'top-down' strategies of action and the inclusion of participation and participatory methods of interaction as an essential dimension of development.

At the other end of the line, the Development Establishment was obliged, some years later, to recognize a structural crisis. Donors and recipient national governments were witnessing the fact that the billions spent on development projects had failed to produce the expected results, often even adding new problems to the old. Even McNamara, then President of the World Bank, had to admit, in 1973, that 'growth [was] not equitably reaching the poor.' In his view, growth had been accompanied by 'greater maldistribution of income in many developing countries'.[4]

Following the recommendations of many of their own experts, a number of major international aid organizations agreed that development projects had often floundered because people were left out. It was found that, whenever people were locally involved, and actively participating, in the projects, much more was achieved with much less, even in sheer financial terms.

The consensus thus reached amongst the planners, NGOs and field workers brought about an important change in the relationships between the different parties to development activities. A word which had been systematically discarded earlier by economists, planners and politicians suddenly lost its earlier subversive connotation. ECOSOC itself recommended to member states 'to adopt participation as a basic policy measure in national development strategies'. As it stands now, participation is a most accepted concept which even very repressive regimes in the 'Third World', such as the ones led by Pinochet and Mobutu, have tried to promote as one of their objectives.

Six reasons, at least, can be identified for the unprecedented interest governments and development institutions have recently taken in the concept of participation.

1. The concept is no longer perceived as a threat: Governments and institutions interested in greater productivity at low cost are increasingly in need of 'participation' for their own purposes. Their interest is also largely sustained by the fact that they have learned to control the risks inherent in possible 'unruly abuses' of participation.

It is a fact that the bulk of the assistance programmes provided by donor states to their developing partners is allocated to the strengthening and modernization of their national needs. These are, firstly, the needs related to the power of the state — i.e. the army, the police and security forces, the administration, transport and communication services, and the mass media; secondly, the infrastructural requirements of modernization and economic development; and, finally, at the very bottom of the list, the social and cultural needs of the populations most seriously hit by the first two categories of 'needs'. Without ever being admitted openly, the scale and content of foreign assistance agreements reflect the degree to which recipient countries are prepared to 'participate' in the global efforts and needs of their developed partners. One result is that this kind of 'co-operation' has already provided most developing countries, including the poorest, with relatively sophisticated systems of control over their populations. These allow governments to be present everywhere, and especially whenever powerful means are felt necessary to bring about 'democratic and orderly' participation. In such a context, participation is easily transformed into manipulative designs totally opposed to what the people want it for.

On the other hand, development policies tend to create induced and addictive needs, many of which strongly condition the minds of their 'target populations'. Once the latter are made dependent on such needs and other modern services, their 'participation' in public activities and policy-making decisions is mostly used to secure general support for the same needs and services. Thus, development or modernizing projects which serve mainly the interests of the few, continue to receive popular support, only because they perpetuate the illusion that, some day, similar advantages will be extended to all.

On the whole, processes of economization of people's lives, coupled with the gradual disintegration of vernacular spaces, seem to have reached a point where governments and development institutions are no longer scared by the outcome of people's participation. As more people are made addicted to public services and consumer goods, they have no difficulty in proposing to them, at the national level, programmes aimed at an acceleration of the processes of economization. At that level, a good number of people are manipulated into supporting those in power, hoping that the promised increase in the size of the national cake will ultimately also increase their share.

2. Participation has become a politically attractive slogan: In situations where governments have learned to control and contain participation, important political advantages are obtained through the ostentatious display of participatory intentions. Participatory slogans create feelings of complicity between the public manufacturers of illusions and their consumers. Politicians give their constituencies the impression that they are really sensitive to all their problems, often inviting the latter to enlighten them on their needs and aspirations.

On another plane, peacefully negotiated forms of participation can take the heat out of many situations where development policies create tension and resistance on the part of their victims.

3. Participation has become, economically, an appealing proposition: Most so-called developing countries are broke or nearly broke, often as a direct result of various financial and economic 'assistance' programmes. They are selling what remains of their soul to anyone who provides them with money to pay their debts. In a situation where they have to 'adjust' their economies, nothing can accommodate them more than passing on the costs to their poor — which is done in the name of participation and its corollary, self-help.

The World Bank alone has invested over $50 billion in so-called poverty alleviation programmes since 1975. Analysing the results, the most informed Bank analysts have come to the conclusion that: 'The long-term "sustainability" of projects is closed linked to active, informed participation by the poor.'[5] Such projects as the Grameen Bank in Bangladesh and other credit arrangements for small farmers have demonstrated that, contrary to the opinion which was held by bankers until the late 1970s, the poor have proved to be more reliable clients than many of the rich, particularly when they are boxed into cleverly organized 'local participatory set-ups'. 'In the last five years,' writes Sheldon Annis, 'extraordinarily powerful new tools have come of age, especially policy-based tools. These have evolved in response to the default anxiety of commercial lenders.'

4. Participation is now perceived as an instrument for greater effectiveness as well as a new source of investment: Participatory processes bring to development projects what they need most in order to avoid the pitfalls and failures of the past, that is: (a) a close knowledge of the 'field reality' which foreign technicians and government bureaucrats do not have; (b) networks of relations, essential both to the success of ongoing projects and long-term investments in rural areas; and (c) the co-operation, on the local scene, of organizations able to carry out developmental activities. These 'investible' organizations also increase the economy's capacity to absorb 'poverty-oriented' investments. In this context, grassroots organizations are becoming the infrastructure through which investment is made, or they help provide the human 'software' that makes other kinds of investments work.[6]

5. Participation is becoming a good fund-raising device: Particularly in the last ten years, the electorate and the media in donor countries have demonstrated increasing interest in development-oriented NGOs. According to a DAC report, already in 1983, no less than $3.6 billion in NGO support was granted by European countries, a sum almost three times larger than the total funds allocated to developing countries through UNDP. This is perhaps due to the reputation acquired by NGOs that their 'participatory' and less bureaucratized approaches have allowed them to meet the needs of people with greater efficiency and at less cost. In order to avoid such views leading to further cuts in their own financial resources, government and inter-governmental organizations now seek to demonstrate their ability to be, at one and the same time, professional *and* participatory. Finally, as the governments of the recipient countries also sense the new advantages of bending with the participatory wind, they are all paying lip service to participation in the hope of continuing to increase their chances on the foreign aid market.

6. An expanded concept of participation could help the private sector to be directly

involved in the development business: Private corporations and consulting agencies associated with development and equipment-producing companies have been lobbying lately for the privatization of development, using authoritative reports that governments and international aid agencies are wasting taxpayers' money. It has been argued that their bureaucracies are not only absorbing a substantial part of programme funds for unjustified salaries and other overhead expenses, but are also preventing voluntary and non-governmental organizations from helping the people. For those advocating the positive aspects of participation, not only to the populations concerned, but to private organizations, these being allegedly in a better position to deliver more competitive services. Not only some donor governments, but also leading United Nations special agencies, are already using this expanded concept of participation, with a view to sharing with the private sector a greater part of their public responsibilities.

In its present context, to borrow from Karl Polanyi's description of the modern economy, participation has come to be 'disembedded' from the socio-cultural roots which had always kept it alive. It is now simply perceived as one of the many 'resources' needed to keep the *economy* alive. To participate is thus reduced to the act of partaking in the objectives of the economy, and the societal arrangements related to it. It is in this sense that one should understand Daniel Lerner and others, when they consider that 'traditional societies are not participant'. For the modern construct of participation, a person should be part of a predefined project, more specifically, an economic project, in order to qualify as a participant.

To sum up, participation is no longer the taboo it was only two decades ago. On the contrary, all developers seem to have definitively adopted the new child as a reliable asset for their own future development.

Popular participation

Activists strongly favouring participatory development argue that they are fully aware of the reasons why politicians and development planners try to co-opt the concept of participation for their own ends. In their view, the types of interaction they propose are precisely intended to prevent all such hegemonistic and manipulative designs. They therefore believe the concept should be further refined — 'popular participation' being able to save development from its present crisis and give it new stamina for enabling the grassroots populations to regenerate their life spaces.

An UNRISD discussion paper defines popular participation as 'the organized efforts to increase control over resources and movements of those hitherto excluded from such control'.[7] For Orlando Fals-Borda, Anisur Rahman and many other PAR theorists,[8] the aim of such a participation is to achieve power:

a special kind of power — people's power — which belongs to the oppressed and exploited classes and groups and their organizations, and the defence of their just interests to enable them to advance towards shared goals of social change within a participatory system.[9]

As a rule, participation is advocated by PAR theorists as the only way to save development from degenerating into a bureaucratic, top-down and dependency creating institution. They do not question the validity of the institution, *per se*, which most of them consider could be a powerful instrument in the hands of the oppressed. They do insist, however, that, for development to play its historical role, it should be based on participation. Genuine processes of dialogue and interaction should thus replace the present subject-object relationships between intervenors and the intervened, thereby enabling the oppressed to act as the free subjects of their own destiny.

The assumptions underlying the popular participatory approach can be summarized as follows:

(a) Present obstacles to people's development can and should be overcome by giving the populations concerned the full opportunity of participating in all the activities related to their development.

(b) Participation is justified because it expresses not only the will of the majority of people, but also it is the only way for them to ensure that the important moral, humanitarian, social, cultural and economic objectives of a more humane and effective development can be peacefully attained.

(c) 'Dialogical interaction', 'conscientization', 'PAR' and other similar activities can make it possible for all the people to organize themselves in a manner best suited to meet their desired ends.

When the concept of popular participation was initially advanced by its promoters as a key element in creating an alternative, human-centred development, it was intended to perform at least four functions: a cognitive, a social, an instrumental and a political one.

In *cognitive* terms, participation had to regenerate the development discourse and its practices, on the basis of a different mode of understanding of the realities to be addressed. It expressed the belief that the cognitive bases of conventional development not only belonged to an irrelevant *episteme*, representing an ethnocentric perception of reality specific to Northern industrialized countries, but were also no longer able to serve the objectives of a sound development. They had to be replaced by a different knowledge system, representing people's own cultural heritage, in particular the locally produced *techne*. Popular participation was to carve out a new meaning for, and a new image of, development, based on different forms of interaction and a common search for this new 'popular' knowledge.

The *political* function of participation was to provide development with a new source of legitimation, assigning to it the task of empowering the voiceless and the powerless, and also eventually, of creating a bridge between the Establishment and its target populations, including even the groups opposing development.

The *instrumental* function of the participatory approach was to provide the 're-empowered' actors of development with new answers to the failure of conventional strategies, and to propose new alternatives, with a view to involving the 'patients' in their own care.

Finally, in *social* terms, participation was the slogan which gave the development discourse a new lease of life. All institutions, groups and individuals involved in development activities rallied around the new construct in the hope that the participatory approach would finally enable development to meet everyone's basic needs and to wipe out poverty in all its manifestations.

The Pitfalls of Empowerment

The new methodologies of interaction inspired by the PAR and conscientization approaches did initially create waves of enthusiasm and hope, mainly amongst fieldworkers engaged in grassroots activities. The rush for the rapid creation of a 'popular knowledge', aimed at destroying the pernicious monopoly of the dominant paradigm, served as a contagious incentive to promote often inspiring activities in such fields as literacy and regeneration of traditional know-how. Particularly in a number of technical areas, it succeeded in denouncing the often dangerous and inhibitive impacts, on people's lives, of imported and irrelevant technologies. Here and there, but mainly at the local level, it served to keep alive the population's resentment against the most visible aspects of political and social discrimination. It also helped some bright elements to be recognized as local leaders, and gain a wider perception of their communities' possibilities of action.

Yet, there is not enough evidence to indicate that a new kind of knowledge did emerge from the process, 'in such a way that the dominated, underdeveloped societies can articulate their own socio-political position on the basis of their own values and capacities.'

While participatory thinkers do admit that all knowledge systems carry a number of values and biases,[10] they seem to exclude the possibility that, as products of a certain knowledge born out of the economic/developmental age, they could be, themselves, the carriers of very questionable values and biases. Neither do they pay enough attention to the fact that traditional or local knowledge systems suffer, too, from similar, sometimes even more inhibitive prejudices. The fact that the latter have been distorted and confused by the processes of change in the colonial and development eras does not change the picture. As such, any attempt to realize a mix of the two knowledges,[11] represented by local and outside persons interacting with each other, is not only a conceptually reductionist and patchwork type of exercise, but also may turn out to be a strange mix of very heterogeneous biases. The exercise tends, finally, to disregard the following very basic principle of learning — that no one learns who claims to know already in advance. Reality is the unknown which has to be '*dis*-covered' together, free from all the presuppositions and influences of the known.

The notion of empowerment was intended to help participation perform one main political function — to provide development with a new source of legitimation. As already made clear in the first part of this essay, the intentions of the pioneers of participation were, indeed, pure and noble. They were right to consider that the tremendous abuses of power by oppressors had to be stopped, and the victims be provided with new possibilities of defending themselves. Yet, in practice, the empowerment discourse raised a number of important questions, both at the theoretical and practical levels. As some of these issues suggest that the discourse can eventually produce opposite results, the matter deserves to be more deeply explored.

When A considers it essential for B to be empowered, A assumes not only that B has no power — or does not have the right kind of power — but also that A has the secret formula of a power to which B has to be initiated. In the current participatory ideology, this formula is, in fact, nothing but a revised version of state power, or what could be called fear-power.

The crux of the matter is that the populations actually subjected to this fear-power are not at all powerless. Theirs is a different power which is not always perceived as such, and cannot be actualized in the same manner, yet it is very real in many ways.[12] It is constituted by the thousands of centres and informal networks of resistance which ordinary people put up, often quietly, against the prevailing power apparatuses. Amongst others, it manifests itself in the reality of 'tax payers cheating the state, young people evading conscription, farmers accepting subsidies or equipment from development projects and diverting them to their own ends, technicians or repairmen working without permits or licences, government paid teachers using the classroom to denounce government abuses of power.'[13]

As a result, there is little evidence to indicate that the participatory approach, as it evolved, did, as a rule, succeed in bringing about new forms of people's power. Instead, there are indications that the way many an activist interpreted their mission contributed to dis-valuing the traditional and vernacular forms of power. More often than not, they helped replace them with a most questionable notion of power, highly influenced by that of the leftist traditions in Europe. This vision of power did, in practice, prove useful to the development establishment. For it helps it to persuade its target populations that not only are economic and state authorities the real power, but that they are also within everyone's reach, provided everyone is ready to participate fully in the development design.

Professionalizing Grassroots Activities

To involve the 'patients' in their own care was the instrumental task which the participatory concept has been assigned by development. 'Change agents' and NGOs were identified as suitably qualified instruments for this function. The notion of 'change agent' was introduced, mainly, as a substitute for the professional expert hired by a development project. The intention was to do away, through this non-professional grassroots-oriented intermediary, with subject/object relationships and to replace the alien authority of the outsider with a 'co-actor' whose role was to intervene, primarily, as a catalyst in an endogenous process of self-regeneration.

In reality, however, the change agent often ended up by exceeding his role as a catalyst beyond all recognition. Acting, in most cases, as a *promoter* or professional of participation, rather than a sensitive party to a process of mutual learning, he became sometimes a militant ideologue, sometimes a self-appointed authority on people's needs and strategies to meet them, and often a 'barefoot developer' lacking the professional competence of the expert. Few were actors genuinely seeking to learn from the people how *they* defined and perceived change, and how *they* thought to bring it about. The change, of which they considered themselves the agents, was only the projection of a predefined ideal of change, often highly affected by their own perception of the world and their own ideological inclinations.

There were indeed cases where some external agents, using their personal gifts, acted as sensitive and compassionate catalysts. Yet, studies made on the subject

> point to the potential drawbacks of such an interaction with external activists, due to the seemingly inherent tendency of the latter to manoeuvre and manipulate the movements and to impose on them their own ideological frameworks and definitions of the aims of the struggle.[14]

As for NGOs, they were given a special status, on the ground that, being non-governmental organizations, they could avoid many of the pitfalls of development projects implemented by bureaucratized government agencies. Yet, here too, most of these organizations became only better agents for the *delivery* of similar projects. As such, the main donors did not take much time to conclude that they could become their best allies in all projects needing a participatory source for marketing purposes.

On the whole, neither the promises of change agents, nor those of NGOs, succeeded in genuinely involving the 'patients' in their own care. With a few exceptions due to the personal qualities of the mediators, the new instrumentalities of participation served to promote a kind of 'fast food' or do-it-yourself development, made out of the same old ingredients. On the other hand, the very patients who were encouraged to go back to their self-care traditions, became dependent on the new breed of barefoot specialists, either parachuted in from abroad as volunteers, or trained on the spot. In short, more refined and deceitful means of action and persuasion came to be added to the paraphernalia of development institutions. The growing role of NGOs in development activities, and the great financial means at their disposal, give them, now, unprecedented possibilities for further professionalizing grassroots activities.

Thus, as one goes on digging into the archaeological site of the many development constructs that are falling apart, trying to see more clearly in the rubble that once impressed so many because of their solid appearance, a number of questions come to mind. Did the new participatory approaches actually lead to any substantial change in the nature of development, or did they serve only as band-aid operations to give a new lease of life to an ageing institution? Did (or can) such methods as dialogical interaction, conscientization and participatory action research really succeed in halting the processes of domination, manipulation and colonization of the mind? Can they really help bring about new forms of knowledge, power, action and know-how, needed to create a different type of society? Or is the new participatory myth acting more like a Trojan horse which may end up by substituting a subtle kind of teleguided and masterly organized participation for the old types of intransitive or culturally defined participation, proper to vernacular societies? Looking at the facts, rather than at the good intentions behind them, it seems difficult to answer these questions in the affirmative.

Conscientizing from Without?

Praxis, or action and reflection, was advanced by the participatory movement as a means to precisely give those wider dimensions to participation. As such, Freirian methods of dialogical action and conscientization are perceived by the movement as a crucial instrument of interaction, aimed not only at liberating the oppressed, but eventually also the intervenor from his own conditioning as a 'bourgeois' thinker. These methods are intended to create new forms of knowledge, power and understanding of reality, proper to the fighting of oppressive trends.

Yet reports coming from the field, some of which have already been highlighted here, point out that conscientization exercises have not always led, in practice, to the types of dialogical interaction persistently advocated by Paulo Freire. A closer look at his theory of 'historical conditioning and levels of consciousness'[15] may perhaps give us some idea of the reasons for this inadequacy.

Elaborating on this question, Freire states that, in dependent societies and during transitional phases, the oppressed do not yet have a 'critical consciousness', but rather a 'semi-transitive', or 'naive transitive', or 'popular' consciousness. This 'historical–cultural reality' leads them to 'internalize the values of the dominant groups', to have a distorted perception of their own condition. Hence, the necessity for 'progressive' groups of non-alienated intellectuals to transcend their class interests and to engage in conscientization exercises.

The 'existential duality of the oppressed', as a phenomenon of economic modernity, was indeed an important Freirian contribution to the understanding of the colonized mind. And it was right to identify the syndrome as one of the main reasons for the 'false perception' of reality. Yet, in his rather long chapter devoted to this issue, no mention is made of the possibility that many an outsider working with the oppressed, namely the activists in charge of other people's conscientization, might eventually themselves suffer from the same syndrome. The omission particularly weakens the importance of the concept. It may, namely, explain the many cases where highly ideologized 'agents of change' or 'vanguards', have tried to use conscientization or participatory methods, simply as new and more subtle forms of manipulation.

The theoretical classification of these change agents as participant actors in the dialogue further facilitates such abuses whenever the outsiders tend to act, not only as bearers of higher forms of consciousness, but also of the ideologies they have internalized. In this context, some participatory activists have been seen to outdo the paternalistic arrogance of the conventional expert/evangelizer. When the common sense of grassroots people prompts them eventually to disagree with a solution offered them by vanguard leaders, their lack of co-operation or outright resistance is attributed to their primary consciousness, if not to counter-revolutionary influences.

Participation: Boon, Myth, or Danger?

The fact that entire populations are robbed of their possibilities of relating and acting together, in their own best interest, is indeed a most serious question. This represents a state of violence which cannot leave anyone indifferent, and it, no doubt, calls for action. Whenever people confront such situations, they do act, collectively or individually, within the limits of their possibilities. 'There are no motion-less people,' says Gustavo Esteva quite rightly.[16] Only the actomaniac, the missionary, the obsessional intervenor and the mentally programmed do-gooder think they alone care about the situation, while the victims do not. And because of the arrogance and lack of sensitivity implied in this attitude, their mediation turns out usually to be manipulative and counterproductive.

Participation, which is also a form of intervention, is too serious and ambivalent a matter to be taken lightly, or reduced to an amoeba word lacking in any precise meaning, or a slogan, or fetish or, for that matter, only an instrument or a methodology. Reduced to such trivialities, not only does it cease to be a boon, but it runs the risk of acting as a deceptive myth or a dangerous tool for manipulation. To understand the many dimensions of participation, one needs to enquire seriously into all its roots and ramifications, these going deep into the heart of human relationships and the socio-cultural realities conditioning them.

As has already been noted, 'relating' is intrinsic to the very act of being and living. To live is to relate, or to participate in the wider living world of which one is only a part. To relate to that world, and to the human beings composing it, is an act of great consequence which cannot and need not be mediated. As such, one's inability fully to assume this vital necessity should only be *understood*. Only this understanding, by the subject and the others interacting with him, can enable one to overcome that predicament. No democratic or participatory panacea can give an ailing society of dead or conditioned persons what they individually do not have. Contemporary history is particularly rich in cases where induced participation in projects of an ideological, national or ethnic nature had repeatedly led to frightfully self-destructive tragedies. After all, slogans of participation have accompanied the events which led to the physical or mental destruction of millions of innocent people in Germany, the USSR, Cambodia, India, Iran, Iraq and elsewhere.

All these difficulties point to a basic dilemma facing the participatory phenomenon. How to reconcile two facts: the fact that no form of social interaction or participation can ever be meaningful and liberating, unless the participating individuals act as free and un-biased human beings; and the second fact that all societies hitherto have developed commonly accepted creeds (religions, ideologies, traditions, etc.) which, in turn, condition and help produce inwardly un-free and biased persons? The dilemma is particularly difficult to resolve at a time when the old ways of socio-cultural conditioning have taken on new and frightening forms. The economization of life with all its implications (cultural, political and social) — is subjecting its participants, all over the world, to often invisible and structural processes of addictive manipulation. As a result, people are led to believe that their very biases, their conditioning and their inner lack of freedom, are not only the expressions of their freedom, but also of an even greater freedom still to be achieved.

Beyond Participation

In real life, the dilemma is addressed differently, according to the great diversity of situations and cultures. In recent years, a number of grassroots movements have demonstrated particular creativity, both in bringing up new forms of leadership and 'animation', and in combining the inner and outer requirements of participation.

In relation to the first achievement, the presence within such movements of sometimes very sensitive 'animators', able to listen to their own people, to the world at large, and to the roots of their common culture, has enabled them to cultivate the possibilities of action and self-discovery dormant in the 'common man'. To take only the Indian scene, the Gandhian, the Chipko, the Lokayan and Swadhyaya movements are good examples of the way such inspiring animators have interacted with their fellow countrymen. Drawing on the most enduring and inspiring aspects of people's traditions, some of them have been able to use these as living instruments of socio-cultural regeneration. New ways of working, acting and hoping together have been found, which have also given new meanings and expressions to modernity, in its real sense of *belonging to the present*. The fact that specially trained change agents do not play a major role in these movements, has not generally prevented them from being highly animated by their own members, most of them acting as their own agents of change.

In the second area of achievement, a new feature, common to most of these genuine grassroots movements, seems to be the substitution of various modern methodologies, project designs, organizational schemas and fund-raising constraints, by more traditional and vernacular ways of interaction and leadership. As a rule, the necessity for a spiritual dimension, and for the revival of the sacred in one's everyday relationships with the world, seems to be rediscovered as a basic factor for the regeneration of people's space. Wherever this spiritual dimension[17] has been present, it has, indeed, produced a staggering contagion of intelligence and creativity, much more conducive to people's collective 'efficiency' than any other conventional form of mass mobilization. In the above mentioned grassroots movements, this dimension has served as a most powerful instrument in reviving the old ideals of a livelihood based on love, conviviality and simplicity, and also in helping people to resist the disruptive effects of economization.

In that sense, to participate means to live and to relate differently. It implies, above all, the recovery of one's inner freedom, that is, to learn to listen and to share, free from any fear or predefined conclusion, belief or judgment. As inner freedom is not necessarily dependent on outer freedom, its recovery is an essentially personal matter, and can be done even in a jail, or under the most repressive conditions. Yet it enables one not only to acquire a tremendous life power for the flowering of one's own life, but also to contribute, in a meaningful way, to everyone else's struggle for a better life. As such, inner freedom gives life to outer freedom, and makes it both possible and meaningful. On the other hand, while outer freedom is often a great blessing, and a necessity to protect people from violence and abuse, it remains hollow and subject to decay, in the absence of inner freedom. It can never, *per se*, help alienated persons to flower in goodness, or live in wisdom and beauty. Anyhow, participation soon turns into a parody, and an invitation to manipulative designs, when it represents only a ritual amongst alienated persons acting as programmed robots.

To live differently implies, secondly, that change be perceived as a process which starts from within, and defines as one pursues one's creative journey into the unknown. It does not mean to conform to a preordained pattern or ideal designed by others, or even one designed by one's own illusions and conditioned ideals. For change to happen and to make sense, it should represent the open-ended quest and interaction of free and questioning persons for the understanding of reality.

In a situation where these crucial dimensions of change are disregarded, or artificially severed from it, organized forms of participation or mobilization either serve illusory purposes, or lead to superficial and fragmented achievements of no lasting impact on people's lives. Even when these seem to be beneficial to a particular group or region, their effects remain inevitably limited, in time and space, sometimes even producing opposite effects in many unforeseen and unexpected areas.

On another plane, planned macro-changes (which are generally the *raison d'être* of development projects) are more the indirect result of millions of individual micro-changes, than of voluntarist programmes and strategies from above. In fact, they often represent a co-option of the unplanned micro-changes produced by others and elsewhere. When these reach a critical mass, and appear as a threat to the dominant knowledge/power centres at the top, they are co-opted and used by their professionals as an input for planned changes, aimed at turning the potential threat posed to the top into a possible asset for it. Hence, major projects of change from above generally represent an attempt, by those very forces under threat, to contain and redirect change, with a view to adapting it to their own interests, whenever possible with the victims' participation. This is how the real authors of most revolutions are, sooner or later, robbed of the changes they have provoked, and ultimately victimized by the professional ideologues and agitators acting on their behalf. This is how the pioneering participatory mendicants of the early development years were also robbed of their participatory ideal, as the latter was transmogrified into the present-day manipulative construct of participatory development.

Should that mean that anything any free human being does for change, even in its genuine and holistic sense, will inevitably be countered and/or co-opted by vested interests? Or should such realities invite those who seriously want to remain free, to live and to relate as such, to continue partaking in the world, free from fears of all kinds, including the fear of co-option? If the participatory ideal could, in simple terms, be redefined by such qualities as attention, sensitivity, goodness or compassion, and supported by such regenerative acts as learning, relating and listening, are not these qualities and gifts precisely impossible to co-opt? Are they not, also, the same which always help flower, in others, their potentialities of inner transformation? To stay with this question could perhaps serve as a good companion to the activist looking for an answer to his or her life and to better ways of participating in other people's lives.

References

1. See Daniel Lerner, *The Passing of Traditional Society*, Glencoe, Illinois: 1958, p. 50.

2. See Norman H. Nie, 'Social Structure and Political Participation', *American Political Science Review*, June 1969, No. 63, p. 369.

3. This is one of the definitions given by the Webster Dictionary for the verb 'to develop'.

4. Robert S. McNamara, *Address to the Board of Governors*, Washington, D.C.: World Bank, 25 September, 1973.

5. See Sheldon Annis, 'The Next World Bank? Financing Development from the Bottom Up, *Grassroots Development*, 1987, Vol. II, No. 1, p. 25.

6. Ibid. p. 26.

7. In a document produced by Matthias Stiefel and Marshall Wolfe, 'The Quest For Participation', UNRISD, Mimeographed Preliminary Report, June 1984, p. 12, the authors conclude that: 'The central issue of popular participation has to do with power, exercised by some people over the people, and by some classes over other classes . . .'

8. PAR — i.e. Participatory Action Research — is a methodology, or approach, to both action and research. It was introduced in the '70s, first in Asia and Latin America, by different groups of activists/theorists working in grassroots developmental activities. PAR seeks to set in motion processes of social change by the populations themselves, as they perceive their own reality. Orlando Fals-Borda, one of its founders, views it as 'a methodology within a total existential process', aimed at 'achieving power and not merely growth for the grassroots populations'.

9. Orlando Fals-Borda, *Knowledge and People's Power*, New Delhi: Indian Social Institute, 1988, p. 2.

10. 'Any science as a cultural product has a specific human purpose and therefore implicitly carries those biases and values which scientists hold as a group'. See Orlando Fals-Borda, op. cit., p. 93.

11. The gist of this design can be found in the following statement by Orlando Fals-Borda: 'Academic knowledge combined with popular knowledge and wisdom may give, as a result, a total scientific knowledge of a revolutionary nature (and perhaps a new paradigm), which destroys the previous unjust class monopoly.' Ibid., p. 88.

12. The Gandhian movement was based on the assumption that Indian rural communities were invested with a much more forbidding power than that of the British administration. As such, Gandhi's persistent message to them was neither to oppose that illusory and corruptive power through violence, nor to try to seize it. Many of the present grassroots movements of India and elsewhere similarly believe that the narrow politics of capturing state power is often a last resort. For more on the question of power, see Majid Rahnema, 'Power and regenerative processes in micro-spaces', in *International Social Science Journal*, August 1988, No. 117, pp. 361–75.

13. Ibid., p. 366.

14. Carlos Fortin and Matthias Stiefel, 'People's Participation — Problem or Promise?, Summary of a Panel of the World Conference', in *Development* [SID], 1985, No. 3, p. 75.

15. See Paolo Freire, *Cultural Action for Freedom*, Harmondsworth: Penguin Books, 1975, pp. 57–71.

16. See Gustavo Esteva, 'Beware of Participation', in *Development*, [*SID*], 1985, No. 3, p. 77.

17. Short of a less controversial word, 'spiritual' is used here to express the following qualities: sensitivity; the art of listening to the world at large and within one, free from the hegemony of a conditioned 'me' constantly interfering in the process; the ability to relate to others and to act, without any pre-defined plan or ulterior motives; and the perennial qualities of love, compassion and goodness which are under constant assault in economized societies. The spiritual dimension has nothing to do with the so-called religious, atheistic or scientific perceptions of the world. It expresses mainly the belief that human beings, in their relations with the world, are moved not only by material, economic, or worldly interests. It recognizes the sacred dimension of life which transcends the latter, giving a higher meaning to such awesome acts as living, relating and loving. The spiritual dimension, it may be said, is generally inhibited by fanatical beliefs in the superiority of one religion over another. As such, contrary to its promoters' claims, it is totally absent in religious fundamentalist movements based on hate and violence.

Bibliography

Burt Alpert & P.A. Smith, 'How Participation Works' and S.M. Miller, 'Planning for Participation', both published in *The Journal of Social Issues*, Vol. 5, No. 1, 1949, are amongst the first writings on participation in the development age. Sporadic studies, like G. M. Beal, 'Additional Hypotheses in Participation Research', in *Rural Sociology*, Vol. 21, Sept.–Dec. 1956; T.R. Black, 'Formal Social Participation: Method and Theory', same journal, Vol. 22, March 1957; and J.W.C. Johnstone & R.J. Rivera, *Volunteers for Learning*, Chicago: 1965, keep alive interest in the subject. The publication, outside Brazil, of Paulo Freire's three major works: *Cultural Action for Freedom*, originally produced as Monograph Series No. 1 of the *Harvard Educational Review*, 1970; *Pedagogy of the Oppressed*, New York: 1970; and *Education for Critical Consciousness*, New York: 1973, provided development activists and theorists with the new concept of conscientization.

The 1970s witnessed a blossoming of ideas and practices aimed at defining and implementing social change by, and with, the populations concerned, in accordance with their own aspirations. PAR (Participatory Action Research) was born as a new methodology for 'dialogical intervention'. Some of the earlier statements are: B. Hall, 'Participatory Research: An Approach for Change', *Convergence*, Vol. 8, No. 2, 1975; F. Haque, S. Mehta, A. Rahman & P. Wignaraja, 'Towards A Theory of Rural Development', *Development Dialogue*, No. 2, 1977; M. R. Hollnsteiner, 'People Power: Community Participation in the Planning of Human Settlements', *Assignment Children*, No. 40, Oct.–Dec. 1977. Experiences from different regions are presented in M.L. Swantz, 'Participatory Research as a Tool for Training: The Jipemoyo Project in Tanzania', *Assignment Children*, No. 41, Jan.–March 1978; R.B. Charlick, 'Animation rurale: Experience with Participatory Development in Four West African Nations', *Rural Development Participation Review*, Vol. 1, No. 2, Winter 1980; H. Masharraf, *Conscientizing Rural Disadvantaged Peasants in Bangladesh: Intervention through Group Action: A Case Study of Proshika*, ILO, Working Paper No. WEP 10/WP.27, 1982. Summaries from a decade of experiences are drawn in Md. A. Rahman (ed.), *Grassroots Participation and Self-Reliance*, Delhi: 1984; M. Stiefel & M. Wolfe, *The Quest for Participation*, Geneva: UNRISD, 1985; O. Fals-Borda & A. Rahman (eds.), *Action and Knowledge: Breaking the Monopoly with PAR*, New York: Apex, 1991.

While the intention of most of the above writers was to impart an endogenous direction to social change, participation soon became a favourite 'amoeba' or plastic word of the development age. For an understanding of this phenomenon, see Uwe Pörksen, *Plastikwörter: Die Sprache einer internationalen Diktatur*, Stuttgart: 1988, with a list of the words in p. 41. A counter-current, mainly composed of planners, experts and economists, sought to co-opt the participatory discourse with a view to carving out a 'human face' for development. See for instance D. Gow & J. VanSant, 'Beyond the Rhetoric of Rural Development Participation: How Can it Be Done?', *World Development*, Vol. 11, No. 5, 1983; D.C. Korten & F.B. Alonso (eds.), *Bureaucracy and the Poor: Closing the Gap*, Singapore: 1981; J. VanSant et al., 'Managing Staff to Promote Participation', *Rural Development Participation Review*, Vol. 3, No. 3, 1982.

The 1980s witnessed a variety of critical reflections on participation, coming from different, sometimes opposite, directions. L. Rao and A. Bhaiya, 'Building Up People's Faith in Themselves', *Ideas and Action*, Vol. 119, No. 7, 1977; N. Long and D. Winder, 'The Limitations of "Directive Change" for Rural Development in the Third World', *Community Development Journal*, Vol. 16, No. 2, 1981; Jacques Bugnicourt, 'Popular Participation in Development in Africa', *Assignment Children*, Vol. 59/60, 1982; and R. Kidd and M. Byram, 'Demystifying Pseudo-Freirian Development: The Case of Laedza Batanani', *Community Development Journal*, Vol. 17, No. 2, April 1982, find out that, in the cases under their consideration, the participatory discourse is now being used for manipulative and domesticating designs. B. Dogra & A. Curucharan, 'Behind the Facade', *The Illustrated Weekly of India*, March 1984, provide a journalistic investigation of one case of abuse, made in the name of people's participation, by a rich international NGO. The co-optation of protest by agencies is further analysed in G. Esteva, 'Beware of Participation' and M. Rahnema, 'NGO's: Sifting the Wheat from the Chaff', both in *Development*, No. 3, 1985; and S. Annis, 'The Next World Bank? Financing Development from the Bottom Up', *Grassroots Development*, Vol. 11, No. 1, 1987. Also the protagonists of PAR are increasingly attempting to reflect upon this ambivalence. For instance, O. Fals-Borda, *Knowledge and People's Power: Lessons with Peasants in Nicaragua, Mexico, Colombia*, Delhi: 1988, in particular pp. 41–50.

Planning

Arturo Escobar

Planning techniques and practices have been central to development since its inception. As the application of scientific and technical knowledge to the public domain, planning lent legitimacy to, and fuelled hopes about, the development enterprise. Generally speaking, the concept of planning embodies the belief that social change can be engineered and directed, produced at will. Thus the idea that poor countries could move more or less smoothly along the path of progress through planning has always been held as an indubitable truth, an axiomatic belief in need of no demonstration, by development experts of most persuasions.

Perhaps no other concept has been so insidious, no other idea gone so unchallenged. This blind acceptance of planning is all the more striking given the pervasive effects it has had historically, not only in the Third World, but also in the West, where it has been linked to fundamental processes of domination and social control. For planning has been inextricably linked to the rise of Western modernity since the end of the 18th century. The planning conceptions and routines introduced in the Third World during the post-World War II period are the result of accumulated scholarly, economic and political action; they are not neutral frameworks through which 'reality' innocently shows itself. They thus bear the marks of the history and culture that produced them. When deployed in the Third World, planning not only carried with it this historical baggage, but also contributed greatly to the production of the socio-economic and cultural configuration that we describe today as underdevelopment.

Normalizing People in 19th Century Europe

How did planning arise in the European experience? Very briefly, three major factors were essential to this process, beginning in the 19th century — the development of town planning as a way of dealing with the problems of the growing industrial cities; the rise of social planning, and increased intervention by professionals and the state in society, in the name of promoting people's welfare; and the invention of the modern economy, which crystallized with the institutionalization of the market and the formulation of classical political economy. These three factors, which today appear to us as normal, as natural parts of our world, have a relatively recent and even precarious history.

In the first half of the 19th century, capitalism and the industrial revolution brought drastic changes in the make-up of cities, especially in Northwestern Europe. Ever more people flooded into old quarters, factories proliferated, and industrial fumes hovered over streets covered with sewage. Overcrowded and disordered, the 'diseased city', as the metaphor went, called for a new type of planning which would provide solutions to the rampant urban chaos. Indeed, it was those city officials and reformers who were chiefly concerned with health regulations, public works and sanitary interventions, who first laid down the foundations of comprehensive urban planning. The city began to be conceived of as an object, analysed scientifically, and transformed according to the two major requirements of traffic and hygiene. 'Respiration' and 'circulation' were supposed to be restored to the city organism, overpowered by sudden pressure. Cities (including the colonial chequerboards outside Europe) were designed or modified to ensure proper circulation of air and traffic, and philanthropists set out to eradicate the appalling slums and to bring the right morals to their inhabitants. The rich traditional meaning of cities and the more intimate relationship between city and dweller were thus eroded as the industrial–hygienic order became dominant. Reifying space and objectifying people, the practice of town planning, along with the science of urbanism, transformed the spatial and social make-up of the city, giving birth in the 20th century to what has been called 'the Taylorization of architecture'.[1]

Just like planners in the Third World today, the 19th century European bourgeoisie also had to deal with the question of poverty. The management of poverty actually opened up a whole realm of intervention, which some researchers have termed the social. Poverty, health, education, hygiene, unemployment, etc. were constructed as 'social problems', which in turn required detailed scientific knowledge about society and its population, and extensive social planning and intervention in everyday life. As the state emerged as the guarantor of progress, the objective of government became the efficient management and disciplining of the population so as to ensure its welfare and 'good order'. A body of laws and regulations was produced with the intention to regularize work conditions and deal with accidents, old age, the employment of women, and the protection and education of children. Factories, schools, hospitals, prisons became privileged places to shape experience and modes of thinking in terms of the social order. In sum, the rise of the social made possible the increasing socialization and subjection of people to dominant norms, as well as their insertion into the machinery of capitalist production. The end result of this process in the present day is the welfare state and the new professionalized activity known as social work.

Two points have to be emphasized in relation to this process. One, that these changes did not come about naturally, but required vast ideological and material operations, and often times plain coercion. People did not become accustomed to factory work or to living in crowded and inhospitable cities gladly and of their own volition; they had to be disciplined into it! And two, that those very operations and forms of social planning have produced 'governable' subjects. They have shaped not only social structures and institutions, but also the way in which people experience life and construct themselves as subjects. But development experts have been blind to these insidious aspects of planning in their proposals to replicate in the Third World similar forms of social planning. As Foucault said, 'the "Enlightenment", which discovered the liberties, also invented the disciplines.'[2] One cannot look on the bright side of planning, its modern achievements (if one were to accept them), without looking at the same time on its dark side of domination. The management of the social has produced modern subjects who are not only dependent on professionals for their needs, but also ordered into realities (cities, health and educational systems, economies, etc.) that can be governed by the state through planning. Planning inevitably requires the normalization and standardization of reality, which in turn entails injustice and the erasure of difference and diversity.

The third factor in European history that was of central importance to the development and success of planning was the invention of the 'economy'. The economy, as we know it today, did not even exist as late as the 18th century in Europe, much less in other parts of the world. The spread and institutionalization of the market, certain philosophical currents such as utilitarianism and individualism, and the birth of classical political economy at the end of the 18th century provided the elements and cement for the establishment of an independent domain, namely 'the economy', apparently separated from morality, politics and culture. Karl Polanyi refers to this process as the 'disembeddedness' of the economy for society, a process which was linked to the consolidation of capitalism and which entailed the commodification of land and labour. There were many consequences of this development, besides generalized commodification. Other forms of economic organization, those founded upon reciprocity or redistribution, for instance, were disqualified and increasingly marginalized. Subsistence activities became devalued or destroyed. And an instrumental attitude towards nature and people became the order of the day, which in turn led to unprecedented forms of exploitation of people and nature. Although today most of us take for granted the modern market economy, this notion and the reality of how it operates have not always existed. Despite its dominance, even today there persist in many parts of the Third World subsistence societies, 'informal' economies, and collective forms of economic organization.

In sum, the period 1800–1950 saw the progressive encroachment of those forms of administration and regulation of society, urban space and the economy that would result in the great edifice of planning in the early post-World War II period. Once normalized, regulated and ordered, individuals, societies and economies can be subjected to the scientific gaze and social engineering scalpel of the planner, who, like a surgeon operating on the human body, can then attempt to produce the desired type of social change. If social science and planning have had any success in predicting and engineering social change, it is precisely because certain economic, cultural and social regularities have already been attained which confer some systematic element and consistency with the real world on the planners' attempts. Once you organize factory work and discipline workers, or once you start growing trees in plantations, then you can predict industrial output or timber production. In the process, the exploitation of workers, the degradation of nature, and the elimination of other forms of knowledge — whether it be the skills of the craftsman or those who live off the forest — are also affected. These are the kind of processes that are at stake in the Third World when planning is introduced as the central technique of development. In short, planning redefines social and economic life in accordance with the criteria of rationality, efficiency and morality which are consonant with the history and needs of capitalist, industrial society, but not those of the Third World.

Dismantling and Reassembling Societies

Scientific planning came of age during the 1920s and '30s, when it emerged from rather heterogeneous origins — the mobilization of national production during World War I, Soviet Planning, the scientific management movement in the USA, and Keynesian economic policy. Planning techniques were refined during the Second World War and its aftermath. It was during this period, and in connection with the War, that operations research, systems analysis, human engineering, and views of planning as 'rational social action' became widespread. When the era of development in the Third World dawned in the late 1940s, the dream of designing society through planning found an even more fertile ground. In Latin America and Asia, the creation of a 'developing society', understood as an urban-based civilization characterized by growth, political stability and increasing standards of living, became an explicit goal, and ambitious plans were designed to bring it about with the eager assistance of international organizations and experts from the 'developed' world.

To plan in the Third World, however, certain structural and behavioural conditions had to be laid down, usually at the expense of people's existing concepts of social action and change. In the face of the imperatives of 'modern society', planning involved the overcoming or eradication of 'traditions', 'obstacles' and 'irrationalities', that is, the wholesale modification of existing human and social structures and their replacement with rational new ones. Given the nature of the post-war economic order, this amounted to creating the conditions for capitalist production and reproduction. Economic growth theories, which dominated development at the time, provided the theoretical orientation for the creation of the new order, and national development plans the means to achieve it. The first 'mission' — note its colonial, Christian missionary overtones — sent by the World Bank to an 'underdeveloped' country in 1949, for instance, had as its goal the formulation of a 'comprehensive program of development' for the country in question, Colombia. Staffed by experts in many fields, the mission saw its task as 'calling for a comprehensive and internally consistent program. . . . Only through a generalized attack throughout the whole economy on education, health, housing, food and productivity can the vicious circle of poverty, ignorance, ill health and low productivity be decisively broken.' Moreover, it was clear to the mission that:

> One cannot escape the conclusion that reliance on natural forces has not produced the most happy results. Equally inescapable is the conclusion that with knowledge of the underlying facts and economic processes, good planning in setting objectives and allocating resources, and determination in carrying out a program for improvement and reforms, a great deal can be done to improve the economic environment by shaping economic policies to meet scientifically ascertained social requirements. . . . In making such an

effort, Colombia would not only accomplish its own salvation but would at the same time furnish an inspiring example to all other underdeveloped areas of the world.[3]

That development was about 'salvation' — again the echoes of the colonial civilizing mission — comes out clearly in most of the literature of the period. Countries in Latin America, Africa and Asia were seen as 'relying on natural forces', which had not produced the 'most happy results'. Needless to say, the whole history of colonialism is effaced by this discursive way of putting it. What is emphasized instead is the introduction of poor countries to the 'enlightened' world of Western science and modern economics, while the conditions existing in these countries are constructed as being characterized by a 'vicious circle' of 'poverty', 'ignorance' and the like. Science and planning, on the other hand, are seen as neutral, desirable and universally applicable, while, in truth, an entire and particular rationality and civilizational experience was being transferred to the Third World through the process of 'development'. The Third World thus entered post-World War II Western consciousness as constituting the appropriate social and technical raw material for planning. This status of course depended, and still does, on an extractive neo-colonialism. Epistemologically and politically, the Third World is constructed as a natural–technical object that has to be normalized and moulded through planning to meet the 'scientifically ascertained' characteristics of a 'development society'.

By the end of the 1950s, most countries in the Third World were already engaged in planning activities. Launching the first 'Development Decade' at the beginning of the 1960s, the United Nations could thus state that:

> The ground has been cleared for a non-doctrinaire consideration of the real problems of development, namely saving, training and planning, and for action on them. In particular, the advantages in dealing with the various problems not piecemeal, but by a comprehensive approach through sound development planning, became more fully apparent. . . . Careful development planning can be a potent means of mobilizing . . . latent resources for a rational solution of the problems involved.[4]

The same optimism — and, at the same time, blindness to the parochial and ethnocentric attitudes of the planners — was echoed by the Alliance for Progress. In President Kennedy's words:

> The world is very different now. For man (sic) holds in his mortal hands the power to abolish all forms of human poverty and all forms of human life. . . . To those people in the huts and villages of half the globe struggling to break the bonds of mass misery . . . we offer a special pledge — to convert our good words in good deeds — in a new alliance for progress — to assist free men and free governments in casting off the chains of poverty.[5]

Statements such as these reduce life in the Third World simply to conditions of 'misery', overlooking its rich traditions, different values and life styles, and long historical achievements. In the eyes of planners and developers, people's dwellings appear as no more than miserable 'huts', and their lives — often times, especially at this early point in the development era, still characterized by subsistence and self-sufficiency — as marked by unacceptable 'poverty'. In short, they are seen as no more than crude matter in urgent need of being transformed by planning. One does not need to romanticize tradition to realize that, what for the economist were indubitable signs of poverty and backwardness, for Third World people were often integral components of viable social and cultural systems, rooted in different, non-modern social relations and systems of knowledge. It was precisely these systems that came under attack first by colonialism and later on by development, although not without much resistance then as today. Even alternative conceptions of economic and social change held by Third World scholars and activists in the 1940s and '50s — the most notable being that of Mahatma Gandhi, but also, for instance, those of certain socialists in Latin America — were displaced by the enforced imposition of planning and development. For developers, what was at stake was a transition from a 'traditional society' to an 'economic culture', that is, the development of a type of society whose goals were linked to future-oriented, scientific–objective rationality and brought into existence through the mastering of certain techniques. 'So long as everyone played his part well,' planners believed, 'the system was fail-safe; the state would plan, the economy would produce, and working people would concentrate on their private agendas: raising families, enriching themselves, and consuming whatever came tumbling out from the cornucopia.'[6]

As Third World elites appropriated the European ideal of progress — in the form of the construction of a prosperous, modern nation through economic development and planning; as other surviving concepts of change and social action became even more marginalized; finally, as traditional social systems were disrupted and the living conditions of most people worsened, the hold of planning grew ever stronger. Elites and, quite often, radical counter-elites found in planning a tool for social change which was in their eyes not only indispensable, but irrefutable because of its scientific nature. The history of development in the post-World War II period is, in many ways, the history of the institutionalization and ever more pervasive deployment of planning. The process was facilitated time after time by successive development 'strategies'. From the emphasis on growth and national planning in the 1950s, to the Green Revolution and sectoral and regional planning of the 1960s and '70s, including 'Basic Needs' and local level planning in the '70s and '80s, to environmental planning for 'sustainable development' and planning to 'incorporate' women, or the grassroots, into development in the '80s, the scope and vaulting ambitions of planning have not ceased to grow.

Perhaps no other concept has served so well to recast and spread planning as that of the Basic Human Needs strategy. Recognizing that the goals of reducing poverty and ensuring a decent living standard for most people were 'as distant as ever', development theorists — always keen on finding yet another gimmick which they could present as a 'new' paradigm or strategy — coined this notion with the aim of providing 'a coherent framework that can accommodate the increasingly refined sets of development objectives that have evolved over the past thirty years and can systematically relate these objectives to various types of policies',[7] including growth. The key arenas of intervention were primary education, health, nutrition, housing, family planning, and rural development. Most of the interventions themselves were directed at the household. As in the case of the mapping of 'the social' in 19th century Europe, where society first became the target of systematic state intervention, Third World people's health, education, farming and reproduction practices all became the object of a vast array of programmes introduced in the name of increasing these countries' 'human capital' and ensuring a minimum level of welfare for their people. Once again, the epistemological and political boundaries of this kind of 'rational' approach — aimed at the modification of life conditions and inevitably marked by class, race, gender and cultural features — resulted in the construction of an artificially homogeneous monochrome, the 'Third World', an entity that was always deficient in relation to the West, and so always in need of imperialist projects of progress and development.

Rural development and health programmes during the 1970s and '80s can be cited as examples of this type of biopolitics. They also reveal the arbitrary mechanisms and fallacies of planning. Robert McNamara's famous Nairobi speech, delivered in 1973 before the boards of governors of the World Bank and the International Monetary Fund, launched the era of 'poverty-oriented' programmes in development, which evolved into the Basic Human Needs approach. Central to this conception were so-called national food and nutrition planning and integrated rural development. Most of these schemes were designed in the early 1970s at a handful of US and UK universities, at the World Bank, and at United Nations technical agencies, and implemented in many Third World countries from the mid 1970s until the late 1980s. Comprehensive food and nutrition planning was deemed necessary, given the magnitude and complexity of the problems of malnutrition and hunger. Typically, a national food and nutrition plan included projects in primary health care, nutrition education and food supplementation, school and family vegetable gardens, the promotion of the production and consumption of protein-rich foods, and integrated rural development generally. This latter component contemplated measures to increase the production of food crops by small farmers through the supply of credit, technical assistance and agricultural inputs, and basic infrastructure.

How did the World Bank define integrated rural development? 'Rural development', the World Bank's policy dictated:

is a strategy designed to improve the economic and social life of a specific group of people — the rural poor. It involves extending the benefits of development to the poorest among those who seek a livelihood in rural areas. A strategy of rural development must recognize three points. Firstly, the rate of transfer of people out of low productivity agriculture into more rewarding pursuits has been slow. . . . Secondly, . . . their position is likely to get worse if population expands at unprecedented rates. . . . Thirdly, rural areas have labor, land and at least some capital which, if mobilized, could reduce poverty and improve the quality of life. . . . [Rural development] is clearly designed to increase production and raise productivity. It is concerned with the monetization and modernization of society, and with its transition from traditional isolation to integration with the national economy.[8]

That most people in the 'modern' sector, namely those living under marginal conditions in the cities, did not enjoy 'the benefits of development' did not occur to these experts. Peasants — that 'specific group of people' which is in reality the majority of the Third World — are seen in purely economic terms, not as trying to make viable a whole way of life. That their 'rate of transfer into more rewarding pursuits' had to be accelerated, on the other hand, assumes that their lives are not satisfying — after all, they live in 'traditional isolation', even if surrounded by their communities and those they love. The approach also regards peasants as suitable for moving around like cattle or commodities. Since their labour has to be 'mobilized', they must surely have just been sitting about idly (subsistence farming does not involve 'labour' in this view), or perhaps having too many babies. All of these rhetorical devices that reflect the 'normal' perceptions of the planner contribute to obscure the fact that it is precisely the peasants' increasing integration into the modern economy that is at the root of many of their problems. Even more fundamentally, these statements, which become translated into reality through planning, reproduce the world as the developers know it — a world composed of production and markets, of 'traditional' and 'modern' or developed and underdeveloped sectors, of the need for aid and investment by multinationals, of capitalism versus communism, of material progress as happiness, and so forth. Here we have a prime example of the link between representation and power, and of the violence of seemingly neutral modes of representation.

In short, planning ensures a functioning of power that relies on, and helps to produce, a type of reality which is certainly not that of the peasants, while peasant cultures and struggles are rendered invisible. Indeed the peasants are rendered irrelevant even to their own rural communities. In its rural development discourse, the World Bank represents the lives of peasants in such a way that awareness of the mediation and history inevitably implicated in this construction is excluded from the consciousness of its economists and from that of many important actors — planners, Western readers, Third World elites, scientists, etc. This particular narrative of planning and development, deeply grounded in the post-World War II global political economy and cultural order, becomes essential to those actors. It actually becomes an important element in their insular construction as a developed, modern, civilized 'we', the 'we' of Western man. In this narrative, too, peasants, and Third World people generally, appear as the half-human, half-cultured benchmark against which the Euro-American world measures its own achievements.

Knowledge as Power

As a system of representation, planning thus depends on making people forget the origins of its historical mediation. This invisibility of history and mediation is accomplished through a series of particular practices. Planning relies upon, and proceeds through, various practices regarded as rational or objective, but which are in fact highly ideological and political. First of all, as with other development domains, knowledge produced in the First World about the Third gives a certain visibility to specific realities in the latter, thus making them the targets of power. Programmes such as integrated rural development have to be seen in this light. Through these programmes, 'small farmers', 'landless peasants' and the like achieve a certain visibility, albeit only as a development 'problem', which makes them the object of powerful, even violent, bureaucratic interventions. And there are other important hidden or unproblematized mechanisms of planning; for instance, the demarcation of new fields and their assignment to experts, sometimes even the creation of a new sub-discipline (like food and nutrition planning). These operations not only assume the prior existence of discrete 'compartments', such as 'health', 'agriculture', and 'economy' — which in truth are no more than fictions created by the scientist — but impose this fragmentation on cultures which do not experience life in the same compartmentalized manner. And, of course, states, dominant institutions, and mainstream views are strenthened along the way as the domain of their action is inevitably multiplied.

Institutional practices such as project planning and implementation, on the other hand, give the impression that policy is the result of discrete, rational acts and not the process of coming to terms with conflicting interests, a process in which choices are made, exclusions effected, and worldviews imposed. There is an apparent neutrality in identifying people as 'problems', until one realizes first, that this definition of 'the problem' has already been put together in Washington or some capital city of the Third World, and second, that problems are presented in such a way that some kind of development programme has to be accepted as the legitimate solution. It is professional discourses which provide the categories in terms of which 'facts' can be identified and analysed. This effect is reinforced by the use of labels such as 'small farmer' or 'pregnant women', which reduces a person's life to a single trait and makes him/her into a 'case' to be treated or reformed. The use of labels also allows experts and elites to delink explanations of 'the problem' from themselves as the non-poor, and assign them purely to factors internal to the poor. Inevitably, people's lives at the local level are transcended and objectified when they are translated into the professional categories used by institutions. In short, local realities come to be greatly determined by these non-local institutional practices, which thus have to be seen as inherently political.

The results of this type of planning have been, for the most part, deleterious to Third World people and economies alike. In the case of rural development, for instance, the outcome was seen by experts in terms of two possibilities: '(a) the small producer may be able to technify his productive process, which entails his becoming an agrarian entrepreneur; and (b) the small producer is not prepared to assume such level of competitiveness, in which case he will be displaced from the market and perhaps even from production in that area altogether.'[9] In other words, 'produce (for the market) or perish'. Even in terms of increased production, rural development programmes have had dubious results at best. Most of the increase in food production in the Third World has taken place in the commercial capitalist sector, while a good part of the increase has been in cash or export crops. In fact, as has been amply shown, rural development programmes and development planning in general have contributed not only to growing pauperization of rural people, but also to aggravated problems of malnutrition and hunger. Planners thought that the agricultural economies of the Third World could be mechanically restructured to resemble the 'modernized' agriculture of the United States, overlooking completely not only the desires and aspirations of people, but the whole dynamics of economy, culture and society that circumscribe farming practices in the Third World. This type of management of life actually became a theatre of death (most strikingly in the case of the African famine), as increased production of food resulted, through a perverse shift, in more hunger.

The impact of many development programmes has been particularly negative on women and indigenous peoples, as development projects appropriate or destroy their basis for sustenance and survival. Historically, Western discourse has refused to recognize the productive and creative role of women and this refusal has contributed to propagating divisions of labour that keep women in positions of subordination. For planners and economists, women were not, until recently, 'economically active', despite the fact that a great share of the food consumed in the Third World is grown by women. Moreover, women's economic and gender position frequently deteriorated in the 1970s as a result of the participation in rural development programmes by male heads of household. It is not surprising that women have opposed much more actively than men these rural development programmes. With the 'technological packages', specialization in the production of certain crops, rigid lay-out of fields, pre-set cultivation routines, production for the market, and so forth, they contrast sharply with the more ecological and varied peasant farming defended by women in many parts of the Third World — in which production for subsistence and for the market are carefully balanced. Unfortunately, the recent trend towards incorporating women into development has resulted for the most part in their being targeted for what in all other respects remain conventional programmes. 'Target group categories are constructed to further development agency procedures to organize, manage, regulate, enumerate and rule the lives of ordinary women.'[10] Thus the development industry's clientele has been conveniently doubled by this shift in representation.

Another important recent instance of planned development is the industrialization schemes in so-called free trade zones in the Third World, where multinational corporations are brought in under very favourable conditions (e.g., tax breaks, assurances of cheap, docile labour and a 'stable' political climate, lower pollution standards, etc). Like all other forms of planning, these industrialization projects involve much more than an economic transformation, and on an ever larger scale. What is at stake here is the rapid transformation of rural society and culture into the world of factory discipline and modern (Western) society. Brought into Third World countries in the name of development, and actively promoted and mediated by Third World states, the free trade zones represent a microcosm in which households, villages, traditions, modern factories, governments and the world economy are all brought together in unequal relations of knowledge and power. It is no accident that most of the workers in the new factories are young women. The electronics industries in South East Asia, for instance, rely heavily on gender forms of subordination. The production of young women factory workers as 'docile bodies' through systematic forms of discipline in the factory and outside it, does not go, however, without resistance, as Aihwa Ong shows in her excellent study of Malaysian women factory workers. Women's forms of resistance in the factory (destruction of microchips, spirit possession, slow-downs etc.) have to be seen as idioms of protest against labour discipline and male control in the new industrial situation. Moreover, they remind us that, if it is true that 'new forms of domination are increasingly embodied in the social relations of science and technology which organize knowledge and production systems', it is equally true that 'the divergent voices and innovative practices of subjected peoples disrupt such cultural reconstructions of non-Western societies.'[11]

Knowledge in Opposition

Feminist critics of development and critics of development as discourse have begun to join forces, precisely through their examination of the dynamics of domination, creativity and resistance that circumscribe development. This hopeful trend is most visible in a type of grassroots activism and theorizing that is sensitive to the role of knowledge, culture and gender in supporting the enterprise of development and, conversely, in bringing about more pluralistic and egalitarian practices. As the links between development, which articulates the state with profits, patriarchy and objectivizing science and technology on the one hand, and the marginalization of people's lives and knowledge on the other, become more evident, the search for alternatives also deepens. The imaginary ideas of development and 'catching up' with the West are drained of their appeal as violence and recurrent crises — economic, ecological, political — become the order of the day. In sum, the attempt by states to set up totalizing systems of socio-economic and cultural engineering through development is running into a dead end. Practices and new spaces for thinking and acting are being created or reconstituted, most notably at the grassroots, in the vacuum left by the crisis of the colonizing mechanisms of development.

Speaking about ecology movements in India, many of them started by women at the grassroots level, Vandana Shiva, for instance, sees the emerging process as:

a redefinition of growth and productivity as categories linked to the production, not the destruction, of life. It is thus simultaneously an ecological and a feminist political project that legitimizes the ways of knowing and being that create wealth by enhancing life and diversity, and which delegitimizes the knowledge and practice of a culture of death as the basis for capital accumulation. . . . In contemporary times, Third World women, whose minds have not yet been dispossessed or colonized, are in a privileged position to make visible the invisible oppositional categories that they are custodians of.[12]

One does not need to impute to Third World women, indigenous people, peasants and others a purity they do not have, to realize that important forms of resistance to the colonization of their life world have been maintained and even nurtured among them. And one does not need to be overly optimistic about the potential of grassroots movements to transform the development order to visualize the promise that these movements hold, and the challenge they increasingly pose to conventional top-down, centralized approaches or even to those apparently decentralized, participatory strategies which are geared for the most part towards economic ends. ('Participatory' or local level planning, indeed, is most often conceived not in terms of a popular power that people could exercise, but as a bureaucratic problem that the development institution has to solve.) Shiva's argument that many groups of Third World people, especially rural women and indigenous peoples, possess knowledge and practices opposite to those that define the dominant nexus between reductionist science, patriarchy, violence and profits — forms of relating to people, knowledge and nature which are less exploitative and reifying, more localized, decentred and in harmony with the ecosystem — is echoed by observers in many parts of the world. These alternative forms, which are neither traditional nor modern, provide the basis for a slow but steady process of construction of different ways of thinking and acting, of conceiving of social change, of organizing economies and societies, of living and healing.

Thus Western rationality has to open up to the plurality of forms of knowledge and conceptions of change that exist in the world and recognize that objective, detached scientific knowledge is just one possible form among many. This much can be gleaned from an anthropology of Reason that looks critically at the basic discourses and practices of modern Western societies, and discovers in Reason and its key practices — such as planning — not universal truths but rather very specific, and even somewhat strange or at least peculiar, ways of being. This also entails, for those working within the Western tradition, recognizing — without overlooking the cultural content of science and technology — that:

(1) The production of universal, totalizing theory is a major mistake that misses most of reality, probably always, but certainly now; (2) taking responsibility for the social relations of science and technology means refusing an anti-science metaphysics, a demonology of technology, and so means embracing the skilful task of reconstructing the boundaries of daily life, in partial connection with others, in communication with all of our parts.[13]

As we have shown, planning has been one of those totalizing universals. While social change has probably always been part of the human experience, it was only within European modernity that 'society', i.e. the whole way of life of a people, was open to empirical analysis and made the object of planned change. And while communities in the Third World may find that there is a need for some sort of organized or directed social change — in part to reverse the damage caused by development — this undoubtedly will not take the form of 'designing life' or social engineering. In the long run, this means that categories and meanings have to be redefined; through their innovative political practice, new social movements of various kinds are already embarked on this process of redefining the social, and knowledge itself.

The practices that still survive in the Third World despite development thus point the way to moving beyond social change and, in the long run, to entering a post-development, post-economic era. In the process, the plurality of meanings and practices that make up human history will again be made apparent, while planning itself will fade away from concern.

References

1. M. McLeod, ' "Architecture or Revolution": Taylorism, Democracy, and Social Change', *Art Journal*, Summer 1983, pp. 132–47.
2. M. Foucault, *Discipline and Punish*, New York: Pantheon Books, 1979, p. 222.
3. International Bank for Reconstruction and Development, *The Basis of a Development Program for Colombia*, Baltimore: Johns Hopkins University Press, 1950, pp. xv and 615.
4. United Nations, Dept. of Economic and Social Affairs, *The United Nations Development Decade: Proposals for Action*, New York: United Nations, 1962, pp. 2, 10.
5. Presidential Address, January 20, 1961.
6. J. Friedmann, *Venezuela: From Doctrine to Dialogue*, Syracuse: Syracuse University Press, 1965, pp. 8, 9.
7. M. J. Crosswell, 'Basic Human Needs: A Development Planning Approach', in D. M. Leipziger and P. Streeten (eds), *Basic Needs and Development*, Cambridge, Mass: Oelgeschlager, Gunn and Hain Publishers Inc., 1981, p. 2.
8. The World Bank, *Assault on World Poverty*, Baltimore: Johns Hopkins University Press, 1975, pp. 90, 91, 16.
9. Depto. Nacional De Planeación de Colombia, Programa de Desarrollo Rural Integrado, *El Subsector de Pequeña Producción y el Programa DRI*, Bogota: DNP, July 1979, p. 47.
10. A. Mueller, 'Power and Naming in the Development Institution: The "Discovery" of "Women in Peru" ' presented at the 14th Annual Third World Conference, Chicago, April 1987, p. 4.
11. A. Ong, *Spirits of Resistance and Capitalist Discipline*, Albany, New York: SUNY Press, 1987, p. 221.
12. V. Shiva, *Staying Alive: Women, Ecology and Development*, London: Zed Books, 1989, pp. 13, 46.
13. D. Haraway, 'A Manifesto for Cyborgs': Science, Technology, and Socialist Feminism in the 1980s', *Socialist Review*, 15(2), 1985, p. 100.

Bibliography

Edward Said's *Orientalism*, New York: Vintage Books, 1979, still constitutes the point of departure for examining European or Euro-American representations of non-Western peoples. The general orientation for the discursive critique of representations is provided by Foucault, especially in *The History of Sexuality*, Vol. I, New York: Vintage Books, 1980, and *Power/Knowledge*, New York: Pantheon Books, 1981. These works provide the general framework for analysing development as a discourse, i.e. as a Western form of social description. Extensions of these works in connection with development are I. Gendzier, *Managing Political Change: Social Scientists and the Third World*, Boulder: Westview Press, 1985; P. Morandé, *Cultura y Modernización en América Latina*, Santiago: Pontificia Universidad Católica de Chile, 1984; V. Y. Mudimbe, *The Invention of Africa*, Bloomington: Indiana University Press, 1988; and A. Escobar, 'Power and Visibility: Development and the Invention and Management of the Third World', *Cultural Anthropology*, 3(4), November 1988.

On the origins of town planning, see L. Benevolo, *History of Modern Architecture*, Cambridge: MIT Press, 1971; and F. Choay, *The Modern City: Planning in the Nineteenth Century*, New York: George Bazillier, 1969. The rise of the social is documented in J. Donzelot, *The Policing of Families*, New York: Pantheon Books, 1979, and *L'Invention du Social*, Paris: Fayard, 1984. I. Illich discusses the professionalization of needs in *Toward a History of Needs*, Berkeley: Heyday Books, 1977. More recently, P. Rabinow has tackled the management of space and the normalization of the population in the context of French Colonial North Africa in *French Modern: Norms and Forms of the Social Environment*, Cambridge: MIT Press, 1989. The role of bio-politics and the narratives of science in the articulation of nature, gender and culture is examined in D. Haraway's *Primate Visions: Gender, Race, and Nature in the World of Modern Science*, New York: Routledge, 1989. The two most insightful books on the origins of the modern economy, on the other hand, are K. Polanyi, *The Great Transformation*, Boston: Beacon Press, 1957 and L. Dumont, *From Mandeville to Marx: The Genesis and Triumph of Economic Ideology*, Chicago: The University of Chicago Press, 1977.

Perhaps the most comprehensive (retrospective and prospective) look at planning is J. Friedmann's *Planning in the Public Domain*, Princeton: Princeton University Press, 1987. The critical analysis of institutional practices has been pioneered by D. Smith, *The Everday World as Problematic: A Feminist Sociology*, Boston: Northeastern University Press, 1987, and extended by A. Mueller in her doctoral dissertation, *The Bureaucratization of Development Knowledge: The Case of Women in Development*, Ontario Institute for Studies in Education, University of Toronto, 1987. E. J. Clay and B. B. Schaffer provide a thorough analysis of the 'hidden' practices of development planning in *Room for Manoeuvre: An Exploration of Public Policy Planning in Agriculture and Rural Development*, Rutherford: Fairleigh Dickinson University Press, 1984, while G. Wood focuses on the relation between labels and power in his article, 'The Politics of Development Policy Labelling', *Development and Change*, Vol. 16, 1985. A. Ong provides a complex view of the manifold practices and effects of development as biopolitics in *Spirits of Resistance and Capitalist Discipline: Factory Women in Malaysia*, Albany: SUNY Press, 1987. An insightful general treatise on practices of domination and resistance is M. de Certau's *The Practice of Everyday Life*, Berkeley: University of California Press, 1984.

Important elements for redefining development, especially from the vantage point of grassroots alternatives, are found in D. L. Shet, 'Alternative Development as Political Practice', *Alternatives*, XII(2), 1987; V. Shiva, *Staying Alive: Women, Ecology, and Development*, London: Zed Books, 1989; O. Fals Borda, *Knowledge and People's Power*, Delhi: Indian Social Institute, 1988; R. Kothari, 'Masses, Classes, and the State', *Alternatives*, XI(2), 1986; A. Nandy, *The Intimate Enemy*, Bombay: Oxford University Press, and *Traditions, Tyranny and Utopias*, Delhi: Oxford University Press, 1987; G. Esteva, 'Regenerating People's Space', *Alternatives*, XXI(1); and M. Rahnema, 'A New Variety of AIDS and Its Pathogens: Homo Economicus, Development and Aid', *Alternatives*, XIII(1), 1988. The role of social movements in articulating alternative visions of social and political change is explored in A. Escobar and S. Alvarez (eds), *New Social Movements in Latin America: Identity, Strategy, and Democracy*, Boulder: Westview Press, 1991.

Population

Barbara Duden

For the purpose of this essay, I take the development discourse since 1949 as the context within which to discuss the concept of population. To do so is a difficult task since for most people the term seems today to denote a natural entity, an issue about which neutral statements can be made, an object open to human control and management. I shall investigate the epistemological status of this 'object' in public policy statements, as well as commenting on the new connotations the term has acquired in ordinary English, for instance in public controversies about birth control, women's status and ecology.

In ordinary English the term 'population' evokes images of an explosion, mainly of uneducated Third World people, in countries that cannot repay their debts. Population also evokes the notion of pressure which pushes people beyond their borders and into camps. Population evokes anger at irresponsible procreation, insufficient funding for birth control programmes, and against the Catholic Church for opposing contraception and abortion. Feminists stress that population will remain a problem as long as its origin is not seen, namely the exclusion of women from the development process. As for ecologists, they connect population with the 'carrying capacity' of the planet. Generally, use of the term increasingly triggers alarm, symbolized in its most common composite, 'over-population'.

High school students learn from their geography books that the 'population explosion' is a result of development. In the wake of development came vaccines, antibiotics, improved sanitation and better nutrition. These were accepted faster than condoms, loops, the pill or sterilization, especially by non-white people. Population has come to evoke something threatening, something which casts a shadow over the future and something which in Northern latitudes looks yellow or brown.

These emotional, value-laden and often paranoic connotations are obviously absent whenever abstract formulae like 'let P = population' appear in the algorithms of statisticians or demographers. As soon, however, as their data are transferred out of the context of pure science and inserted into the models of policy makers, 'P' acquires a life of its own. 'P' ceases to represent simply an arbitrarily chosen class of entities. 'P' now refers to the ability to count real people and 'let P = population' amalgamates the sick child, the pregnant woman and even the census-taker into the subject of a sentence whose predicate attributes to 'population' the semblance of reality. 'Populations' grow, consume, pollute, need, demand, are entitled. 'Populations' become objects that can be acted upon, controlled, developed, limited.

Our subject is, therefore, this pseudo-entity, how it has been transformed during 40 years of development discourse, and the social realities engendered by its use. The misuse of population by statistics and unwarranted demography, however, are not my themes. Instead I want to describe how the use of the term 'population' has become a tool for what amounts to the verbal extermination of people.

How People Became Populations

'Population' calls for a different historical analysis than 'development'. Development is a term coined within the discourse on progress when, after World War II, social change was redefined as the task of a new, multi-professional establishment of experts. Population, on the contrary, was at that moment already a well established term in political discourse, but one which, from this point on, began profoundly to change its meaning.

Gilbert Murray's *Oxford English Dictionary* documented the state of the English language on the eve of the 20th century. The entry on population consists of half a column. Most of it is taken up by the action noun, well known for example from the American Declaration of Independence, in which the King of England 'has endeavoured to prevent the population of these states . . .' 'Population' was still a verbal noun: England wanted to prevent the populating of the colony, i.e. the generative, homesteading action of real people.

The *OED* of 1889 also reports the emergence of another meaning, this time technical. According to Malthus (1798), 'population increases in a geometrical ratio, subsistence in an arithmetical ratio'. In this sense, the term appears as part of ordinary English when Macaulay in 1849, for example, states that: 'The population of England in 1685 cannot be ascertained with perfect accuracy.' A generation later, Mendel. brazenly refers to pink and blue 'populations' of beans. The original *nomen actionis* fades as population for the next hundred years in political discourse designates an entity, an agent or claimant.

This transition takes place against the background of the evolution of a new branch of mathematics. The subsequent most recent mutation in the meaning of population in the age of development, and of systems thory, cannot be understood without first grasping the relationship between the concept and early statistics. Not census taking, but the first attempt at political arithmetic in the 17th century, is the ancestor of statistics. William Petty, influenced by Hobbes who spoke about society *more geometrico*, conceived the idea of quantifying society. 'Instead of using only comparative and superlative words, and intellectual arguments, I have taken the course . . . to express myself in terms of Number, Weight and Measure.'[1] In doing so, he aimed at creating a *Political Arithmetic* (London: 1690). He wanted to continue Bacon's attempt to draw a parallel between the 'body natural' and the 'body politic'. He tried to demonstrate that the wealth and power of the state depends on the number and character of its subjects. Yet, even after the first census of modern times was taken in Ireland in 1703, political arithmetic did not seek to calculate data but to reason about them. Even for Peter Suessmilch, who argued very early on for the importance of enumeration as a basis of a government's bureaucracy, statistics remained a speculative science.

The transition from general reasoning about numerical data culled from parish registers to their mathematical treatment is an event that happened almost instantaneously around 1800. For 18th century political arithmetic, quantitative reasoning had been a mere adjunct to observation. Now the mathematical treatment of data became the basis of new theory and new concepts. In this transition a new language came into being, created to observe people in quantitative contexts. These new concepts made it possible to uncover general truths about mass phenomena even though the cause of each particular action was unknown and remained inaccessible. Populations were attributed forms of 'behaviour', explained now by 'probability'. Statistics became the new 'Latin' of all modern sciences and the term 'population' lost its tie to actual people.

In the Supplement to the *OED*, published 80 years after the first edition, the entry for population lists more than two columns of new meanings. Clearly the word that had been originally derived from *populare*, 'to people', had not only lost its active usage; in most contexts it no longer had anything to do with people. It now refers to a totality of objects which may as well be so many pellets as people. It refers to a reproductive community that meets and mates with a defined probability. It can refer as much to mosquitoes as humans. In physics it refers to particles that exist in a particular energy state. In astronomy the metal-rich stars at the centre of galaxies form a population distinct from the stars in globular clusters. Penologists and the like distinguish the inmate population of their clients from those on parole. And, under a fourth and entirely new section, the *OED Supplement* lists population -census, -control, -cycle, -distribution, -explosion, -growth, -planning, -policy, -pressure, -survey, -trend, and still other words for functions and factors studied and supposedly managed.

All these new composite words nowadays occur frequently in the daily papers. Population is a prime example of what Uwe Pörksen calls the creolization of language by the pseudo-language of statistics.[2] The term we now are saddled with is a result of this colonization which took place in three stages.

In the first stage, around the turn of the century, statistics became an autonomous subject within mathematics. Its rigorous terminology became foreign to ordinary speech. Among the founders of mathematical statistics were demographers who wanted to create a tool by which they could give a political interpretation to Darwin's theory of evolution. This political commitment of demographers was, arguably, one of the means which led the scientific world, physicists as much as biologists, to familiarize themselves with the use of aggregate numbers and mean values for studying inherently independent and variable, but collectively predictable, objects.

In the second stage, statistics became a lingua franca. Its assumptions were integrated into physics as much as into biology and sociology. Textbooks that teach students the application of statistical methods surreptitiously tend to inculcate the idea that the procedures and variables they learn to manipulate are somehow natural givens. They learn, for example, to construct graphs that correlate population size to variables like nutritional status, GNP and genetic endowment. They learn to manipulate these variables and gradually come to believe that people can be managed just as dependent variables can be controlled.

Only then, in a third stage, did statistical concepts creolize ordinary English. The editor's box rather than the textbook is the typical device by which reporters' stories about famines, epidemics, or discrimination are transformed into readily visualized representations of aggregate numbers. On one page, a magazine shows a woman surrounded by her seven starving children. On the next, three boxes provide a visual interpretation of the author's text. There are bar charts, pie charts and graphs which compare US and Nigerian contraception, nutrition and abortion rates.

Most of the key concepts of the development discourse are statistical driftwood like population. They are immigrants into ordinary speech from the language of statistics, algorithms which are used outside of their original context. They are used to generate the semblance of a referent which may only be a pseudo-reality, but which at the same time gives the impression of something very important and obvious, and which the layman cannot understand without an explanation by experts. The growth of 'GNP', for example, as much as its alternative 'aggregate real use value' suggests to the layman a measure of wealth and simultaneously demands professional interpretation. Among these amoeba-like words, population has a special status. It does not aggregate things, but people. It does not reduce things to dollars, but persons to bloodless entities that can be managed as characterless classes that reproduce, pollute, produce or consume, and for the common good, call for control.

Birth Control for Development

Between 1950 and 1990, three periods can be distinguished in each of which the reference to populations obliterates ever more thoroughly the consideration of real people. In the first, ten years after Truman's Point Four Message (January 1949), the term 'population' continues to be used in policy statements as the equivalent to a concrete social collectivity. It designates the inhabitants of a country, a region or a continent. Statements designate populations as the beneficiaries of the economic, technical or even cultural developments by which they are affected but from which, as subjects, they remain distinct. Population control is not yet mentioned as a public policy goal. Even during the second period, the 1960s, when population control first appears in the speeches of ministers and heads of state, population is still treated as one of the *external* factors in the development calculus, a given like a country's rivers or subsoil. Only in a third stage, during the mid-1970s, does population growth come to be seen as one among many inter-related processes. Population then comes to be treated as an endogenous factor of the developing 'system'.

During the 1960s US policy shifted 180 degrees. In December 1959 President Dwight D. Eisenhower declared that: 'Birth control is not our business. I cannot imagine anything more emphatically a subject that is not a proper political or governmental activity, or function or responsibility.' Only ten years later, in July 1969, President Nixon issued the First Presidential Message on Population. After discussing US and world population growth and the need for family planning, he stated that: 'This Administration does accept a clear responsibility to provide essential leadership.' Another five years later and leadership had turned into a manifest mandate. George Bush, the then US Representative to the United Nations, declared in 1973 that: 'Today, the population problem is no longer a private matter . . . . (It) commands the attention of national and international leaders.'[3] Eisenhower's hands-off policy in regard to *birth control* was followed by Nixon's commitment to *family planning* and then the concern of Bush with the *population problem.*

This remarkable shift in US policy can at least in part be explained by an unusually effective private philanthropy. In 1952 John D. Rockefeller III established the Population Council with a large personal gift. This agency — since 1982 an NGO — served from its very beginning as a forum and lobby for activist demographers committed to redefining the goals of contraception in an age of explosive population growth. Fabians, Social Democrats, the Margaret Sanger League and public health agencies since the 1920s had organized to motivate women to use birth control in the interest of their own health and the wellbeing of their families. The new lobby insisted during the 1950s that private motivation had now to be mobilized in the service of nothing less than the world's survival. Given development and the consequent rapid reduction in infant and puerperal mortality, the Population Council's publications argued that 'over-population' was now undermining the achievement of development's goals. Further, explosive population growth threatened underdeveloped countries with previously unknown levels of famine, disease and violent disorder. Henceforth birth control had to be seen as the one and only desirable means to reach a newly defined goal — *'control' of populations.*

During the late 1950s, for the first time, 'over-population' came to be understood as an imminent threat. The speed of population growth came as a surprise even to Frank Notestein, one of the great figures of modern demography. At the close of World War II, this Princeton professor had foreseen a world population of three billion by the year 2000. In fact the three billion mark was passed by 1960. In 1964 in an address to the Ceylon Association for the Advancement of Science, Notestein recognized that a further doubling by the end of this century could not be avoided.[4] Modernization reduces the death rate long before it reduces the birth rate. As a result, development may increase GNP and at the same time reduce GNP per capita.

While, as of 1968, the US population would double in 63 years, Great Britain's in 140 years, Austria's in 175 years, the doubling time for Kenya and Turkey was 24 years, the Philippines and Mexico 20, El Salvador 19. What is more, even if in a period of 15 years the birth-rate of an Egypt or a Mexico could be halved, a large enough number of female children already born in the interim would have reached fertility to ensure a further doubling of the population in the next 30 years. Even in spite of an extraordinary decline in the average number of children per woman, the population would continue to grow. Population was said to have a momentum which added to the problem of controlling it. The 'underdeveloped' — only recently defined as a distinct class of populations by the development discourse — were henceforth perceived as outbreeding the North and at the same time frustrating their own development.

In the 1950s demographers were still on the fringes of the development discourse. Then politicians discovered the 'potentially important contribution to development from an induced change in demographic behaviour.'[5] Demographers were recognized as experts and demography acquired the status of a technique at the service of development. Reduction in the rate of population growth was now seen as a condition for successful investments in development. High rates of population growth create unemployment faster than jobs, increase the number of mouths to be fed faster than the productivity of rice paddies, squatters faster than people housed in modern facilities, excrement faster than sewers can be built. A population growing faster than the output of modern goods and services not only frustrates development goals; it undermines the credibility of promises made in the name of development and the political will to pay the price of progress.

When demographers were first seated alongside the other development experts, an assumption which now seems incredible was still very common. Policy makers spoke as if large proportions of any rapidly increasing population were inclined to reduce the number of their children, but only lacked the knowledge how to do so. The first generation of demographers confidently made forecasts about the number of 'acceptors of proffered contraceptives' and projected the 'net costs of births averted'.

In 1964 President Johnson endorsed the temerity of his population advisers. At the twentieth anniversary celebration of the UN, he claimed that each five dollars spent on population control was worth a hundred dollars invested in economic growth (at an estimated cost of five dollars per 'birth averted'). In his next State of the Union message he promised 'to seek new ways to use our knowledge to help deal with the explosion in world population'.[6] In 1966 Martin Luther King accepted the Margaret Sanger Award in Human Rights. It is remarkable that, unlike the President who had used economic language, this black American leader used medical language to discuss population: 'Unlike plagues of the Dark Ages, or contemporary diseases we do not yet understand, the modern plague of over-population is soluble by means we have discovered and with resources we possess.' During the early part of the 20th century, condoms had been associated with individual defence against unwanted children or syphilis in the pursuit of personal pleasure. In the late 1960s and early 1970s, they connoted a public defence against a new epidemic called the population explosion. The goal of sexual intercourse without issue in poor nations acquired the status of a public health measure.

The popularization of the algorithmic 'P' for Population now appeared in the media as the spectre of over-population. The population lobby helped to redefine sexual behaviour as a matter of public policy. This, in turn, led to the creation of a well-financed establishment whose task consisted in trying to bring about a worldwide change in sexual behaviour.

In 1958 Sweden became the first government to provide international assistance for population control, first to Sri Lanka and then to Pakistan. The aid programme, however, was still coyly labelled 'assistance for family planning'. In 1966 the General Assembly of the UN reached a consensus about 'population assistance'. This label also eschewed control and limitation. It henceforth became a euphemistic label for all international funding of condoms, IUDs, the pill and Karman tubes, as well as US university demography departments, international bureaucracies and local workshops. Total official assistance for 'population assistance' between 1961 and 1979 increased from $96 million to $455 million annually. 'Population assistance' as a percentage of total development assistance rose from 0.1 per cent (when total aid was $5 billion a year) to 1.7 per cent by 1979 (by which time ODA had reached $26 billion).[7]

In the early 1960s most large Asian countries and several countries in Latin America mounted modern large-scale tax funded family planning programmes. Under the aegis of population control and in the name of family planning, the promotion of contraception became a veritable growth sector on its own, providing jobs and incomes for semi-professionals and lay organizers at village level who had to try to induce popular acceptance of freely distributed contraceptive foam, pills and rubbers. Most of the employees in this new worldwide sector were poor and female, while most of the funds for international assistance went to bureaucrats, experts and pharmaceutical researchers. Activist demographers not only helped to publicize the political relevance of population dynamics and to define positive, even aggressive, population policies in countries like India and Egypt as much as in the US; they now provided the leadership in a highly financed worldwide programme.

In the 1990s, two decades after public discussion of the unwanted side-effects of the large-scale use of contraceptive pills, it is not easy to remember how recently the IUD and the pill hit the market. In his 1964 address, Notestein could still say: 'All of you have heard, I am sure, that certain steroid pills, if taken each day . . . unfailingly prevent pregnancy . . . (and that there) is accumulating evidence that new plastic inter-uterine devices are virtually ideal contraceptives.'[8] Barely five years later the promise seemed an indisputable fact. Gunnar Myrdal in 1969 took the effectiveness of the new methods for granted and urged governments 'to make millions of individual couples change their most intimate sexual behaviour.'[9] During the 1970s even conventional wisdom considered population size amenable to a technical fix.

The expert opinion of social anthropologists, however, had passed beyond this naivety as early as the late 1950s. Their research results contradicted the assumptions underlying the new population programmes, namely that: 'In the developing countries individuals are already motivated to limit births, but lack the means to do so. When these means are supplied, the eligible population will use them and thereby control fertility. The best way to provide such means is through a large-scale voluntary family planning programme.'[10] Field studies showed that contraceptives — even when they were accepted by the client — simply did not work as long as deeply rooted traditional perceptions of fertility did not change. Such a change would usually imply and require a transformation in the experience and meaning of love and lust, the cultural meaning of womanhood, attitudes towards the female body, and the context in which private acts take place. And these changes, according to the anthropologists' case studies, were the psychological result of an advanced stage of development: they came with stable employment, urban living, and the motivation to keep children in school. While infant mortality and mothers' deaths in childbirth could be dramatically reduced with low levels of expenditure, even costly family planning programmes did not show perceptible results unless the 'target population' had already benefited from development.

From an anthropological perspective population programmes were the most arrogant part of all externally imposed development strategies. Factories, dams and schools may produce respectively jobs, kilowatts and dropouts without having to prove that they have changed attitudes or behaviour. Sulfadrugs, penicillin and rehydration salts significantly reduce mortality at little cost. But the distribution of equally cheap contraceptives makes an impact on fertility rates only after a central pillar of culture has crumbled.

Economists, early on, tended to trust conventional wisdom about the cost of children. They recognized that, for the subsistence farmer, many children were an asset and family limitation made little sense. But in the early 1960s they began to assume that, with increasing dependence on cash incomes, even poor people would soon forego the feeding of many mouths. This over-simplified assumption had to be qualified, as studies began to show that, for the recently urbanized in most parts of the world, fertility had a direct and positive correlation with insecurity. One study showed that unionized workers had fewer children than those equally paid workers for whom children were the only insurance of a roof over their heads in their old age.

Population Control for Survival

The complex inter-relationships among fertility, literacy, spread of the media, job security and housing were one of the reasons why, by the early 1970s, population came to be treated as just one more endogenous factor in the development calculus. This happened in the context of the debates aroused by *The Limits to Growth*, published by the Club of Rome in 1972. This bestseller popularized the idea of the world as a 'system' whose 'survival' was threatened. In this discourse the 'human species' acquired a new sacredness and its protection was recognized as an international management responsibility. The new stress was on *world* population as a whole. A new logic moved to the fore. Paul Ehrlich argued, for example, that the earth's 'carrying capacity' was endangered by population growth. Not the hope of development but the fear of global disaster gave a new motivation to the attempts at population control. Paul Ehrlich began his book:

> The battle to feed all humanity is over. In the 1970s the world will undergo famines — hundreds of millions of people are going to starve to death inspite of any crash program embarked upon . . . . These programs will only provide a stay of execution unless they are accompanied by determined and successful efforts at population control. The birth rate must be brought into balance with the death rate or mankind will breed itself into oblivion . . . . Population control is the only answer.[11]

During the 1970s the people versus resources perspective took a hold of political reasoning. This perspective pits people against finite resources and population comes to be seen as a factor that threatens the earth's capacity to support human life.

The United Nations Fund for Population Activities was created as a specialized agency in 1969 and quickly its budget soared to $1 billion. The agency defined its task as exploring:

> The complex ways in which population variables interact, reciprocally, with socio-economic development variables and to show how action programmes can be mounted to integrate population activities with health care, educational, rural development organization of agriculture, industrial development and other . . . programmes.[12]

UNFPA prided itself on the 'maturation and sophistication of population thinking (that) put an end to simplistic models'.[13] By the late '70s population appears in policy statements as a variable in the algorithm to which the whole immensely complicated development process had been reduced. Population had become a variable analogous to capital, labour, technology or infrastructure in a 'world system'.

In retrospect, we know that the development decades brought an unexpected growth in the world's population. This was an unprecedented phenomenon and gave rise to equally unprecedented concepts about human beings. Populations came to be conceptualized as actors, processes, objects of development planning, obstacles to successful investment, sources of qualified manpower and threats to the world's ecosystem. First hesitantly, and then by consensus, almost all Third World nations built up powerful population programmes that absorbed the earlier small movements which had campaigned for family limitation and provided access to contraception and abortion. A survey covering 114 'developing' countries in 1977 showed that 83 of these had entrusted a central government planning authority with the task of 'integrating population factors with development planning'.[14]

Between 1974 and 1984 the global population growth rate in fact declined from 2.34 per cent to 1.67 per cent per annum, which corresponds to an extension of the doubling rate of the world's population from 30 to 42 years. During the same decade, the absolute numbers of those defined by World Bank criteria as absolutely poor became as large as the entire world's population had been in 1974 at the beginning of the period. And this occurred despite the decline in the global growth rate. Population growth, and with it the growth of those who are absolutely poor, is expected to continue. By 1990, all the 1.6 billion women who will reach childbearing age by the year 2000 had been born and 1.3 billion of them are in Third World countries. Ninety per cent of the world's population increase will occur there.

Looking back on the last 25 years, all statements about the likely large-scale impact of population programmes remain speculative, if one excepts the case of China. Even in those instances where birth rates have declined according to plan, this reduction stands in no proven causal relationship to the family planning programmes that have been funded. The new technologies promoted by various agencies, including foam, the pill or IUDs, played almost no proven role in those countries that have successfully reduced their fertility rates. Even if we grant that 'assessing program effects on national fertility thoroughly and quantitatively has proven to be extraordinarily difficult',[15] one thing is clear: the population activities launched since the 1960s have turned out to be dreams that brought forth monsters. First, a social commitment to useless public controls over sexual behaviour. And, second, a widespread acceptance of the formula 'a community of people = a population = P.' And P (like radiation, poisoning, the ozone hole and global warming) is one of the invisible threats to humanity.

References

1. Quoted in M. J. Cullen, *The Statistical Movement in Early Victorian Britain: The Foundations of Empirical Social Research*, New York: Harvester Press, 1975, p. 2.

2. U. Pörksen, *Plastikwörter: Zur Sprache einer internationalen Diktatur*, Stuttgart: Klett-Cotta, 1988.

3. P. T. Piotrow, *World Population Crisis: The United States Response*, New York: Praeger, 1973, pp. x and vii.

4. This lecture, delivered September 22, 1964, in Colombo, Sri Lanka, was reprinted in *Population and Development Review*, Vol. 9, No. 2, June 1983, pp. 345–60.

5. P. Demeny, 'Social Science and Population Policy', in *Population and Development Review*, Vol. 3, 1988, p. 45.

6. P. T. Piotrow, op. cit., p.89.

7. 'International Population Assistance', in *International Encyclopedia of Population*, New York: Free Press, 1982, Vol. 1, p. 375.

8. F. Notestein in *Population and Development Review*, Vol. 9, No. 2, June 1983, p. 359.

9. G. Myrdal, *The Challenge of World Poverty*, New York: Pantheon, 1970, partially reproduced in *Population and Development Review*, Vol. 13, No. 3, September 1987, p. 536.

10. D. P. Warwick, *Bitter Pills*, Cambridge: Cambridge University Press, 1982, p. 34.

11. P. Ehrlich, *The Population Bomb*, New York: Ballantine, 1968, p. 3.

12. R. Salas, *International Population Assistance: The First Decade*, New York: Pergamon Press, p. 140 (Doc., August 8, 1977).

13. Op. cit. p. 147 (Doc., April 3, 1978).

14. D. L. Nortman and J. Fisher, *Population and Family Planning Programs: A Compendium of Data through 1981*, New York: Population Council, 1982.

15. 'Family Planning Programs' in *International Encyclopedia of Population*, op. cit., p. 214.

Bibliography

The International Encyclopedia of Population, New York: Free Press, 1982, 2 vols., is the standard reference tool for concepts, action programmes and institutional support of research on population up to the year 1982, while *The New Palgrave Dictionary of Economics*, London: Macmillan, 1987, helped me to understand subsequent economic models recasting the family, children, fertility and private actions in the development decades. The best single visual introduction to the imaginary relationship between 'population' and 'development' is a set of coloured computer illustrations published as *Population Images*, New York: UNFPA, 1987. Its glossy graphs and tables portray visually energy consumption, deforestation, water resources, income levels and demographic facts and trends for teachers and students. A critical distance to these kinds of graphic representations of quantitative data is provided by Edward R. Tufte, *Envisioning Information*, Cheshire, CT: Graphics Press, 1990.

The conception, perception and imagination of 'human populations' would have been impossible without the spread of statistical terminology and reasoning into ordinary English, which, albeit with some delay, went hand in hand with the evolution of statistical concepts. For this history I found helpful Th. M. Porter, *The Rise of Statistical Thinking, 1820–1900*, Princeton: Princeton University Press, 1986, where on pp. 17–90, 'The Social Calculus', you find a good introduction to the first phase in the government's centralized bureaucratic efforts to collect numbers on numerous subjects and D. A. Mackenzie, *Statistics in Britain 1865–1930: The Social Construction of Scientific Knowledge*, Edinburgh: Edinburgh University Press, 1981. Most courses on statistics implicitly inculcate the idea that the indicators used are natural givens. W. R. Arney, *Understanding Statistics in the Social Sciences*, New York: Freeman, 1989, alerts the student to the inescapable political dimensions of statistical reasoning.

Ever since Malthus, demographic concepts have been subjected to criticism. Paradoxically, most substantive criticisms of statistical methods, and their application to demographic phenomena, lead to the technical refinement of these methods and not to an understanding of the relevance of their results in ordinary experience and daily perception. Thus the critique of population policies focused on policy, and occasionally on techniques, and did not touch upon the legitimacy of using statistical results in the shaping of policy or legislation. As a result, principled opposition — be it anti-colonial, feminist, Marxist or theological — of 'population policies' often operated with a popularization of concepts taken from statistics and demography, such as 'world', 'distribution', 'control'. Thus, a factitious mathematical category is used to shape fictitously manageable fetishes, such as 'populations'. Only with this caveat in mind do I want to mention books that I am indebted to.

D. Warwick, *Bitter Pills: Population Policies and their Implementation in Eight Developing Countries*, Cambridge: Cambridge University Press, 1982, juxtaposes high-level policy declarations and 'low-level implementation records' in 'successive decades of failure' and finds hypocrisy and arrogance on the one side and reasoned cultural resistance on the other. Dom Moraes, with funds from UNFPA, travelled through four continents, visited myriads of rural birth control centres and vividly describes the manifold resistance to contraceptive promotion in *A Matter of People*, New York: Praeger, 1974. In the 1970s it was characteristic for research on 'parental motivation' for birth control to explore the economic value of children. The cost of their education, their speculative future value as producers and their perceived value to their procreators were distinguished and analysed in population studies and a high contraceptive acceptancy rate predicted. For a critique I found excellent Mahmood Mamdani, *The Myth of Population Control: Family, Caste and Class in an Indian Village*, New York: Monthly Review Press, 1972. Mamdani found at village level that children were essential not despite, but because of, poverty. A redistribution of the means of living would be the inevitable precondition for 'responsible procreation'. The growing belief in the '80s that the decline in birth rates is primarily dependent on the social and political milieu in which power, rather than contraceptives, is made available to all on an egalitarian basis is cogently argued by Frances Moore Lappe and Rachel Schurman, *The Missing Piece in the Population Puzzle*, San Francisco: Institute for Food and Development Policy, 1988. The popular revulsion against the violence in India's population programme in the '70s is analysed by Debabar Banerji, 'The Political Economy of Population Control in India', in *Poverty and Population Control*, edited by Lars Bondestam and St. Bergstroem, London: Academic Press, 1980, pp. 83–102.

Women as the targets of contraceptive campaigns within population policies have been the subject of numerous studies. The ILO sponsored a research project that resulted in a volume which related changes in fertility to development-initiated changes in the status of specific groups of women as workers. See Richard Anker, M. Buvinic and N. Youssef (eds.), *Women's Roles and Population Trends in the Third World*, London: Croom Helm, 1982. I found much more helpful Betsy Hartmann, *Reproductive Rights and Wrongs: the Global Politics of Population Control and Contraceptive Choice*, New York: Harper, 1987. Women social anthropologists investigated different perceptions and conceptions of the female body as a clue to resistance to the use of contraception: Susan C. M. Scrimshaw, 'Women's Modesty: One Barrier to the Use of Family Planning Clinics in Equador', in *Culture, Natality and Family*

Planning, edited by John F. Marshall and Steven Polgar, Chapel Hill, N.C.: University of North Carolina Press, 1976, pp. 167–83 and Lucile F. Newman (ed.), *Women's Medicine: A Cross-Cultural Study of Indigenous Fertility Regulation*, New Brunswick: Rutgers University Press, 1985. The most useful recent literature includes Gisele Maynard-Tucker, 'Knowledge of Reproductive Physiology and Modern Contraceptives in Rural Peru', in *Studies in Family Planning*, Vol. 20, No. 4 (July/August 1989), pp. 215–24. Christa Wichterich, 'From the struggle against "Overpopulation" to the Industrialization of Human Production', in *Reproductive and Genetic Engineering*, Vol. I, No. 1 (1988) pp. 21–30, calls attention to the 'racist eugenic and patriarchal tradition' inherent in the perception of the 'population catastrophe'.

Poverty

Majid Rahnema

Destitution, or imposed poverty, no doubt hurts, degrades and drives people into desperation. In many places, hunger and misery cry out to heaven. Indeed, few development concepts find their proof in such a glaring reality. Yet poverty is also a myth, a construct and the invention of a particular civilization.

There may be as many poor and as many perceptions of poverty as there are human beings. The fantastic variety of cases entitling a person to be called poor in different cultures and languages is such that, all in all, everything and everyone under the sun could be labelled as poor, in one way or another. The list could include not only the weak, the hungry, the sick, the homeless, the landless, the crippled and the beggar; not only the mad, the prisoner, the enslaved, the fugitive, the exiled, the street vendor and the soldier; not only the ascetics and the saints, but also all the losers of the world, including the millionaire after the crash of the stock exchange, the fired executive and the artist who finds no buyer for his works.

Many Perceptions, Countless Words

World languages compete with each other for the number of words referring to the stations and conditions associated with the different perceptions of poverty.

In Persian, for instance, there are more than 30 words for naming those who, for one reason or another, are perceived as poor. In most African languages, at least three to five words have been identified for poverty.[1] The Torah uses eight for the purpose.[2] In the Middle Ages, the Latin words covering the range of conditions embraced by the concept were well over forty.[3] To this impressive variety of words found at the national or dictionary level, many more should be added from the corresponding dialects, slang or colloquial expressions used at the vernacular level. A whole universe of insights into the murky depths of poverty is to be explored in the many thousands of related proverbs and sayings.[4] In most cases, it is extremely difficult for the outsider to grasp the full meanings and nuances of all those words and expressions, let alone to translate them into other languages.

For long, and in many cultures of the world, poor was not always the opposite of rich. Other considerations such as falling from one's station in life, being deprived of one's instruments of labour, the loss of one's status or the marks of one's profession (for a cleric, the loss of his books; for a noble, the loss of his horse or arms), lack of protection, exclusion from one's community, abandonment, infirmity, or public humiliation defined the poor. The Tswana people of South Africa recognized their poor by their reactions to the appearance of locusts. Whereas the rich were appalled lest the locusts ate the grass needed by their cattle, the poor who had no cattle rejoiced because they could themselves eat the locusts.[5]

In Europe, for ages, the pauper was opposed to the *potens* (the powerful), rather than the rich. In the 9th century, the pauper was considered a free man whose freedom was imperilled only by the *potentes*. In the texts of peace movements of the 11th century, the pauper had become the *inermis* who had to respect the force of the soldiers, the *miles*. The word, poor, could be applied to the owner of a little *alleu* (a tax-free property), a wandering merchant, and even to any non-fighter, including the unescorted wives of knights.[6] On the whole, the poor were quite respectable persons who had only lost, or stood in the danger of losing, their 'berth'.

In that same period in Europe, a whole new category of poor appeared on the social stage — the voluntary poor who chose to share the life of the destitute and the berthless. For these, living poorly was a sign of elevation rather than degradation.[7] Respect and admiration for the voluntary poor had, of course, always existed in Eastern traditions.[8]

It was only after the expansion of the mercantile economy, the processes of urbanization leading to massive pauperization and, indeed, the monetization of society that the poor were defined as lacking what the rich could have in terms of money and possessions.

A common denominator for most perceptions of poverty remains the notion of 'lack' or 'deficiency'.[9] This notion reflects only the basic relativity of the concept, for a utopian 'complete man' would not be lacking anything. Besides, when poor is defined as lacking a number of things necessary to life, the questions could be asked: What is necessary and for whom? And who is qualified to define all that?[10] In smaller communities, where people are less strangers to one another and things are easier to compare, such questions are already difficult to answer. In a world of the mass media, the old familiar horizons and communally defined bases of comparison are all destroyed. Everyone may think of themselves as poor when it is the TV set in the mud hut which defines the necessities of life, often in terms of the wildest and fanciest consumers appearing on the screen.

In the same way, the ambiguity of the concept takes on new proportions as the old familiar horizons fade away. There was nothing ambiguous about the pauper who lived on what he earned from some humble trade in his village, notes Mollat.[11] 'His face was familiar, and despite his misfortune he remained, in his suffering, a member of the social group.' Ambiguity starts when one crosses the vernacular boundaries. Are these strangers rebels, vagabonds, disease carriers, really poor or genuinely ill? Are they saints or sinners? These questions not only deepen our ignorance about who the poor really are, but face us with serious cognitive problems as to what people are actually thinking.

Four Dimensions of Poverty

1. The materialities: The facts or materialities on which the various constructs of poverty are based are those 'things', the lack of which is perceived as poverty. These lacks, deficiencies, or deprivations are either of a non-material and existential kind, or of a material nature.

To the first category belong such factors as one's inability to meet one's end, lack of good fortune or self-confidence, not being respected or loved by others, being neglected or abandoned, etc. As to material factors, these could include discrimination, inequality, political or other forms of oppression and domination, absence of entitlements,[12] non-availability of the minimum of 'necessaries'[13] required for economic or biological survival, as defined by one's particular culture; also, all other forms of deprivation, destitution, hunger, malnutrition, homelessness, ill health, and exclusion from educational possibilities, etc.

Although the materialities referred to are relative to various societies and cultural spaces, it could be argued that: 'There is an irreducible core of *absolute* deprivation in our idea of poverty, which translates reports of starvation, malnutrition and visible hardship into a diagnosis of poverty, without having to ascertain first the relative picture.'[14]

2. The subject's own perception of his condition: The materialities referred to are indeed essential to the understanding of poverty in its different perceptions. Yet none of them should be confused with the concept itself. It is only when one or a combination of these materialities is perceived by a subject as an expression of poverty, that they acquire the particular meaning attached to that word. And that perception is quite a personal and socio-cultural affair. It is, in fact, part and parcel of the subject's wider perception of the world and his place in it.

It has been noted that the poor — leaving aside voluntary mendicants — tend generally to attribute what they lack to conditions independent of their will and beyond their control — whether defined by metaphysical causes such as God's will, one's *karma* or *qismat*, or the unjust constitution of society. Their perception of the deprivations from which they suffer is also often aggravated by the feeling that they lack the necessary ability to overcome their condition.

The lack of particular material means is not, however, always perceived in negative terms. The case of the mendicants in medieval Europe, already referred to, is not the sole exception. For the Iranian sufis, the Indian sanyasin, and some contemporary schools of thought, such as the Gandhians, to be free from alienating material possessions is a blessing indeed, and an opportunity for reaching higher forms of riches. The Prophet of Islam has been widely quoted as saying: 'Al faqro faxri' [Poverty is my pride and glory].

It remains true, however, that the destitute and materially deprived generally perceive their predicament in negative terms.[15] Even when they attribute their condition to metaphysical or ontological reasons, they spare no effort in trying to put an end to their deprivations, if necessary through violence. Often, they tend to establish relations of dependency with more powerful persons, groups, faiths or ideologies, a relationship which gives them an inner feeling of security and, sometimes, of false strength.

3. How the others view the poor: The poor's perception of their predicament is inevitably affected by how others view them. The two perceptions are seldom identical.

Poverty is sometimes perceived as a virtue by others when it represents a free choice on the part of those subject to it. Otherwise, the poor are generally looked upon with feelings ranging from embarrassment to contempt and even violence. On another plane, while pauperism[16] was perceived as abnormal and calling for remedial action, poverty in vernacular and pre-industrialized societies was considered, by contrast, as a rather natural human predicament, if not an irremediable and unavoidable fact of life.

Different views of the poor have led to basically two types of reaction. The first represents a variety of forms of direct or indirect intervention, based on social, cultural or ethical reasons such as charity, assistance, education, confinement, repression, etc. The second is grounded on philosophies of non-intervention, either justified by the belief that nothing should be done for the poor for they somehow deserve their condition, or on the assumption that nothing can be done, for all forms of intervention ultimately produce negative results, or no change at all, in their lives.

4. Spimes (socio-cultural space-times) affecting various perceptions of poverty: While the above dimensions are mutually interactive in shaping the construct of poverty, they are all, in turn, affected by the space-times to which they belong. This explains why, in different communities and at different times, the same materialities are perceived differently, both by those referred to as poor and by society at large. To take an example, Helena Norberg-Hodge mentions how the notion of poverty hardly existed in Ladakh when she visited that country for the first time in 1975. 'Today,' she says, 'it has become part of the language.' When visiting an outlying village some eight years ago, Helena asked a young Ladakhi where were the poorest houses. 'We have no poor houses in our village,' was the proud reply. Recently, Helena saw the same Ladakhi talking to an American tourist and overheard him say, 'if only you could do something for us; we are so poor!'[17]

The Global Construct

Global poverty is an entirely new and modern construct. The basic materials which have gone into the construct are essentially the economization of life and the forceful integration of vernacular societies into the world economy.

In one of its first reports in 1948, the World Bank closely correlates the problem of global poverty with countries' gross national products. It postulates that countries with an average per capita income of less than $100 are, by definition, poor and underdeveloped. It expresses the responsibility of the richer nations, the richest of them being the United States, to help the poor countries raise their living standards.

Thus, for the first time in history, entire nations and countries came to be considered (and consider themselves) as poor, on the grounds that their overall income is insignificant in comparison with those now dominating the world economy. Consequently, national income was introduced as a new global measure for expressing the various stages of economic development, the latter process being proposed as the final answer to poverty.

On another plane, the new construct no longer embraces the view that poverty is a multi-faceted human predicament. It considers it as a single pathological phenomenon of universal character, but particularly acute in pre-economized societies. Following a consensus reached amongst the world elites on the diagnosis of the disease (underdevelopment and lack of income,) as well as its cure (economic and technological development), armies of experts, politicians, planners, bureaucrats, socio-economists and even anthropologists started acting as pauperologists, seeking to refine the discourse and practices related to world poverty. The gist of the new approach was expressed in President Harry Truman's famous Point Four Declaration: The economic life [of the poor] is primitive and stagnant. . . . Their poverty is a handicap and a threat both to them and to more prosperous areas.' Greater production, development, assistance, and a wider and more vigorous application of science and technological knowledge are recognized as the answer and the 'key to prosperity and peace'.

The new construct has indeed had a long gestation. The industrial era accelerated the breakdown of vernacular societies. It led to 'the great transformation' which dramatically reversed the traditional relationship between society and economy and, for the first time in history, *disembedded* the latter from its socio-cultural roots, thus subjecting society to its own economic rules and dynamics, rather than the other way round. 'Man, under the name of labor, nature under the name of land, were made available for sale,' notes Polanyi.[18] The ensuing economization of society brought about, first, the hegemony of national economies over vernacular activities, then, that of the world economy over all others. These drastic changes affected largely the ways in which the materialities underlying the various perceptions of poverty came to be reinterpreted and reconstructed.

Firstly, the advent of a world economy, with all its realities and accompanying myths (the existence of unlimited resources, technological miracles, endless consumer goods, induced needs, etc.) created a set of universal referents. To go back to a case previously mentioned, this is how the Ladakhis came to perceive themselves as poor, once development and other national and strategic considerations had led to the economization of Ladakh. Similarly, not only individuals and communities, but entire nations and continents were led to believe that they were poor, and in need of assistance, only because their per capita income was below a universally established minimum.

Secondly, while the traditional answers to poverty were, in the past, often based on the pluralistic, culturally established and holistic perceptions of each particular space, the new programmes of action represented a universalist, one-track, income-based, and totally acultural recipe for abstract 'patients'. The recipe was composed of a mix of technicalities and 'neutral' economic referents which only experts and planners could master and use with authority. The new technologized approach to poverty developed its own cognitive bases in such new fields of study and intervention as employment policy, production strategy and the measurement of poverty, etc. It certainly overshadowed the exploration of such deeper and more sensitive issues as the processes of political and cultural domination, the pervasive role of institutions, and the very nature of the industrial production system.

Thirdly, the new fetish of a healthy global economy destined to save all the world's poor, not only helped the pauperizing economic and political systems to reinforce and legitimize their positions, but it also led their victims to perceive their own situation in the same terms. Thus, the new proletarians and impoverished wage earners, particularly in urban areas, focused their actions and struggles on such limited objectives as employment, income raising and access to public services. And, to this end, they sought to protect themselves through labour unions, sometimes totally disregarding the informal, and formal, community organizations which had traditionally helped the poor. Following the same patterns, even non-wage earning workers in rural areas came to think that earning cash or receiving economic assistance and public services were the most logical ways of alleviating their deprivations.

Finally, as more people were manipulated into sharing the new economic myth that poverty could now be finally conquered through increased productivity and the modern economy's 'trickle down' effects, the search for new modes of life and social organization based on simplicity, or on voluntary or moral forms of povery, were devalued and discredited.[19]

Most traditional societies had resisted the view that all poverty reflected personal inadequacy. This view, that became characteristic of every capitalist society, especially in its Protestant versions, was now advanced as a major component of the new value system. Economic poverty was now to be perceived and acted upon, on a global level, as a shame and a scourge. The vast increases in wealth offered, or achieved, by modern societies fostering greed and profit-making, played a significant role in the sharp devaluation of moral poverty. Thus, the race for enrichment became not only a desirable goal for the economy but also a morally justified end.

The Construct in Action

Assumptions

To translate the construct into action, a particular discourse and set of programmes were initiated. Looking back at what actually occurred during the nearly 50-year old history of the exercise, it seems to have rested on the following assumptions.

Firstly, the poor are assumed to be 'underdeveloped' and — momentarily at least — deprived of their capacity to define their own interests. It is up to those in a superior position of knowledge and power (governments, institutions, professionals, competent authorities) to assist them on their behalf. People's 'participation' is indeed welcomed whenever that could help the populations concerned to manifest their support for the professionally designed programmes.

Secondly, the discourse on global poverty recognized the fact that the perceptions of poverty differed according to cultures. Yet it assumed that the perceptions in question all shared a common belief — that economic growth and prosperity was a *sine qua non* for coming out of poverty. Thus it posited economic development as the key to poverty eradication programmes, assuming further that the resolution of all non-economic or cultural problems of the poor could be tackled later.

The above assumptions served, in turn, to justify three basic tenets of interventionist practices. Firstly, that poverty was too global and sensitive a matter to be taken out of the hands of professionals and institutions trained and empowered for this purpose. Secondly, that the programmes in question had to be mapped, basically, in terms of economic resources and needs. Finally, that the agents mainly responsible for the design and execution of such strategies would, naturally, be the governments and other institutions officially in charge of both the identification of needs and the production of the required solutions. Eradication of global poverty was thus considered yet another reason for consolidating the present structures of governance, both at the international and national levels.

Operations

Assessment of needs: Poverty alleviation programmes claim to be based on an assessment of 'needs'. Yet, what planners, politicians and economists tend to consider as their needs, has little or nothing to do with what different categories of the poor perceive as their needs.

In the global context, needs are first identified in an abstract manner, on a regional or national basis. To take an example, for UNDP, a golden rule was set in the mid '70s that 80 per cent of the organization's resources should automatically be allotted to the needs of LDCs (or Least Developed Countries), i.e. countries where the people's annual per capita income is lower than $300. The rule has now been extended to some other countries which, at their explicit request, are recognized, literally, 'as if they were LDCs' and, hence, given the same 'privileges'! The fact which is totally disregarded by the bureaucracies concerned is that, according to their own statistics and criteria, a much larger number of persons considered to be poor actually live elsewhere. The needs of these individuals are treated differently only because they happen to be citizens of countries where per capita GNP is higher.

As for the assessment of specific needs, these are evaluated on the basis of other sets of globally established economic criteria and systems of comparison. For Unesco, for instance, to have a percentage of illiterates above a certain figure, or a percentage of radios, books or newspapers below another, represents a set of needs calling for action. For WHO, the criteria of poverty are expressed in terms of the ratio of doctors, nurses, and health centres to the population. For FAO, the needs are evaluated in terms of per capita calorie or protein intake. In all these cases, needs are perceived as figures or combinations of elements disembedded from the particular mode of livelihood characteristic of each culturally defined vernacular space.

The promotion of institutions and professional skills at the country level: A major long-term component of all national and international programmes of poverty eradication has been what UN jargon likes to call 'institution building', the latter being generally coupled with the reinforcement of 'national capacities' and professional skills.

As in the case of needs assessment practices, this policy also represents a consensus reached amongst donors and recipients of economic and technical assistance. The policy is supposed to provide the governments concerned with the instruments necessary for them to design their plans of action and put an end to their structural dependence on foreign expertise. Strong ministries of planning and parastatal organizations were — at least until the 'roll-back' of the state that took place during 'structural adjustment' in the 1980s — presented as essential for assessing people's needs and responding to them. For the donors, the policy served not only to provide them with professionally respected counterparts, but also with institutions assumed to be in a better position to guarantee the protection of foreign economic and political investments, and in particular the further integration of these economies into the global one.

Production of goods and services: The production of economic goods and services is a major component of all poverty eradication programmes — economic growth being the general talisman.

Sectoral reforms: The need for more diversified and expanded services has led many of these programmes to reserve a leading place to sectoral reforms, particularly in such areas as unemployment, population control, co-operatives, and educational and health services.

Redistributive policies: For more progressive or democratic states, redistributive policies are considered to be the most effective and dignified means of stopping the structural processes of pauperization generally triggered by the dynamics of economic development. In this context, Japan, India and China represent three very different countries where interesting results have been achieved through political and legislative measures.

Assistance programmes: These programmes are the last of the activities which are generally pursued in the context of present day poverty eradication campaigns. They are meant to come closer to the actual and pressing preoccupations of the deprived. Whatever their value in practice, welfare states consider assistance to the poor as an obligation on society and an act of solidarity. More conservative governments, together with economists, tend to question the relevance of assistance to the long-term interests of a modern state.

Results

The actual impact of the above policies and programmes on the lives of the deprived are often very different from the planners' expectations. We shall try to explore them briefly, in the same order as above.

The needs which development and poverty-eradication programmes seek to identify and assess through their experts and planning institutions are basically the needs of a certain 'economy', a certain idea of poverty, and a particular category of consumers and tax payers whose rights and interests should be protected. They do not correspond to what the people at large need, confronted by the fact of having been cut off from their vernacular spaces. While these needs remain unmet, the very economic activities deployed in the name of the poor impute to them different needs of a more insatiable nature. On another plane, the problematization of the poor's needs in modern economic terms further contributes to the disintegration of vernacular spaces, thereby exposing the poor to situations of even more complete helplessness.

To sum up, the whole exercise of needs assessment is justified on the ground that it provides the planners with a 'scientific' basis for their anti-poverty planning. In practice, it is often an irrelevant exercise. The very idea that it should start with an allocation of funds on the basis of the economic development of the particular country where the poor live, rather than the location and condition of the poor themselves, is enough to indicate the bureaucratic and highly irrelevant nature of the exercise. After separating the poor person's 'needs' from him as an active and living human being, it reduces him to only an inadequate ingredient of economic growth.

The absurdity of the situation is increased by the fact that the whole task is entrusted to predatory governments which happen to be in power in the designated poorer countries. While the sovereignty of these governments is often a matter of pure fiction, the fact is that their power resides, on the one hand, in their capacity to 'milk' their own people and, on the other hand, in the assistance they receive from their richer foreign patrons. For these governments, poverty, like underdevelopment, is a catchword for legitimizing their claims for more centralized forms of control over their populations and, also, for more funds to implement their objectives. Foreign assistance, in particular, helps them to enrich themselves and strengthen their army, police, security and intelligence services. The latter operate to make the population pay for the services relating to their own exploitation and accept their forcible integration into the national and world economies, as well as the heavy burden of debts contracted for those very purposes.

On a different plane, the objectives of institution building and skill training create additional barriers between the vernacular world of the poor and the new economized world of their protectors/predators. Much more than serving the poor, the new institutions and their professionals help the rich to better organize themselves against their victims.

On the central issue of the production of economic goods and services, it is still difficult for many to agree that poverty is *not* a question of 'resources', in the sense given it by economists and planners. Yet it is a fact that, in most developing countries, neither the production of economic resources and commodities, nor the extension of social services have ultimately served the poor. More often than not, they have resulted in further diminishing their capacity to meet their real needs which they used to do in the context of their vernacular livelihood — which is a way of life under constant erosion by the forces of the modern economy.

In fact, there is no evidence that affluence has, anywhere, improved the poor's condition. Notwithstanding the fact that the so-called affluent societies are presently the ones posing the greatest threats to the very life of the planet, the reservoirs of plenty they produce create, at the same time, new islands of poverty. The United States, the richest country in the world, has to recognize that 30 million of its citizens live below the poverty line.[20] Similarly, in the richest city in Brazil, a country of the South whose development was once called miraculous, five out of its 15 million inhabitants 'live in extreme poverty, earning less than 65 dollars a month'.[21]

In short, what the poor need is not the production of economic resources or services which ultimately benefit others or the generations to come. It is rather the recovery of their actual capacity to tap their own vernacular, locally available resources — which are totally different from what economists call resources.

Sectoral reforms in the various fields of unemployment, population, education, health, etc., seem also to have had little or no positive effect in reducing discriminatory trends. Here again, even when these reforms have achieved their objectives, they have proved to be of little relevance to the specific needs of the deprived. 'Good' schools have generally served to produce greater numbers of drop-outs belonging to poor families. Contrary to their vocation, health centres, and hospitals in particular, have seldom given hospitality to the poor. Employment policies have hardly succeeded in stopping the mass exodus of millions of people from their communities to the slum areas of big cities.

In this long list of 'answers which are not', it could be argued that redistributive policies at least have achieved partial success in some important cases. The experiences of Japan, India and China might suggest, each in a different way, that political measures aimed at fostering the principles of justice and equity as integral dimensions of development policies, have reduced some of the impoverishing side-effects of economy. The fact remains, however, that the dynamics and goals of a 'resource' generating economy (principles of profit, productivity, capital accumulation, etc.) diverge, by definition, from socially defined objectives. As such, it is perhaps too early to conclude that such redistributive policies will be able to keep pace with the more powerful pauperizing trends of economy. In any case, they may only succeed in replacing traditional poverty with the forms of modernized poverty proper to all 'developed' countries. Finally, there is no evidence to indicate that the successful economization of life, in these countries, can ultimately prevent the destructive side-effects of the process on people's livelihood, including the destruction of their natural environment.

Assistance policies, finally, have failed in many ways. It is now clear that all systems of aid ultimately serve to perpetuate processes of pauperization. As Georg Simmel has pointed out:

> The goal of assistance is precisely to mitigate certain extreme manifestations of social differentiation, so that the social structure may continue to be based on this differentiation. If assistance were to be based on the interests of the poor, there would, in principle, be no limit whatsoever on the transmission of property in favor of the poor, a transmission that would lead to the equality of all.[22]

A World Economy against Vernacular Villages

Using the striking image of 'one world' or the 'global village', the development discourse invites its 'target populations' to look at their predicament in a 'modern', 'realistic' and indeed comparative way. It asks them to consider that the world has changed, and to learn from the experience of those who have finally made it. If the poor would only understand what historically brought the people of the North to higher standards of living and greater political, economic and technological power, they, too, would no longer hesitate to take the main highway of development. This is presented as the only transcultural and universal road for all would-be travellers to reach their modern destination.

In reality, what is proposed serves only the interests of the highway designers and their management system. For as one enters into it, one becomes a prisoner of its rules and logic. Not only does one have to use a car to drive on it, not only are the road, the destination, and the exits predefined, but the person engaged on the highway is no longer a free and incomparable human being. He becomes only a passenger in a car with a more or less powerful engine whose speed and performance henceforth define for him his comparative position and power on the common road.

As to the notion of the global village, it uses a vernacular concept only to destroy it. For it aims precisely at wiping out the thousands of villages whose great diversity has actually made the world's singularity and richness. The proposed 'one world' seeks to substitute the thousands of real and living worlds with a single non-world, a totally acultural and amoral economic corporation whose only purpose is to serve the interests of its shareholders.

Certainly, the economic approach to life may well lead for a time to a massive or more efficient production of goods and commodities, that is, a development of things. Yet both the resources and the needs it creates inevitably lead to a situation of permanent scarcity where not only the poor and the destitute, but even the rich, have always less than they desire. Moreover, regardless of the level of wealth reached by a society, it is a fact that the poor are always the ones who suffer the most from the gap generated between their needs and the economically produced scarce resources. This is particularly so as the same economy increasingly imputes to them new needs of its own, ever more difficult to meet. Thus, it is becoming clearer to many that, however their needs may be defined, it is not only an illusion, but a contradiction in terms, to expect that economy could ever satisfy their needs.

Economy can indeed produce a lot of commodities and services to relieve a particular set of needs. But as it disvalues and often destroys a whole range of other human activities which, for the majority of people, continue to be vital for meeting their needs, the disabling effects of those relief operations are indeed highly negative in the long run. The overwhelming majority in the world still shape and satisfy their needs thanks to the network of human relationships they preserve within their vernacular spaces, and thanks to the many forms of solidarity, co-operation and reciprocity they develop within their communities. Their activities are generally concrete responses to concrete and immediate problems, enabling the people involved to produce both the changes and the things they need. The modern economy disvalues these activities and presses, or forces, people to abandon them. It seeks to reduce everyone into becoming the agent of an invisible national or world economy, geared only to producing things for whoever can pay for them. In other words, in the name of poverty alleviation, it only forces the poor to work for others rather than for themselves.

In vernacular societies, abundance is perceived as a state of nature, inviting all living species to draw on it for meeting their specific needs. These are, in turn, perceived as limited, insofar as they represent a mix of organic and socio-cultural 'necessaries' for life. To share such plentiful resources as air, water and land, arrangements are generally made, similar to the original commons in Europe, which make it possible for everyone to have access to them. The extent to which a community organizes itself for drawing on nature's abundant resources and sharing them with its members defines the relative prosperity of that community.

Whenever the populations concerned are, for some natural or socio-political reason (drought, natural calamity, economic status, political or cultural oppression, etc.), prevented from drawing freely on those resources, they suffer from scarcity. Yet they continue to refine and diversify their activities. Their success in dealing with such situations is, however, more often than not, due to the non-economic aspects of these activities.

The modern economic construct of reality is based on a different, if not opposite, set of assumptions. It assumes that natural resources are scarce; that human needs, in particular those of *homo economicus* are unlimited; and finally, that a sound economy can make it possible for everyone ultimately to meet all their needs. This particular perception of reality tends to reduce human beings and their societies to their economic dimension alone. It strips the vernacular space of all its powerfully alive potentialities. It seeks to transform it into a mere economic machine, and one controlled and operated by others. In the same construct, human beings are perceived as simply one of the many resources required by economy for its own needs.

The insidious effects of the destruction of vernacular space are particularly dangerous at a time when many other alternatives need to be explored, taking into account both the incredible advance of certain autonomous and convivial technologies and the often very imaginative solutions that some grassroots movements are offering in terms of the regeneration of their people's life spaces.

Signals from the Grassroots

The way planners, development actomaniacs and politicians living off global poverty alleviation campaigns are presenting their case, gives the uninformed public a distorted impression of how the world's impoverished are living their deprivations. Not only are these people presented as incapable of doing anything intelligent by themselves, but also as preventing the modern do-gooders from helping them. Were these preposterous misrepresentations really true, three-quarters of the world's population would already have perished.

In the last couple of decades, promising signals are being received from the grassroots indicating their still amazing vitality — in many areas, in fact, where the outsider would normally expect total resignation or submission. Not only in Asia where imaginative movements have been consistently witnessed since the Gandhian revolution, or in Latin America where much has equally been happening,[23] but in Africa, too, interesting and original grassroots movements are now emerging. These movements vary greatly in their approaches to the regeneration of people's space and in their size. As a rule, they are localized and rather small in number. Yet the rapid growth of some, like the Chipko, or the Swadhyaya,[24] which already embrace several million people, indicate that even their size is growing in importance. Let me outline their significance and message.

Indigenous responses: For a couple of decades, the development discourse and its practices succeeded in manipulating and bullying their 'target populations'. Many of the present grassroots movements represent people's rejection of this. The victims now want their poverty or riches to be defined by themselves, and to deal with that, free from unwanted pressures.

Growing resistance to governments and their modernizing policies seems to have fostered the trend towards a return to roots. It is true that such trends have often been co-opted by a new breed of manipulators linked with fundamentalist or ethnic interests. Yet, as a whole, most grassroots movements are now aware of the dangers of sectarian ideologies. The lessons of the past, including the most recent coming from Eastern Europe, prompt them, more than ever, to rely on their own creative wisdom and cultures in responding to their reality.

Surfing over the threats: Another expression of this growing distance toward established ideologies is the rejection, by many a grassroots movement, of the old-established notions of power, including the much sought after objective of seizing power. Here, too, these movements have not only learned much from their own experiences, but from all the other revolutions. These have convinced them that violence only leads to superficial changes, to a transformation of the former victims into new victimizers, and often to new structural forms of violence. As the praxis of grassroots movements leads them to understand better the dynamics of violence and power, they seem continuously to discover new and more artful ways of looking at the world and themselves. As the common man realizes that the dominant Western form of modernity has, in fact, lost touch with the present it claims to represent, he becomes truly modern, in the original sense of the word, that is, one who is *of the present*. As such, he constantly refines his traditional, vernacular ways of facing the many waves threatening his life. To the thousands of tricks each culture has developed in order to preserve itself from such passing waves, the new grassroots are adding the art of *surfing over and inside* the waves.

Vernacular universes: As in the case of power, grassroots movements seem to differ considerably from planners and politicians on their approach to the macro dimensions of change. What essentially matters for them is to bring about, within the horizons with which they are familiar, changes which are both possible and meaningful to their own lives. It matters little to them whether what they do is replicable elsewhere, or in conformity with ideal models of society constructed elsewhere. As a rule, grassroots populations resent the man-made macro world to which they are asked to conform. The more they feel its artificiality and the danger it poses to all their dreams and aspirations, the more they consider themselves as parts of macro worlds of their own. These are the vernacular or religious universes which give them hope and strength, and in which they like to find refuge. The particularly subtle Hindu concept of dharma well expresses the relationship between everyone's 'micro' life and the 'macro' cosmic order, a relationship which also defines one's responsibilities and duties toward both.

Here lies another fundamental difference separating the grassroots universe from that of modern technology. The latter starts with a 'macro' blueprint, a predefined idea of what should be done and how. The technocrat's design consists, then, in transforming everything to meet that blueprint. For the communities at the grassroots level, what matters is, by contrast, what is,[25] and life, as it designs its own course. What finally decides is the living 'nose' of the people directly concerned for what is appropriate and sensible to do. In the other, the technocratic approach, the deciding factor is the dead data of an alien, often ideologically biased, knowledge system.

Spiritual dimension: Most contemporary grassroots movements have a strong spiritual dimension. It is not only in India where such movements, starting from the Gandhian Sarvodaya, to Manavodaya[26] and Swadhyaya, have attached seminal importance to such factors as inner transformation, moral purity, self-discovery, self-knowledge, or the notion of God in its many different interpretations. For other movements inspired by Islam, Christianity and/or Marxism (as in the Theology of Liberation), the outer and the inner conditions of freedom have also been closely linked together. The sense of sharing common spiritual ideals of a purifying nature can create new and contagious forms of enthusiasm and solidarity, which in turn greatly increase the operational effectiveness of the group. A reason for people's indifference to the dominant development ideology, and hence its failure, could well be the latter's utter insensitivity to this crucial dimension.

Convivial poverty: A last point of importance seems now common to most genuine grassroots movements — the belief that the answer to imposed forms of material poverty has to be found in the people's own ethical and cultural approach to poverty. In other words, as long as the present race for material riches continues, on the ground that nothing but technological limitations should stop human beings from wanting and having more, not only will the race itself continue to breed the most dehumanizing forms of imposed poverty, but it will ultimately impoverish and destroy the very planet which gives us our common riches. By contrast, convivial poverty — that is, voluntary or moral poverty — implies the ideal of a livelihood based on the age-old moral principles of simplicity, frugality, sufficiency and respect for every human being and all forms of life. It does not mean asceticism or the monastic life. It only tries to give back to everyone that holistic and compassionate dimension of being, without which no human relationship is possible, in the true sense of the word. As such, convivial poverty could perhaps serve both as a means and an end to pauperizing economism.

In conclusion, the time has come to look at poverty in a different way. The time has come to regenerate the age old tradition of voluntary poverty as both a new form of individual liberation and a major instrument for reducing all other forms of brutalizing poverty. A tragic form of poverty, often perceived as an expression of modernity, is that of a world of economically obsessed individuals and nations fighting with each other over more greed, more violence, more exploitation and more destruction of the inner and outer life forces of humankind. That poverty, of both perception and lifestyle, is now being challenged by the ideals of a different form of poverty. Increasingly, more compassionate and informed human beings are realizing that the earth can only provide enough to satisfy all the needs of persons if they are liberated from greed. The Economic Age, like all its predecessors, is not an eternal state. The deep crises it is traversing in all its fields of activity and, above all, the threats it is now posing to the very existence of our planet, are already preparing for the coming of a new age. The flourishing of other, higher forms of convivial poverty may then appear as the last hope for creating different societies based on the joys of 'more being', rather than the obsession of 'more having'.

References

1. John Iliffe, *The African Poor: A History*, Cambridge: Cambridge University Press, 1987.

2. *Encyclopaedia Judaica*, under 'Poverty'.

3. Michel Mollat, *The Poor in the Middle Ages*, New Haven: Yale University Press, 1978, p. 3. This study is a classic for the history of poverty in Europe. Besides the word 'pauper', Mollat has listed the following words: referring to impecuniosity and destitution in general (*egens, egenus, indigens, inops, insufficiens, mendicus, miser*); shortage of food (*esuriens, famelicus*) or clothing (*nudus, pannosus*); physical defects such as blindness (*caecus*), lameness (*claudus*), arthritic deformity (*contractus*), infirmity in general (*infirmus*), leprosy (*leprosus*), injury (*vulneratus*), feebleness due to poor health or old age (*aegrotans, debilis, senex, valetudinarius*); mental deficiency (*idiotus, imbecillis, simplex*); temporary weakness affecting women during pregnancy and childbirth (*mulier ante et postum partum*); situations of adversity such as those involving the loss of one's parents (*orphanus*), husband (*vidua*), or liberty (*captivus*), and, finally, banishment and exile (*bannus, exiliatus*).

4. Here are some samples of proverbs and sayings from Africa: For the Igbos, 'The rich man puts down his basket in the market, the poor man fears'; 'The poor man gets a friend; the rich man takes him away'; 'Those who have money are friends of each other.' For the Tswana, 'Where is no wealth, there is no poverty.' In Iliffe, op. cit., pp. 91, 78, 28, 85.

5. A letter from Hughes to Ellis, 13 March 1836, *Council for World Mission; Incoming Letters*, South Africa 15/1E/34, quoted by Iliffe, op. cit., p. 78.

6. Michel Mollat, *Etudes sur l'Histoire de la pauvreté*, publication de la Sorbonne, Serie Etudes, Tome 8, Vol. 2, Paris: 1974, p. 15.

7. St Francis of Assisi considered that charity did not consist in 'leaning over' the poor, but in 'elevating oneself' to their level.

8. For the Iranian mystic A. Nasafi, the only shortcoming of poverty is apparent, while its virtues are all hidden. In the case of wealth, it is exactly the opposite. Hence, he exhorts upon the dervish: 'Poverty is a great blessing; wealth, a great pain. But the ignorant ignores this, escaping poverty and sticking to wealth. Our prophet . . . chose poverty, for he knew it and its

effects, as he knew wealth and its effects.' Translated from A. Nasafi, *Le Livre de l'homme parfait*, Paris: Fayard, 1984, p. 268.

9. The French Robert Dictionary defines the word as follows: 'Qui manque du nécessaire ou n'a que le strict nécessaire' (Lacking what is necessary or having only what is strictly necessary).

10. What is necessary to a peasant in a rural area is quite different from a city dweller. And while a Ladakh family in the Himalayas can still live lavishly on an average 'income' of much less than $1,000 a year, an American family of the same size living in the US could hardly meet their needs with a yearly income of $10,000, which represents the officially recognized 'poverty line'.

11. Michel Mollat, 1987, op. cit., p. 8.

12. The notion of 'entitlement relations' was coined by Amartya Sen, first in 1967, later elaborated in *Poverty and Famines*, Oxford: 1981.

13. For Adam Smith, the necessities were, interestingly enough, 'not only the commodities which are indispensably necessary for the support of life, but whatever the custom of the country renders it indecent for creditable people, even the lowest order, to be without.' See *An Inquiry Into the Nature and Causes of the Wealth of Nations*, 1776, p. 351.

14. Amartya Sen, op. cit., p. 1714.

15. 'Savanna Muslims viewed poverty with much ambivalence. Their traditions stressed the values of wealth and generosity. At their best, traditions evoked the largesse of the rich and the hospitality of common people which many European travellers admired. At their worst, the same traditions bred contempt for poverty, both in others, expressed sometimes in mockery of the handicapped, and in oneself, for the shame of poverty could lead men (but apparently not women) to suicide. John Iliffe, op. cit.

16. Pauperism describes 'a category of people unable to maintain themselves at all, or to maintain themselves at the level conventionally regarded as minimal, without outside assistance . . .' 'Poverty', as a social phenomenon, implies only economic and social inequality, 'that is, a relation of inferiority, dependence, or exploitation. In other words, it implies the existence of a social stratum definable by, among other things, lack of wealth.' See E. J. Hobsbawm, op. cit., pp. 398, 399.

17. Peter Bunyard, 'Can Self-sufficient Communities survive the onslaught of Development?' *The Ecologist*, Vol. 14, 1984, p. 3.

18. 'Traditionally, land and labor are not separated; labor forms part of life, land part of nature, life and nature form an articulate whole. Land is thus tied up with the organizations of kinship, neighborhood, craft and creed — with tribe and temple, village, guild and church.' Polanyi, op. cit., p. 178.

19. In this tradition, Michel Mollat quotes a great teacher of the first millennium, the sixth century North African abbot, Julianus Pomerius, who believed that: 'once an individual ensured his own survival and the survival of his family, he had the duty to give whatever he owned beyond his own needs to the *debiles* and *infimi*, that is, to the poor.' See Mollat, op. cit., p. 23.

20. For Michael Harrington, already in 1963, the deprived in the US numbered nearly 50 million people. Some startling facts on the phenomenon of poverty amidst affluence in the US were recently reported in an article by Dolores King, a correspondent of the *Boston Globe*. 'Twenty years after a White House Conference was "to put an end to hunger in America itself for all time", as President Nixon phrased it, hunger is making a comeback in vengeance.' See 'Hunger's Bitter Return: Working poor, children seen as newest victims', in the *Boston Globe*, December 9, 1989.

21. See Cardinal Paulo Evaristo Arns, 'Sincerity is Subversive', *Development*, No. 3, 1985, pp. 3–5.

22. Georg Simmel, 'The Poor', *Social Problems*, Vol. 13, 1965.

23. There is an abundant literature on the grassroots movements and networks in Latin America. Already in the '60s, some came to public attention which had been initiated in Chile and Mexico. Between the '60s and the '70s, the Freirian methods of 'conscientization' were used by a large number of them in other parts of the continent.

The mid-'70s witnessed the birth of the Participatory Action Research (PAR) methodology, conceived by a group of activists from different regions of the world, in particular Latin America and Asia. Their intention was, amongst others, to create with the populations concerned, the most favourable conditions for the creation and dissemination of 'grassroots knowledge'. The methodology was soon adopted by, and spread to, many grassroots movements, not only in Latin America, but all over the world. In April 1986, many networks of grassroots movements signed a solidarity agreement for working together.

Lately, a most innovative movement found its expression in the Mexican ANADEGES (Analysis, Decentralism & Gestion). This movement considers itself as a 'hammock' for peasants, marginals and 'deprofessionalized intellectuals'. Around 500,000 persons are said to be involved in this 'hammock', whose discourse and practices take the opposite course to those of 'development'.

24. Although Swadhyaya had its first tiny seeds planted in the early '50s by Dada (an affectionate nickname for the Rev. Pandurang Athvale Shastri), the movement is less known outside the Swadhyayi *parivar* (family). It took the first 'seeds' some 20 years to become 'seedlings', and finally an impressive human forest of over 3 million people. 'Swadhyaya' means 'self-knowledge' or 'self-discovery'. The movement is entirely self-reliant and based on the Vedic belief that there is a God within each person. Swadhyaya has generated great material wealth without any assistance from anywhere. The 'family' has been using that 'wealth' and its regenerated relationships to improve the condition of its poorer members, in a most ingenious and graceful manner. See also, Majid Rahnema, 'Swadhyaya: The unknown, the peaceful, the silent, yet singing revolution of India', in *IFDA Dossier*, No. 73, April 1990.

25. A vivid illustration of this approach is given in an article on Chodak, a movement of 'self-organization' of the poor and the marginalized in Dakar. In this excellent case study, the author indicates how the key to success, for this movement, became the people's concern 'to see and to understand "what is".' See Emmanuel Seyni Ndione, 'Leçons d'une animation au Senegal', *IFDA Dossier*, No. 74, Nov./Dec. 1989.

26. 'Manavodaya', in Hindi, means 'human awakening'. This is another grassroots movement whose 'organizing philosophy and practice start with self-awakening and awareness, leading to family, community and social awakening. . . . Recognizing a unity of purpose in all life and evolution, the end goal of development is seen by this movement as a society based on self-discipline and love.' See the mimeographed Preliminary Report of the International Workshop, *People's Initiatives to Overcome Poverty*, March 27–April 5, 1989, organized by the East–West Centre, Honolulu, Hawaii.

Bibliography

To compose a bibliography for this particular entry on poverty is an almost impossible task, as the two major means of expression for the poor are either silence or the spoken word. The written material on poverty is, at best, an accumulation of knowledge *about* the world of the poor and their needs. As such, the present bibliography represents only a poor selection of the sources on which the author has relied for his own personal reflections.

To obtain a wider view of the perception of poverty in vernacular, or pre-economic, societies, I found it useful to start by refreshing my memory of poems and old classical writings familiar to Iranians and other people of my region. Amongst these, the following are available in English and French: *The Mathnawi of Jalalu'ddin Rumi* (translated by R. A. Nicholson), Cambridge, 1977; *The Gulistan of Saadi* (translated as *Kings and Beggars* by J. Arberry, London: 1945); Farid al Din 'Attar, *Tadhkirat al-Awlia* (translated by Ed. Nicholson), London: 1905; Abd-ar Rahman Al Jami, *Vie des Soufis ou les Haleines de la familiarité*, (translated by Sylvestre de Sacy), Paris: 1979; A. Nasafi, *Le Livre de l'homme parfait*, Fayard, 1984; Ibn Khaldûn's *Muqaddima* (partly translated in French in Ibn Khaldûn, Paris: Seghers, 1968) and Rabi'a al-'Adawiyya's teachings in Margaret Smith's *Rabi'a al-'Adawiyya: The mystic Saint of Basra*, Cambridge: 1928.

For more recent views on poverty in the pre-industrialized societies of the South, see, for the African region, A. Tevoedjré, *Poverty: Wealth of Mankind*, Oxford: 1979; R. Palmer and N. Parsons, *The Roots of Rural Poverty in Central and Southern Africa*, Berkeley: 1977; and John Iliffe, *The African Poor*, Cambridge: 1987. For Asia, see R. R. Singh (ed.), *Social Work Perspectives on Poverty*, Delhi: 1980, and Leela Gulati, *Profiles in Female Poverty*, Delhi: 1984. And for Latin America, Gustavo Gutierrez, *The Power of the Poor in History*, New York: 1984, and the well-known studies of Oscar Lewis, *The Children of Sanchez*, New York: 1961, and *La Vida*, New York: 1966. Marshall Sahlin, *Stone Age Economics*, Chicago: 1972, provides unusual insight into the relation of poverty with material wealth as these were perceived in the earliest vernacular societies. On another plane, Richard Wilkinson demonstrates in his *Poverty and Progress*, London: 1973, that economic poverty, little known in societies with an ecological equilibrium, appears when man-made pressures of an economic or cultural nature disrupt the latter.

There are authoritative books on the historically changing perceptions of poverty in Europe. A classic is Michel Mollat's edited series entitled *Etudes sur l'Histoire de la pauvreté: Moyen Age-XVIème siècle*. The studies were later compiled in a concise and revised English version bearing the name *The Poor in the Middle Ages*, Yale, 1987. Of similar importance is Bronislaw Geremek's work, *Litosc i szubienica*, as yet unpublished in its Polish original, although translations of it have appeared in Italian, *La Pieta e la forca*, Rome: Laterza, 1986, and French, *La Potence ou la pitié*, Paris: 1987. See also G. Himmelfarb, *The Idea of Poverty: England in the Early Industrial Age*, New York: 1984.

For the processes leading to the 'modernization of poverty' (a term coined by Ivan Illich in 'Planned Poverty: The End Result of Technical Assistance', a chapter of his *Celebration of Awareness*, London: 1971), Karl Polanyi, *The Great Transformation*, New York: 1944, and *The Livelihood of Man*, New York: 1977, remain outstanding references. Amartya Sen's important book, *Poverty and Famines: An Essay on Entitlement and Deprivation*, Oxford: 1981 expresses a thoughtful and convincing demonstration of the dangers of reducing the causes of famine and poverty to food supply. Charles Valentine, *Culture and Poverty*, Chicago: 1968, substantiates the concerns of a soul-searching anthropologist about the dangerous consequences of 'ill-founded conclusions and recommendations from the academic experts [which] are being accepted and acted upon by the public and policy makers alike'.

The phenomenon of poverty in the midst of affluence has been abundantly explored. For the United States, see Robert H. Bremner, *From the Depths: The Discovery of Poverty in the United States*, New York: 1956; Mollie Orshansky's numerous studies, in particular, his earlier often quoted article 'Recounting the Poor: A Five Year Review' in *Social Security Bulletin*, December 1960; Michael Harrington's two major works, *The Other America*, Baltimore: 1963, and *The American Poverty*, New York: 1984; Robert E. Will & Harold G. Vatter, *Poverty in Affluence*, New York: 1970; The Physician Task Force On Hunger in America, *Hunger In America: The Growing Epidemics*, Wesleyan University Press, 1985. B. S. Rowntree, *Poverty and Progress: A Second Social Survey of York*, London: 1941, and Peter Townsend, 'The Meaning of Poverty', *British Journal of Sociology*, September 1962, describe the same phenomenon in England. P. de la Gorce in *La France pauvre*, Paris: 1965, deals with the case of his own country. Finally, Cardinal Paulo Evaristo Arns describes the Brazilian drama in his short and moving article in the SID Journal, *Development*, No. 3, 1985.

Amongst the studies known to this author on the traditional wisdom of the poor in responding to their predicament, the following works are particularly useful. James Scott, *The Moral Economy of the Peasant*, Yale University Press, 1976, demonstrates, in the cases of Burma and Vietnam, how the peasants' 'moral economy' allows them to preserve and enrich their culture while safeguarding at the same time their security. Michael Watts, *Silent Violence*, Berkeley: 1983, is a remarkable study on the ways the Hausa in Northern Nigeria had always organized their poverty with intelligence and wisdom, until their mode of life was shattered by the rise of capitalist development. See also Louis Dumont, *Homo Hierarchicus*, Paris: 1966, and D. H. Wiser, *The Hindu Jajmani System: A socio-economic system inter-relating members of a Hindu village community in services*, Lucknow: 1936. Both studies reveal the subtleties of vernacular societies in dealing with their 'poorest' members.

In the abundant literature on more recent grassroots movements initiated by the poor, the following selected readings are suggested to give a bird's eye view of the situation in some of the areas exposed to rapid economization of life: Anisur Rahman (ed.), *Grassroots Participation and Self-reliance: Experiences in South and SE Asia*, New Delhi: Oxford & IBH Publishing Co., 1984; G. V. S. de Silva al., 'Bhoomi Sena: A Struggle for People's Power', in *Development Dialogue*, No. 2, 1979, pp. 3–70; Vandana Shiva, *Staying Alive: Women, Ecology and Development*, London: 1989; Majid Rahnema, '*Swadhyaya*: the unknown, the peaceful, the silent, yet singing revolution of India', *IFDA Dossier*, No. 73, April 1990; Gustavo Esteva, 'A New Call for Celebration', *Development*, No. 3, 1986, and 'Regenerating People's Space', *Alternatives*, Vol. XII, 1987; Albert Hirschmann, *Getting Ahead Collectively: Grassroots Experiences In Latin America*, New York: 1984; Emmanuel Seyni Ndione, *Dynamique urbaine d'une société en grappe: un cas, Dakar*, Dakar: 1987; also his more recent article, 'Leçons d'une animation au Sénégal', *IFDA Dossier*, No. 74, Nov.–Dec. 1989.

On the general question of poverty as an offshoot of the development discourse and practices, see the thought-provoking text of Wolfgang Sachs, 'Poor not different' in 'The Archaeology of the Development Idea', *Interculture*, Vol. 23, No. 4, Fall 1990.

Production

Jean Robert

A Man and A Concept

Don Bartolo lives in a shack behind my house. Like many other 'displaced persons' in Mexico, he is a squatter. He constructed his dwelling of cardboard, together with odd pieces of plastic and tin. If he is lucky, he will eventually build walls of brick and cover them with some kind of cement or tin roofing. Stretching behind his hut, there is an expanse of barren unused land. From the owner he got permission to cultivate it, to establish a *milpa*: a field of corn planted just when the rains start so that a crop can be harvested without irrigation. Bartolo's action may appear to us profoundly anachronistic.

After World War II, Mexico and the rest of the 'Third World' were invaded by the idea of development. According to President Harry Truman — whose inaugural address in 1949 did much to popularize the term — development consists principally in helping 'the free peoples of the world, through their own efforts, to produce more food, more clothing, more materials for housing and more mechanical power to lighten their burdens'.[1] The key to development is greater production and 'the key to greater production is a wider and more vigorous application of scientific and technical knowledge.' Don Bartolo does not produce more than his father did nor does he use mechanical power to lighten his burden. Experts say that he is underdeveloped.

Once defined as the application of science and productivity, production gradually came to mean productivity itself — more outputs at less cost. And, according to mainstream Mexican economists today, Bartolo's behaviour is clearly *not* productive. But do they have the last word? Perhaps we should take a look at the history of the concept.

Production comes from the Latin verb, *producere* which meant 'to stretch', 'to spend', 'to prolong', 'to draw into visibility'. It generally referred to an actualization of possible existence. In terms of this ancient meaning, production is a movement from the invisible to the visible, an emanation through which something hitherto hidden is brought within the range of man's senses. This idea of emanation fitted ordinary people's experience, the awareness that nature, husbanded by man, brings forth a people's livelihood.

In the European Middle Ages, production retained its ancient sense of emanation. The exceptions are found in the writings of those philosophers who tried to reformulate Christian thought in Aristotelian terms. They sometimes used production as a synonym for creation and, of course, God, not man, was for them the 'Producer'. However, most theologians insisted that God's creation must not be expressed by the same word as the products of nature. In the 15th century, Nicholas of Cusa clarified the difference between creation and production further by stating that God created the world out of nothing, while nature only brings forth what God has previously created.

The Renaissance called a man wise if he, like Prometheus, sought to emancipate himself from the bounds of nature and to act following his free will, while the unwise remained 'nature's debtor'. This Promethean mood, however, was still not called productive.[2] Nature, and nature alone, was 'the great queen and mother of all production'.

Until the eve of modernity, the term continued to be used primarily in its ancient meanings where it designated an emanation of nature or the bringing forth of something hidden. In that second sense of 'making visible', the term, by the mid 18th century, had acquired the status of a technical term in jurisprudence. For example: 'The books must be produced, as we cannot receive parole evidence of their content.' (1776, from the *Oxford English Dictionary*). From the early 17th century, however, a change can be noted. The term production begins to imply the notion that certain combinations of any two elements can generate a third — something entirely new which is not reducible to its components. For Milton, the outcome of such unions was still evil. In *Paradise Lost* (1667), for example, he wrote: 'These are the Product of those ill-mated Marriages thou saw'st, where good and bad were matcht, who of themselves Abhor to joyn.'[3] And well into the next century, the terms 'creation', 'production' and 'fabrication or manufacture' still had strictly defined domains of application. God was the Creator, nature the producer and man the manufacturer. Though man could sometimes be its subject, the verb 'to produce' had not yet become the neutral synonym, 'to realize', that it has today.

The modern sense of production, where man is the producer and the product is a new entity, required a break with the word's traditional meanings.[4] The first step to that Promethean understanding of production was taken by the writers and philosophers of the Romantic period at the end of the 18th century. For them, the artist became the archetype of the producer, since the Romantics ascribed the generative powers of nature to him.[5] Kant in philosophy and Goethe in literature thus coined a new sense of production which is best exemplified in Kant's concept of the *Einbildungskraft*, the power of the imagination. This power is productive not because it conjures up an object's image in its absence, but because, Kant insisted, it is capable of conceiving the formal characteristics of an object before any empirical perception of it is possible.[6] Kant thought that the morphological description of natural phenomena was an integral part of the productive activity of nature — it was nature acting in the scientist.

Inspired by Kant, Goethe wrote: 'Man does not feed himself and enjoy without, at the same time, becoming productive. This is the most inherent property of human nature.' For Goethe, the artist was productive because nature was productive in him: 'Nature, who spontaneously produced in me great and small work of her kind, rests sometimes for long periods.'[7] He was attentive to his own 'productive mood' as if it were a natural phenomenon and observed the moments of an 'accumulation of productive force'. He also devised productive maxims with which he admonished himself, and made lists of production-enhancing 'technical details', like the good effects of solitude, springtime, the early morning, some bodily motions, certain colours, and music. His social vision, also, was permeated by 'the dichotomy between the productive and consuming classes', a projection of his interest in the relation between the productive artist and his public.

This was new. In contrast to this Promethean view, Daniel Defoe — not yet the renowned author of *Robinson Crusoe* but an obscure pamphleteer — still insisted (in 1704) that production belonged to nature's power, not man's industry: 'When we speak of it [wealth] as the Effect of Nature, 'tis *Product* or Produce; when as the Effect of Labour, 'tis Manufacture.' In another pamphlet, he refers to what we would call the products of a region as its 'manufactures'.[8] David Hume also insisted that man could not match nature: 'His utmost art and industry can never equal the meanest of nature's productions, either for beauty or value.'

Of Character and the Earth

I approached Bartolo's field one day while he was ploughing. When he reached the end of a furrow, I greeted him. After exchanging the customary formalities, I told him I was writing an article in which I discussed a *milpa*. I asked him why some neighbours appeared able to plant one while others, seemingly, could not. Is there a name for that quality, I wondered, which some possess and others lack? He was silent for a while, and I felt that he unobtrusively watched me from the corner of his shrewd eyes. Then he answered with one of those words which mestizo peasants use every day, but which urban people only meet in Cervantes. He said that the *milpa* requires *enjundia*. In his vocabulary, this forgotten word of Latin origin (*exunguo*: I anoint) refers to a man's constitutional strength and virtue, to qualities with which he was anointed at birth. I understood that being born with *enjundia* means having a taste for good corn — along with the talent 'to produce' it.

Production became an economic concept when it was made into the source of value. The concept of economic production was popularized by the Physiocrats, a group of French philosophers for whom all wealth ultimately stemmed from the earth's generative powers. In their *Tableau Economique* they described the three orders which contribute to 'the annual produce of the land and labour' (the expression is Adam Smith's) of any nation: (1) The landed proprietors (owners); (2) The cultivators of the land — the farmers and country labourers; (3) The 'artificers, manufacturers and merchants'. This third group they called 'the unproductive class', since it contributed no new value — in terms of this theory — to 'the value of the whole annual amount of the rude produce of the land'.[10] The first two groups are the 'productive' classes of society, since they do contribute, or produce, new value. In this economic tableau, the earth was clearly the matrix of the nation's wealth and the state's power.

Of Labour and the Earth

Don Bartolo is a rural migrant from the state of Guerrero. He is proud that he can supply his family with the high quality and good taste of the corn they enjoyed in their native village. And he wants to eat *tortillas que saben*, not the insipid substitutes now sold in government-sponsored stores. He also wants to say who he is: a man of qualities, one who knows how to work the land, how to tend a *milpa*.

The modern concept of economic production turns the Physiocrats' relationship between earth and industrial labour upside down. The first step toward the primacy of labour over the land was taken by de Condillac, a contemporary. In opposition to the Physiocrats, he wrote:

> Exactly speaking, the farmer doesn't produce anything; he only enhances the earth's disposition to produce. On the contrary, the craftsman produces a value, inherent in the forms he gives to the new materials. To produce is, indeed, to give new forms to matter; the earth, when she produces, doesn't do differently.[10]

With a team of borrowed oxen, Bartolo first ploughs the furrows where he will plant his seed. Observing the signs in the sky since the *cabañuelas* — the light rains of January — he learns when he has to sow so that his crop will receive sufficient rain while it is growing, and a week of dry weather when the cobs are ripe. When the young plants come up, he gently banks up the earth so that the roots will not be exposed to the sun. At the proper time, he and his family go to work on the *limpias*, the weeding. Weeding is tiring work and festive celebrations accompany it.

Adam Smith, who was critical of the Physiocrats, pointed out that their system 'at present exists only in the speculations of a few men of great learning and ingenuity in France' and developed a counter-argument similar to de Condillac. The wealth of a nation results in the production of necessities ('not only those things which nature, but those things which the established rules of decency, have rendered necessary to the lowest rank of people') and luxuries ('all other things . . . without meaning by this appellation to throw the smallest degree of reproach on the temperate use of them).[11] The principal human factor in the creation of wealth seems to be, he said, the division of labour. And for Smith, labour is either productive or unproductive. The former comprises workers on the land, in manufacturing and trade. The latter includes 'some of the most respectable orders in the society' as well as 'some of the most frivolous professions', reaching from churchmen, lawyers, physicians to buffoons, musicians and opera singers.[12] Smith's great work, *The Wealth of Nations*, is important — from the perspective of this essay — for its reversal of the Physiocrats' concepts and the important place given to labour, and hence its impact on the modern world's notion of production.

Of Use Value and Exchange Value

Like many suburban dwellers, Don Bartolo does his best to maintain something of his traditions under hostile conditions. He grows his *milpa* on marginal land. He has no monetary expenses, for he selects his seed from the largest kernels of the preceding season and uses little bought-in fertilizer. He relies on his and his family's labour. If his behaviour were evaluated according to the norms of economic profit, it would be characterized as non-profitable. Mexican economists would tell him that he is much better off hiring himself out on some construction site and buying imported corn in the market with his wages. And experts go on advocating this in spite of the fact that the unemployment of men who have abandoned the *milpa* is rampant. Today, these experts point out, corn imported from the US grain belt is cheaper than the product of the local *milpas* because North American grain is produced following the norms of economic productivity. But some Mexicans insist that the *milpa* obeys another logic, incarnates another kind of life. Further, they know that corn from the *milpa* has a different taste; it *has* taste, they say.

The next step was taken by Ricardo. His ideas tended to reduce the earth's generative powers to merely quantifiable factors — we would say inputs — of productive labour. And he equated welfare and wealth with exchange value. With these ideas, the link between *economic* production and the old sense of production as emanation was definitively broken. Production could now be understood as a purely human creation — resulting in exchange value and its expression in money — on which everyone would be dependent for survival. The economy is then the dependence of man's concrete subsistence on abstract value. Subsistence is implicitly redefined as the individual producer's socio-biological survival under conditions of the accumulation of capital. The commons — formerly contributing to people's subsistence — could now be destroyed through enclosure in the name of a productive imperative. For the commons are an obstacle to production since they allow people to subsist independent of producing economic value.[13]

Looking at the *milpa*, I imagined a cycle of moving energies, but I was wrong. Energy is quantitatively conserved and dissipated; not so the peasant's *enjundia*. This is not conserved, nor is it dissipated. It emanates from a man's body and, if the weather and other factors are favourable, is recreated by the plant. It does not circulate in a closed system, but is given and taken. Sometimes it is lost, sometimes given back abundantly — *con creces*. The strength which flows from a man's body calls for other, natural flows or emanations — the warm caressing of the sun, the showers of rain from the sky, like successive anointings of earth and crop. In the *milpa*, labour is an act of propitiation, not an input. The exchange is open, each year nature will follow her mood, good weather can only be hoped for, controllable factors are few.

It should be noted that at the time when Ricardo's ideas led to a view of the earth as a passive input for production (a factor of production), chemists were redefining soil as a compound of minerals, and Liebig, the father of the fertilizer industry, began his experiments with growing plants in a soil-less chemical preparation. Moreover, there is a conceptual similarity between Ricardo's disregard of the earth's productive powers and the substitution of a chemical theory of agriculture for the ancient notion of the earth as the stomach, the nurturer, of growing organisms. Agriculture's 'need' for fertilizer inputs can be seen as an ultimate consequence of Ricardian economics. Then, as labour also became an increasingly abstract concept — just another input like fertilizer or irrigation, but simultaneously the secret of all the other inputs' value — economics came to disengage itself from a consideration of actual local production procedures. The major problem of economics was no longer the material production of goods, but their distribution — as the condition for the realization of their exchange value.

Of Theory and Memory

Don Bartolo has little understanding of or interest in economic theory. Near his shack, he has built a *troja*, a small corncrib of clay, straw and palm branches in which he stores his corn during the dry season. Each day his wife, daughters and daughters-in-law can take what is needed for the *tortillas* and — on feast days — for the *pozole*, the *tamales* or the *tlaxcales*. Bartolo is motivated by memories of good, simple meals and family traditions. Cost-benefit analysis and economic profit are completely alien considerations for him.

For Marx, production was a two-faced Janus. In a narrow economic sense, he built on Smith and Ricardo, making labour into a kind of paradigm for production, the source of all value. But his originality consists in the way in which he embraced the philosophical and Romantic meanings of production and turned them into the hub of his theory of history. To do this, he took up production in its ancient meaning of 'bringing forth', of 'actualizing a hitherto only potential shape'. In this way production came to be the fundamental concept and hinge in his work. As Hentschel notes, Marx 'saw production as the shape-giving force of History and, ultimately, as the fulcrum for the necessary and unavoidable transformation of the world'.[14] The term assumed a reflexive overtone when, in harsh opposition to Hegel's idealism, he wrote: 'Men start to distinguish themselves from the animals as soon as they begin to produce the material conditions of their living', when 'they indirectly produce their material life itself'.[15]

But I want to emphasize another, less known aspect of Marx's thinking about production — its relationship to his ideas on the origin of exchange value. Marx was a witness to the first railroads and wrote the initial sketch of *Capital* (*Grundrisse*) during the decade of railroad mania in Europe. He said:

This locational movement — the bringing of the product to the market, which is the necessary condition for its circulation, except when the point of production is itself a market — could more precisely be regarded as the transformation of the product into a commodity.[16]

This is one of Marx's most powerful insights into the nature of commodities and their production. Defined technically, economic production is the chain of transfers and transformations which take place between the moment when given substances or goods are uprooted from a region and when they are offered on the market somewhere else. But the historical emergence of commodities does not require the whole chain of industrial transformations, but only the uprooting, since uprooted local goods were already commodities even before they were produced by industrial methods. It is important to see the effect of the movement itself:

> With the spatial distance that the product covers on its way from its place of production to the market, it also loses its local identity, its spatial presence. Its concretely sensual properties, which are experienced at the place of production as a result of the labour process (or, as in the case of the fruits of the land, as a result of natural growth) appear quite different in the distant marketplace. There the product, now a commodity, realizes its economic value, and simultaneously gains new qualities as an object of consumption.[17]

Of Goods and Movement

The *milpa* has high use value, modern production high exchange value. Working in the *milpa*, needs are shaped by the activities which satisfy them — one cannot speak of distinguishing production from consumption. Modern production, on the other hand, separates needs from satisfaction and clearly creates two spheres, one of production and the other of consumption. The *milpa*, unless carried out on a large scale, contributes little to economic indicators, wages and employment. However, production, by definition, increases the GNP as well as other economic indicators.

The perception of goods — and, *a fortiori*, subsistence goods — as commodities has a history. From the point of view of the history of this perception, 'commodity' is the *form* of uprooted goods. To have understood this is one of Marx's more brilliant — and less acclaimed — insights. In order to document the historical appearance of the commodity form of goods, he allowed the ancient sense of emanation to complement the modern narrow economic meaning of production. By uprooting all goods, transportation literally actualizes the commodity form into their substance.

But what does this mean? Marx rejects both Platonism and Hegelian idealism. Forms or ideas have no existence independent of the act that 'actualizes' them. Hence the commodity form of goods is given to them precisely in the movement which uproots them, bringing them to market. And the possibility of that movement makes all goods potential commodities, with transportation being the realization of that form. Commodities do not require transportation because their site of production is distant from the place where they are consumed. Rather, we first separate a sphere of production from a sphere of consumption because we perceive all goods as commodities. Transportation is not, in the first place, a material or locational necessity, but a hidden axiom of our representation of goods. It is not a 'need', but a requirement for the social construction of a commodity-intensive productive order. It is this order which then transforms uprooted goods — commodities — into everybody's needs.

Of Progress and History

Economists tend to define the *milpa* by what it lacks. The labour involved is characterized as a subsistence activity — hard work with inefficient tools to generate only a few goods, that is, little or no surplus. Subsistence production is seen by them as the poor relation of modern economic production. They define subsistence as a situation of endemic scarcity, not realizing that they thereby project the foundational axiom of Western economics — scarcity — on to a setting which obeys a non- or pre-economic logic. The *milpa* is a historical activity rooted in millennial traditions. An economist's certainties can only enter this world at great risk. They can colonize the past — thus distorting it, and falsify the present — thus not understanding it.

In *Capital* (Ch. 7), Marx showed that violence is a historical precondition for the establishment of production relations in which accumulation can be realized 'peacefully' by the play of economic laws. He saw that the historical violence which he calls 'original accumulation' is also an uprooting of people from their place, their customs, their identity. But because he believed in progress, he was convinced that the productive forces unleashed by that very uprooting would ultimately bring about a more human world in which 'everyone will receive according to his needs'.

In the scenario of original accumulation, traditional forms of domination and physical violence characteristically exploit and uproot people. In Marx's dialectic, this original overt violence brings on the development of productive forces. And a belief in progress prevents the adherent of this idea from raising questions about the possibly irreversible losses inherent in such a development. Class struggle is thus seen as a contest for a pie whose goodness is beyond doubt.

Of Gifts and Service

My conversations with Don Bartolo led me to elaborate some tentative characteristics to distinguish his behaviour from what economists today call production. The *milpa* worker's view of the weather — with his corresponding behaviour — acknowledges and accepts the world's essentially contingent nature — in some sense, everything rests in God's hands. Modern economics, on the other hand, attempts to identify, isolate and control all 'the productive factors'. The *milpa* farmer hopes; the modern producer has quantitative expectations of profit. Bartolo growing corn is part of a natural drama; the producer is mentally outside nature, attempting to manage her. The *milpa* is giving and receiving; modern production matches benefits against costs. The *milpa's* gifts are both concrete and multiple — immediately sensible to the taste, socially joyful in the festivals it elicits. The single abstract value, money, overshadows all other evaluations of production. The economic 'pie' has no taste, only a quantifiable value.

It is the goodness of that pie which is now in question. Marx's schema, by its very construction, prohibits assessment of any destructiveness possibly inherent in economic production. Today, awakening from four decades of development dreams, we are forced to confront the credibility of the association of production with happiness or welfare. For we can now see the worldwide dislocation, suffering and alienation resulting from these dreams — or delusions. We are the witnesses of a war, a war against subsistence embedded in specific cultures, a war against nature itself.

This war became obvious only some decades after World War II. The experience of wartime production revealed unsuspected possibilities for increasing productivity. A whole bevy of experts united in 'interdisciplinary' efforts to explore the potential for increases in efficiency. Alongside these endeavours there was an explosive growth in wholly new areas of production — in ever more 'imaginative' and differentiated services, in the very actions which Adam Smith had explicitly characterized as *unproductive*. And it seemed that there were no limits to the variety and extension of services which professionals could devise and promote. Government, business, the people themselves were all convinced that these ministrations, vanities and pleasures were so worthwhile that it was necessary to institutionalize their production, so that people could pay for them. These newly proliferating forms of production — of 'services' rather than material goods — then became the most important growth sectors of the economy, the ones that most contributed to the Gross National Product.

At the end of the 19th century, the idea that a small set of numbers could express which nations were well off and which were lagging behind had led some economists to estimate the income of a nation as if it were a single household. Before the First World War, only nine countries were reported to have attempted such an evaluation, and since there was no consensus about the relevant criteria, these first national income estimates hardly allowed for comparisons. It was Keynes who, in his *General Theory of Employment, Interest and Money* (1936), first suggested that a country's total expenditures on final products — goods and services ready for consumption — could be the measure of its 'national product'. Three years later the League of Nations was already producing estimates of the national product of 26 countries.

My neighbour's *milpa* does not contribute to Mexico's GNP. In order to include it, economists would have to imagine a fictitious market situation in which Don Bartolo sells his corn at the low autumn price — when Mexican corn is abundant — and then buys it again from his own granary at the going price during the dry season. But officials prefer to devise policies which really do force peasants to sell their corn cheap after the harvest and then buy imported corn from the government's supplies later in the year. And both these operations then appear in the GNP. When such policies do not drive peasants off the land — as probably will happen with Don Bartolo — Mexican corn looks more 'productive' in the GNP when it is sold as gourmet food abroad than when eaten locally by the people.

Comparative national income accounting systems developed during the Second World War and spread rapidly afterwards. In 1947, an International Association for Research in Income and Wealth was founded, and by 1953, the Association had devised a uniform System of National Accounts and Supporting Tables (SNA) which became the standard procedure for the calculation of the GNP — a nation's annual output of goods and services valued at current market prices.[18]

This concept of GNP expresses the belief that the world is one big marketplace in which nations compete for rank and economic respectability. Considered as a norm of behaviour, productivity has become the new anthropological condition of each person's legitimacy. The GNP expands that condition to become a nation-wide scale. Thanks to the magic of numbers, experts can now view even the global economy as a game in which a country's GNP is its score.

Of Light and Shadow

Don Bartolo, who produces high quality maize for his own family, is, indeed, an anachronism. Economists say that a subsistence mode of living is long dead. I am fascinated by my neighbour; he forces me to ask questions. I see that his *milpa*, from seed to table, entails the alternation of masculine and feminine domains, the intertwining of hard labour and festive celebration, the mysterious intermingling of husbandry and nature — all these complementarities essentially belonging one to another. Their existence and complexity place the 'production' of corn within a cosmology where nature is not reduced to resources but respected in *its* autonomy. And, as every sky in every place is a different sky, so each *milpa* calls for a different care, its proper propitiation. No single perspective can be true to the diversity of forms through which nature is induced to bring forth her fruits. Is economics, then, an impoverishment?

Eventually, during this same period — the post-war era — shadows began to appear on the balance sheets. In the production of goods and services, unexpected side-effects began to dampen the universal optimism. People saw that the productive processes themselves polluted the environment. Further, institutionalized help and concern appeared to make clients more needy, more dependent. Then the experts redefined these effects as 'costs' and, when they were not too conspicuous, tried to hide or internalize them. Alternatively, they could be exported to the countries of innocent third parties (like the dumping of toxic waste in the Third World) or included in the price of the product or service.

But the growth of the service sector of the economy manifested a different kind of negative effect that cannot be reduced either to 'pollution' or to an 'external cost'. It became increasingly evident that the very institutions which provided the major services of industrial societies — health, education, transportation and so on — were inherently counter-productive, no matter how modern and up-to-date they were. That is, they tended to achieve the very opposite of the goals for which they were designed. Everybody could experience that, besides producing new social polarizations, schools also rendered their clients stupid; medicine made doctors rich and prestigious, but also generated new varieties and incidences of sickness; transportation not only built freeways, but also piled up horrendous traffic jams and a mounting toll of accidents.

As this counter-productivity spread throughout the productive sectors of society, the suspicion arose that the primary product of the economy — in the philosophical sense of 'prior' — is actually waste. Perhaps the modern economy is essentially a way of organizing reality in a way that actually transforms both nature and people into waste. For modern production to function, the economy must first establish a system in which people become dependent upon goods and services produced for them; and to do this, it must devalue historically determined patterns of subsisting and corrupt cultural webs of meaning. The mass production of modern goods, services and images demands cultural blight through the spread of *disvalue*, that is, the systematic devaluation of the goods found in traditional cultures.

Disvalue, to the extent that the economy is productive, entails a degradation which touches everything and everyone affected by or involved with this modern mode of organizing reality. A person is less a person, the more he or she is immersed in the economy. And less a friend. Less a participant in leisure — that is, in culture. The air is less pure, the wild places fewer, the soil less rich, the water less sparkling.

Of Women and the East

Mexican women know many ways to prepare meals with corn. In October, some cobs are picked while they are still tender, boiled in water and eaten on a wooden stick; these are called *elotes*. The other cobs are left on the stalk to ripen fully, letting the sun dry out the kernels. They are then picked, shelled and put in a mixture of lime and water to soak. Corn softened overnight in this way constitutes what is called *nixtamal*. Ground up in a *metate* — a flat stone with a shallow concave hollow, used as a mortar — the *nixtamal* becomes *masa* — a heavy paste — from which *tortillas* are made. But mature dry corn can also be ground up into a fine powder which, mixed with water, becomes *atole*, the most popular Mexican drink — known in the southern states as *pozol*. In the North, *pozole* is a soup made from corn kernels boiled all day. All these operations take place in the feminine domain of the patio, between the outdoor kitchen and the *milpa*. The *tamales*, *tlaxcales* and *chalupas* sold on Mexican streets by women who are independent pavement traders, are the results of still other ways to prepare corn. What wheat and bread are to Europeans, corn and *tortillas* are to Mexicans — necessary ingredients of all meals.

For some people today, the most evident signs of the character of modern productivity are found in actual and potential eco-catastrophes. A theoretical perspective on these phenomena has been provided by a group of Japanese scientists. The late Professor Tamanoy and his colleagues at the Japanese Entropy Society have suggested that the degradation of natural substances into waste is to industrial production what the flow of heat from higher to lower temperatures is in Carnot's model of the steam engine. The Frenchman, Carnot, around 1830, attempted to describe the economy of heat flow in a steam engine. He showed that, as water naturally runs from a higher to a lower place — thus making a water mill turn — so heat — which he conceived as a substance, the *calorique* — will only flow from a hotter to a cooler 'place', thus making a steam engine run. The Japanese argue that, not unlike Carnot's engine, modern economic production requires a kind of irreversible downhill motion in order to run. This is true since, on the whole, industrially processed material can only flow from the state of a valuable resource to a state of waste. Water which has passed through a millrace can only be pumped back to its source through an expenditure of energy, and industrial waste can only be recycled at the cost of more waste somewhere else.[19]

The balance sheet of economic production can only appear to be positive so long as islands of production are immersed in large spaces which can absorb their waste without visible cost. But the current generalization and intensification of production worldwide makes these spaces ever more scarce. This means that the West's market economies seemed to produce goods more valuable than waste when they were 'lost' in a world of non-market subsistence which could absorb the waste and supply the West with cheap inputs. If economic production were generalized so that everyone's subsistence depended on the market, the balance sheet would be negative. The current economic and ecological crises reveal that there are limits. Economic production cannot grow forever without disrupting and destroying men's livelihood and the biosphere. The Japanese scholars referred to above insist that the limits have already been passed, and that to regain some balance, economic production must be reduced worldwide.

Tamanoy's explanation of the inherent destructiveness of economic production may appear awkward because he took entropy, a concept from thermodynamics, to be the sign of inevitable waste. High entropy means low quality and low entropy the opposite. Carnot's image of a mill powered by a downhill flow of water becomes industrial production fed by a general flow of energy and matter from a state of low to high entropy. As economic production expands, nature is less able to cope with the high entropy. It is not simply waste, therefore, but the necessary embodiment of a principle of destruction which feeds economic production and causes its ultimate nemesis.

Tamanoy and his colleagues show that economic production can be described in two completely different ways. On the screen of economic science, production is a generation of value, essentially an abstract concept materialized on paper. Economists are interested in the formation of value under the assumption of scarcity, not in the sociogenesis of scarcity. In contrast to this, Tamanoy attempts to get at the very origins of scarcity. He does so by comparing the economic tableau of value production with another tableau where the economy is seen to 'produce' the very opposite of a value, a disvalue. Seen through the eyes of the natural scientist, economic production is an increase in entropy, and this entropy — as a depletion of nature — is the ultimate symbol of scarcity.

Of Nature and History

The *milpa* and economic production are not situated on the same continuum, ranging from small to large. The beauty of the *milpa* is not to be sought in its size. And yet there is something in it which draws me, which attracts me. Don Bartolo's *milpa*, probably disappearing next year because of encroaching urbanization, may be one man's lonely protest against the consumption of tasteless, imported food which is a staple in his diet. Or his *milpa* may be a poor man's construction of a living symbol for a remembered way of life, the annual source of his renewed *enjundia*, the restoration of what is most vital in his being as a *historical* man. What his *milpa* most certainly is not is a field for the abstract action of producing a commodity called food. In the end it is perhaps simply Bartolo's quixotic attempt to make sense of the crazy world in which he has had to grow up.

For four decades, development has been the central concept mediating relationships between the industrialized North and the South. Production was the operational concept of this relationship. By becoming economically productive, the South would develop, indeed, would be transformed. The development era sustained itself with the belief that economic growth generated in the North could help the South to be better off. Further, southern elites enthusiastically embraced the idea of production, since it still retained some of its romantic connotations. When an African or Latin American leader spoke of the development of his country's productive forces, he imagined the realization of its destiny, its emergence as an actor on the world scene.

We now know, however, that it is necessary to look at both production and its shadow, disvalue. Industrial production requires, it seems, as its necessary condition, a principle of irreversible degradation. But this principle is not the outcome of some inexorable law of nature; rather, of historically identifiable processes. These processes are the progressive denial of traditions favouring subsistence, denial of the human condition as culturally determined. Disvalue, which makes industrial production possible, is also the historical root of the modern ecological catastrophes.

References

1. Harry S. Truman, Inaugural Address, January 20, 1949, in *Documents on American Foreign Relations*, Connecticut: Princeton University Press, 1967, pp. 103, 104.

2. F. Kaulbach, 'Produktion, Produktivität', first part in Joachim Ritter and Karlfried Gründer, *Historisches Wörterbuch der Philosophie*, Basel: Schwabe & Co., 1989, Vol. 7, p. 1419ff.

3. 'And by imprudence mixt, Produce prodigious Births of bodie or mind. Such were these Giants, men of high renown', John Milton, *Paradise Lost*, Book XI, pp. 680–85.

4. See Volker Hentschel, 'Produktion, Produktivität' in Otto Brunner et al. (eds.), *Geschichtliche Grundbegriffe*, Stuttgart: Klett-Cotta, 1984, Vol. 5, S. 1–26.

5. Productivity was for them a force of nature which existed independent of man and could embody itself in the genius. See Kaulbach, op. cit.

6. See Kaulbach, op. cit., p. 1421.

7. J. W. Goethe, *Dichtung und Wahrheit*, IV, 16 (WA I, 29, p. 16 or Inselausgabe p. 487).

8. Daniel Defoe, *Giving Alms no Charity, And Employing the Poor: A Grievance to the Nation, Being an Essay Upon this Great Question*, London: 1704 (Republished in J. R. McCulloch, ed., *Select Collection of Scarce and Valuable Economical Tracts*, London: 1859; the book also contains Townsend's 'Dissertation on the Poor Laws' and Burke's 'Thoughts and Details on Scarcity'.

9. See F. Quesnay, *Analyse du Tableau*, Paris: 1766. For a critique of the Physiocrats by Adam Smith, see Adam Smith, *The Wealth of Nations*, London: 1776, Book 4, Ch. IX.

10. E. B. de Condillac, *Le Commerce et le Gouvernement* in *Oeuvres Complètes*, Paris: 1921–22, Vol. 4, p. 59.

11. Adam Smith, op. cit., Book 5, Ch. II.

12. Ibid., Book 2, Ch. III.

13. David Ricardo, *On the Principles of Political Economy and Taxation*, London: 1817, Ch. 1.

14. V. Hentschel, op. cit., p. 17.

15. Karl Marx & Friedrich Engels, *Die deutsche Ideologie* (1845–46), MEW, Vol. 3 (1958), p. 21.

16. Karl Marx, *Grundrisse: Foundations of the Critique of Political Economy*, London: 1973 (1844), p. 534.

17. Wolfgang Schivelbusch, *The Railroad Journey: Trains and Travel in the 19th Century*, Oxford, Basil Blackwell, 1980 (1978), p. 46.

18. *The New Encyclopaedia Britannica*, 15th edition, London: 1986, Vol. 20, p. 207.

19. Yoshiro Tamanoy, Atsushi Tsuchida Takeshi Murota, 'Towards an entropy theory of economy and ecology' in *Economie appliquee*, 37, 1984, p. 279.

Bibliography

The story of the concept of production may be summed up as a progressive transition from a sense of emanation or actualization to the promethean meaning of man-made creation which it acquired in modern times. F. Kaulbach, 'Produktion, Produktivität', in Joachim Ritter and Karlfried Gründer (ed.), *Historisches Wörterbuch der Philosophie*, Basel: Schwabe and Co., 1989, Vol. 7, p. 1419ff., gives a fresco-like picture of that transition from antiquity to modernity; insists that the modern economic meaning of the term builds, since the late 18th century, on an already — but recently — constituted promethean meaning. Volker Hentschel, 'Produktion, Produktivität', in Otto Brunner et al. (ed.), *Geschichtliche Grundbegriffe*, Stuttgart: Klett-Cotta, 1984, Vol. 5, pp. 1–26, divides the history of the concept into a 'pre-theoretical' and a 'theoretical' era; and stresses the importance of a previously constituted juridical meaning for the emergence of the term as a technical one in economics.

For the progressive translation of 'production' into a technical term of economic parlance, the following authors' contributions constitute decisive steps: François Quesnay, *Analyse du Tableau*, Paris: 1766, establishes the term's economic meaning, but still reserves it for the works of nature: land and labour on the land are for him the sources of production. E. B. de Condillac, 'Le Commerce et le Gouvernement', *Oeuvres Complètes*, Paris: 1921–22, Vol. 4, p. 59, is apparently the first author to put the work of a craftsman on a footing of equality with nature's production. Adam Smith, *The Wealth of Nations*, London: 1776, Book 5, Ch. II and Book 4, Ch. IX, where he criticizes Quesnay and the Physiocrats, makes 'labour' the source of production. David Ricardo, *On the Principles of Political Economy and Taxation*, London: 1817, disengages 'production' from the consideration of concrete activities, a step that can be compared with Liebig's theory of agriculture, in which chemicals, and no longer the actual earth, nurture the plants. For a collection of early economic pamphlets, including Defoe's, see J. R. McCulloch (ed.), *Select Collection of Scarce and Valuable Economical Tracts*, London: 1859.

H. Immler, *Natur in der ökonomischen Theorie*, Opladen: Kiepenheuer, 1985, points out how, in the perception of classical economists, nature has been submerged by human labour power as the primary source of value. J. Burkhardt, 'Das Verhaltensleitbild "Produktivität" und seine historisch-anthropologischen Voraussetzungen' in *Saeculum*, 25, 1974, pp. 277–305, emphasizes that 'productive' could become a dominant value only after man was thought to be capable of continuously increasing more wealth through time. W. Schivelbusch, *The Railroad Journey: Trains and Travel in the 19th Century*, Oxford: Blackwell, 1980, builds on Marx's insight that it is transportation which transforms goods into commodities, illustrating the part played by the railroad.

H. W. Arndt, *The Rise and Fall of Economic Growth: A Study in Contemporary Thought*, Chicago: University of Chicago Press, 1984, traces the emergence of 'growth', as a policy objective, while *The New Encyclopedia Britannica*, 15th edition, London: 1986, Vol. 20, p. 207, gives a concise history of the concept 'Gross National Product', showing the steps by which the competitive comparison between nations helped generalize the concept of production. S. Gudeman, *Economics as Culture: Models and Metaphors of Livelihood*, London: Routledge, 1986, illustrates how different cosmologies shape the meaning of production, and D. Groh, 'How Subsistence Economies Work', in *Development*, No. 3, 1986, describes the rationale for the so-called underproductivity of pre-modern economies. For a powerful historical treatise on the meaning of work in Western thought, see H. Arendt, *The Human Condition*, Chicago: University of Chicago Press, 1957.

Ivan Illich, *Medical Nemesis*, New York: Random House, 1976, launched a new reflection on the structural counter-productivity of service-producing agencies and illustrated it with the modern spread of 'iatrogenesis', the effect of the health institutions to produce ill health. Jean-Pierre Dupuy and Jean Robert, *La Trahison de l'Opulence*, Paris: Presses Universitaires de France, 1976, build on Illich's distinction between clinical and symbolic (or paradoxical) counter-productivity and test that conceptual distinction in several realms of the modern service industries, in particular transportation. Another version of counter-productivity can be found in F. Hirsch, *Social Limits to Growth*, London: Routledge, 1978. The concept of disvalue was also introduced by Ivan Illich, 'Disvalue and the social creation of waste', conference paper, Tokyo: Meji University, as an answer to Yoshiro Tamanoi, Atsushi Tsuchida and Takeski Murota, 'Towards an entropic theory of economy and ecology', *Economie Appliquée*, Vol. XXXVII, 1984, No. 2, pp. 279–94.

Progress

José María Sbert

With the rise of the modern world, a distinctly modern faith — faith in progress — arose to make sense of, and give ultimate meaning to the new notions and institutions that were now dominant. Our deep reverence for science and technology was inextricably linked up with this faith in progress. The universal enforcement of the nation-state was carried out under the banner of progress. And increasing conformity with the rule of economics, and intensified belief in its laws, are still shadows of this enlightened faith.

Though today faith in progress is largely unacknowledged, and probably weaker than at any other time in contemporary history, a definite breakdown in the plausibility of this faith — which many people think has already occurred — would confirm a crucial turning point in modern culture, and one pregnant with threats to the spiritual survival of persons.

The gradual obsolescence of the development ideal and sudden implosion of bureaucratic state socialism certainly represent a reduction in the pre-eminence, as well as concrete manifestations, of faith in progress. For it has been 'development' and 'revolution' which were supposed to actually embody progress during the greater part of the 20th century.

Two Offspring: Revolution and Development

The term 'progress' had suffered heavily in prestige, along with 'civilization', as a result of the two World Wars and the Great Depression. Politicians and experts could no longer brandish it about without some traces of embarrassment, especially in Europe.

But progress retained some messianic force in the Soviet Union and other socialist countries, where communism was thought to be 'establishing on earth peace, labour, liberty, equality, fraternity, and happiness for all nations', as the Soviet Party Programme proclaimed in 1961. North Americans, coming out of the Second World War with little damage and less guilt, still found the word, progress, suitable for describing the achievements of the American way of life, including their own generosity which at the beginning of the 1960s took the form of the aptly-named Alliance for Progress.

In the United States, assassinations at home and accusations of genocide abroad, however, soon poisoned the optimism of the period. The sacred lamp of progress seemed no longer to illuminate the political scene. It then withdrew to purer and more transcendent spheres: to the conquest of space as the culmination of the glorious power of science, and of disease and death — that other infinite realm — as the culmination of technology's redemptive humanism.

In the late 1960s faith in progress was kept smouldering mostly through its Lady Macbeth-like daughter — revolution. Revolution may not have 'killed the sleep' of modern civilization, but it had certainly turned its dreams of progress into recurrent nightmares. From the beginning, the new faith was fanatical enough to justify not only conquests and foreign adventures, but murder, widespread destruction and civil war. Revolution, in line with progress, was also handily sacralized. So from the 19th century onwards, revolution had to be held in check through the promotion of less draconian ideas such as evolution and some early political uses of development.[1]

Revolution as people saw it in the 1960s — perhaps in 1789 as well — was not the ultimate answer to unprecedented despotism or unbearable injustice. Rather, it was the rejection of irrational obstacles to cashing in on the promises of a rational faith. In the 1960s, from both sides — amidst socialist successes and Keynesian prosperity, Marxist messianism and liberal generosity — the hopes of progress appeared ripe and luxuriant, imminent and inevitable, and certainly not to be senselessly surrendered.

For the *contestataire* products of the baby boom, there were only two kinds of people — those few screwed up through having achieved progress themselves and the many screwed up by the progress of others. And the claims, even to power, of underprivileged groups — whether majorities or minorities — were acceptable, for a while at least. There was black power, student power and a war on poverty — until, that is, real power felt it had had enough and shrugged off any feelings of guilt and unnecessary scruples and set out to establish the monopoly of money power, abstaining only from street demonstrations flaunting as placards their mink coats and diamond necklaces.[2] For money power did not have to march in the streets to bring back into line — as it did so effectively — the universities, the media, the political parties and governments.

Apparently, there was something faulty in the simple and irrefutable logic of progress. Intellectual fashion moved away from utopian thinking and plunged into the structural complexities of language, the unconscious and the microphysics of power. Progress flew even further away from the scene. Under 'progress', the 1983 edition of the *Columbia Concise Encyclopaedia* states only: See *space exploration*.

But, as an export commodity, the moon was not a satisfactory replacement for progress. The pristine credo of faith in progress had been constantly preached to the Third World. As expressed originally by Condorcet, prior to the depths and refinements added by Hegel, Marx and Comte, such a credo promised:

> The destruction of inequality between nations, the progress of equality within one and the same nation, and finally, the real perfecting of mankind . . . We shall find, from past experience . . . that nature has assigned no limits to our hopes . . . The time is doubtless approaching when we shall cease to play the role of corrupters and tyrants in the eyes of these people (in Africa and Asia) . . . Then will the Europeans respect that independence which they have hitherto violated with such audacity . . . and those thieves' counting houses (established by Europeans) will become colonies of citizens who will propagate, in Africa and in Asia, the principles and the example of freedom, and the reason and learning of Europe.[3]

Integration of progress and national culture in fact followed many different paths throughout the world — among them, the strategy of defensive modernization, first attempted by Peter the Great in Russia and then carried out successfully by the Japanese. But this route was not available to the rest of the world, which had been 'heavily impacted by the Western imperial era'.[4] In most of Asia and Africa, where colonialism lasted only a century or so, Western domination did not entirely submerge the original cultures, while it did effectively transmit to local leaderships a faith in progress 'rendered ambivalent . . . by its very association with Westernization'.

In the Spanish colonies, established in Latin America as early as the 16th century, a very different situation obtained. Indigenous cultures were submerged and, in time, the new local elites adopted the idea of progress without any 'sense of moral ambivalence'. Indeed they 'viewed themselves as culturally European'.[5] The very words that summarized Auguste Comte's ideal, 'order and progress', were written on Brazil's flag and in Mexico they became the slogan of the late 19th century 'liberal dictatorship' that consolidated the nation-state.

By the middle of the 20th century, however, what had been called by Europeans uncivilized, uneducated and backward all over the world had a new name: *underdeveloped*. Apparently, while faith in progress had already created great expectations, the term itself had become somewhat tainted and worn-out by both its imperial and indigenous champions. So the new word 'development' came in handy.

Within this new development scheme of things, the idea of progress remained implicit as a crude dogma, debasing the sublime and fascinating elaborations of its 18th and 19th century philosophers and ideologues. The development discourse was now the work of 'experts'. Their perspective is well expressed by C. E. Ayres in the 1962 Foreword to his 1944 book which is entitled *The Theory of Economic Progress*, but which is already devoted to development:

Since the technological revolution is itself irresistible, the arbitrary authority and irrational values of pre-scientific, pre-industrial cultures are doomed. Three alternatives confront the partisans of tribal values and beliefs. Resistance, if sufficiently effective, though it cannot save the tribal values, can bring on total revolution. Or ineffective resistance may lead to sequestration like that of the American Indians. The only remaining alternative is that of intelligent, voluntary acceptance of the industrial way of life and the values that go with it.

We need make no apology for recommending such a course. Industrial society is the most successful way of life mankind has ever known. Not only do our people eat better, sleep better, live in more comfortable dwellings, get around more and in far greater comfort, and . . . live longer than men have ever done before. In addition to listening to radio and watching television, they read more books, see more pictures, and hear more music than any previous generation or any other people ever has. At the height of the technological revolution we are now living in a golden age of scientific enlightenment and artistic achievement.

For all who achieve economic development, profound cultural change is inevitable. But the rewards are considerable.[6]

What was added later to the premises of development — intelligent and sensitive as they so obviously already were — amounted only to a cosmetic touching up. Nonetheless, in a frequent confusion, critical analysis of development generally reached a point where an unacceptable loss was confronted. To proceed with the critique down to the very core of the concept would have been experienced as the abandonment of faith in progress itself.

With the timely arrival of development, the term 'progress' was subsequently applied only to what the self-designated First World had already achieved and to the infinite potential conquests still to be secured through its economy, science and technology, and not yet available to the rest of the world. The Third World had to develop first — before even thinking about real progress. The term 'development' would be one in a series of words to describe — and rally people to — the ever more elusive path to progress. Only a path, not an arrival — and one, for that matter, that would be proved utterly inadequate.

A Theodicy and an Imperative of Power

But progress is more than just a journey or an ideal. It is modern destiny. To modern man, and to those who want to share his identity, rejecting faith in progress is unbearable. Modern man is defined by progress. His self-esteem is rooted in it and it is his deepest justification for the ruthlessness he displays towards his fellow men and nature.

A portentous faith built on progress is the real spiritual foundation of modern man, the tradition he stands on. The idea has been the most influential and ubiquitous notion in the formation of modern thought, merging the power of the modern world with the spell of a chimerical metamorphosis of Christian faith.

Progress possesses the brightness derived from its close link with the sacred — even when, as here, the sacred is not presented as such. It has the lustre of transcendence. Consequently, it has to be enshrined nowadays in achievements that would seem to confirm that man, the terminator of the gods, is indeed supplanting them through the conquest of the heavens in space and time. But its proper home base on earth remains the First World. There it reveals that man no longer needs a creator, but constantly re-fashions himself.

Progress, whether because it was forced by historical inertia into 'reoccupying positions' established by Christianity — as Hans Blumenberg[7] contends — or because of the advantage obtained from such positions, turned into a quite typical theodicy. Progress explains current phenomena inconsistent with its promise by reference to future perfection. The sufferers will be consoled and the unjust punished, just as in 'the different manifestations of religious messianism, millenarianism, and eschatology'.[8] Progress as theodicy is associated in times of crisis with revolutionary promises and, when these promises are proved hollow by events, the locus of compensation is transposed to remove scientific conquests, quite similar in fact to the kind of other-worldly explanations and realizations characteristic of conservative theodicies.

Down here on earth, however, progress remains the irresistible imperative of power. It is imperative to the powerless in order to enforce their submission, and just as imperative to the powerful because they wish to retain their positions. Progress is felt to be a matter of survival. Who would dare risk turning his back on progress? As Hobbes understood long ago, freedom can only be guaranteed by the capacity to dominate others, and happiness cannot lie in *having* progressed, but in progressing here and now.

Progress is an imperative that outlasts the failure, no matter how recurrent, of particular stratégies. Its model is modified constantly, as well as the path to attain it. But the path will be followed, no matter what the resistance of American Indians, the people of the subcontinent, the Shogun or *mafiosi* politicians. Progress redefines reality through the manifold influence of power. Those who have progressed more, and continue progressing, are stronger and wealthier and inexorably prevail, no matter whether the instrument be missionary and educational institutions, or the East India Company, or Commodore Perry or, equally well, simply the spontaneous and overpowering desire to imitate the rich and the famous.

Virtues into Vices

To disguise inevitable submission and make the new faith accessible, progress has to redefine man, time and the world. It has to present history as following a *vector*, replacing the cyclical conception of time and discarding faith in destiny or providence. It portrays other religions as contemptible schemes for obedience, practised by oligarchical priests who invoke ghosts to humiliate man and who induce him to waste his life on searches far removed from the perfectly feasible construction of a paradise on earth. It offers the world as a *resource* to a unified *humanity* — headed, of course, by those who have already progressed, but open to all races and nations provided they jettison their tribal and traditional bonds which are but the capricious obstacles to universal redemption.

Progress highlighted hope — a vision of a future of plenty, freedom and justice — and excluded, along with beliefs in powers superior to man, the traditional notions of man's limitations. Humility turned from a saintly virtue into a rare heresy. Condemnations of greed, innate to the Christian religion and to all traditional systems of wisdom and philosophy, were transformed into leniency bordering on approval toward such a sin, which is now perceived as the veritable psychological engine of material progress.

So, greed and arrogance in individuals turn into prosperity and justice for nations and all mankind. Such a miraculous feat does not even require the intervention of divine providence. Supra-individual man — the 'humanity' invented by the Christian Church of Imperial Rome and ultimately consecrated by the Enlightenment — is led by an invisible hand, a cunning reason that will do him good even if its members indulge in evil.

Thus, mortal sins contribute to progress and famine, plague, war and death are nothing but small accidents along the road — provided the advancement accumulated in history as a whole is considered. And such accumulated capital, which keeps on growing ever faster, will permit those who fail again and again, and even those who move backwards — always the majority — eventually to obtain a share in the promised land, even if only through their descendants.

The creed of progress bloomed exuberantly as an ideological force and seemed destined to prevail over the decadent spiritual power of established religion in 18th century Europe. A new galaxy of social forces and institutions, led by the capitalist or entrepreneurial class and the modern state — the great binomial of modern political economy — found in religion an obstacle to further advancement. So waving the flags of progress, the new social forces snatched away the banners of religion.

Likewise, progress championed the fight against the moral power of those traditions representing an obstacle to the expansion of the market, industry and the modern state. Once the causes of the wealth of nations had been properly assigned to the novel Western way of subordinating society to the market and technological innovation, the idea of progress provided the new justification for inequality at home and Western self-assertion abroad. It was progress which had permitted Europeans to 'discover' the whole world, and progress which would explain their growing hegemony over the global horizon.

In European history, and in the history made by Europeans worldwide, the new faith in progress may have been a decisive weapon in the conflict between, on the one hand, the modern economy, modern institutions and the *humanity* they sought to create and, on the other, *men and women* deeply rooted in their respective cultures and places. Progress impelled these people to become their own God and make their own history. It ridiculed their old beliefs, fears and superstitions as well as their reverence for nature, the past and their ancestors. It dismissed vernacular gender — the all embracing division of the person's inner and outer worlds into the asymmetrical complementarity of men and women — as irrational, pigheaded and unjust.

Faith in progress is entrusted with stripping the common man — who as yet has not progressed, but has already been cut off from his common land and deprived of his traditional means for autonomous subsistence — of all the cultural footholds that could give him spiritual autonomy and personal confidence as he faces the market, industry and the nation-state. Disembedded from his community and caring only for himself, free from his elders' beliefs and fears, having learned to look down on his parents and knowing he will find no respect in what they could teach him, he and his fellows can only become *workers* for industry, *consumers* for the market, *citizens* for the nation and *humans* for mankind.

Eclipse of Providence and Wisdom

Western faith in progress is rooted in historical experience as much as in the oft cited Judaeo-Christian view of time, history and man's place in the world. What got the modern Europeans hooked on the idea of progress was probably their peculiar history, mostly in the quite poor Northwestern parts of the Continent. Between the fall of the Roman Empire in the West and Scottish prosperity in the time of Adam Smith, lie more than fifteen centuries of advancement, enough to feel that progress is deeply grounded in their experience, and to ride out ups and downs of fortune and to scoff at the greater grandeur of more ancient civilizations.

Plagues and wars at home, and mighty enemies on their boundaries, forged their character to be able to face diversity successfully in a never ending confrontation with all things foreign — beliefs, ideas, weapons, even disease. Fierce competition in the market and constant war on the frontiers contributed to a prodigious rate of technological advancement which eventually made Europeans invincible in every field. As today's fashionable historiography sees it, the arms race combined with the rat race was a mighty formula for the rise of great powers, provided, of course, it was compatible with modern financial wisdom.

Thus, the Western penchant for progress and hegemony has deep roots in historical experience. As Karl Löwith puts it, the big question remains:

> Whether this tremendous sweep of Western activity has anything to do with the non-secular, religious element in it. Is it perhaps Jewish messianism and Christian eschatology, though in their secular transformations, that have developed those appalling energies of creative activity which changed the Christian Occident into a worldwide civilization? It was certainly not a pagan but a Christian culture which brought about this revolution. The ideal of modern science of mastering the forces of nature, and the idea of progress, emerged neither in the classical world nor in the East, but in the West. But what enabled us to remake the world in the image of man? Is it perhaps that the belief in being created in the image of a Creator God, the hope in a future Kingdom of God, and the Christian command to spread the gospel to all the nations for the sake of salvation, have turned into the secular presumption that we have to transform the world into a better world in the image of man and to save unregenerate nations by Westernization and re-education?[9]

In response to his own question, he formulated the influential thesis that:

> The eschatological outlook of the New Testament has opened the perspective toward a future fulfilment — originally beyond, and eventually within, historical existence. In consequence of the Christian consciousness, we have a historical consciousness which is as Christian by derivation as it is non-Christian by consequence.[10]

From this point of view we could add that, ever since the 12th century, technological innovation in both production and learning combined with a process of Church institutionalization which, by providing services and written records, controlled peoples lives, establishing thus the organizational model of the modern state. The secularization of the world that ensued is the actual history of progress, where *transmogrified religious beliefs, rituals and institutions undertook a 'reform' of the world* through major scientific, economic and political breakthroughs.

What the Christian creed demanded was a *spiritual reform of the believer* which, had it become prevalent, would have led to a serious challenge to the worldly passions for riches and power which, for Christians, headed the incarnations of evil. If Christianity in practice contributed to an opposite orientation on the part of Western civilization, we might conclude, with Jacques Ellul, that it was because it was subverted by its own power, and because the radical nature of Christian faith is so intolerable that, for it to become a dominant cultural force, it had to be transformed into its opposite

> since it is really intolerable to think that peace, justice, and an end to poverty cannot take place on earth . . . . However, that is precisely what Jesus himself has said.[11]

But notwithstanding:

> Christ has said: 'Do whatever you can to make this world liveable and share with everybody the joy of salvation, but without any illusions about what you can really achieve.' But that is what man cannot hear or accept. If he acts, he wants his doings to work, to succeed, to progress. He wants to achieve by himself. In that context the word of Christ is actually demobilizing, not deriving from the fact of Christ's truth, but from the realities of man's indigence, his pride and his foolishness![12]
>
> The difficulty arises since we cannot say: 'Indeed, our practice is faulty, but look at the beauty, the purity, the truth of Revelation!' *No Revelation can be known outside the life and testimony of those who carry it* . . . Not being that which Christ demands, we turn all of the Revelation into something mendacious, delusory, ideological, imaginary.[13]

Free from the radical demands of praxis — which is essential to the very meaning of the principle of faith — Christian revelation was turned instead into a philosophical and cultural instrument of the Western world.

And it was precisely in the link with 'praxis' that characterized 'wisdom', that progress, by eclipsing that central notion, was most revolutionary. Instead progress, as the new Polar Star in the firmament of ideas, became closely associated from its beginnings with the splendour of science, that boast of the Moderns over against the knowledge of the Ancients:

> In the tradition of the great books, the moderns usually assert their superiority in all the arts and sciences. They seldom claim superiority in wisdom. The phrase 'modern science' needs no elucidation, but if anyone were to speak of modern wisdom, he would have to explain his meaning. . . . A distinctive mark of wisdom is that it cannot be misused. . . . Rabelais's Gargantua admonishes (his son) in the words of Solomon: 'knowledge without conscience is but the ruin of the soul'.[14]

Besides obliterating the ideas of destiny, fortune and providence, the new star of modernity or progress overshadowed the importance of wisdom as existential, cultural experience. Formerly, the practice of virtue and fidelity to sacred principles embraced and gave meaning to intellectual knowledge, which could only be enriched thereby. But faith in progress is faith in a purely intellectual, mathematical, scientific knowledge 'liberated' of all moral constraint and ethical context.

Doctrines of progress, at first, had a difficult time filling the gap left by the flight of wisdom and providence. Quite differently from wisdom, progress no longer trusted in the individual will to virtue — which had probably already been disheartened by the intolerable demands of Christian praxis. Instead the new doctrines seemed to rest their hope for the moral perfection of humans on the exhaustion of greed through the satiation of appetites, or on some prodigious balancing act of egotistical forces. This last presumed that stasis would be worked out by reason, but of a kind which had no known locus since it rested neither on God's providence, nor individual experience, nor revealed truth, nor moral tradition.

The processes leading to collective good and excellence would be harder to grasp for the devotees of progress than spiritual reform had been, and as inscrutable as providence, despite the efforts of modern thinkers to explain how 'the invisible hand' of the market or 'cunning reason' might automatically attain these ends. Eventually, the job of reason was taken on by the managerial and bureaucratic systems of industrial society. And social reality had to be remodelled to fit the 'laws' of economics and efficient administration.

The subversion of Christianity, well under way in the medieval alliance of feudal and Church power, was thus perfected by a faith in progress that now placed the opportunities it had opened up, its philosophical and cultural synthesis, and its worldview and hopes of the future — so richly nourished for centuries — at the service of the market, industry, the modern state and their agents — the merchants, bankers, princes; politicians, intellectuals, mass leaders; scientists, entrepreneurs and revolutionaries.

In this way the notion of progress came to be used and propagated most patently through the action of the masters of modern history, from Frederick the Great and Queen Victoria to Lenin, Castro and Reagan. It was elaborated and diffused through the writings of brilliant adherents, from Voltaire and Darwin to Sartre, Regis Debray and Vargas Llosa. The register of thinkers which enthusiastically believed in progress is huge and includes the roll of honour of the last three centuries. Indeed, some historians of progress manage to include almost every eminent thinker in history although a distinction tends to be made — most explicitly by Bertrand Russell and Robert Nisbet — between those stressing rationality, freedom and the market — such as Turgot, Hume, Smith, Kant, Mill — and those emphasizing feeling, equality, power and the state — Rousseau, Fichte, Hegel, Marx, Nietzsche.

The roots of the ideological quarrels of the 20th century, however, may be traceable to the fervent hope that all held in common and the related differences about how best to reap the unlimited promises of industrial society. Nevertheless, no matter how great the distinctions or antagonisms among this large majority of modern thinkers may appear, as a group they turn out to be quite homogeneous in their thinking, especially when confronted with the central notions related to the nature of man and history — in contrast to the Ancients and Medievalists. Their worldview is even more radically incompatible with the cultures of those in other parts of the world who have not yet joined industrial society, and the partisans of tribal and indigenous peoples' values and beliefs who question the designs of progress before being ready to bless any further immolation.

Still a Search for the Beyond

Progress is a faith that is not recognized as such, but remains the genuine soul of the modern West and whatever comes to resemble it in the present world. Modern man has to believe that his ideas and actions are entirely grounded in what is rational and not supported by revelation, or a vision, or hope. His very identity has been forged in the conquests of progress, and centred on the conviction that he can know reality through science, thus overcoming obscurantist dogmas.

Nonetheless, trust in progress may in truth pertain to the realm of *faith* in a sense similar to the Christian *assurance of things hoped for* in the beyond. Certainly, faith in progress turns in practice mostly into mere 'false consciousness' — into ethnocentric, class-oriented and self-interested self-deception.

Paradoxically, this unacknowledged faith, this false consciousness — often labelled materialistic or even hedonistic — flagrantly contradicts true attachment to the world. It is a desperate search for transcendence that, again and again, *annihilates the world as it is* and substitutes for any real sense of place, rhythm, duration and culture a world of abstractions, a *non-world* — of homogenous space, linear time, science and money.

Originally, progress was a term referring to place, as in the destination of a journey. Later it came to mean an advancement in time, in vectorial measurable time. And as progress evolved further as a result of the need for calculation in industrial economics, it condemned us to live in a 'worldly' future, to build *there* an always elusive fulfilment 'under the sun' — which turned out to be a quite neurotic over-extension of the reality principle, which was apparently already making modern society feel there was something wrong by the time of Freud.

Just as being in the present lost meaning, so did every defined place — we do not, for example, build on a plot or in some town but instead convert it into 'value': a figure in our heads or some record kept on paper or in a computer. And it is there, and only there, *in an abstract record of values*, that most material progress really is, utterly removed from the truly worldly aim set down in *Ecclesiastes* by Kohelet, the voice of a tribal assembly:

> Eat thy bread with joy, and drink thy wine with a merry heart. . . . Live joyfully with the wife whom thou lovest all the days of the life of thy vanity . . . for that is thy portion in this life.[15]

As for spiritual progress, the accumulation of scientific knowledge and technical achievement seems to ignore its own meaning and direction and is prone to be misused. It is detached from the flesh, the heart and the soul. Man, therefore, cannot be any wiser today, since the knowledge he so massively acquires cannot be integrated into either culture or the person.

What is more, progress can rarely be enjoyed during the lifetime of a person; rather it is mostly to be hoped for, for his descendants. For the believer in progress falls into a sort of inverted Confucianism — a cult of the descendants, not the ancestors. And now this faith in progress faces a traumatic nemesis. For the glory of sacrifice for the sake of a better world for future generations is in danger of turning into its opposite — fear of not bequeathing them anything but a shambles, and the guilt that goes with that tragic anticipation.

The Bourgeois and His Feedback

Perhaps it was these sorts of paradoxes that inspired Paul Valéry to write: 'The bourgeois has invested his funds in ghosts and gambles with the ruin of common sense.'[16] And today, we would have to add with the ruin of the biosphere, the new mother Goddess of our eco-computers. Gaia, the suffering planet, must halt the 'strategy of the progress culture' because its 'basic values act as a great complex of positive feedback forces' that are 'self-amplifying, like a fire burning out of control'.[17]

With this new systems management mentality, faith in progress may turn out to be fighting its last round in history. Myriads of 'side-effects', mutually reinforcing each other in their devastating power, are creating serious doubts about the feasibility of spreading further the Western style throughout the world. Besides, those who run world models on their computers are repeatedly led to the discovery that programmed progress turns out to be less efficient than the 'cultural strategy' of the bees, or, when it comes to environmental adaptation, far less 'developed' than, say, that of the Australian aborigines. Thus, nobody admits any more to ever having believed in utopia. Some even see the future as a time where nothing but incalculable catastrophies loom. The time-arrow, the axis of faith in progress, is in the process of shifting its angle: if anything, it now points downward.

Avoidance of outright planetary disaster may soon top the global agenda. This very different prospect calls for a different conceptualization — hence the resort to systems language which best expresses man's current preoccupation with stability. For it directs attention away from highflying hopes to the nitty-gritty conditions of systems maintenance here and now. 'Feedback cycles' show on the computer screen the hideous workings of 'side-effects', forcing their official recognition by governments, while the search for the conditions of 'equilibrium' aims at identifying the break points. In terms of this perspective, the affairs of people are not at the centre of politics any more, which instead has become preoccupied by the abstract requirements of systems maintenance as defined by the new experts in survival. As for the idea of progress, it will have come a long way and may in the end mean simply avoiding the worst.

Progress was an illusion; but a great illusion. It contained much more than anyone had ever dared to dream — justice, and even immortality on earth, achieved by man himself. As the vital and creative self-assertion responding to the previous overriding emphasis on divine omnipotence',[18] progress was a great path of achievement. Facing both fears of eternal damnation and feelings of impotence in the utter contingency of his existence in the world — both ideas hammered into him by theological absolutism — modern man managed to gain confidence by way of self-realization, a confidence finally felt as the all-powerful free seeker after perfection. Progress was still a dream of persons, not of bees.

Sadly, the utopian ethos of progress lost its chance to come to terms with reality. It became overwhelmed by the undiscerning forces of economics and technology, or led along the political road to totalitarian straitjackets. Along with utopia, progress shed most of the layers that had sculpted its tragic beauty and conceptual richness, and fled instead into the realms of science fiction. Today it merely shields the blind conceit of the post-modern world from serious critical thought and any doubts about sense and meaning. Reduced to the childish fantasies of scientists — pervertedly polymorphous indeed — faith in progress is nothing today but a fortress of contemporary folly which wards off our multiple fears of annihilation from modern weaponry, economic growth and cultural indigence. It has shrunk to a foolish confidence that the predicaments of modern civilization will be solved through a psychotic delirium of abstractions and technological creations which have been given a life of their own.

The new wisdom of systems theory, now taking charge of reconciling the biosphere and the economy in some impossible balance — having one's cake and eating it — has to accept the humiliating assumption that man is just one among many forms of life. What greater vanity and vexation of the spirit? The harder it is for man to recognize that what he has placed under the sun has not made him much better, the harder it is for him to recognize his basic reality, an always tragic reality. And it is only human, too human, to try to change or forget this reality, as Solomon himself admits:

> And I gave my heart to seek and search out by wisdom concerning all things that are done under heaven . . . So I was great and increased more than all that were before me in Jerusalem.[19]

But Solomon did not conclude that his kind could become omnipotent. Modern man, having ventured so deeply into that delusion, finds it ever more difficult to accept his frailty, to live in *this* world and to search for his truth. Jacques Ellul sums it up in a quote from George Bernanos:

> In order to be ready to hope for what will not deceive, we must first despair of all that already deceives.[20]

There may be much more involved in despairing about progress than we have glimpsed in this essay. As I have suggested, faith in progress has been built into modern man to such an extent that he is not aware of it any more, like a fish is not aware of the water till drawn out of it. And, like fish out of water, we may eventually realize the importance of our faith in progress only after emerging from it — at the point of again dying in awe as persons or — in a world of systems maintenance — at the point of turning into just another 'life' managed by abstract systems moving towards some 'steady state'.

References

1. Wolfgang Wieland, 'Entwicklung, Evolution', in Otto Brunner, Werner Conze, Reinhart Koselleck, (eds.), *Geschichtliche Grundbegriffe: Historisches Lexicon zur politisch–sozialen Sprache in Deutschland*, Volume 2, Stuttgart: Klett-Cotta, 1975, pp. 199–228.

2. As in a cartoon by Quino, the Argentinian creator of Mafalda, the *contestataire* replica of Peanuts. In *'A mi no me grite'*, Buenos Aires: Siglo XXI, 1972.

3. Condorcet, 'An historical picture of the progress of the human mind', in *The Idea of Progress: A Collection of Readings*, selected by F. J. Teggart, Berkeley and L.A.: University of California Press, 1949, pp. 337–8.

4. Crawford Young, 'Ideas of progress in the Third World', in Almond, Chodorow and Pearce, eds., *Progress and its Discontents*, Berkeley: University of California Press, 1982, p. 90.

5. Ibid., p. 88.

6. C. E. Ayres, *The Theory of Economic Progress: A study of the fundamentals of economic development and cultural change*, New York: Schocken Books, 1962, pp. xxiv–xxv.

7. Hans Blumenberg, *The Legitimacy of the Modern Age*, Cambridge, Mass.: MIT Press, 1986, Part I, *Chapter 3*.

8. Peter L. Berger, *The Social Reality of Religion*, London: Faber and Faber, 1967, p. 68.

9. Karl Löwith, *Meaning in History: The theological implications of the philosophy of history*, Chicago: University of Chicago Press, 1949, pp. 202–3.

10. Ibid., p. 197.

11. J. Ellul, *La Subversion du Christianisme*, Paris: Editions du Seuil, 1984, p. 201.

12. Ibid., p. 201.

13. Ibid., p. 13.

14. *'Wisdom'*, in *The Britannica Great Books: A Syntopicon*, Chicago: 1952, pp. 1102–3.

15. *Ecclesiastes*, King James' Version. Chapter 9 (7 & 9).

16. 'Le bourgeois a placé ses fonds dans les phantasmes et spécule sur la ruine du sens commun' in 'Propos sur le progrès', 1929, collected in *Regards sur le monde actuel*, Paris: Gallimard, Col. folio-essais, 1988, p. 142.

17. Bernard James, *The Death of Progress*, New York: Alfred A. Knopf, 1973, p. 10.

18. Robert M. Wallace, translator's introduction to Hans Blumenberg, *The Legitimacy of the Modern Age*, op. cit., p. xviii.

19. *Ecclesiastes*, Chapters 1(3) and 2(9).

20. 'Pour être prêt à espérer en ce qui ne trompe pas, il faut d'abord désespérer de tout ce qui trompe.' In Jacques Ellul, *La Raison d'Être: Méditation sur l'Ecclésiaste*, Paris: Editions du Seuil, 1987.

Bibliography

As a starting point, the historical review by S. Pollard, *The Idea of Progress: History and Society*, New York: Basic Books, 1968, which contains a separate bibliography, and R. Nisbet, *History of the Idea of Progress*, New York: Basic Books, 1980, where the sources are commented on in the text, are the most accessible and useful, as well as the collection of readings by F. J. Teggart, *The Idea of Progress*, Berkeley and L.A.: University of California Press, 1949, and the related article and quotes in *Britannica World Books* which contains also the basic traditional bibliography. To my knowledge, the most recent comprehensive effort on the subject was edited by G. A. Almond, M. Chodorow and R. H. Pearce, *Progress and its Discontents*, Berkeley: University of California Press, 1982. Divided into five parts related to the historical, scientific, economic, social and humanistic dimensions, it covers 25 different themes by as many authors. P. Chaunu, *Histoire, Science Sociale: La Durée. L'Espace et L'Homme à l'Epoque Moderne*, Paris: SEDES, 1974, and G. Duby, *Guerriers et Paysans, VII–XII siècle: Premier Essor de l'Economie Européenne*, Paris: Gallimard, 1973, gave me a rich portrait of the experience of progress in Western Europe, which can be complemented by the strategic outlook of P. Kennedy, *The Rise and Fall of the Great Powers: Economic Change and Military Conflict from 1500 to 2000*, New York: Random House, 1989.

The closest approximation to ancient wisdom in dealing with substantially the same subject — that is, progress — is contained in the Greek literature about Prometheus and in *Ecclesiastes*. J. Ellul devotes an entire book to *Ecclesiastes, La raison d'Etre*, Paris: Edition du Seuil, 1987. E. Bickerman, *Four Strange Books of the Bible*, New York: Schocken Books, 1967, and H. I. Leiman, *Koheleth: Life and Its Meaning*, Jerusalem and New York: Feldheim Publishers, 1980, also approach this biblical book at length. I. Illich, in a call to put hope above expectation, deals with Prometheus and Pandora in the last chapter, 'Rebirth of Epimethean Man', of *Deschooling Society*, New York: Harper and Row, 1970. Illich's books, among their innumerable facets, prompt a continuous meditation on the concept of progress.

The key book on Christianity, secularization and progress is K. Löwith, *Meaning in History*, Chicago: University of Chicago Press, 1949. W. W. Wagar, 'Modern Views of the Origins of the Idea of Progress', *Journal of History of Ideas*, Vol. 28, 1967, pp. 55–70, gives a panoramic view of various authors on the subject of secularization, among them the less pessimistic outlook of J. Maritain's books. Ch. Dawson, *Progress and Religion*, New York: Doubleday, 1960, rather celebrates the worldly orientation of Western civilization as fully consistent with its Judaeo-Christian religious heritage. The rich outlook and fine thread that G. B. Ladner, *The Idea of Reform: Its Impact in Christian Thought and Action in the Age of the Fathers*, Cambridge: Harvard University Press, 1959, started to weave is regrettably cut short at an early historical period. H. Blumenberg, *The Legitimacy of the Modern Age*, Cambridge, Mass.: MIT Press, 1983, does not succeed in upsetting Löwith's thesis, but glances deeply into the soul of the modern age at its intellectual starting point. E. Castelli, *Hermeneutique de la Secularisation: Actes du colloque organisé par le Centre International d'Etudes Humanistes et par l'Institut d'Etudes Philosophiques de Rome*, Paris: Aubier, 1976, contains rich and abundant material, including a paper by J. Ellul, whose books constitute a wide-ranging and up-to-date critique of modern progress by a Christian theologian.

Among the classical sociologists, a reflection on progress demands, especially, a review of Weber's work, and of those who followed him as well as his critics.

Resources

Vandana Shiva

'Resource' originally implied life. Its root is the Latin verb, *surgere*, which evoked the image of a spring that continually rises from the ground. Like a spring, a 're-source' rises again and again, even if it has repeatedly been used and consumed. The concept thus highlighted nature's power of self-regeneration and called attention to her prodigious creativity. Moreover, it implied an ancient idea about the relationship between humans and nature — that the earth bestows gifts on humans who, in turn, are well advised to show diligence in order not to suffocate her generosity. In early modern times, 'resource' therefore suggested reciprocity along with regeneration.

Gifts, Inputs and Substitutes

With the advent of industrialism and colonialism, however, a conceptual break occurred. 'Natural resources' became those parts of nature which were required as inputs for industrial production and colonial trade. John Yeates in his *Natural History of Commerce* offered in 1870 the first definition of the new meaning: 'In speaking of the natural resources of any country, we refer to the ore in the mine, the stone unquarried, the timber unfelled (etc.).'[1] In this view, nature has been clearly stripped of her creative power; she has turned into a container for raw materials waiting to be transformed into inputs for commodity production. Resources are now merely 'any material or conditions existing in nature which may be capable of economic exploitation.'[2] With the capacity of regeneration gone, the attitude of reciprocity has also lost its ground: it is now simply human inventiveness and industry which impart value to nature. For natural resources require to be 'developed'. Only once capital and technology have been brought in, will nature find her destiny. From now on, it will become common sense that: 'natural resources cannot develop themselves; it is only through the application of human knowledge and skill that anything can be made of them, and most of the necessary work requires skill of a very high order.'[3]

Nature, whose real nature it is to rise again, was transformed by this originally Western worldview into dead and manipulable matter. Its capacity to renew and grow had been denied. It had become dependent on people. The development of people was thus essential for the development of nature. This was particularly true for nature and the colonies. Before industrialism and colonialism, nature and society had evolved. Colonial policy, which ensured capital and raw material flows for the empire, aimed at 'developing' natural resources in a planned manner, to facilitate the generation of revenues and growth of capital.

This created a new dualism between nature and humans. Since nature needed to be 'developed' by humans, people had also to be developed from their primitive, backward states of embeddedness in nature. Nature's transformation into natural resources needed to go hand in hand with the transformation of culturally diverse people into 'skilled human resources'. As the UN report on Science and Technology for Development states: 'The development of human resources must go hand in hand with that of natural resources.'[4] The white man's 'civilizing' burden was thus an essential part of developing natural resources, and making them available for commercial exploitation. The relationship of people to nature was transformed, from one based on responsibility, restraint, and reciprocity to one based on unrestrained exploitation.

In every case, the exploitation of nature in the colonies appears to have taken place in two phases. In the first phase, when nature's wealth was considered abundant and freely available, 'resources' were exploited rapaciously. They were not husbanded. In the second phase, once exploitation had created degradation and scarcity, the 'management' of 'natural resources' became important in order to maintain continued supplies of raw material for commerce and industry. So, first land was turned into a resource, then forests and water, and now with the onward march of technology, it is the turn of seeds to be converted into what are called today 'genetic resources.'

'Management of natural resources' has therefore been a managerial fix for resource scarcity resulting from the uncontrolled destruction of nature.

The first decades of the post-colonial, post-war period were characterized by silence about resources. Nature seemed to have gone into oblivion, probably under the spell of the technological euphoria of the post-war period, in which technology was viewed as offering a miracle of limitless abundance through the *substitution* of plentiful materials for scarce ones. The replacement of silk, wool and cotton by synthetic fibres, and organic manures by chemical fertilizers, seemed to free society from the limited availability of land and its produce, and appeared to make available unlimited reserves of substitutes.

This period of post-war recovery in the North also coincided with the need to invest surplus capital in the Third World. Successive 'development decades' saw the emergence of development as the overriding reason for the transformation of Third World societies and their natural wealth. Development was equated with economic growth and the rise of per capita incomes. The material inputs needed for this process seemed to be in abundant supply — the scarcity was of capital and technology. Aid and technological transfer, therefore, became the mobilizing forces for the early years of planned development. There was a euphoria about capital and technology having self-regenerative powers. Growth was seen as being able to create an end to scarcity, and an end to the struggle for survival.

In the 1970s, however, a new scarcity of non-renewable natural resources was perceived as a result of rising oil prices. The arguments created by the 'limits to growth' debate brought back concern about natural resources in the development discourse. However, since the debate had merely been based on the alleged distinction between exhaustible and renewable resources, and had focused exclusively on the non-renewable (i.e. exhaustible) resources, economists were very rapidly able to shift the discussion of natural resource scarcity into issues around substitutability. 'Even suppose we are running out of some resoures, can we not substitute others?' they asked. 'New investment is a substitute for a currently partly depleted stock such as coal,' they proclaimed. 'Maintaining high levels of consumption can be sustained provided current investment equals the value of current depletion of the finite homogeneous stock.'

Money and investment had completely replaced the life processes of nature in the economists' equations and debates about scarcity. Gone was the ancient wisdom that had gently cautioned that money is ontologically not convertible into life, a truth captured graphically in the native American saying that: 'Only when you have felled the last tree, caught the last fish and polluted the last river, will you realize that you can't eat money.'

The theology of the market, and the belief in technological miracles, allowed modern economists like Robert Solow to argue that: 'The ancient concern about the depletion of natural resources no longer rests on any firm theoretical basis.' Solow was even awarded the Nobel Prize for Economics for stating that production and growth can completely do away with the notion of exhaustible natural resources and that resource exhaustion is not a problem As he put it:

If it is very easy to substitute other factors for natural resources, then there is, in principle, no problem. The world can, in effect, get along without natural resources, so exhaustion is just an event, not a catastrophe.[5]

The great scarcity debate generated in the 1970s was thus economized, so to speak, through the promise of a technological fix for scarcity. However, this optimism faded almost at once. The next decade saw the 'ecologizing' of the scarcity discourse, with the growing awareness that the development process and its unrestrained appetite for destruction and consumption of resources was not merely depleting non-renewable stocks but was also transforming renewable resources into non-renewable ones as a result of ecological disruption. The self-renewing capacity of the forests, the atmosphere, the oceans, the soils and rivers had been severely impaired. The attempt at removing nature's limits by means of technological growth, which had characterized the previous 40 years of the development era, was now precipitating an ecological crisis. It was this violation of nature's limits that then brought forth the most recent phase in the ever-changing development recipe — the notions of 'sustainable development' and 'sustainable growth'. New limits are now to be *imposed* on nature's processes in order to sustain development and growth. The crisis of scarcity is now being formulated in the language of sustainability.

The different connotations of the word 'resources' express changing attitudes to nature. All these modern connotations, however, have in common the desacralization of nature and destruction of the commons.

Desacralization of Nature

Francis Bacon (1562–1626) has been called the father of modern science, the originator of the concept of the modern research institute, and of industrial sciences as a source of economic and political power. His contribution to modern science and its organization is critical.

In Bacon's experimental method, there was a fundamental dichotomizing between male and female, mind and matter, objective and subjective, the rational and the emotional. His was not a 'neutral', 'objective', 'scientific' method. Rather it was a peculiarly masculine mode of aggression against nature and domination over women and non-Western cultures. The severe testing of hypotheses through controlled manipulations of nature, and the necessity of such manipulations if experiments are to be repeatable, were formulated by Bacon in clearly sexist metaphors. Both nature and the process of scientific inquiry appear conceptualized in ways modelled on rape and torture — on man's most violent and misogynous relationships with women. And this modelling was advanced as a reason to value science. According to Bacon, 'the nature of things betrays itself more readily under the vexations of art than in its natural freedom.'[6] The discipline of scientific knowledge, and the mechanical inventions it leads to, do not 'merely exert a gentle guidance over nature's course; they have the power to conquer and subdue her, to shake her to her foundations.'[7]

In *Temporis Partus Masculus*, or 'The Masculine Birth of Time', translated by Farrington in 1951, Bacon promised to create 'a blessed race of heroes and supermen' who would dominate both nature and society. The title is interpreted by Farrington as suggesting a shift from the older science, represented as female, passive and weak, to a new masculine science of the scientific revolution which Bacon saw himself as heralding. In New Atlantis, Bacon's Bensalem was administered from Solomon's House, a scientific research institute from which male scientists ruled over and made decisions for society, and decided which secrets should be revealed and which remain the private property of the institute.

Science-dominated society has evolved very much in the pattern of Bacon's Bensalem, with nature being transformed and mutilated in modern Solomon's Houses — the corporate labs of today and university research programmes they sponsor. With the new biotechnologies, Bacon's vision of controlling reproduction for the sake of production is also being realized, while the Green Revolution and the Bio-Revolution have already created what in New Atlantis was only a utopia. For Bacon, nature was no longer Mother Nature, but a female nature, conquered by an aggressive masculine mind. As Carolyn Merchant points out, this transformation of nature from a living, nurturing mother to inert, dead and manipulable matter was eminently suited to the exploitation imperative inherent in nascent capitalism. The old nurturing earth image acted as a cultural constraint on the new exploitation of nature. 'One does not readily slay a mother, dig her entrails or mutilate her body.'[8] But the mastery and domination images created by the Baconian programme and the scientific revolution that followed removed all restraint and functioned in fact as cultural sanctions for the denudation of nature and her conversion into a 'resource'.

The removal of animistic, organic assumptions about the cosmos constituted the death of nature — the most far-reaching effect of the scientific revolution. Because nature was now viewed as a system of dead, inert particles moved by external, rather than inherent forces, the mechanical framework itself could legitimate the manipulation of nature. Moreover, as a conceptual framework, the mechanical order had associated with it a framework of values based on power, fully compatible with the directions taken by commercial capitalism.[9]

In contrast to the knowledge system created through the scientific revolution, ecological ways of knowing nature are necessarily participatory. Nature herself is the experiment and ordinary people are the scientists, as sylviculturalists, agriculturists and water experts. Their knowledge is ecological and plural, reflecting both the diversity of natural ecosystems and the diversity in cultures that nature-based living gives rise to. Throughout the world, the colonization of diverse peoples was, at its root, a forced subjugation of ecological concepts of nature, and of the earth as the repository of all forms, latencies and powers of creation, the ground and cause of the world. The symbolism of *Terra Mater*, the earth in the form of the Great Mother, creative and protective, has been a shared but diverse symbol across space and time, and ecology movements in the West today are inspired in large part by the recovery of the concept of Gaia, the earth goddess.

Destruction of the Commons

Parallel to the destruction of nature as something sacred was the process of the destruction of nature as commons — i.e. something all have access to and responsibility for. The destruction of the commons was essential for the creation of natural resources as a supply of raw materials for industry. A life support base can be shared; it cannot be owned as private property or exploited for private profit. The commons, therefore, had to be privatized, and people's sustenance base in the commons had to be appropriated for feeding the engine of industrial progress and capital accumulation.

The commons, which the Crown in England had called wastelands, were not really waste. They were productive lands, providing extensive common pastures for the animals of established peasant communities, timber and stone for building, reeds for thatch and baskets, wood for fuel, wild animals and birds, fish and fowl, berries and nuts for food. These areas supported large numbers of small peasants by means of these common rights. And these areas received the poorer and landless peasants who migrated from the overcrowded open field villages of the corn-growing districts.

But at the same time these wastes and unimproved commons were 'the richest seams of untouched wealth that a landlord could hope to find on his estate in the 17th century', apart from minerals.[10] By clearing trees, draining marshes, fertilizing barren soils and enclosing the ground thereby improved in this way, and parcelling it out into large farms for lease at competitive rents, the lords of the manor could tap great new wealth. This process would benefit not only the landlords, but also those who could afford to lease the 'new' land. But it would be at the expense of the landless peasant, and the medium and smaller peasants, who would be impoverished by the loss of some of their pasture and common rights on which the viability of their little farms so often depended. Also losing out would be the cottagers, labourers and industrial workers who would be deprived of the resources that kept them from being entirely dependent on wages or poor relief. So there developed a head-on clash between the lords of the manor and the main body of the peasantry in many parts of the country over their respective rights and shares in the unimproved commons and wastes. This conflict was to decide whether the landlords and big farmers or the mass of the peasantry were to control and develop these lands. This was the central agrarian issue of the 1630s and 1640s and of the English Revolution.

The enclosure movement was the watershed which transformed people's relationship both to nature and one another. It replaced the customary rights of people to use the remaining commons by laws of private property. The Latin root of the word 'private', interestingly enough, means 'to deprive'.

The fate of the forests was similar to the pastures. The Crown possessed the forests, while the peasants had customary rights to some kinds of forest produce. With the resource demands of capitalist growth, however, the king adopted a policy of deforestation. The peasants lost their rights, and the Crown and the lords of the manor enclosed their deforested land and parcelled it out into large farms for lease at economic rents. This policy of deforestation and the enclosure of the forest commons led to 'perhaps the largest single outbreak of popular discontent in the 35 years which preceded the start of the Civil War.'[11] In the period 1628 to 1631, large crowds attacked and broke down the enclosures and entire regions of England were in a state of rebellion.

The policy of deforestation and enclosure of the commons was later replicated in the colonies. In India, the first Indian Forest Act was passed in 1865 by the Supreme Legislative Council, which authorized the government to declare forests and wastelands (*benap* or unmeasured lands) as reserved forests. The introduction of this legislation marked the beginning of what is called today the 'scientific management' of forests. It amounted basically to the formalization of the erosion both of the forests and of the rights of local people to forest produce.

Breaking Nature's Limits

The treatment of nature as a resource which acquires value only in exploitation for economic growth has been central to the project of development. It is also central to the development crisis. Philosophically, the desacralization of nature entailed the violation of nature's integrity by violating the limits which had to be maintained for the resurgence and renewal of nature's life. In the relationship of an ecological culture with resurgent nature, limits are recognized as inviolable and human action has to be *restrained* accordingly. This relationship is primarily ethical.

In complete contrast is the relationship of an industrial culture with a 'natural resource'. Here limits are viewed simply as constraints to be removed.

All ethical aspects of relating to nature are destroyed and the relationship is reduced to merely commercial concerns. Yet this Baconian triumph over natural conditions is the reason for nature's regenerative capacities being impaired. As the limits of nature's renewability are violated, and its ability to 'rise again' is damaged, so real scarcity is generated — forests disappear, rivers dry up, soils lose fertility, water, soil and air are polluted. Most environmental problems which are described as 'natural disasters' are not in fact works of nature but were created as a result of scientists and planners overstepping boundaries in order to create limitless growth and limitless consumption.

However, this much vaunted possibility of limitless growth does not take place in practice because the conditions of sustainability have been violated. New limits are now faced by the development process itself, and more seriously, survival itself is threatened, especially of the poor. New poverty is created, and this growing poverty itself becomes evidence of the development crisis. To see it involves, first, a recognition that the categories of productivity and growth, which have been taken to be positive, progressive and universal, are in reality politically, spatially and temporally restricted in character. When viewed from the point of view of nature's productivity and growth, and people's production of sustenance, they are actually found to be ecologically destructive and a source of class, cultural and gender inequality.

It is no accident that the modern, efficient and productive technologies created within the context of growth in market economic terms are associated with heavy ecological costs. The resource- and energy-intensive production processes they give rise to demand ever increasing withdrawals from the ecosystem. These withdrawals disrupt essential ecological processes and convert renewable systems into non-renewable 'resources'. A forest, for example, provides inexhaustible supplies of biomass in different forms over time, if its diversity is maintained and used to satisfy a variety of needs. The heavy and uncontrolled demand for industrial and commercial timber, however, requires the continuous overfelling of natural trees, which destroys the regenerative capacity of the forest ecosystem, and eventually converts the renewable forests into a non-renewable resource. As a result, new scarcities are created of water, fodder, fuel and food.

Sometimes the damage to nature's intrinsic regenerative capacity is impaired not by over-exploitation of a particular resource but, indirectly, by damage caused to other related natural resources through ecological processes. Thus the excessive overfelling of trees in the catchment areas of streams and rivers destroys not only forests but also renewable supplies of water, through hydrological destabilization.

Resource-intensive industries disrupt essential ecological processes not only by their excessive demands for raw materials, but also their excessive creation of waste which leads to the pollution of air and water and soil. Often such destruction is caused by the raw material demands of luxury consumption.

In spite of severe ecological crises, the dominant modern paradigm of viewing nature as a resource continues to operate because, for the North and for the elites of the South, the destruction remains largely hidden. For they have become more affluent through the privatization of nature's commons, and through their affluence, they have been able to create protective barriers between themselves and an impoverished nature and impoverished peoples. The ecological costs of the economic processes consequently still remain largely invisible to them.

Since the scientific and industrial revolution, technology and economics have mutually reinforced the assumption that nature's limits must be broken for the creation of abundance. Agriculture provides an illustrative example, however, of how breaking away from limits has led to a breakdown of ecological and social systems. For centuries, agricultural societies have been based on working in accordance with nature's limits for the renewability of plant life and soil fertility. Natural processes of the renewal of plants and fertility of the land were, however, considered a hurdle by modern Western man, a constraint which had to be removed. Industrially produced fertilizer and scientifically engineered seed strains were considered superior substitutes for nature's fertility and seed. Yet these inventions rapidly transformed renewable soil fertility and plant life into a non-renewable resource. Soil and seeds were used as raw material and inputs for the Green Revolution and industrial agriculture. The result was to create waterlogged or salinized wastelands, and pest and disease infested crops.

The ultimate step in converting nature into a resource is the conversion of seed — the source from which plant life rises again — into a 'genetic resource', a commodity to be genetically engineered, patented and owned for corporate profit. Nature's ways of renewing plants are now viewed as primitive and slow. Limits put by nature on the reproduction of life by species barriers are now to be crossed by the engineering of transgenic life-forms whose impact on the biosphere and life cannot be known or imagined.

The scientific revolution was to have rolled back the boundaries of ignorance. Instead, a particular knowledge tradition, one which views nature only as a resource and nature's limits as constraints, has created unprecedented man-made ignorance, and ignorance which is becoming a new source of threat to life on this planet.

Undermining of Sustenance

The transmutation of nature into a resource goes hand in hand with alienating the ancient rights of people to nature as a source of sustenance. When forests, land, water or plants are 'developed' or 'scientifically managed' in order to supply industrial inputs, they are appropriated from communities whose lives and livelihoods they have supported for centuries.

The dispossession of the local people of their rights, their resources and their knowledge has, however, not gone unchallenged. Forest struggles have been taking place throughout the world for over two centuries to resist the colonization of the people's forests for the supply of commercial and industrial timber.

In India the access and rights of the people to forests were first severely encroached upon with the introduction of the Forest Acts of 1878 and 1927. The following years witnessed the spread of forest satyagrahas (non-violent struggles) throughout India, as a protest against the reservation of forests for exclusive exploitation by British commercial interests and their concomitant transformation from a common resource into a commodity. Villagers ceremonially removed forest products from the reserved forests to assert their right to satisfy their basic needs. The forest satyagrahas were especially successful in regions where survival of the local populations was intimately linked with access to the forests, as in the Himalayas, the Western Ghats and the Central Indian hills. These non-violence protests were systematically crushed by the British. In Central India, Gond tribals were gunned down for participating in the protests and in 1930 dozens of unarmed villagers were killed and hundreds injured in Tilari village, in Tehri Garhwal, when they had gathered to protest against the Forest Laws of the local rulers. After enormous loss of life, the satyagrahas were successful in reviving some of the traditional rights of the village communities to various forest products.

The forest policy of post-colonial India continued, however, on the colonial path of commercialization and reductionism, and with its continued people's resistance to a denial of their basic needs as a result of both alienation of their rights and ecological degradation. In the mountain regions of the Himalayas, the women of Garhwal started to protect their forests from commercial exploitation, even at the cost of their lives, by starting the famous Chipko movement, embracing the living trees as their protectors. Beginning in the early 1970s in the Garhwal region of Uttar Pradesh, the methodology and philosophy of Chipko has now spread to Himachal Pradesh in the north, Karnataka in the south, Rajasthan in the west, Orissa in the east and the Central Indian highlands.

The Penans of Borneo are one of the last of the hunting and gathering tribes left in the world's tropical forests. For centuries, the Penan have lived in and with Borneo's forests — in Sarawak in Malaysia and in Kalimantan in Indonesia. Wild sago (*u'ud*) has been their staple food, along with fish and game. Everything they need comes from the forest. Today, their survival is threatened because the forests which give them life, which are the dwelling place of their gods and ancestors, have been made into sources of commercial tropical timber and foreign exchange. Loggers from across the world have been attracted to the dipterocarps of these Asian forests — the red merantis, shorea and the yellow and white anisopetra. Eighty per cent of the tropical hardwoods traded globally now come from Malaysia and Indonesia where the biological diversity of the forests is reflected in the cultural diversity of the forest peoples. If the destruction caused by logging continues at current rates, the natural forests of the region will be exhausted by the end of this decade. And the destruction of the forests means the annihilation of the peoples of the forest.

In March 1987, the Penan along with the Kelabit and Kayan decided to fight back — peacefully. They formed human barricades across logging tracks in a bid to stop the destruction of their forest homelands by the timber companies. By June they had set up 12 blockade sites along a 150 km. length of road in Sarawak's timber-rich northern districts of Limbang and Baram, and they have since continued their struggle against commercial logging.

Traditional economies based on principles of providing sustenance with a stable ecology have shared with industrially advanced, affluent economies the ability to utilize nature to satisfy basic vital needs of food, clothing and shelter. But the former differ from the latter in two essential ways. First, the same needs are satisfied in industrial societies through much longer technological chains requiring higher energy and resource inputs and greater creation of waste and pollution, while at the same time excluding large numbers of people lacking purchasing power and access to means of sustenance. Second, affluence and overproduction generates pressure to create new and wholly artificial needs, and hence the impulse for over-consumption, which in turn requires an even greater exploitation of natural resources. Traditional economies are not 'advanced' in terms of wasteful consumption, but as far as the satisfaction of basic and vital needs is concerned, they are often what Marshall Sahlins has called 'the original affluent society'. The needs of the Amazonian tribes are more than satisfied by the rich rainforest; their poverty begins with its destruction. The story is the same for the Gonds of Bastar in India or the Penans of Sarawak.

The paradox and crisis of development arises from the mistaken identification of the culturally perceived poverty of earth-centred economies with the real material deprivation that occurs in market-centred economies, and the mistaken identification of the growth of commodity production with providing better human sustenance for all. In actual fact, there is less water, less fertile soil, less genetic wealth as a result of the development process. Since this natural wealth is the basis of nature's economy and the people's survival economy, its scarcity is impoverishing people in an unprecedented manner. The new impoverishment lies in the fact that nature, which always did support their survival, is being exploited by the market economy from which the people are themselves excluded and displaced as control of man-made capital over nature and people's lives expands through the process of development.

The dominant ideology of post-war development has been exclusively concerned with the conversion of nature into a resource and the use of natural resources for commodity production and capital accumulation. It ignores the ecological processes that have been regenerating nature outside the domain of human activity. It also ignores the requirements of the huge numbers of people whose needs are not being satisfied through market mechanisms. The ignorance or neglect of these two vital economies of nature's processes and people's survival has been the reason why development has posed such a threat of ecological destruction and a threat to human survival, both of which have, however, remained the 'hidden negative externalities' of the development process.

Modern economics and its concepts of development span a negligible portion of the history of human interaction with nature. Principles of sustenance have given human societies the material basis of survival over countless centuries by deriving livelihoods directly from nature through self-provisioning mechanisms. Limits in nature have been respected, and have guided the limits of human consumption. In most Third World countries large numbers of people continue to derive their sustenance in the survival economy which remains invisible to market-oriented development. And, in any case, *all* people in *all* societies depend on nature's economy for survival. The market economy is not the primary one in terms of the maintenance of life. When sustenance is the organizing principle of society's relationship with nature, nature exists as a commons. It only becomes a resource when profits and capital accumulation become the organizing principles and create an imperative for the exploitation of resources for the market. Yet without a clean atmosphere and clean water, fertile soils and crop and plant genetic diversity, human survival is not possible. These common resources have been destroyed by economic development. This, in turn, has created a new contradiction between the economy of natural processes and people's survival economy, since those pushed out by development are forced to survive on an increasingly eroded nature.

Limits of Nature — Limits to Development

Limits are not unidirectional. They work reciprocally between nature and society. Recognition of the limits of nature implies limits on society, and notions that no limits are necessary in society imply a breakdown of limits in nature. Either nature's limits are respected, and human activity is limited within ecological bounds, or nature's limits are disregarded and violated in order to exploit nature for society's limitless greed and consumption. 'Development' of natural resources has basically involved a breaking down of nature's limits in order to meet the unlimited demands of a market that sees limitless expansion as essential for profit.

In the market economy, the organizing principle for relating to nature is the maximization of profits and capital accumulation. Nature and human needs are managed through market mechanisms. The ideology of development is in large part based on a vision of bringing all of nature's products into the market economy as raw materials for commodity production. When these resources are already being used by nature to maintain her renewability and by people for providing sustenance and livelihood, their diversion to the market economy generates a condition of scarcity for ecological stability and creates new forms of poverty for people.

The organizing principle of economic development based on capital accumulation and economic growth renders valueless all properties and processes of nature and society that are not priced in the market and are not inputs to commodity production. This premise very frequently generates economic development programmes that divert or destroy nature and people's base for survival. While the diversion of resources, like diversion of land from multipurpose community forests to monoculture plantations of industrial tree species, or diversion of water from production of staple food crops and provision of drinking water to cash crops, are viewed by the modernizers and businessmen as 'development' in the context of the market economy, they actually lead to a shrinkage in nature's space and people's space. The endless growth of markets and production processes at the cost of nature's stability is at the root of the crisis of sustainability. Sustainability demands that markets and production processes be reshaped in line with nature's logic of returns, not the logic of profits, capital accumulation and returns on investment. 'Development' must be restrained by limits set by nature on economy.

There is, however, another — and dangerous — meaning being given to sustainability. This meaning refers to sustaining not nature, but development itself. Sustainability in this context does not involve recognition of the limits of nature and the necessity of adhering to them. Instead it simply means ensuring the continued supply of raw materials for industrial production, the ongoing flow of ever more commodities, the indefinite accumulation of capital — and all this to be achieved by setting arbitrary limits *on* nature. Thus the dangerous original shift in the meaning of 'resources' is now being reproduced in an equally disastrous shift in the meaning of 'sustainability'. The original concept refers to nature's capacity to support life. Sustainability in nature implies maintaining the integrity of nature's processes, cycles and rhythms. It involves the recognition that the crisis of sustainability is a crisis rooted in neglecting nature's needs and processes and impairing nature's capacity 'to rise again'. In a finite, ecologically interconnected and entropy-bound world, nature's limits need to be *respected*; they cannot be *set* by the whims and conveniences of capital and market forces, no matter how clever the technologies summoned to their aid.

References

1. *Oxford English Dictionary*, Second Edition.
2. Joseph Meeker, 'Misused Resources', *Resurgence*, No. 125, December 1987.
3. Science and Technology for Development, *Report on the United Nations Conference on the Application of Science and Technology for the Benefit of Less Developed Areas, Vol. II: Natural Resources*, New York: United Nations, 1963, p. 18.
4. Ibid.
5. Robert Solow, quoted in Narendra Singh, 'Robert Solow's Growth Hickonomics', *Economic and Political Weekly*, Vol. XXII, No. 45, November 7, 1987.
6. F. H. Anderson (ed., *Francis Bacon: The New Organon and Related Writings*, Indianapolis: Bobbs-Merrill, 1960, p. 25.
7. Quoted in Evelyn F. Keller, *Reflections on Gender and Science*, New Haven: Yale University Press, 1985, pp. 38–9.
8. Carolyn Merchant, *The Death of Nature: Women, Ecology and the Scientific Revolution*, New York: Harper and Row, 1980, p. 182.
9. Ibid., p. 193.
10. Brian Manning, *The English People and English Revolution*, Harmondsworth: Penguin Books, 1976, p. 133.
11. Ibid., p. 134.

Bibliography

The Chipko movement was my first exposure to alternative worldviews that do not see nature merely as a resource but as a living system with self-generating capacity and its own integrity. The spoken words of village women were most significant for insights, but there were also little pieces of 'grey' literature which provided inspiration, like R. Tagore, *Tapovan* (Hindi), Tikamgarh: Gandhi Bhavan, undated; S. Behn, 'From Revolt to Construction', in *Uttar Ke*

Shikharo Mein Chetna Ke Ankur (Hindi), New Delhi: Himalaya Seva Sangh, 1975; or her 'Blueprint for the Survival of the Hills', supplement to *Himalaya: Man and Nature*, New Delhi: Himalaya Seva Sangh, 1980. I have drawn together my experience and research in V. Shiva, *Staying Alive: Women, Ecology, and Development*, London: Zed Books, 1989.

An introduction to the economist's reasoning about resources can be found in 'Exhaustible Resources', *New Palgrave Dictionary of Economics*, Vol. 1, New York: Macmillan, 1987. K. Tribe, *Land, Labour and Economic Discourse*, London: Routledge, 1976, explored how, in the 18th century, the economic perception of land and other resources was formed, while E. Wrigley, *People, Cities and Wealth: The Transformation of Traditional Society*, Oxford: Blackwell, 1987, explains how the shift from vegetative and animal resources to fossil resources has shaped the thinking of classical economists. The conversion of commons into commodities, in the course of the enclosure movement in England, has been analysed by B. Manning, *The English People and the English Revolution*, Middlesex: Penguin, 1976.

Resource use by foreign powers and socio-economic subordination of indigenous peoples went hand in hand during the history of colonialism. E. Wolf, *Europe and the People Without History*, Berkeley: University of California Press, 1982, offers a wide-ranging synthesis of this transformation. Moreover, colonialism also changed the face of nature itself. A. Crosby, *Ecological Imperialism: The Biological Expansion of Europe, 900–1900*, Cambridge: Cambridge University Press, 1986, documents the shifts in flora and fauna caused by European intrusion. R. Tucker, 'The Depletion of India's Forests under British Imperialism: Planters, Foresters, and Peasants in Assam and Kerala' and T. Weiskel, 'Toward an Archaeology of Colonialism: Elements in the Ecological Transformation of the Ivory Coast', both in D. Worster (ed.), *The Ends of the Earth*, Cambridge: Cambridge University Press, 1988, pp. 118–40 and 141–71, and S. Bunker, *Underdeveloping the Amazon: Extraction, Unequal Exchange and the Failure of the Modern State*, Chicago: University of Chicago Press, 1988, describe typical examples of colonial forest exploitation. About the role wood has played in the history of civilization, see J. Perlin, *A Forest Journey*, New York: Norton, 1989.

The change in the image of nature from a living organism to raw material has been powerfully traced by women writers like C. Merchant, *The Death of Nature: Women, Ecology and the Scientific Revolution*, New York: Harper & Row, 1980; S. Griffin, *Women and Nature*, London: The Women's Press, 1984; and C. Von Werlhof, 'Concept of Nature and Society in Capitalism', in M. Mies et al., *Women: The Last Colony*, London: Zed Books, 1988. With regard to the position of Third World women in the international division of labour, see M. Mies, *Patriarchy and Accumulation on a World Scale*, London: Zed Books, 1986.

Science

Claude Alvares

I was born into a culture that continues to exercise greater influence and power over behaviour than modern science does, or will ever do. If *that* were properly understood, then this obituary would not appear either scandalous or scurrilous. Every culture enjoins on its members respect for certain entities. Modern science does not find a place in *our* pantheon.

Far from it. From this side of Suez, in fact, modern science appears akin to an imported brand of toothpaste. It contains elaborate promises and much sweetness and glamour. It can be used, is often used (many times pointlessly), yet can be dispensed with at any time precisely because it is still largely irrelevant to *life*.

Toothpaste has become a significant universal commodity: for some, it has even evolved into a category of mind. For decades now, it has remained (with the toothbrush) an essential adjunct of modern civilization, available from Managua to Manila. Those who have ingratiated themselves with modernity are prone to find any absence of toothpaste (either for themselves or for others) a source of acute anxiety.

In *our* society, however, the moment we find toothpaste unavailable, we return to neem sticks, or cashew or mango leaves, or mixtures composed of ginger, charcoal and salt. All excellent, locally available and dependable materials for keeping the mouth fresh and disinfected and the teeth clean.

Now modern science is a universal commodity too, also distinctly recognizable from Managua to Manila, also approved by many whose devotion to its tenets and its propagation is more often than not related to its ability to provide a high living wage and, often, in addition, power, prestige and a chauffeur-driven car. Like the early morning toothbrush, science is considered a precondition for a freshly minted worldview uncontaminated by unlearned or unemancipated perceptions. For its part, it offers to flush out the many disabling superstitions from all those hidden crevices of a society's soul, to eliminate any and every offending bacteria, to produce a clean and ordered world. Most important, it promises a materialist paradise for the world's unprivileged through its awesome, magical powers. But not for any reason difficult to understand, it also continues to require as big an advertising budget as toothpaste. There is something about modernity's leading prestige product that is actually so bland it has to be rendered spectacular by sensational copy and a fertile imagination.

Such an irreverent view of modern science will not be comfortable for those who have chosen to remain imprisoned within the dominant present-day perceptions of the age. But for us, it always was *another* culture's product, a recognizably foreign entity. We eventually came to see it as an epoch-specific, ethnic (Western) and culture-specific (culturally *entombed*) project, one that is a politically directed, artifically induced stream of consciousness invading and distorting, and often attempting to take over, the larger, more stable canvas of human perceptions and experience. In a world consisting of dominating and dominated societies, some cultures are bound to be considered more equal than others. This heritage of inequality, inaugurated and cemented during colonialism, has remained still largely intact today. So the culture products of the West, including its science, are able to claim compelling primacy and universal validity only because of their (as we shall see later) congenital relationship with the political throne of global power.

Colonialism, we know, subjects, undermines, subordinates, and then replaces what it eliminates with its own exemplar. It is natural to expect that Western science, an associate of colonial power, would function not any less brazenly and effectively: extending its hegemony by intimidation, propaganda, catechism and political force. In fact, being a culture product, it was only to be expected that it would be associated with the various (mostly aggressive) thrusts of that culture. It would attempt to extend its hegemony to other cultures through an elite class, which social commentators today call 'modernizers', whose distinguishing characteristic, following a period of schooling at Oxbridge, was a thoroughgoing alienation from the life and culture of their own people. And true to its origins, this science has remained in the service of Western culture to this day, a crucial component in the hysterically active hegemony of the West.

However, due to stupendous and unrecognized inner strengths, the cultures on which modern science was sought to be imposed were able to prevent themselves from being fully incorporated. Its inability to deliver the goods and its general incompetence to deal with specific problems have also led to its decline. A global overview today of its actual hegemony would, in fact, be quite distressing to its devotees. In many areas of the non-Western world, it has been reduced to the status of a commodity (like toothpaste) or a gadget (to be purchased with money). Its promise to transform the world into a materialist paradise and thereby put an end to poverty and oppression has lost all credibility. There is evidence indeed to show that it has accomplished just the contrary. As for its offer of a new metaphysical worldview to provide us with ethical guidance, this has also been largely rejected. *Dharma*, conversation, community, interaction with sacred entities and their associated symbols, still remain prime movers within our societies. One even encounters significant desertions from the imperium of science in the very citadels of Western culture.

Thus, the geographical area of its influence has turned out to be far less than was originally desired or attempted. In comparison, other ideas have dominated (and sometimes unsettled) human societies for far longer periods of time. Buddhism, for example, which like Western science had its own theory of causation, was born on Indian soil, from where it was exported to entire civilizations. In societies like Japan, it exercised influence for centuries. It unsettled most South and South East Asian societies with its radically new notions of what a society should be like and of the relationship between the sangha and the state. In comparison with Buddhism, the sway of modern science is impressive, but less pervasive. We should also remember that Buddhism, in contrast to science, was not propagated and imposed by violence.

The actual self-perception of modern science as a recognizably distinct human activity does not go back more than 200 years in Western society. The very term 'scientist' (used as an analogy to the word 'artist') was first suggested by William Whewell as late as 1833 at a meeting of the British Association for the Advancement of Science. It was only used without distaste by its practitioners towards the end of the first quarter of this century.

This is not to deny that the world's citizenry did suffer greatly from the temptations of modern science. It did. Just as it did until recently from the promises of development. But just as one now routinely encounters the 'stink of development', one is also compelled to concede that three centuries of science have raised their own trail of disturbing odours. Not surprisingly, therefore, one discovers that whatever is being said in obituaries about development can equally be said about modern science.

Science and Development: A Congenital Relationship

What has been responsible for the gross influence of science over the imagination of men in our times? One major factor has been the intimate relationship between science and development. They cannot be understood in isolation from each other, as India's policy makers made clear 30 years ago:

> The key to national prosperity, apart from the spirit of the people, lies, in the modern age, in the effective combination of three factors, technology, raw materials and capital, of which the first is perhaps the most important, since the creation and adoption of new scientific techniques can in fact make up for a deficiency in national resources and reduce the demands on capital.[1]

Generally speaking, development was merely modern science's latest associate in the exercise of its political hegemony. Earlier, science had linked itself with enlightenment and millennial claims, before going on to associate itself with racism, sexism, imperialism and colonialism, and then settling down with development, *an idea in which most of these earlier inheritances are encoded*.

If one, in fact, reflects on the events of recent decades, one is indeed reminded that development and science have run through the period, tied together as intimately as a horse and carriage. Development was desired by us non-Western societies precisely because it was associated with science. What obtained prior to development, either in the form of pure nature or non-Western subsistence, did not have, we were told, the rationality, slickness and efficiency of modern science. People, societies, nature itself were backward because of its absence. Planners labelled entire zones 'backward' simply because they lacked factories. (The factory has remained until today a concrete symbol of the new processes developed by science.) Backwardness was to be substituted by development, an allegedly better way of organizing man and nature based on the rich insights of up-to-date science.

Science, in turn, was desired because it made development *possible*. If one developed its associated skills, one could have unlimited development and riches. Science and development both reinforced the need for each other; each legitimized the other in a circular fashion popularly rendered: 'I scratch your back, you scratch mine.'

If development had had no special relationship with science, there would have been no need to displace subsistence and the new standard of living that development proposed.

However, the relationship between modern science and development was much more than merely intimate: it was congenital. This congenital relationship can be traced back to the industrial revolution when a relationship was first established between science *and industry*. This should not unduly surprise the reader. Some of the principal laws of science arose originally out of industrial experience. For instance, the Second Law of Thermodynamics resulted from efforts to improve the working of the steam engine with a view to advancing industry.

The Indian scientist, C. V. Seshadri, in a paper on 'Development and Thermodynamics', has provided some original clues to the historical development of this relationship between industry and science. Seshadri found the Second Law of Thermodynamics, on close scrutiny, *ethnocentric*. He charged that, due to its industrial origins, the Second Law had consistently favoured the definition of energy in a way calculated to further the allocation of resources solely for big industry purposes (as opposed to craft). In a related paper, co-authored with V. Balaji, Seshadri wrote:

> The law of entropy, backed by its authority, provides a criterion for utilization of energy available from various resources. This criterion, known as the concept of efficiency, is a corollary to the law of entropy and came into existence along with the law. The efficiency criterion stipulates that the loss of available energy in a conversion becomes smaller as the temperature at which the conversion is effected is higher above the ambient. Therefore, high temperatures are of high value and so are resources such as petroleum, coal, etc., which can help achieve such temperatures. In this sense, the law of entropy provides a guideline for the extraction of resources and their utilization.[2]

Efficiency, perceived in such terms, came to be the leading criterion for judging technologies and productive work. In the light of modern science, more efficiency of this kind was considered synonymous with more development. Yet, in reality, this central concept of modern science is thus fused with a particular kind of resource utilization.

An economy based on this kind of science not only provides itself with a self-serving criterion with which to legitimize itself, it also assumes thereby that it has a justification for taking over all resources hitherto outside its domain and untouched by modern science. Just as economics invented the idea of scarcity to further its domain, so science assumed the idea of thermodynamic efficiency in order to dislodge competition.

Bias Against Nature and Handicraft

As Seshadri pointed out, both nature and non-Western man proved to be losers when the thermodynamic definition of efficiency became *the* criterion for development. Both, by definition, overnight became undeveloped or underdeveloped. A tropical monsoon, for example, transporting millions of tonnes of water across the tropics became by definition inefficient since it performed work at ambient (and not high) temperatures.

S. N. Nagarajan agrees:

> This is not merely confined to the organic world. Even the evaporation of water, which forms clouds and desalinizes, is not done at 100°C. Life could not have emerged by a process similar to what scientists use, at high temperatures. Scientists are incompetent to construct higher organizations at low temperatures. Tropical agricultural practices were built upon such a kind of knowledge. The two different kinds of approaches have different criteria of efficiency. So the two have a different understanding of development.[3]

And he adds:

> Nature's way is slow, peaceful, non-harmful, non-explosive, non-destructive, both for others and for itself. Take for example, the production of fibre by plants and animals, compared to machines. The end result of plant and machine processes may appear to be the same: fibre and rayon. The machine also produces a large quantity in a short time. But at what cost? The costs are borne by the weaker sections and by nature. The people who are chained to the machine (workers) are also consumed by it.

In fact, all processes or work effected at ambient temperatures are discounted in the suzerainty of modern science. Thus tribals, bamboo workers, honey bees and silkworms all process the resources of the forest at ambient temperatures, and hence without the polluting side-effects of waste heat and effluent associated with big industrial processes. However, in the eyes of development, it is only the high energy input rayon and pulp units that really process the forest resources and contribute to economic growth and production.

Yet modern science still insists: *'The efficiency criterion stipulates that the loss of available energy in a conversion becomes smaller as the temperature at which the conversion is effected is higher above the ambient.'*. By this means, it in fact destabilizes and exorcizes entire industries and livelihoods. A final illustration from the production of various kinds of sugar in India can drive home the point.

India produces different forms of sugar. The most important of these are white sugar and *gur*. According to official opinion, the processes used for the extraction and production of white sugar are superior to those that lead to *gur*. Not only is the extractive efficiency of large mills higher, the product (white sugar) stores well. It can be transported and hoarded, and otherwise abused for reasons of state. The attendant pollution wreaked by sugar mills is acknowledged, but is considered a small price to pay for the benefits of progress.

Gur, on the other hand, is mostly manufactured in open furnaces, using agricultural waste, timber or bagasse. The extraction of sugar cane juice is not as high as in the big industry process. The final product also does not keep well beyond a certain period. However, no pollution results from the production process: neither the earth nor its atmosphere is damaged. And, of course, hoarding and speculation in *gur* is less easy.

From a bare accounting of the two processes, it would seem to be in the public interest for the state to support the replacement of *gur* production with modern sugar mills. *Development is white sugar.* And this is what has occurred in countries like ours in the post-independence period. Credit policy towards farmers in the vicinity of large sugar mills stipulates that if farmers take loans for growing sugar cane from government financial institutions, they are duty bound to sell all their sugar cane only to the large refineries. They may not make *gur* out of it. Special officers of government, designated Sugar Commissioners, actually oversee such development. Indeed, this authoritarianism of development has been upheld by the Supreme Court of India. A farmer was ordered by a Sugar Commissioner to deposit all his sugar cane with a large sugar mill. He refused because he wanted to process it into *gur* instead. The matter went up to the Supreme Court. The Court upheld the orders of the Sugar Commissioner.

A different picture emerges, however, when a closer investigation is made of the *qualities* of the two processes and their end products. We then discover how modern science highlights certain qualities to the exclusion of others and how the blind adoption of its procedures can lead us to emphasize the wrong values. White sugar is dangerous to health for a number of reasons long tested and proven. The bodily processes involved in the metabolism of white sugar end up destabilizing the health of the consumer. In addition, the human body has no physiological requirement for white sugar as such. It is recognized that white sugar is, after all, nothing but empty calories. *Gur*, on the other hand, is a food. It contains not merely sugar, but iron and important vitamins and minerals.

Thus, if the two sugars are compared in the round, *gur* would make a positive contribution to human welfare, whereas white sugar would not. This, however, is not apparent in any comparison of the mere production processes that produce white sugar and *gur*, and in any case the criterion of this comparison resides only in the particular, and biased, terrain of modern science's view of efficient energy conversion. The technology for white sugar production is simply assumed to be more efficient than the technology used in the production of *gur*. Besides, whether it is worth producing a commodity that is harmful to human health and also damages the environment (waste heat and effluents) is not part of the efficiency debate.[4]

Symbolic, nevertheless, of the new status sought for modern science by Third World ruling elites was an international conference on the *Role of Science in the Advancement of New States* held in August 1960, in Israel. At that conference, S. E. Imoke, Minister of Finance for Eastern Nigeria, told his audience:

> We do not ask for the moon nor are we anxious for a trip there with you just yet. All we seek is your guidance, assistance and co-operation in our efforts to gather the treasures of our lands, so that we may rise above the subsistence level to a life more abundant.[5]

Revamping Society

The drive to advance big industry in the West was paralleled by an equally powerful project to reorganize society along scientific (i.e. efficient) lines. August Comte set out the general design. His vision of applying the principles of rationality, empiricism and enlightenment to human society in every detail has already had a pervasive influence on the so-called advanced societies.

A roughly similar Comtean vision received a fresh lease of life with the political independence of Third World nations. Here science (the archetypical instrument) was entrusted with the turn-key role of promising undreamed of standards of material well-being to the so-called poor of the planet.

The most well-known specimen of this innocent worldview was Jawaharlal Nehru, the first Prime Minister of free India. No leader of the Third World was as enamoured of the glamour and promise associated with modern science as Nehru. For him development and science were synonymous. The original Comtean vision is starkly revealed in Nehru's insistence on scientific temper as a *sine qua non* of material advancement. According to him (in his *Discovery of India*), it was science and science alone that 'could solve the problems of hunger and poverty, of insanitation and illiteracy, of superstition and deadening custom and tradition, of vast resources running to waste, of a rich country inhabited by starving people.'

This alarming naivety was passed on by him to the country's leading bureaucrats. India adopted a science policy resolution in March 1958, which read in part:

> The dominating feature of the contemporary world is the intense cultivation of science on a large scale, and its application to meet a country's requirements. It is this which, for the first time in man's history, has given to the common man in countries advanced in science, a standard of living and social and cultural amenities, which were once confined to a very small privileged minority of the population. Science has led to the growth and diffusion of culture to an extent never possible before. It has not only radically altered man's material environment, but, what is of still deeper significance, it has provided new tools of thought and has extended man's mental horizon. It has thus even influenced the basic values of life, and given to civilization a new vitality and a new dynamism.
>
> Science and technology can make up for deficiencies in raw materials by providing substitutes or, indeed, by providing skills which can be exported in return for raw materials. In industrializing a country, a heavy price has to be paid in importing science and technology in the form of plant and machinery, highly paid personnel and technical consultants. An early and large development of science and technology in the country could therefore greatly reduce the drain in capital during the early and critical state of industrialization.
>
> Science has developed at an ever-increasing pace since the beginning of the century so that the gap between the advanced and backward countries has widened more and more. It is only by adopting the most vigorous measures and by putting forward our utmost effort into the development of

science that we can bridge the gap. It is an inherent obligation of a good country like India, with its tradition for scholarship and original thinking and its great cultural heritage, to participate fully in the march of science, which is probably mankind's greatest enterprise today.[6]

Likewise, the authors of the country's First Five Year Plan noted: 'In the planned economy of a country, science must necessarily play a specially important role . . . Planning is science in action, and the scientific method means planning.'

These great 'self-evident truths', however, did not seem so obvious to many ordinary people in the Third World, particularly tribals, peasants and others not yet converted to the Western paradigm. In fact, if the benefits of modern science were not immediately obvious to them, neither did development seem to symbolize a better way of doing routine tasks. On the contrary, development seemed more of a con-game to ordinary folk. To these perspective observers, it actually demanded greater sacrifices, more work, and more boring work, in return for a less secure livelihood. It required the surrender of subsistence (and its related autonomy) in exchange for the dependence and insecurity of wage slavery.

Left to its own, development would have made little headway across the globe. That it did eventually get moving was due purely to the coercive power of the new nation-states which now assumed, in addition to their earlier *controlling* function, a *conducting* function as well. Every nation-state stepped in voluntarily to force development, often with the assistance of police and magistrates. If their citizens were so ignorant that they were unable on their own to recognize the 'benefits of development', the new states would have no option but to 'force them to be free'.

Development became coercion: forced relocations to *ujamaa* villages, compulsory co-operatives, and tying people up in new forms of organization 'for their own good'. Said Abel Alier, Sudan's Southern Regional President, during an Assembly discussion of the controversial Jonglei Canal: 'If we have to drive our people to paradise with sticks, we will do so for their good and the good of those who come after us.'[7] The modern state does not understand, much less accept, the right of people not to be developed.

We must recognize that the state's commitment to development stemmed from its equal commitment to modern science. Science was an ideal choice because it claimed to be able to *remake* reality. It redefined and invented concepts and laws, and thereby remade reality as well. It manufactured new theories about how nature worked, or more important, should work.

Therefore, when the state in the non-Western world assumed the role of developer, desirous of creating a new society and economy, with an entirely new set of temples and all, science naturally became the most attractive and crucial instrument for the purpose. It was Nehru, after all, who called mammoth development projects the 'temples of today'.

Neither people nor nature have been spared as victims of a science-fuelled developmentalism driven on by the state. Today, the remaking of nature has become a major preoccupation of officialized ecology. A classic illustration comes from the approach of scientists to what is called forest development. Foresters are unable to recreate natural forests. But that does not bother them. Instead they redefine forests as plantations, and carry out monocultures under the label of scientific forestry. Nature is thus replaced with a substandard substitute. In reality, the afforestation engineered by modern science becomes the deforestation of nature.

The state claims its right to 'develop' people and nature on the basis of a vision of progress set out in blueprints supplied by modern science, itself a cultural product of the West. The people have no role other than as spectators or cogs in this 'great adventure'. In exchange, they, or some of them at least, are privileged to consume the technological wonders that result from the heady union of development and science. In the eyes of a patronizing state, this is adequate compensation for a surrender of their natural rights. As for those who cannot or will not participate, they must lose their rights. They can be displaced from the resource arena, their resources being transferred instead to big industry.

A Totalitarian Edge

The democratic idea remains the one potential element available to counter these twin oppressions of modernity. For democracies are based on the principle of fundamental human rights. Let us turn to how this potential for checking the totalitarianism of modernity was, however, effectively undermined.

We have probed the congenital links between modern science and development, and the implied bias in science against both nature and handicraft production. We have also discussed how the new nation-states, heavily committed to development, found in this science an attractive instrument for their project of remaking their people in the image of what they believed was an advanced form of man.

Both these features of the modern science/modern state relationship indirectly undermined the natural rights of man. In the first instance, science dismissed all existing processes in nature and traditional technics as inferior or of marginal value, thus enabling big industry (capitalist or statist) to substitute the blueprints supplied by science. Yet in human history, at least up until the scientific and industrial revolutions, the technical knowledge necessary for survival had mostly remained non-centralized and radically dispersed. Literally millions of arts and technologies existed — all using a vast variety of accumulated knowledge and productive of a huge quantum of goods, cultural ideas and symbols stemming from the rich diversity of human experience, and based principally on exploiting processes at ambient temperatures. In many ways, this technical diversity of the human species more or less paralleled the genetic diversity of nature itself.

In the second instance, the very conception of what constituted human normality was itself redefined. People lost the right to claim that they could function as competent human beings unless they underwent the indoctrination required by modernity. It was *a priori* assumed that they were deficient as human beings and had to be remade. As the scientific policy resolution quoted earlier noted: '*India's enormous resources of manpower can only become an asset in the modern world when trained or educated.*' If in the process they emerged as pale caricatures of human beings in more powerful cultures, this was nothing to worry about. Science and its experts would decide how human beings would be brought up, trained, and entertained, and what they should consume.

This is not too difficult for modern science to achieve primarily because it claims to be associated not only with greater efficiency, but also to have greater explanatory power. What is more, it claims its explanatory power to be superior to anything ever achieved before in the human past, because it alone is impartial and therefore objective. Objectivity was also easy to associate with equality and democracy, since neutrality was beneficial to all. (The biases of monarchical forms of administration, for instance, were notorious.) Modern science therefore seemed ideally suited for modern democracies.

By implication, everything 'non-scientific' was devalued as subjective and arbitrary, of marginal value, and could hardly be made the foundation of public policy.

The so-called scientific revolution of the 17th century constituted a watershed in thinking about thinking. The revolution was successful in insinuating a general consensus that, for the first time in human history, human beings had succeeded in unravelling a method of gaining knowledge as certain as the knowledge that earlier had only been available via revealed scripture. This technique of knowledge acquisition was so reliable that the knowledge acquired thereby was for all practical purposes non-negotiable. It was this claim which would soon conflict with the natural rights of man.

The indisputable knowledge that science presumed to offer was kept outside the arena of politics: in no way was it the consequence of bargaining or choice. In fact, one was no longer at liberty to choose scientific knowledge as an option from among other systems of knowledge. Scientific knowledge was a given. No one was any longer free to reject its statements, as one was free (and often encouraged) to reject the statements of religion or art. The individual who refused to accept the basic scientific worldview risked being labelled not merely ignorant, but obscurantist, deviant or irrational.

Two important points here. First, fallible beings, equipped with an equally fallible instrumentality, reason, were now staking a claim to an infallible method of generating and certifying knowledge. Second, rationality itself was being reduced to nothing more than a narrow and biased scientific rationality which has precious little to do with how the human mind actually thinks, although much to do with how some people think the mind ought to think.

We have to acknowledge that, in its drive for power, modern Western science could hardly afford to be diffident about the nature of its claims. It was compelled by its own premises to concentrate and arbitrate all epistemes, and to pretend to do so impersonally. As the need for certification increased, so did modern science become less democratic and access to knowledge itself turned into a matter of privilege and special training. The layman was now seen as an empty receptacle to be filled up with the contents of science. He was to forgo his own knowledge and knowledge-rights.

Another curious paradox here. Scientific reason operated with a logic that was allegedly independent of personal factors or whims. It aimed at the formulation of laws existing independently of persons. Yet its certifiers were persons, often persons who had a vested interest in the power of science, and who were dependent on it for their livelihood. Fallible individuals thus exploited the prestige associated with their discipline to gain a share of political power. The ballot was surreptitiously replaced, increasingly by the new scientific priesthood indoctrinated by its shared assumptions.

This, of course, was diametrically opposed to democratic functioning where rights are unique and universal and belong to individuals primarily because they are members of the species. Such rights include the right to claim true knowledge and the right to reject impersonal knowledge. A right which, in other words, includes the power to certify knowledge. Under the new tyranny of modern science, such rights were first assaulted, then extinguished, and ordinary people were no longer considered as being capable by the fruit of their own activity of providing or obtaining true and certain knowledge of the world. This political right was taken away from all people falling within the ambit of science's dictatorship. In fact, for the ruling classes which felt that human rights had been too early democratized, or unnecessarily so, science now provided an instrument by which they could take back with the one hand what they had earlier been compelled to give away with the other.

Thus planning, science and technology — the technocracy — now became the principal means for usurping the people's rights to the domains of knowledge and production, for dismissing the people's right to create knowledge, and diminishing their right to intervene in matters of public interest or affecting their own subsistence and survival.

The non-negotiability of modern science, the much vaunted objectivity of scientific knowledge, the seeming neutrality of its information, all these seemed positive features to most reasonable and educated men of different religions, values and nations. Rationality, the scientific temper and modern education seemed indisputable and necessary assets to human life.

However, while science itself advanced its knowledge by dissent, by the clash of hypotheses, it summarily dismissed dissent from outside the scientific imperium regarding either its content or its methods and mode of rationality. The non-negotiability of scientific assumptions, methods and knowledge became a powerful myth elaborately constructed over several centuries, fed by a feigned ignorance among its propagandists concerning how it had actually negotiated its rise and apparently unassailable position.

Scientific knowledge — seen as above emotion, caste, community, language, religion, and transnational — became the preferred and primary instrument for transformation not only above the interest of all, but more importantly, enforceable on all. Never, in fact, was there so much agreement among the intellectuals of so many nations, whether liberals, communists, reactionaries, Gandhians, conservatives, or even revolutionaries: all succumbed to the totalitarian temptation of science.

What we have said concerning the power relationship of modern science with other epistemologies is also true of what came to obtain between it and technics. Development based on it came to constitute a dynamic (actively colonizing) power, committed to compromising the survival possibilities and niches of larger and larger masses of people. By and large, it found the people's knowledge competitive and therefore offensive. And since it maintained a contemptuous attitude towards folk science, it also treated people's rights to use resources in their own way with scant respect.

Most important of all, the modern state's interest in such development itself owed much to the latter's constant search for ways and means to compromise, erode, and oftentimes severely diminish, personal autonomy, and the creativity and political freedom that went with it. In a democracy, people can govern themselves, but they can hardly do so if their governments are seriously attempting at the same time to see whether they can be successfully managed and changed.

Once the ordinary people's epistemologic rights were devalued, the state could proceed to use allegedly scientific criteria to supplant such rights with officially sponsored and defined perceptions and needs.

Science's propaganda, that it alone provided a valid description of nature, was turned into a stick with which to beat trans-scientific, or folk-scientific, descriptions of nature. The various 'people's science movements' in India took this job quite seriously, by functioning as an unofficial establishment, gallantly attempting to replace the science of the village sorcerer or *tantrik* with the barbarism of modern science's electric shock treatment or frontal lobotomies.

This expansion of the domain of scientific epistemology involved the most sustained deprivation of others' epistemologic rights. State policy being committed to this one epistemology exclusively, abused or ignored others. In medicine, to take just one example, the bias exercised against Indian systems of healing in favour of imported allopathy needs little documentation.

All imperiums are intolerant and breed violence. The arrogance of science concerning its epistemology led it actively to replace alternatives with its own, superimposing on nature new and artificial processes. Naturally, the exercise provoked endless and endemic violence and suffering as the perceptions of modern science sat clumsily and inappropriately on natural systems. Thus, just as the Europeans eliminated millions of indigenous Indians from North and South America and other indigenous populations elsewhere to make place for their own kind, and just as their medicine uprooted other medicine, and their seeds displaced other seed, so their knowledge project called modern science attempted to ridicule and wipe out all other ways of seeing, doing and having.

Knowledge is power, but power is also knowledge. Power decides what is knowledge and what is not knowledge. Thus modern science actually attempted to suppress even non-competitive, but different ways of interacting with man, nature and the cosmos. It warred to empty the planet of all divergent streams of episteme in order to assert the unrivalled hegemony of its own batch of rules and set of perceptions, the latter being clearly linked with the aggressive thrusts of Western culture.

It is an illusion to think that modern science expanded possibilities for real knowledge. In actual fact, it made knowledge scarce. It over-extended certain frontiers, eliminated or blocked others. Thus it actually narrowed down the possibilities for enriching knowledge available to human experience. It did *appear* to generate a phenomenal information explosion. But information is information, not knowledge. The most that can be said of information is that it is but knowledge in degraded, distorted form. Science should have been critically understood not as an instrument for expanding knowledge, but for colonizing and controlling the direction of knowledge, and consequently human behaviour, within a straight and narrow path conducive to the design of the project.

Is, then, the defeat total? No. The planet has not succumbed to appropriation by modern science everywhere. Indeed the outward symbols of science — agribusiness food, nuclear reactors, gigantic dams — are facing rebellion across the globe. And if those who have tasted the empty fruits of modern science are disillusioned with them, others have refused to taste them at all. Millions of farmers, for instance, reject the modern rice strains manufactured by cereal research centres controlled by agribusiness. Citizens across the planet are rejecting modern allopathic medicine to varying degrees. Millions of ordinary people reject the idea of living by the distorting (and distorted) values associated with modern science.

In a country like India, 40 years of state sponsorship of science and all its works have been unable to bolster its failing reputation. In 1976, the late Prime Minister Mrs Indira Gandhi made the propagation of the scientific temper one of the fundamental duties of Indian citizens, and amended the Constitution accordingly. Despite this there is an even greater sense of crisis among the Indian scientific community, which finds itself every decade more and more out of tune with Indian society's principal preoccupations.

This sense of failure has irreversibly crippled much of the thrust to push India into the straitjacket prepared for it by the project of modern science. The people in non-Western societies do not merely not co-operate with its principal designs, they indicate they do not care a fig for the West and its creations.

In many areas, the non-co-operation has become aggressive. People, groups, villages have openly rejected modernizing development and stubbornly insisted on maintaining their ways of life, their ambient interactions with nature, and the arts of subsistence. The revolt against development is bound to be at another level a revolt against modern science and the violence it symbolizes. This was Mahatma Gandhi's view. It will eventually become the view of those interested in protecting the natural rights of man and nature everywhere.

References

1. Indian Science Policy Resolution, 1958, in W. Morehouse, *Science in India*, Bombay: Popular Prakashan, 1971, p. 138.

2. C. V. Seshadri and V. Balaji, *Towards a New Science of Agriculture*, Madras, MCRC, undated, p. 4.

3. S. N. Nagarajan, in a personal communication to the author dated 7 May 1990.

4. See Claude Alvares, *Science, Development and Violence*, New Delhi: Oxford University Press, forthcoming, for a detailed argument.

5. In Ruth Gruber (ed.), *Science and the New Nations*, London: Andre Deutsch, 1963, p. 34.

6. The entire Science Policy Resolution is to be found in Ward Morehouse, op. cit., pp. 138–40.

7. Quoted in E. Goldsmith and N. Hildyard, *The Social and Environmental Effects of Large Dams*, Wadebridge: Wadebridge Ecological Centre, 1984, p. 18.

Bibliography

Mahatma Gandhi's vigorous attack on the claim of modern science to truth in M. K. Gandhi, 'Hind Swaraj', in *Collected Works of Mahatma Gandhi*, Delhi: Government of India, Vol. 4, pp. 81–208, has been most important to me. A few decades later, a kindred spirit, Lewis Mumford, examined similar trends and pointed to the violence inherent to science in L. Mumford, 'Reflections', in *My Works and Days*, New York: Harcourt B. Jovanovitch, 1979, and, of course, in his *The Myth of the Machine*, New York: Harcourt B. Jovanovitch, 1964. Among the more recent inquiries into the epistemological limitations of science, see for instance P. Feyerabend, *Against Method: Outline of an Anarchistic Theory of Knowledge*, London: Verso, 1975, or K. Hübner, *Critique of Scientific Reason*, Chicago: University of Chicago Press, 1985. It is also worthwhile consulting L. Fleck, *Genesis and Development of a Scientific Fact*, Chicago: University of Chicago Press, 1979, an early essay (written in 1936) on science as a social construction.

The vicious link between science and development has been explored in A. Nandy (ed.), *Science, Hegemony and Violence: A Requiem for Modernity*, New Delhi: Oxford University Press, 1988, and by myself in C. Alvares, *Science, Development and Violence*, New Delhi: Oxford University Press, forthcoming. I found very insightful C. V. Seshadri's seminal work *Development and Thermodynamics*, Madras: Murugappar Chettiar Research Centre, 1986, and also J. P. S. Uberoi, *Science and Culture*, New Delhi: Oxford University Press, 1978. For two case studies in India, see D. Sharma, *India's Nuclear Estate*, New Delhi: Lancers, 1983, and V. Shiva, *The Violence of the Green Revolution: Ecological Degradation and Political Conflict in Punjab*, Penang and London: Third World Network and Zed Books, 1991.

Stunning critiques of science have emerged from gifted practitioners of life husbandry. In the field of agriculture there is M. Fukuoka, *The One Straw Revolution*, Hoshangabad: Friend's Rural Centre, 1985, and in the field of health M. Kothari & L. Mehta, *Cancer: Myths and Realities*, London: Boyars, 1979, and *Death*, London: Boyars, 1986. I. Richards, *Indigenous Agricultural Revolution: Ecology and Food Production in West Africa*, London: Hutchinson, 1985, testifies to the appropriateness of indigenous knowledge of cultivation, while F. Apffel-Marglin, 'Smallpox in Two Systems of Knowledge', in F. Apffel-Marglin & S. Marglin, *Dominating Knowledge*, Oxford: Clarendon, 1990, pp. 102–44, shows the inner cultural logic of a non-scientific way of seeing smallpox. Furthermore, there is obviously a long history of non-Western science. Thanks to the monumental work of J. Needham et al., *Science and Civilization in China*, Vols. 1–7, Cambridge: Cambridge University Press, 1954, rich material on China is available, while Dharmapal, *Indian Science and Technology in the 18th Century*, New Delhi: Impex, 1971, highlights the Indian patrimony of knowledge before colonization. S. Goonatilake, *Aborted Discovery: Science and Creativity in the Third World*, London: Zed Books, 1983, discusses the attempts and difficulties in redefining science from a non-Western perspective.

But no work of academia can be as compelling as human experience. Enmeshed in day to day village cosmology, it was not too long before the scales fell off quickly from my eyes. If one attempts to live close to the peasants or within the bosom of nature, modern science is perceived differently: as vicious, arrogant, politically powerful, wasteful, violent, unmindful of other ways. Life in Thane, a village north-east of the state of Goa, on India's West Coast, and for the past six years in Parra, a more accessible coastal village, provided me with enough education to see through the emperor's new clothes.

Socialism

Harry Cleaver

One of the longest standing critiques of capitalist development has been that of the socialists. From pre-Marxian analyses of the way capitalist development generates extreme poverty and suffering alongside extreme concentrations of wealth, through Marx's dissection of capitalist exploitation and class antagonism, through Luxemburg, Bukharin and Lenin's work on imperialism as the highest stage of capitalism, to more contemporary critiques of dependency, socialists have lambasted the international expansion of capitalist social relations as a process which has brought misery rather than improvements in living conditions for the vast majority of the world's peoples. Rather than 'developing' the Third World, they say, capitalism has 'underdeveloped' it — made things worse than they were when it was still 'undeveloped', i.e. free of the imposition of capitalist class relations.

Yet, at the same time, rather than abandoning the development project, socialists have consistently proposed the adoption of an alternative 'socialist development'. This has been the case primarily since the construction of socialism in the USSR provided a real life alternative to capitalism, and not just a theory. The extremely rapid (by historical standards) industrialization of the USSR, which at the time of the Revolution of 1917 was still an overwhelmingly agrarian society, convinced many of the superiority of socialist over capitalist development, of socialism over capitalism, *tout court*.

This was particularly true in the Third World where anti-colonialism often came to include anti-capitalism and many intellectuals in the independence movements were impressed with Soviet efforts to foster socialist development and began to consider ways such measures might be adapted to their own circumstances. Such intellectuals included both revolutionaries and those who sought more peaceful change. Already, by 1920, Mao Zedong had been drawn to Marxism and the struggle for socialism, in part by the Soviet example. By 1927 Jawaharlal Nehru, returning from the Brussels Congress of Oppressed Nationalities and a visit to Moscow, was ready to proclaim that his goal was socialism, as well as the independence he had hitherto pursued as a disciple of Mahatma Gandhi. In 1936, he enunciated a view of the relationship between socialism and development which would be shared by a generation of leaders throughout the Third World: 'I see no way of ending the poverty, the vast unemployment, the degradation and the subjection of the Indian people except through socialism.'

Elsewhere in the British Empire, similar socialist visions would be repeated, as with Kwame Nkrumah in the Gold Coast (Ghana), Julius Nyerere in Tanganyika (Tanzania), and Eric Williams in Trinidad & Tobago. Against the French Empire, leaders such as Ho Chi Minh in Indochina, Ben Bella in Algeria, Léopold Senghor in Senegal, Modibo Keita in Mali, and Sékou Touré in Guinea, also sought some form of socialism or communism beyond colonialism. Among the many other Third World leaders who turned to various (and often quite different) forms of socialism, we must also mention Fidel Castro and Che Guevara in Cuba, Patrice Lumumba in the Belgian Congo, Amilcar Cabral in Portuguese Guinea, Camilo Torres in Colombia, Muamar Qaddafi in Libya, Michael Manley in Jamaica, Pol Pot in Cambodia, Salvador Allende in Chile, the Sendero Luminoso in Peru, the Sandinistas in Nicaragua and Nelson Mandela in South Africa. The adoption of Soviet-style socialism by China and Cuba after their revolutions, as well as the introduction of such methods into Eastern Europe after World War II, and their apparent success in eliminating the most obvious evils of capitalist development — starvation, dramatic extremes of wealth and poverty, illiteracy — which continued unabated elsewhere, reinforced the case for socialist forms of development.

In short, throughout the four decades since World War II, a contest between capitalist and socialist development has raged in the Third World that paralleled the contest between capitalism in the First World and socialism in the Second. While Americans and the ex-colonial powers of Western Europe pushed their own development strategies under Point Four and other foreign aid programmes, the Soviets (mostly after Stalin's death), the Chinese and to some degree the Cubans sought to extend their development models, partly through the support of various revolutionary movements, partly through their own foreign aid packages. Paralleling Western methods, the socialist countries financed trade and infrastructure development, from dams to roads and agricultural research, built schools and brought thousands of Third World students to the socialist countries for education. Only in the absence of private foreign investment could socialist foreign aid methods be differentiated sharply from those of the West. Within the context of this history, it is not an exaggeration to say that the majority of revolutionary movements in the Third World aimed at overthrowing local institutions of capitalist power have turned to the socialist countries for both help and alternative models of development.

The Popular Revolts of 1989

In the wake of the wave of popular struggles that swept across Eastern Europe in 1989 overthrowing self-proclaimed socialist governments, in the midst of equally widespread popular upheaval in the Soviet Union itself — from the Baltic through the Russian to the Central Asian Republics — it is nevertheless impossible to avoid recognizing that Soviet-style socialism is being torn apart from the inside. In the West, the ideologues of capitalism are trumpeting the death of socialism, the final burial of the God who failed, and the triumph of freedom, democracy and free markets. The Cold War is over, they gleefully proclaim; capitalism has won, socialism has been defeated and history is at an end.

At the same time, socialists and communists throughout the world have clearly been thrown on the defensive. On the one hand, the hard-line opponents of reform, especially in China, where Deng and his friends responded to a similar popular rising by bathing Tiananmen Square in the blood of their children, are condemning the mass movements as reactionary and counter-revolutionary and are proclaiming themselves to be the last bastions of the socialist alternative to capitalism. On the other hand, vast numbers of other socialist and communist opponents of capitalism, who recognize the movements in Eastern Europe as truly popular, are being forced to retrench and rethink.

Indeed, for all of us who struggle for a better world beyond capitalism, whether we call ourselves socialists or not, for all of us who claim to believe in the power of common people to reshape their world, this dramatic upheaval in the socialist world must be the occasion for serious thinking about the issue of socialism as an alternative to capitalism. We may reject the claims of both capitalist ideologues and Communist hardliners as self-serving propaganda, but we can certainly agree that something very significant is happening. Should we read in the actions of the people of Eastern Europe the definitive rejection of socialism by the only people who count — the masses — and therefore, taking their lesson to heart, stop talking about socialism and socialist development as desirable alternatives to capitalism? Or, are the regimes being rejected because they are Stalinist rather than because they are socialist? If that is the case, then what is there left of socialism to hang on to as a guide to thinking about moving beyond capitalism?

There is no better place to begin, therefore, than with a brief examination of just what the people of Eastern Europe and the Soviet Union are rejecting. At first glance, the demands that have been enunciated are such as to warm the hearts of capitalists everywhere. At the top of the agenda has been the destruction of the monopoly power of the Communist Party over not only the formal political process but over all of social and economic life. The cry has reverberated from one end of the Soviet empire to another: 'end the monopoly, lift the heavy hand of the Communist controlled state from our lives!' In Eastern Europe the mass movement has already implemented multiparty political systems and the revolts in the Soviet Republics have forced Gorbachov to accept similar changes in the Soviet Union itself. At the same time, the repressive state apparatus is being dismantled — the secret police disbanded, political prisoners released. Hard on the heels of these dramatic political changes, are emerging intense debates over economic and social policy. Here again the emphasis of the popular reformers has been, so far, on the reduction of state control over the economy and social life in general. In some areas state planning and subsidies are being reduced or eliminated, in other areas restrictive state social policies, such as the Romanian state's attempt to force women to have more children, are being abolished.

On the other hand, it is clearly too soon to see exactly which of the old policies will be retained and what the full range of new policies will look like. Already public discussions throughout the area, such as the heated debates in the new Hungarian parliament, have shown that a great many people there are not interested in giving up many of the benefits of socialism such as guaranteed employment and wages, subsidized housing, free health and child care, or old age pensions. Around such issues the debates have barely begun and will determine much about the future shape not only of East European society but also the Soviet Union.

The existence of such debates gives credence to socialists who are presently maintaining that the popular upheavals have been directed not against socialism *per se* but against its Stalinist perversion. For such socialists emphasize the ideals of equality and social justice which, for them, socialism has always borne within it, as well as the real material benefits even Soviet-style socialism, at least until the recent collapse of its over-centralized and bureaucratic system of economic management, has brought to many. While one approach to deciding what, if anything, is left of socialism that is worth defending and using as a guide to moving beyond capitalism, is to examine the nature of those benefits, and compare them with the alternative set of benefits available within the capitalist world, I would rather, in the context of this essay, examine the other side of the socialist argument.

That is to say, as against Soviet or Chinese style socialism with their characteristic monopoly of power by the Communist Party, other socialists, who often call themselves democratic socialists or social democrats, have long maintained that the essence of socialism has been its humanistic social ideals. As opposed to the capitalist ideology, and practice, of individualistic competition at the levels of persons, firms and nation states, they argue socialism has always, from its earliest formulations, affirmed the centrality of the social context of people's lives, the naturalness of social co-operation and joint social action. As opposed to the capitalist ideology of self-serving egotism and narcissism, socialism has always affirmed that personal development and individual satisfaction could only be achieved through the kind of intimate, non-competitive relationships that only exist in the context of co-operative living. Socialist programmes for the reform of economic and social institutions, therefore, have always been aimed at the creation of a framework within which such co-operation could thrive. The real lesson of the upheavals in the East, I suspect most such socialists will argue, is that, while the Soviet and Chinese approaches failed to create it, such a framework is still a desirable goal and can still provide a theoretical perspective for thinking about moving beyond capitalism.

Against such arguments, the more sophisticated of capitalist critics can raise the charge that, even though the concept of socialism can be separated from the Soviet and Chinese experience, in part because it predates both, nevertheless the concept has always had a totalitarian side to it. That side has derived from the misguided notion that capital accumulation, economic growth and social development can be *planned* more efficiently than they can be regulated by the market. Planning has always meant that there had to be those with the power to plan, and such a concentration of power must, and has always, led to totalitarian government.

Is this true? Has socialism always had this element? Or, as the democratic socialists argue, has such been a perversion of the essence of socialism? These are questions to which we can give at least a tentative answer by taking a look at the history of the concept. What we find, it seems to me, is that while the concept of socialism has certainly mutated repeatedly over time, meaning many different things to many different people at different times, there have indeed been within all of its history two contradictory meanings in struggle with each other. The first is that emphasized by its capitalist critics: a tradition that honours intentional social and economic planning over the automatic adjustments of capitalist markets. The second is that emphasized by the proponents of socialism: a tradition of believing that human beings can indeed co-operate to determine jointly their collective future in ways far superior to that possible under the regime of capitalist exploitation and the markets that have always been associated with it. Let's investigate the history of these two meanings as they have been interwoven in the history of the concept of socialism.

Dreams of Liberation and the Totalitarian Legacy

For a long time the idea of socialism was a dream. It was a dream that first appeared in Western Europe simultaneously with the development of capitalism and its industrial revolution. It was a dream conjured up by those oppressed by the violence and exploitation of capitalist society in their work-a-day lives or by those outraged at their observations of misery and injustice around them. Dissatisfied with the coexistence of outrageous wealth and abject poverty, appalled by the destruction of traditional communities with all their intimate personal bonds and their replacement by individualism and the competitive war of all against all, offended by ugly cities crammed with dark factories and dank dwellings, dismayed by the displacement of craft skills by a crippling division of labour, many workers and social reformers yearned for a better world. A few contented themselves with old dreams of the city of God in which they might find peace after a difficult life of toil. But others crafted new dreams of alternatives which did not yet exist — utopias — but which could perhaps be constructed. Dreamers such as Claude-Henri de Saint-Simon, Charles Fourier, Robert Owen, Etienne Cabet, Wilhelm Weitling and their followers designed new and, they believed, better social structures than the ones around them. These dreams were not only fanciful imaginings, they inspired people to act, to struggle for their realization. What could be dreamed today, might be achieved tomorrow and these men and their followers struggled to transform the world either in large, through reform or revolution, or in small, through the founding of experimental communities.

Such struggles, based on dreams of a better world, predated capitalism but seemed to flourish with its growth. Outrage at the excesses and exploitation based on landed property had helped fuel the English Revolution in the 1640s and the French Revolution in 1789. The Levellers and Diggers in England had fought to turn the world upside down. The *enragés* and *sans-culottes* had overthrown the old order and the Parisian radicals and followers of Babeuf in France had battled under the banner of *égalité* against the counter-revolution in the 1790s. These revolutions, however disappointing their immediate outcomes, left a legacy of radical social imagination that spread and evolved, inspiring discontents to political action throughout the 19th century. During the July Revolution of 1830, the Revolutions of 1848, the Chartist Movement of the late 1830s and 1840s through the formation of the First International in the 1860s to the Paris Commune of 1870, men and women fought and bled for the realization of their dreams even in the midst of the massive historical changes that consolidated the power of capitalism throughout most of the world.

The term *'socialisme'* was apparently first used in 1832 by the Frenchman Pierre Leroux, a disciple of Saint-Simon, in his journal *La Globe*. It was also used in the 1830s by the followers of Robert Owen in England. It appeared in the midst of a swirl of revolutionary and reformist ideas and in that confusion its meaning changed and evolved with the development both of capitalism and of the struggle to get beyond it. From the beginning, however, the concept of socialism shared with that of communism the argument that only through a transformation of fundamental social relations could the evils of poverty and unequal, hierarchical distributions of power and wealth be overcome. From Saint-Simon and Owen onward, socialists condemned the destructive antagonisms and anarchy of free market, competitive capitalism. Even when they accepted the Natural Law tradition which underlay the philosophical justifications of capitalism, they rejected the reasoning of men like Thomas Hobbes and Adam Smith that the unrestrained pursuit of individual self-interest was both natural and would lead to an acceptable social harmony. Their emphasis rather was on the naturalness and possibilities inherent in human co-operation and solidarity at the social level. Despite the experience of capitalist competition, they believed, people could learn to co-operate, to work for each other instead of against each other, to conceive their self-interest more broadly in terms of their community instead of narrowly and egotistically. This is the side of their thought that democratic socialists tend to emphasize.

Yet at the same time, even in the concepts of Saint-Simon and Owen, there was another side to their socialism, the side capitalist critics point to as harbouring the seeds of totalitarianism. Owen, it will be recalled, was himself a capitalist, a reform-minded capitalist to be sure, but a capitalist nevertheless. He was certainly no democrat. His was a socialism-from-above in which the oppressed and irrational masses would need to be educated to new habits by a socialist elite. All of society should be taken care of, he thought, 'as the most advanced physicians govern and treat their patients in the best arranged lunatic hospitals.' And as he sought to achieve the kinds of reforms — the reduction of working hours, improved working conditions, greater co-operation between workers and masters — his followers would call socialism, he turned first and foremost to other capitalists and to the aristocracy in an attempt to convince them that such reforms, if implemented by the state, would make British industry more productive and profitable than ever. Eventually, disheartened by his failure to convince his peers of the wisdom of his views, Owen turned his efforts to the organization of trade unions and co-operatives and eventually to utopian community experiments. Nevertheless, even these activities were shaped by his belief that reforms could be achieved through the use of existing state power and the development of British trade unionism was strongly influenced by this belief.

Saint-Simon's concept of socialism, even more than Owen's, had an elitist bias toward centralized, top-down planning. A noble who had survived the

Revolution, his desire to get rid of the poverty and crises caused by what he saw as the anarchy of capitalist markets, led Count Claude-Henri de Saint-Simon to call for the centralized state regulation of production and distribution. With no faith whatsoever in the wisdom and abilities of common working people, he called for bankers and economic experts to control the allocation of investment and the optimal distribution of the product according to people's needs. No leveller, Saint-Simon would maintain a kind of meritocratic hierarchy as the means of organizing his social society. Not surprisingly, like Owen, he also turned to the existing power elite of politicians, bankers and industrial entrepreneurs with his ideas. Both his plans for socialism and his personal politics would lead some later commentators to see in him an ancestor of 20th century technocracy.

We should note, at this point, that the elitist proclivities of these two founding socialists were not entirely inconsistent with the even more radical communist tradition of the time. The Jacobin insurrectionary heritage of the French Revolution which was preserved in the politics of Babeuf, Buonarroti and Blanqui had the same contradictory tendencies between a humanitarian concern with the elimination of poverty and the privileges of property and a belief in the necessity of a highly centralized and tightly controlled governance of their alternative communist society. Their radical egalitarianism called for equality in the distribution of both property and the enjoyment of material wealth. Babeuf drew on the utopian traditions of the Enlightenment to call for the sharing of goods (mainly tools and land), while Buonarroti and Blanqui carried this tradition well into the period of the capitalist industrial revolution so that their communism came to mean the dispossession of not only the landed rich but also the new industrial bourgeoisie. At the same time, despite their radical egalitarianism, their approach to revolutionary activity and to the governance of post-revolutionary society, should they be successful, was quite explicitly elitist. Their Jacobin heritage was, above all, a politics of the seizure of power. However much they may have fought for the poor, the downtrodden and later the working class, their means was the secret conspiratorial organization of a relatively small group of revolutionaries.

This revolutionary heritage was embraced by Karl Marx and Friedrich Engels and their followers, in their call for the overthrow of capitalism. Their understanding of the possibilities of socialism, based upon an analysis of the antagonistic class forces of capitalism, came some years after their earliest socialist forerunners and was developed within the context of a more mature capitalist development. At least from the time of the *Communist Manifesto* on, they mostly rejected the reformist approach to getting beyond capitalism, be it through legal changes or utopian experiments. For Marx and Engels such changes as could be achieved in this manner — like the Factory Acts in England, or later, representation in parliament — might constitute important steps in the development of working-class organization but could not bring about the complete transformation of the system.

Like their socialist forerunners, however, Marx and Engels elaborated a vision of socialism which, although partial — for they rejected utopian speculation — contained most of the earlier socialist preoccupations with the possibilities of creating a more equal and just society. Their analysis of exploitation and alienation in capitalism led them to believe that the working-class overthrow of capitalism would not only lead to workers' control of production and distribution, but to the overcoming of all the aspects of alienation inherent in the capitalist use of work as its fundamental mechanism of social control. Exactly how this would be done, they did not know. Marx studied the extremely brief experience of the Paris Commune for some glimpse of what the proletariat would actually do when it took power. He especially and repeatedly celebrated its moves toward the abolition of the state and toward real democracy — universal suffrage with representatives revocable at short notice. Also, when he was drawn into a debate in Russia over the applicability of his analysis to the class struggle in that land, he studied the Russian peasant commune and saw it as a possible point of departure for the construction of socialism.

Once workers were in command of the means of production, Marx clearly believed they could transform it so that products would once again be an expression of the workers' will, so that the work process itself could become an interesting activity of self-realization (understood both individually and collectively), so that conflicts among workers which had been so much the basis of capitalist ability to control them would be replaced by a real flowering of self-organized co-operation. At the same time, his understanding of both the role of imposed work in capitalism and the long history of the workers' struggle to reduce it led him to believe that in post-capitalist society free time as the basis for the 'full development of individuality' would replace labour as the source of value in society. Thus, post-capitalist society would most likely be characterized, at least in part, by the open-endedness characteristic of 'disposable time', an expanding sphere of freedom which would allow a multi-sided development of the individual and of society. Some of these ideas have remained highly influential in subsequent socialist thought and constitute much of Marxism's continuing attraction to democratic socialists.

At the same time, it must be said, that the conflict in socialist thought between the desire to foster a new kind of social co-operation and the tendency to have recourse to elitist methods did not disappear with the development of Marxism but only took on greater ambiguity. On the one hand, as the foregoing discussion suggests, Marx was very much convinced of the possibilities of a classless, stateless free society. On the other hand, his own political practice, and to some degree his theory, argued in ways ambiguous enough to allow many of his followers to derive justification for an elitist conception of socialism as a prolonged transition to classless communism.

Most important here are two elements of his work and thought: the concept of the dictatorship of the proletariat implemented by a revolutionary communist party and the idea that the central object of that dictatorship should be the replacement of the market anarchy of capitalism by the centralized planning of social and economic life. Certainly, Marx was no elitist in the sense of those socialists like Saint-Simon or Owen who were willing to turn to the capitalist state to achieve the realization of their hopes. Moreover, it is clear that his recurrent use of the term communist party must be understood not in terms of 19th century secret conspiracies or in the contemporary terms of either the Leninist organization of professional revolutionaries or of social democratic electoral politics, but rather in the more general (and more ambiguous) sense of those who represent the most fundamental interests of the working class. This sense is what guided Marx in his work within the workers' movement, first in the Communist League and then in the International Working Men's Association (the First International). While Marx never spelled out in any detail what he felt the role of the working-class (or communist) party would be after the overthrow of capitalism, he clearly felt it should play a leading role in the struggle that would lead to such a victory.

Marx called for greater centralization not only in working-class organization but in the aftermath of revolutionary upheavals. Warning against bourgeois efforts to disperse and weaken, Marx called on workers to strive 'for the most determined centralization of power in the hands of the state authority'. This was one of the central points of contention between him and the anarchists in the First International. While the latter felt that the immediate abolition of the state was the shortest method of ending exploitation and class domination and renounced the call for any working-class 'seizure of power', which they argued would merely reinforce the state, Marx argued first, that the capitalist state was a manifestation of the power of the capitalist class and that without ending that power the abolition of the state would be at best short-lived, and second, that after the overthrow of the capitalist government the workers would need some means to prevent a counter-revolution (such as had occurred in the 1848 Revolutions and the Paris Commune) and to achieve the transformation of society along communist lines.

In his *Critique of the Gotha Programme*, Marx renewed his insistence on the necessity of a workers' state — the dictatorship of the proletariat — yet nowhere in any of these writings is there an attempt to spell out concretely what such a state would entail or to address the objection repeatedly raised by the anarchists that any workers' state would recreate tyranny. The closest Marx ever comes to answering that objection was in his analysis of the Paris Commune where he emphasized how the ability of workers to recall their representatives and the avoidance of any concentration of military power that could be used against the workers were themselves steps in the abolition of the state. The ambiguity of Marx's writing lay in the vagueness of his more abstract discussions of these issues of revolutionary power — a vagueness almost inevitable in a discourse that refused both utopian speculation and *a priori* prescription. Almost unavoidably, that ambiguity left his thought open to the widest possible range of interpretation — to which it was subjected even before his death.

The first great debates about 'what Marx really meant', about the proper 'Marxist' strategy for the achievement of socialism, took place in the context of the Second International (1889–1914) which was a renewed attempt to organize the socialist movement internationally. It was an attempt led and dominated by the German Social Democratic Party which, while seeking power through the electoral process, was also attempting to head off a major European war. The debates within the socialist movement of that period are numerous and touch on many issues which go beyond my immediate concerns here. However, in terms of the contradiction in socialism that I have been tracing, it is easy to identify the most salient issues.

What made it possible to speak of a socialist movement at that point in time was the common vision of the possibility of a more just, democratic and egalitarian post-capitalist society. Among socialists, the central debate was over the best method of overthrowing capitalism. Dominant among the Social Democrats at the time was the view that electoral politics and gradual social reform was the best, perhaps the only, path beyond capitalism. One such argument was put forward by Edward Bernstein who understood that the growing ability of capitalism to regulate and adapt itself dramatically reduced the possibility that a catastrophic crisis would occur to provide the occasion for a working-class revolution. Against such reasoning, other Marxists such as Rosa Luxemburg argued both that the capitalists could not eliminate crisis from the system, and second, that therefore the continuing role of the socialist party must be to prepare the workers for revolution and to be ready to lead them when the time came. With the collapse of the Second International in 1914, when the Social Democrats voted for war credits to support the German war effort, these debates became even more acrimonious. The German radicals around Luxemburg and the Spartacus League were joined in their attack on the Social Democrats by Lenin and the Bolsheviks in Russia. We should note that, on neither side of this debate, was there any call for the socialist party to abdicate its leading role in political struggle: the debate was only over how it should lead, not whether.

Enthronement of the Leviathan

During this whole period, however, all of these debates, about how capitalism could be abolished and what socialism might be like, were largely speculative projections. With the October Revolution and the Bolshevik seizure of power in 1919, however, all that changed. Suddenly, overnight it seemed to most, a socialist society was being constructed in Russia — not as a small, isloated experiment like the Paris Commune or the scattered international communities of the utopians, but on a huge scale, as huge as the fallen Czarist empire. All of a sudden, socialism leaped from the world of dreams and speculation — however rooted it may have been in the workers' movement — into concreteness. The spontaneous creation by Russian workers and peasants of the soviets and factory committees seemed to herald the popular self-governance that so many socialists had long anticipated. All around the world socialists, and even anarchists, celebrated the Revolution as the realization of their dreams.

Immediately after the October seizure of power, however, the Bolshevik leadership moved with blinding speed to consolidate all power in the hands of the party. Step by step they stripped both soviets and factory committees of their autonomy and gathered the reins of control into their own hands. They were not unopposed, there was real resistance among the Russian workers and peasants, even among the Bolsheviks; but they were victorious. While the meaning of the 'dictatorship of the proletariat' may have been ambiguous in

Marx, there was no ambiguity at all for the Bolsheviks. If the widespread dislocation and hardship left in the wake of World War I were not enough, the attack on the Revolution by the white army backed by Western powers provided Lenin and the other Bolshevik leaders with all the excuse they needed to rationalize the need for centralized control — both military and economic — a control they would not relax when the attack was defeated. As a result anarchists, radical communists and social democrats in Western Europe all challenged the legitimacy of Bolshevik power and policies. The anarchists and radical communists, such as Rosa Luxemburg and those who would become known as the council communists, saw in the dismantling of the workers' factory committees and soviets the solidification of a Bolshevik state, a reconcentration of power antithetical to their conception of popular power. The social democrats also decried the concentration of Bolshevik power, lamented the destruction of democracy and, for the most part, reaffirmed their reformist politics against what they saw as the subversion of the Russian Revolution.

While, during the period of (civil) 'war communism' many socialists were willing to give the Bolsheviks the benefit of the doubt, the end of that war brought new criticism, this time not only over the centralization of power but also over the purposes for which that power was being wielded. Little by little it became apparent, at least to some Western Marxists, that the nationalization of industry, the imposition of strict labour discipline, the collectivization of the peasantry and finally the brutality of forced labour in the Gulag, all of which had been carried out in the name of the people, were not merely unfortunate and temporary means to an end but had come to constitute permanent characteristics of Soviet-style socialism. The deliberate diversion of the fruits of rising productivity away from both consumption and less work toward investment and more work had become an endless process. Under such circumstances it became increasingly difficult to take seriously the Soviet claims to be a 'workers' state'. To be sure, certain concessions were made to the workers and peasants in Russia. They were guaranteed employment and a wage. They were provided free education and free health care. But over time at least some socialists began to see these concessions as not all that different from those won by workers in the West. And upon close examination some socialists even concluded that what detailed comparisons of Soviet and Western economies revealed was in fact a striking similarity.

Beneath the veneer of socialist rhetoric lay merely a different method of organizing the accumulation of capital. Some, such as C. L. R. James and Raya Dunayevskaya, went so far as to conclude that what the Bolsheviks under first Lenin and then Stalin had created was a form of 'state capitalism' and not socialism at all. Others, such as Max Horkheimer or Cornelius Castoriadis, would refuse such a characterization, preferring 'authoritarian state' or 'bureaucratic collectivism' or 'state socialism'. Except for those closely wedded to Moscow's line, a great many Marxists have come to see Soviet-style socialism as a new kind of class society, containing severe class antagonisms which, if not exactly the same as those of capitalism, are at least similar and thus remote from any kind of socialism they can identify with. The forced extension of this model of Soviet-style socialism to all of Eastern Europe after World War II, the revelations of Stalinist crimes by Krushchev in 1953 and then the violent suppression of popular uprisings in Germany in 1953, Hungary in 1956 and then Czechoslovakia in 1968 reinforced critics' scepticism about the socialist character of the Soviet model, even before the current series of dramatic popular revolts.

All of this reinforced the already dominant tendency among many Third World socialists to *adapt* socialist ideas rather than to slavishly adopt the Soviet model in any of its permutations: before, during or after Stalin. It is well known how Mao reworked both revolutionary strategy and the building of socialism in a predominantly peasant society; how Nehru embraced the socialist vision, and even state planning, but not the overthrow of private property; how Senghor elaborated his theory of the indigenous roots of African socialism; how Nyerere developed Ujamaa which sought to base socialism in the African family and village, and so on. In part, these adaptations were the outcome of attempting to take account of specific local conditions and history. In part, they were the result of critical assessments of the Soviet experience. They have all contributed to the continuing mutations in the meaning and content of socialism.

Subordination of Diversity

What, in the light of this history, are the implications of the massive upheavals in Eastern Europe, the Soviet Union and China for the concept of socialism? For those who would still like to recuperate the concept from the jumbled ruins of its history, the answer is probably that those meanings of socialism which we have identified as associated with attractive and democratic alternatives to capitalism are worth preserving, while those meanings which have been associated with elitism and then authoritarianism ought to be rejected. This is certainly the project of democratic socialists and is signalled by the adjective 'democratic' which is now being highlighted more than ever to distinguish it from authoritarian or totalitarian socialism — either as it was imagined in the past or practised in the present. I must admit to a certain sympathy with this attempt to preserve a term which has been associated with so many people's best aspirations and sacrifices. On the other hand, it also troubles me. Not only has the very term 'socialism' become one of opprobrium to the millions who are revolting against it, but as a result of the long history of political repression and economic exploitation in regimes which have called themselves socialist, it is really hard to see how the term can now be accepted as designating *only* the best of the ideals and practices that have been associated with it.

Beyond this problem, however, I have yet another difficulty with the continued demand for 'socialism' as an alternative to the existing order. Not with this or that use, but with any use at all. Throughout its history, even when we strip the concept of its immediately authoritarian variations, the concept of socialism has been designed to discuss the replacement of the capitalist social order by the construction of an alternative social order. Social*ism*, it has always been said, will replace capital*ism*. Not just in terms of ideology but in terms of social systems. Even the most casual perusal of the history of the socialist imagination shows a repeated attempt to either design a new social order to replace the present one (as in the case of utopians like Saint-Simon, Owen, Cabet or Fourier), or to discover which social order will most likely replace the current one as a result of the working out of historical forces (the Marxists). Where socialists have actually achieved the power to construct a new 'socialist' society, they have in fact been consistent with this tradition and have sought to design and impose a unified social order. The debates over the nature of the Soviet Union, or those over the Chinese, Cuban or Tanzanian experiences for that matter, are always over whether the particular model is the best that could be designed or, at least, the best under the historical circumstances and material conditions available.

This concept of alternative system building, which is present throughout every concept of socialism and every effort actually to construct a socialist society, seems to me to reproduce one of the most fundamental characteristics of the kind of society that it has always sought to replace. That characteristic is the essence of what has always been meant by domination: the subordination of social diversity to a standard measure. Such subordination was exactly what capitalism has always sought to do to the diverse and variegated societies of the world in which it emerged or over which it has sought to gain control. With capitalism such subordination has in fact meant obliteration of many societies and cultural groups and the partial destruction of all the rest. It was in part against just such destruction that the first socialists raised their voices. Saint-Simon, for example, shared with the Romantics a sense of tragedy and outrage over the destruction of traditional communities and their fabric of intimate human relations. At the same time, he and many other socialists condemned the capitalist reduction of human relations to purely commercial, monetary exchanges and the exploitation of some by others who profited from their labour. Unlike reactionaries, of course, they wanted to go forward, not backward to a lost Golden Age, but when they designed their alternatives their imagination was too limited by their experience in capitalism to let them see beyond the substitution of one social hegemony for another. Indeed, when we look closely at the mechanisms they designed for regulating their alternative social systems, we find that in their attempts to correct the injustices of capitalism, they remained trapped in the capitalist practice of measuring everything in terms of labour and money — in short, in that social reductionism so characteristic of capitalism.

Marx also recognized how capitalism tore apart all old social ties and substituted universal exchange relations. His analysis carried him behind the fetishism of exchange and he was able to show in theory what every worker experiences daily, that every form of alienation in capitalism derives from the universal and unending imposition of work and the extraction of surplus. His labour theory of value expressed perfectly the nature of capitalist reductionism, its tendency to convert every social activity into just one more form of work (disembedded, as Polanyi would say, from the fabric of its social meaning) comparable with every other kind of work and, in that social abstraction, the ultimate measure of every aspect of society. Unlike other socialists, however, both those who came before him and those who came after him, Marx's efforts to see beyond capitalism by carrying the logic of capitalist development, i.e. the logic of class antagonism, to its ultimate conclusion brought him, as I mentioned above, to the insight that the end of capitalism would mean the end of labour value and the emergence of socialism would involve the emergence of a new, open-ended value system based on free or 'disposable' time. He therefore rejected all utopian plans — such as those of Proudhon or Bray and Gray, the followers of Owen — for substituting labour chits for cash money, and imagined instead the socialist abolition of all kinds of money along with a dramatic reduction in the quantity of labour and the substitution of the direct distribution of collectively produced wealth among the producers.

Such insights, however, were mostly lost in the history of post-Marxian socialism as the desire to create a new system led many, from the British Ricardian socialists to the Russian Bolsheviks, not only to maintain labour as the standard of value but also to reproduce the capitalist practice of making the very mechanism of domination into a religious virtue. Indeed, in Soviet and Chinese style socialism, the cult of labour replaced every other religious practice and the Calvinist work ethic that Marx, Weber and Tawney had so identified with capitalism was replaced by a secular socialist work ethic that legitimated the endless subordination of people's lives to work under socialism just as they had been under capitalism.

In short, just as capitalism, by disembedding labour from every social fabric in which it found it, used an increasingly homogenized and abstract labour process as its fundamental means of ordering its society (and in this light, markets and competition must be seen as merely the forms through which this was carried out) so too did 20th century socialists in the USSR, and later in Eastern Europe and China, employ the same methods. Moreover, the tendential effect on the diverse array of social and cultural practices of the hundreds of millions of people of Eastern Europe, the USSR and China was the same as that of capitalism elsewhere: a tearing apart designed to purge those practices of all activities and meanings antithetical to the one overarching goal of socialist development — capital accumulation through endless labour.

It is doubtlessly true that the socialists in every self-proclaimed socialist country have paid lip service to the so-called 'national question' of diverse ethnic nationalities within their borders. They have made a political point of allowing such nationalities to preserve and reproduce those aspects of their cultures which have not been judged obstacles to socialist development. But in reality a great many aspects — including language, religious practices and festivities — have been judged incompatible with socialist development and have been banned. (It is a different point altogether — although a valid one — that the socialist authorities of those countries have actually used ethnic differences to control their own peoples.)

The point is this: it is hard to see how such a result is avoidable given the basic concept of socialism as a unified and homogeneous social system. The openness to social, cultural and ethnic diversity that was at least implicit in Marx's notion of the transcendence of labour value by an indeterminate free time, has been both ignored and contradicted by the very concept of a specific socialist project, as well as by the actual attempts to implement it. Only lately have a few Marxists, such as Antonio Negri or Felix Guattari, sought to recuperate and explore the possibilities of real multilaterality in post-capitalist society. In the language of currently popular post-modern theory (which in its own way also celebrates diversity), Marx's master narrative of capitalism (his theory of capital) was appropriate to capitalism's own attempt to impose its master narrative on the world. But while his refusal of utopian design bespoke a refusal to impose a new master narrative on a post-capitalist future, his persistence in speaking of socialism (or communism) without specifically addressing the issue of social diversity left a fundamental weakness in the heritage he bequeathed, a weakness which, most unfortunately, has barely begun to be remedied by his successors, either in theory or in practice.

From all of this, I conclude that the continued use of the term 'socialism', or the pursuit of any variety of 'socialist development', carries an inescapable, historical baggage of misconception and error. Not only has the history of actually existing socialism failed to provide any real alternative to capitalist development — socialist development has shown itself to be but a modified form of capitalist development which has preserved its most essential and worst aspects — but the history of socialist thought is shot through with fundamental conceptual problems. I certainly believe that it is worthwhile disentangling those elements and insights of past socialist thought (including utopian thought) which seem worth preserving from the more objectionable elements with which they have been interwoven — not only to preserve the memory and ideas of those who have fought and sacrificed so much to better the world, but also because the persistent popularity of many of those ideas shows that they express the real hopes and desires of a great many people. On the other hand, it seems to me that we can avoid a great deal of conceptual and communicative difficulty by stopping using the terms 'socialism' and 'socialist development' as shorthands for what we want. Better we set these terms aside and attempt to figure out, and perhaps later to spell out, without jargon or historically loaded slogans, exactly what characteristics of a post-capitalist world we want to aspire to, including the overriding necessity of recognizing the virtues of a world that encourages diverse social projects and a rich multiplicity of cultural development by its peoples. This, it seems to me, is likely to be the most useful method of proceeding both for those who are currently in revolt against Soviet-style socialism, and those of us who are struggling against Western capitalism.

Bibliography

So mutable has been the meaning of the concept of socialism for its advocates, so biased have been its opponents, and so unsatisfactory have been the many commentaries on the history of the concept and of the socialist movement, that there is really no substitute for reading its proponents' writings in the original and for examining their actual practices as closely as possible.

As a beginning to the study of 19th century socialism, the most important works of the utopian socialists include Henri Saint-Simon: a useful collection of English translations of his writings has been assembled by Keith Taylor (ed.) *Henri Saint-Simon (1760–1825): Selected Writings*, London: Croom Helm, 1975; Robert Owen: fundamental is his *A New View of Society or Essays on the Formation of the Human Character* (1816) reissued by Augustus M. Kelley in 1972; and Charles Fourier: one useful collection is *The Utopian Vision of Charles Fourier: Selected Texts on Work, Love and Passionate Attraction*, Boston: 1971.

The best of Marx and Engels, who opened up a very different approach to the issue of going beyond capitalism, can be found in the essay on unalienated labour in communism, K. Marx, 'Economic and Philosophic Manuscripts of 1944', *Karl Marx and Friedrich Engels: Collected Works (MECW)*, Vol. 3, pp. 272–81; in the vision of the end of labour value and the open-endedness of post-capitalist society: 'Outlines of a Critique of Political Economy (Grundrisse)', (1857–58), *MECW*, Vol. 29, pp. 80–99; in Marx's critical reflections on the limitations of revolutionary efforts in 1848 and 1870: 'Class Struggles in France' (1850), *MECW*, Vol. 10, pp. 118–31; 'Address of the Central Authority of the League', (1850), *MECW*, Vol. 10, pp. 277–87; 'Civil War in France', (1871) *MECW*, Vol. 22, pp. 307–59; and finally for Marx's open view of the possibilities inherent in the Russian peasant commune, 'Letter to Vera Zasulich', (1881) *MECW*, Vol. 24, pp. 346–71 and the various interpretations in T. Shanin (ed.) *Late Marx and the Russia Road*, New York: Monthly Review Press, 1983. A most useful discussion of the evolution of the meaning of the troublesome term 'dictatorship' in the 19th century, especially among socialist reformers and revolutionaries, can be found in Hal Draper, *Karl Marx's Theory of Revolution, Volume III: The 'Dictatorship of the Proletariat'*, New York: Monthly Review Press, 1986.

As a beginning to the study of the debate in 20th century socialism, the arguments of the Second International can hardly be ignored, in part because they are still being repeated. The key revisionist text is Edward Bernstein's *Evolutionary Socialism: A Criticism and Affirmation*, (lacking two critical chapters, see Draper above, pp. 337–43), New York: B. W. Huebsch, 1909, which is, in turn, taken to task by Rosa Luxemburg in her *Reform or Revolution?* (1898–99) New York: Pathfinder, 1974. The subsequent debates around the Russian Revolution were also formative for everything which has followed. The central figure, of course, was Lenin and the following pieces contain his vision of socialism in all its brilliance and all its limitations: (all from *V. I. Lenin Collected Works*), 'The State and Revolution', (1917), Vol. 25; 'Can the Bolsheviks Retain State Power?' (1917) Vol. 26; 'How to Organize Competition', (1917) Vol. 26; 'The Immediate Tasks of the Soviet Government', (1918) Vol. 27. Neither Lenin's vision nor his methods went unchallenged and the best of those challenges from the Left were: Rosa Luxemburg's *The Russian Revolution* (1918) and *Leninism or Marxism?* (1904) Ann Arbor: University of Michigan Press, 1961; Karl Kautsky, *The Dictatorship of the Proletariat* (1918) Ann Arbor: University of Michigan Press, 1964, and *Terrorism and Communism*, London: National Labour Press, 1920; and the Council Communists, of which a useful collection in English is D. A. Smart (ed.) *Pannekoek and Gorter's Marxism*, London: Pluto Press, 1978, pp. 93–148; Paul Mattick, *Anti-Bolshevik Marxism*, White Plains: M. E. Sharpe, 1978; and the material in Douglas Kellner (ed.) *Karl Korsch: Revolutionary Theory*, Austin: University of Texas Press, 1977. Among the many volumes of Leon Trotsky's later work which show how he held to and perpetuated the Bolshevik vision of socialism see: *The Revolution Betrayed: What is the Soviet Union and Where is it Going?* (1936) New York: Pathfinder, 1972.

The battle between Soviet efforts to establish a hegemonic orthodox vision of socialism and the social democratic alternatives continued after World War II in both the North and throughout the rest of the world. In Western Europe and the United States, Marxist critiques emerged of Soviet-style socialism, of which some of the most interesting are: C. L. R. James & Raya Dunayevskaya, *State Capitalism and World Revolution* (1949) New York: Charles H. Kerr, 1986; Part V of Dunayevskaya, *Marxism and Freedom* (1958) New York: Columbia University Press, 1988; Cornelius Castoriadis, 'The Relations of Production in Russia', 'On the Content of Socialism, I', in Vol. 1 and 'The Proletarian Revolution Against the Bureaucracy', 'On the Content of Socialism, II', and 'On the Content of Socialism, III', in Vol. 2 of *Political and Social Writings*, Minneapolis: University of Minnesota Press, 1988; M.

Horkheimer, 'The Authoritarian State', *Telos*, No. 15, Spring 1973, pp. 3–20, and R. Bahro, *The Alternative in Eastern Europe*, London: Verso, 1981.

In the Third World, the ideal of socialism was more or less adapted to local conditions and intellectual traditions. Without a doubt the two most intellectually influential socialists who have shaped most subsequent debates were Mao Zedong, who fought and spoke for a Soviet-style revolutionary communism and Jawaharlal Nehru who fought and spoke for a more peaceful evolutionary parliamentary socialism. Mao's writings are gathered in the *Selected Works of Mao Tse-tung*, Peking: 1967 to 1977, in 5 volumes; Stuart Schram (ed.), *The Political Thought of Mao Tse-tung*, New York: Praeger, 1963; and Stuart Schram (ed.), *Chairman Mao Talks to the People: Talks and Letters, 1956–1971*, New York: Pantheon, 1974. For Nehru see: *Jawaharlal Nehru: An Autobiography, with musings on recent events in India*, London: 1936; 'Whither India?' (1933) and 'The Presidential Address' (1936) in *Selected Works of Jawaharlal Nehru*, New Delhi: Orient Longman, Vol. 6, pp. 1–32, 1974, and Vol. 7, pp. 170–95, 1975 respectively. Also see the selection of writings on 'Planning and Socialism' in S. Gopal (ed.) *J. Nehru: An Anthology*, Delhi: Oxford, 1980, pp. 291–319.

Of the attempts to rethink the issue of the transcendence of capitalism in ways which involve no *a priori* unity of vision or project, see: Antonio Negri, *Marx Beyond Marx*, Bergin & Garvey, 1984, especially 'Lesson Eight: Communism & Transition', *The Revolution Retrieved*, London: Red Notes, 1989; *The Politics of Subversion*, London: Polity Press, 1990; Felix Guattari (with Gilles Deleuze), *Anti-Oedipus: Capitalism and Schizophrenia* and *A Thousand Plateaux: Capitalism and Schizophrenia*, Minneapolis: University of Minnesota Press, 1983 and 1987 respectively.

Standard of Living

Serge Latouche

W hen, on June 24, 1949, in his message to Congress on his Point Four Programme, President Truman announced the necessity 'to assist the people of economically underdeveloped areas to raise their standard of living',[1] he emphasized an objective which was already accepted as obvious and indisputable for all modern states. It was only a few years previously, in 1945, that the Charter of the United Nations had affirmed, in Article 55, the global objective 'to promote higher standards of living'.

According to both popular opinion and scientific usage, 'standard of living' refers to material well-being and constitutes a concept, susceptible to measurement, similar to per capita Gross National Product. 'The standard of living,' wrote Jean Fourastie, 'is measured by the quantity of goods and services which may be purchased by the average national income.'[2] Any increase in the level of this indicator is considered the logical consequence of economic development. It is supposed to derive from an improved exploitation of natural resources through the utilization of science and technology in the form of industrial equipment. Equalizing this standard all over the globe suggested itself as the ideal towards which organizations throughout the world must strive. Bertrand de Jouvenel stated with authority in 1964: 'The improvement of the material condition of the greatest number is, in our times, fact, hope and desire.'[3]

While the hope of a satisfactory life is a very human concern, the obsession with this sort of 'standard of living' is very recent. Interest in salary levels on the part of wage earners and as a general social preoccupation dates from the industrial era. As more and more people were turned into wage earners, the wage became the basic component of the standard of living. However, in the founding proclamation of the League of Nations on June 28, 1919, according to which 'the well-being and the development of . . . people form a sacred mission of civilization,'[4] the concept still did not exist as a measurable index. Nor had it attained the straightforward simplicity of GNP per capita, as first Stalin, and then Krushchev, drew up their ambitious plans for catching up with and overtaking the Americans. Even if one spoke of 'standard of living', the concept was not yet a technical term referring to a precise and statistically determined economic aggregate, but a general notion that remained largely imprecise and subjective. In particular, the concept was still far from being used as a categorical imperative to the exclusion of all others.

Instead, specialists in human geography had long concentrated on studying different modes of living. They attempted to describe the ways of life which were specific to a given region or a given social milieu. Quantitative and normative measures were largely absent; a concern for the different qualities of living predominated. Economists today, however, are able to use the standard of living concept because ways of living have become increasingly uniform with the result that differences in *modes* of living can be more and more translated into differences in *levels* of living.

The widespread acceptance of the concept of standard of living has been the result of recent circumstances and events, although their roots date back a number of years into history. Examination of these circumstances may shed light on the implications and significance of the new concept. What immediately catches one's eye is that the concept's much vaunted universal relevance certainly cannot be assumed without further thought. In fact, looking at the world in terms of 'standard of living' is like looking through dark glasses; they make the rich variety of colours disappear, turning all differences into shades of the same colour. Whoever wants to appreciate the irreducible diversity of ways of realizing human existence, must step back and take off these conceptual spectacles.

GNP Per Head: A Post-war Invention

For the Anglo-Saxon reader, it may seem a travesty to date the emergence of the preoccupation with the standard of living to the period only following the Second World War. The expression itself is in fact very old. However, as we shall now see, its meaning has evolved in the meantime very considerably. Originally it indicated an *irreducible minimum income*, a subsistence level of living, the cost of the reproduction of the work-force, in the tradition of the classical economics of Malthus, Ricardo and Marx. It was still defined in this sense as late as 1934 in the *Encyclopedia of the Social Sciences*.[5] Without totally losing this connotation, and under the influence of the more recent rise in the level of living, the expression came to indicate a *desired* manner of living (plane of living), or normal living conditions (contents of living). It was on this conception that, in February 1945, the economist Joseph Davis insisted in his presidential speech to the American Association of Economics.[6]

It is clear that, in a short time, it became more and more difficult to dissociate the connotation of goal from that of fact. The concept also found itself oscillating uneasily between the two notions of the irreducible minimum and the desired level. The absorption of the descriptive (the actual level) into the normative (setting the standard) is revealing of the gradual degradation from concern with issues of quality to a sole preoccupation with quantity which has come to dominate the Western perspective. At least for once, the French language is less ambiguous than English; the expression *niveau de vie* clearly indicates a positively established fact, and its recent appearance has prevented any semantic ambiguity. The good fortune of this expression derives partly from the fact that it condenses a series of notions — subsistence level, income level, average per capita income, living conditions and a vital minimum wage . . .).

Among the specific circumstances that have led the standard of living to become the daily obsession of our contemporaries and the dominant horizon of economic politics, three phenomena appear to merit particular discussion. These include the general spread of the concept of national accounts, the growth of mass consumerism in the major industrial countries during the 30 'glorious years' (1945 to 1975), and the universalization of the myth of development in the Third World. Let us look briefly at each of these developments.

In the absence of any system of accounting, however imprecise, for the measurement of social conditions, it was vain to consider endowing with a quantitative capacity the concept of standard of living, and to generalize its usage. One cannot truly enjoy one's standard of living unless one is conscious of it. Today this consciousness is pushed extremely far amongst the majority of our contemporaries, engendering a veritable fetishism for the *amount* of income. To make up for lack of time to enjoy the fruits of our labour, the greatest satisfaction can at least be drawn from the contemplation of the amount one has earned in comparison with those lower down on the scale.

Following the Great Depression, with the vogue for Keynesian ideas and the interest in macro-economics, the major industrial countries equipped themselves for the first time with statistical research institutes. Statistical data began to adorn economic concepts and to subvert them from within. As early as 1940, Colin Clark made a comparison between the incomes of different countries, and international organizations propagated the new cult of numbers. Even though certain Third World states were still living in the pre-modern age and did not function as national markets, they were also adorned with arrays of statistics and all the attributes of a nation-state.

The attribution of standarized measurements became a categorical imperative. Living standards could at last be quantified and thus compared. The global ideal of a uniform standard of living ceased to be a futile concept; it now came to be represented by a specific quantum of dollars which could at least be referred to, even if not realized. The utilitarian objective of the greatest happiness for the greatest number had found its scientific expression.

The Universal Declaration of Human Rights of 1948 proclaimed the equality of all human beings. This abstract universalism called for indicators of happiness which would be applicable everywhere. GNP per head provided a convenient measuring rod that claimed equal relevance all over the world. Before the War, under the conditions of colonialism, such a concern could hardly arise for it was meaningless to calculate the average standard of living for citizens of the British Empire, adding up for instance English and Indian incomes. It was only with decolonization that the idea of equality between English and Indian levels of living came to be considered as legitimate.

During the first 30 years after the Second World War, the developed economies experienced a phase of unprecedented growth, resulting in spectacular effects on the standard of living. The centuries-old poverty in the industrialized societies seemed almost to disappear. Work for all in a free society brought forth the spread of well-being under the guardianship of the welfare state. The expectation took root that universal affluence was just around the corner. Everybody, the moment he was conscious of his position, scrambled to catch up with those who were ahead. Disparities — the narrower they appear, the less tolerable they are — were considered likely to disappear soon, as they lacked any democratic legitimacy.

The myth of development was thus born. What had been produced in the industrialized countries would generalize itself across the planet. The differences between countries came to be seen as mere delays, condemned as unjust and unacceptable, and the elimination of these gaps was planned. GNP per head, the basic indicator of the standard of living, became the fundamental criterion for measuring the level of development. Gradually additional criteria were established — non-monetary, but still quantitative, indicators of living standards, ranging from life expectancy to the number of doctors per square kilometre! The compilation of statistics required national accounts. The different indices were most often strongly correlated — which is why GNP per head still tends to have a veritable monopoly in official reports.

Periodically, there were reactions against this abusive reductionism. The World Bank, following the famous speech of Robert McNamara in 1973, called for other indicators. The speech criticized the increasing income disparity which, in most of the developing countries, was camouflaged behind statistics indicating growth in income per head. It called for the inclusion of other objectives besides the increase in the GNP, such as reductions in unemployment and increasing the income of the poor. Eventually, the World Bank approved the adoption of 'a socially oriented measure of economic performance'.[7]

Such a claim was by no means new. Concern with the need to take into account the multiple aspects of reality was present in the remarks of the earliest statisticians of development. A United Nations report in 1954 on the definition and measure of 'standards' and 'levels of living' called attention to 12 possible components of the standard of living for international comparison. They included:

(1) Health, including demographic conditions; (2) food and nutrition; (3) education, including literacy and skills; (4) conditions of work; (5) employment situation; (6) aggregate consumption and saving; (7) transportation; (8) housing, including household facilities; (9) clothing; (10) recreation and entertainment; (11) social security; (12) human freedom.[8]

However, the practical import of such wider conceptions has been largely symbolic. Even where they have led to concrete action in favour of basic needs, self-sufficiency in food production, or appropriate technologies, their overall impact has been questionable. The results have not been without ambiguities and have certainly not attained a sufficient salience to modify the dominant GNP perspective.

In any case, war against misery was thus declared at the start of the so-called Development Decades and it broke out with great force. Has anyone been concerned about the underlying ambiguities? A few isolated voices, at times prestigious, such as G. Myrdal, have made themselves heard, but they were without influence. The struggle, daggers drawn, for the highest standard of living per head has become an obsession in the international arena, while the reduction of the gap between the well-to-do and the wretched has been declared a priority objective. Each country, by any means compatible with the maintenance of world peace, endeavours to increase its advantages over its neighbours and to carve out a slice of the market for itself at the expense of others. Tariff and non-tariff protections, subventions and fiscal policies, industrial policies (that of MITI, the Ministry of Industry in Japan, for example), the dismantling of social security systems, deregulation, and the most brazen instances of competitive wage bargaining comprise the gamut of most visible means in this mad scramble. With a sometimes unconscious hypocrisy, the winners then lend a helping hand to the laggards so that they may catch up. The experts possess miracle prescriptions for any problem, provided at both state and private enterprise levels they are left to operate freely. They hope to succeed (though nobody knows how) in squaring the circle. The notion of the standard of living carries in itself the demand for egalitarianism and at the same time a spirit of competition. All will be saved and everyone will be a winner.

Well-Being and Well-Having

'Standard of living' encapsulates all the dimensions of the dominant paradigm of the West, of modernity and of development. This paradigm constitutes a perfectly auto-referential sphere containing only a very limited number of elements. Need, scarcity, work, production, income, and consumption are the key concepts within an enclosed semantic field that has no need of the outside world. The interaction of these elements is auto-dynamic and supposed to provoke unlimited growth of material wealth. The concept we are dealing with here — the standard of living — thus has the same historical origins as the general economic paradigm itself.

An essential watershed in this history was the reduction of the *good* to the *amount*. This transition simultaneously eliminated the multiplicity of possible social values and allowed the quantification of the only dimension that was retained.

The objective of a 'good life' can manifest itself in a whole host of forms — from the warrior's heroism to asceticism, from Epicurean enjoyment to aesthetic toil. However, as soon as the good life is expressed in terms of the global common good, the manifold personal arts of living and diverse ways of knowing tend to get reduced in favour of a single collective project, which easily leads — concerning its ends and even its means — to an homogenization of individual pursuits. It is not by chance that Truman as well as Kennedy — though themselves separated by a quarter of a century — still referred to the 'common good'.[9] This age-old Aristotelian and Thomist term evokes the ideal of the just and responsible city-state, rather than a rich and individualist society.

But in the modern world, the only good that appears as common to all people, above and beyond cultural differences, is life as a physiological property. Even this cult of life is very different from what can be found in non-Western cultures. In Brahman India for example, life also has pre-eminent value; however, it is envisaged as a cosmic whole. The earthly life of the human individual is of limited importance and animals and the natural world have as much right to live as man. The death of some individuals provides the condition for the life of others, and it is the dynamic flux that assures the order of a glorified cosmos. Death is not excluded from life. The West, on the other hand, has long since declared war on death in all its forms — poverty, violence and natural death. This programme reduced the 'greater life' to a concern with survival. It became the priority to live more, and not well or better. This selection in Western thought of the quantum of life as the sole objective offers itself as both a physiological and a social frame of reference. The two tend to merge in the perspective of naturalism, with 'need' serving as the category joining both frames.

Spiritual needs were the first, if one accepts the analysis of Illich, to give rise during the Middle Ages to the figure of the specialist, capable of providing the answers.[10] Passing into the secular sphere, this concept of needs retained its ambiguity. At the physiological level, it now refers to the number of calories per head along with its correlates like the amount of protein, fat and carbohydrate. At the social level, it is the number of dollars. Survival for all was the goal of the Leviathan, the great technocrat of the 17th century, while on the eve of the French Revolution, happiness ('a new idea in Europe' according to Saint Just) was the objective of the 'enlightened despot'.

The emergence of the utilitarian individual seeking to maximize his pleasure and to minimize his pain did not guarantee the immediate triumph of the pursuit of the highest standard of living for each and all. The logical consequence of the arrival of the calculating subject was rather an unbridled outburst of passions. In England Puritan restraint permitted a channelling of these passions into a search for material accumulation, thus assuring a minimum common interest. This reduction of the drama of life to transactions in the marketplace was achieved with much greater difficulty in France. The Marquis de Sade showed with implacable logic the type of anarchy towards which calculating individualism could lead when the passions were not suppressed. The incommunicability of subjective worlds (the 'no-bridge' problem) becomes insurmountable. Each individual can and should take advantage of the opportunities that his situation offers. It is quite in order to skilfully deceive one's fellow man provided one is not caught. It is acceptable to become a hypocrite (like the depraved monks of *Justine*), and to encourage the virtue and generosity of the weak in order that they may be more easily duped. Such have been the inevitable consequences of the loss of social bonds. Our present world, without faith or law, is an *anti-society*, impossible and unliveable. There is no invisible hand here; the pleasures of the butcher or the brewer do not converge on my satisfaction. It has been necessary for the passion for business to triumph over all others in order to permit a *common measure* of unbridled desires. The economic paradigm has succeeded very well in reducing our perspective to a single point of view. It has resulted in a one-dimensional reductionism.

When human fulfilment is interpreted as only material well-being, the differences between after-life, worldly happiness and physical survival get blurred. The promised after-life existed, in the West as in other societies, in the next world. Loss of contact with the deceased as respect for our ancestors declined in the West resulted in giving the resurrection of the body a more and more abstract content — the abstract eternity of the beyond replaced the concrete immortality of the ancestors. With the subsequent death of God in our own time, life has become the pursuit of a purely secular objective, that of mere physiological survival. The gap was virtually bridged when economic growth elevated physical survival to the height of general 'well-having' as expressed in national consumption.

Well-having aims at the maximization of 'objects' — i.e. maximal material consumption — but the status of these objects is quite ambiguous. For as social objects destined for consumption, the accumulation of physical products lacking any practical use has very limited meaning beyond a certain point. (The accumulation of equipment to be used for the production of other goods of course does have a meaning which consumer goods lack). The standard of living measures itself by the level of consumption, including the amount of waste produced. Our gadget-ridden civilization is the natural result of this process. Abundance carries with it the loss of its proper meaning. In this deluge of objects, it has become almost impossible to desire something for itself, if it is not already the envied possession or object of desire of others. Advertising plays at the heart of this mimesis of desire. And ultimately, the anguish of having nothing more to desire adds to the distress of desire unsatisfied.

The basis for evaluating both physiological and psychological need is *utility*. The triumph of utilitarianism is thus the condition that has to be met to make ambitions like maximization and equalization of living standards conceivable. The reduction of the multiple dimensions of life to what is quantifiable finds its purest mode of expression in money and its locus of realization in the market economy. The generalization of the market accelerates its motion, which in turn facilitates its extension. Utilitarian reductionism and the obsession with consumption push forward the growth of the market, and the commoditization of increasingly large sectors of social life reinforces the calculating and utilitarian perspective. The market reveals the 'preferences' of buyers and sellers and thus provides the otherwise impossible measure of what is useful. It achieves, according to the economists, the 'well' and the 'good', the best usage that can be made of available factors of production. The citizens, having become agents of the economic machine, end up believing in it. Thus the great myth of modernity is able to gain ground, holding out the promise that each and all will be enriched through the advance of economic organization, science and technology, and that, over and above all of this, the accumulation of riches will be infinite.

'The American amassment of riches,' writes Bertrand de Jouvenel, 'is becoming, as it were, the fairy tale of the modern age.'[11] He calculates that, with the near doubling of the standard of living every ten years, a goal generally proposed, the result amounts to an 867-fold increase in a single century!

Blind Spots

The Westernization of the world has by no means created a universal equalization of living standards. Instead, it has imposed the concept of standard of living as the dominant category for perceiving social reality (and therefore underdevelopment), and made the increase of living standards a moral obligation for the leaders of emerging nations.

It has often been demonstrated how the transfer of statistical measurements to the Third World leads one astray. 'The unemployed worker in the slums of Caracas,' writes Jean Chesneaux, 'discovers with amazement that he enjoys a standard of living defined in terms of GDP which is worthy of envy. No less flabbergasted, the fisherman in Samoa who lives quite at ease in relative self-sufficiency, learns that, in terms of GNP, he is one of the poorest inhabitants of the planet.'[12]

The first case illustrates how an unequal distribution of wealth removes all meaning from the figure of an average, while the second example reveals the absurdity of international comparison of indices when lifestyles are very different and in fact non-comparable. Political economy has not been able to construct a satisfactory theory of the objective value of all things, thus making it impossible to proceed to an evaluation and a summation of objective *utilities*. These are subjective and by nature mutually incommunicable (the no-bridge problem). Constant reminders about the limits of national accounting do not appear to have had any impact. Furthermore, arbitrary as the divisions are, even in industrialized societies, which lie at the root of social accounting, it borders on the absurd to apply them outside these developed societies to the Third World.

Competent statisticians have always emphasized the limits of their approach,[13] but in practice these words of caution have served no purpose. For quantitative reductionism has become entrenched in the logic of modernity, and the spirit of the times cannot be held back by precautionary admonitions. Nevertheless we must remind ourselves of some of the absurdities involved.

The standard of living is measured by the volume of goods and services consumed by the inhabitants. However, only the goods and services regularly exchanged on the market enter into this calculation, and they do so even if they are not the object of a genuine exchange. As a result, important aspects of the quality of life are not taken into account. Inversely, those things we 'consume' which imply a degradation in the quality of life are valued and counted as positive contributions.

'The measure of consumption,' writes Bertrand de Jouvenel, 'is none other than a measure of goods and services which are obtained from enterprises by private individuals and which are subject to payment. It is apparent that this measure omits: (1) services rendered by public authorities; (2) free goods and services; (3) external costs inflicted by transformations in the economy.[14] services; (3) external costs inflicted by transformations in the economy.'[14] rendered by mothers to their children, without which, of course, there would be no economy at all! Unpaid domestic work in the home, which in the developed countries remains hidden from the official national accounts, constitutes a large part of the informal economy. For Great Britain, Colin Clark in 1968 calculated the value of free house work (calculated in terms of 1871 GNP values) as amounting to 50 per cent of the GNP of 1956.[15]

On the other hand, and equally subversive of the national accounts as an accurate mirror of economic reality, an increased consumption of fuel due to traffic congestion and increased travel distances between home and work translates into an increase in our consumption of transportation and, therefore, into a rise in the standard of living! As de Jouvenel put it:

> In the United States the food consumption per head measured in constant prices increased by 75% from 1909 to 1957. However, according to the calculations of the Department of Agriculture, the increase in physiological consumption was at most 12 to 15%. Thus, according to the analysis of Kuznets, at least four-fifths of the apparent growth in food consumption is due, in fact, to an increase in transport costs and the distribution of foodstuffs to the urban centres.[16]

The exclusion of the value of material goods when consumed in small quantities, and the inverse practice of taking into account the enormous expenses needed to restore degradation, or to compensate for it, introduces other considerable distortions. 'According to our way of counting', de Jouvenel remarks with humour, 'we would enrich ourselves by making the Tuileries into a parking lot and the Cathedral of Notre Dame into an office building.'[17]

If, as a result of this particular notion of national accounts, which represents a particular Western interpretation of reality, the underdeveloped countries appear to be poor in terms of those things we judge as rendering us rich, they are (and were) infinitely richer in those things in which we are now poor. They have at their disposal goods and services which are non-measurable or undervalued, fragile as they are now becoming — the open space, the warmth of the tropics, leisure, solidarity, and so on. By the prevalent standards of the world system, their purchasing power, which is representative of their power in general terms, is infinitely smaller. But, then, only the Westernized portions of their socio-economic reality are being measured.

At the root of the paternalism of the international agencies dealing with the Third World lies a terrifying ethnocentrism. If we pursued a true and genuine internationalism, or universalism, it would be necessary to invite 'experts' from the last remaining 'primitive' regions of the world to draw up a list of the deficiencies from which we, the people of the *developed* countries, suffer — loneliness, depression, stress, neuroses, insecurity, violence, and so on.

Such considerations, however cogent, do not nevertheless fundamentally challenge the solid foundations of economic reductionism. But they do serve to advocate the wisdom of a certain prudence — something which has been largely ignored today.

Yet the early economists, searching to determine the essence of the economic act behind the appearances of the market, did struggle at length with the paradoxical nature of economic categories. Thomas Malthus spoke of his perplexity:

> If the exertion which produces a song, whether paid for or not, be productive labour, why should the exertion which produces the more valuable result of instructive and agreeable conversation be excluded? Why

should we exclude the efforts necessary to discipline our passions, and become obedient to all the laws of God and man, the most valuable of all labours? Why, indeed, should we exclude any exertion, the object of which is to obtain happiness or avoid pain, either present or future? And yet under this description may be comprehended the exertions of every human being during every moment of his existence.[18]

Indeed, why shouldn't the dance which is staged to ask the spirits for a rich harvest be considered as work? Why shouldn't the tom-tom played next to the campfire be considered as the production of leisure services, or the caresses of a wife as part of national consumption? Is not the use of a personal vehicle the production of a transport service? Its purchase an investment? Isn't the work expended by the labourer at a factory the consumption of accumulated energy — i.e. capital?

All conceptual distinctions break down, and easy assumptions and certainties fade away, as soon as one frees oneself from the taboos which govern the tribe of economists and statisticians. Malthus and the economists who succeeded him and who feel confused, have no choice but to take refuge in common sense. This common sense interprets the practices of the European marketplace on the basis of well-established prejudice. It is simply the Western imagination which has invented this system of classification. Hence the particularistic notions, specific to Western cultural perceptions, of no work (in the modern sense) without the Protestant ethic; no production without the myths of nature, need, scarcity, and a conception of matter borrowed from 18th century physics; no consumption without the generalized market. Out of the infinite variety of human activity, the distinction made between playful and productive gestures on the one hand, and between the object produced and that consumed on the other, is entirely based upon particular cultural values. Rearing an animal, a dog or a cow for example, could be considered as investment, production, or consumption, depending on the animal's habitat and whether it is meant to hunt, plough, provide meat, parade, or show affection.

The currently dominant accounting categories represent a radical form of cultural imperialism. It is not only that happiness and the joy of living in countries of the Third World are reduced to the paltry level of GNP per head by this globally imposed statistical butchery, but the very reality of diverse other arts of living is flouted and misunderstood in their richness and potentialities.

As Ivan Illich noted: 'Until the present, all efforts to substitute a universal commodity for a local value have resulted not in equality but in a hierarchical modernization of poverty,'[19] in other words, misery and dereliction.

Paradoxically, the fascination with a rising standard of living is often greater among the populations of the Third World than in the West. The reason for this is easy to understand. Neophytes to the cult of the gods of modernity as they are, the uprooted social strata of these societies strive to reach the modern life. They see in the increase of their monetary income their only means of gaining social status. Westerners, or at least some amongst us, have already had a chance to acquire a certain distance, which allows for second thoughts and some new wisdom. We have become more aware of the limitations of growth. We are beginning to learn to appreciate certain traditional values, or to invent for ourselves an anti-utilitarian 'post-modernism'.

Many Faces of Wealth

With all the well-intentioned efforts to measure the standard of living in the Third World and to push it to higher levels, a tragic farce has been staged. To bring about well-being has contributed increasingly to the very negation of being. The wealth of the 'other' has not only been denigrated (even in the other's eye), but its very foundations have been torn apart. Wealth and poverty are clearly relative concepts. What they mean varies according to what a culture defines as its reference points and how it models reality.

According to the ethno-geographer Joel Bonnemaison, one of the islands in the New Hebrides named Tanna 'is thus rich and poor at one and the same time, according to the interpretation which is adopted. Its people live in a certain abundance if seen in the context of their traditional milieu, but they look "proletarian" if seen from an imported socio-economic perspective.'[20] All the values which fail to pass through the filter of quantifiable utility, which are foreign to a 'dollarized' life, are downgraded. Their practices, excluded from the definition of standard of living, tend as a result to disappear. This happens to the ideal of heroism which in warrior societies is more highly cherished than any riches. It is also true of communal solidarity, that veritable social treasure trove by which much of the Third World continues to live against all economic logic. For example, practices like ostentatious display, colourful parades, ritual challenges, and the various forms of sensual enjoyment which enrich social life are now in the process of losing their meaning. What sense does a rise in the standard of living have for a nomad society in the desert which aspires to lightness and frugality?

In fact, the obsession with the standard of living and its increase has caused an unprecedented impoverishment of life by neglecting some of its principal dimensions. Death, for one, is struck dead. Instead it has become simply a failure of human enterprise, an inevitable loss entered on the balance sheet.

In many previous societies, wealth was considered a gift left behind by the deceased. Material wealth was not regarded as a means of accumulation, but as a proof that the living recognize their debt to the dead. Now, however, the dead are merely seen as having been expelled from the realm of economics and deleted from the commercial register of the living. The loss of the meaning of death is perhaps the greatest source of impoverishment of modern man. There is no longer a price to buy peace. The Westerner is condemned to live his death as a failure and to deaden his life in order to ease the pain and forget the final absurdity.

Likewise, illness and ageing are also seen as partial failures in the West. It is part of the hidden treasures of societies in the Third World, however, that they still conserve different attitudes towards the old and the sick. Illness and ageing are not considered as natural curses that separate the individual from the world of the living and which must be treated in isolation, shame and guilt. They may be a source of tragic conflict if the cause is attributed to witchcraft, but they are also sources of personal and social enrichment. Suffering has only become unbearable and intolerable in the West because it no longer has meaning. The fact that pain is inherent to the human condition, and perhaps necessary, highlights to what extent its refusal and trivialization contribute to our impoverishment.

This impoverishment culminates in the Western contempt for poverty. Most cultures honour their poor. The much admired ancient Greeks took enjoyment in both their leisure and their meagre resources; it was in these conditions that their culture flourished. Even in the West until the 18th century, poverty was not necessarily seen as a disgrace. 'The poor,' writes Alain Caille, 'were not all poor people, at least in terms of rights.' And he adds: 'Who could be made to believe today in a happy man without a shirt? Nobody. And with good reason, because someone without a shirt can have no other status than that of a failure.'[21]

Frugality and austerity are neither defects nor misfortunes. They are even at times the signs of divine choice. The vow of poverty testifies to the desire for holiness. According to the Stoics, true richness consists in limiting desires. Most schools of wisdom, and in particular Buddhism that still prospers, define the acquisition of self-awareness as the goal of existence, and regard moderation in pleasure and attention to an equilibrium between different values, and never the unlimited accumulation of a single value, as the secrets for a happy life. Material deprivation, which we take as the sole criterion making for a dishonourable poverty, is often no more than a minor aspect alongside other sorts of deprivation in traditional societies. For the Serere, as for many others, it is loneliness that makes for true misery. 'Poverty is not a matter of lacking clothes, but the one who is truly poor is he who has no one,' states a Serere proverb.

All societies have a concept of wealth and this concept is reflected most often by tangible indicators. It includes all the natural or man-made objects and all the cultural gestures and creations (names, dances, chants) accessible to individual or collective appropriation. The possession of these values confers a status, a prestige and a power. If these 'riches' are able to translate themselves into monetary terms through contact with the West, it is because the people realize that money in our world takes the place of their riches. Their riches, however, do not engender a dishonourable poverty and destitution. The failure that is so evident today of development, of modernity and of Westernization opens up the opportunity to view with great scepticism the phantasmal aspects of this fetishistic object, standard of living, and to rediscover the multidimensionality of life. For the concept of the standard of living has imposed itself with the force of a certainty beyond all criticism and has become inscribed in the logic of modernity. The universalism of this concept is as fallacious as that of the West, and its promises are as illusory as those of development.

References

1. Harry S. Truman, Message to the Congress on Point Four, June 24, 1949.
2. Jean Fourastier, 'Standard of Living', in Jean Romoeuf, *Dictionnaire des Sciences Economiques*, Paris: P.U.F., 1958, p. 800 and 'genre de vie', ibid., p. 571.
3. Bertrand de Jouvenel, *Arcadie: Essai sur le mieux vivre*, Paris: Sedeis, 1968, p. 170.
4. Covenant of the League of Nations (June 28, 1919), Article 22.
5. Carl Brinkmann, 'standards of living', in *Encyclopedia of the Social Sciences*, London, 1934, pp. 322–4.
6. J. Davis, 'standards and contents of living', *The American Economic Review*, March 1945, pp. 1–15.
7. Robert McNamara, Address to the Board of Governors, World Bank, Nairobi: September 24, 1973, p. 12.
8. United Nations, *Report on International Definition and Measurement of Standards and Levels of Living*, Doc. E.CN 5/299, 1954.
9. Truman, op. cit., J. F. Kennedy, Inaugural Address, January 20, 1961.
10. Ivan Illich, *Shadow Work*, London: Boyars, 1981, p. 61.
11. Bertrand de Jouvenel, op. cit., p. 132.
12. J. Chesneaux, *La modernité monde*, Paris: La Decouverte, 1989, p. 64.
13. See, in particular, the *Studies in Income and Wealth of the N.N.B.: Problems in the International Comparison of Economic Accounts*, Vol. XX.
14. B. de Jouvenel, op. cit., p. 178.
15. Colin Clark, 'The Economics of Housework', *Bulletin of the Oxford Institute of Statistics*, Vol. XX, No. 2, May 1958, quoted by B. de Jouvenel, op. cit., p. 178ff.
16. Ibid.
17. Ibid., p. 267.
18. Thomas Malthus, *Principles of Political Economy*, London: 1820, p. 42.
19. I. Illich, op. cit., p. 4.
20. I. Bonnemaison, *La dernière île*, Arlea Orstom, 1986, p. 157.
21. A. Caillé, *Critique de la raison utilitaire*, Paris: La Decouverte, 1988, p. 118.

Bibliography

The classic definition of standards of living, along with a methodology of measurement, can be found in United Nations, *Report on the International Definition and Measurement of Standards and Levels of Living*, Doc.E.CN 5/299, 1954. These definitions have subsequently been taken up in most countries. With respect to France, for example, see J. Fourastie, 'Niveau de vie', in J. Romoeuf, *Dictionnaire des sciences economiques*, Paris: Presses Universitaires de France, 1958. It was in 1940 that C. Clark, *The Conditions of Economic Progress*, London: Macmillan, 1940, offered the first international comparison of national incomes. Further bits of information about the history of the concept can be gathered from C. Brinkmann, 'standards of living', in *Encyclopedia of the Social Sciences*, London: 1934, and J. Davis, 'standards and content of living', in *American Economic Review*, 35, 1945, pp. 1–15, while H. W. Arndt, *The Rise and Fall of Economic Growth*, Chicago: University of Chicago Press, 1984, presents a broader history of the notion that growth is a policy objective.

Numerous authors have highlighted the systematic bias built into the concept and its methods of measurement. The essays of B. de Jouvenel, *Arcadie: Essai sur le mieux vivre*, Paris: Sedeis, 1968, are already quite old but unsurpassed in their lucidity and pertinence. His critique, though intended to be constructive, is precise and radical; I owe a great deal to this author. A. Sen, *Standard of Living*, Cambridge: Cambridge University Press, 1987, analyses the tensions and contradictions between pleasure, happiness, welfare, and standard of living, discussing the possibility of expressing them in economic terms. In the same book, K. Hart,

'Commoditization and the Standard of Living', shows the inadequacy of the concept by comparing conditions in West Africa with Great Britain. Probably the best documented critique from an ecological point of view, focusing on the remedial expenditures needed to deal with the cost of progress, has been written by Ch. Leipert, *Die heimlichen Kosten des Fortschritts*, Frankfurt: Fischer, 1989.

Astonishingly, the founding fathers of economics often showed a clear awareness about the limits of those economic categories which are designed to define and measure levels of wealth. Apart from remarks in A. Smith, J. B. Say, D. Ricardo and J. C. de Sismondi, I found most revealing the reflections of Th. Malthus, *Principles of Political Economy*, London: 1840, the first two parts. While these doubts have been entirely consigned to oblivion by economists, they do emerge again and again in the work of anthropologists. For example, M. Sahlins, *Stone Age Economics*, Chicago: University of Chicago Press, 1972, rejects the conventional wisdom that primitive societies lived in permanent scarcity or that, in a way, pre-industrial societies had a low standard of living. In *Culture and Practical Reason*, Chicago: University of Chicago Press, 1976, he uncovers the hidden utilitarian certainties of our worldview which lead to such prejudices. The collection of K. Polanyi and C. Arensberg, *Trade and Market in the Early Empires*, New York: Free Press, 1957, excellently illustrates the historical limits of economic categories. The quarterly *Revue du MAUSS*, published by Editions La Decouverte, 1 place Paul Painleve, Paris, has as its objective questioning the utilitarian and economistic base of the social sciences and modern life, and attempts to develop a non-utilitarian, alternative perspective. A. Caille, *Critique de la raison utilitaire*, Paris: Le Decouverte, 1989, has presented a synthesis of this programme. Finally, my 'Si la misère n'existait pas, il faudrait l'inventer' in G. Rist & F. Sabelli (eds.), *Il était une fois le développment*, Lausanne: Editions d'en bas, 1986, complements the present considerations by exposing the function of misery in contemporary consciousness.

State

Ashis Nandy

The growing interest in the nature of state represents the revival of a major intellectual concern of the 1950s and 1960s: state- and nation-building in the old societies turned new nations. However, the new interest in the state has a different tonal quaity to it, for the world has, during the last two decades, witnessed a major change in the context in which studies of the state were once conducted.

The 1950s and 1960s were a period of optimism. It was widely believed in the modern world, and in the modern centres of the non-modern world, that every society had to pass through clear-cut historical stages to finally conform to the prevalent model of a proper nation-state — exactly as every economy had to go through fixed stages of growth to attain the beatitude of development. It was also believed that to go through these inescapable stages, each society had to restructure its culture, shed those parts that were retrogressive, and cultivate cultural traits more compatible with the needs of a modern nation-state.

Two forces seem to have changed that easy, progressivist view of the relationship between culture and state. First, a huge majority of Third World societies have failed to walk successfully the arduous path of 'progress', laid out so considerately by the dominant school of post World War II social science, and they have failed to develop viable nation-states along the lines prescribed by post-17th century Europe. The state in these societies often looks today like some kind of specialized coercive apparatus or private business venture. Second, culture in these societies has shown more resilience than expected by the learned and the knowledgeable. When pitted against the needs and rationales of the state, it is often the state which has given way to culture. This resilience of culture, also expressed in the spirited resurgence of ethnic self-awareness in many Third World societies, seems to show that what was once possible in the case of small tribes and minorities which were bulldozed by modernization is no longer possible in the case of larger cultural entities without arousing stiff resistance. Increasingly, cultures are refusing to sing their swan songs and bow out of the world stage to enter the textbooks of history. Indeed, cultures have now begun to return, like Freud's unconscious, to haunt the modern system of nation-states.

It is against this background that the recent vicissitudes of the idea or construction of the state in the dominant culture of global politics must be explored.

Fusion of Nation and State

What we have learned to call the state today is actually the modern nation-state. It entered the world scene only really after the treaty of Westphalia in 1648. Though a contractual element had already entered the civic space by the

13th century in parts of Europe, the treaty gave formal institutional status to the emerging concept of the state in Europe. But even then the concept would have never attained the power it later did if the French Revolution had not underwritten it by linking up the story of the state to that of nationalism.

With the spread of republicanism in Europe, there also grew up severe doubts among European elites about the long-term legitimacy of the merging non-monarchical states. Nationalism came in, and was systematically promoted, as an alternative basis of such legitimacy. The Weberian charisma that was previously concentrated in the person of the monarch — supposedly meditating between the sacred and the secular orders — was now distributed among the population and a non-specific nationalism was seen as the best guarantor of the stability of the state.

This sense of insecurity, of which nationalism was supposed to be the cure, persisted in the culture of the nation-state. From the very beginning, nation-building — a polite term for the cultural and ideological homogenization of a country's population — became one of the goals, stated or unstated, of the modern state. Some early nation-states, for instance, even proscribed trade unions for a while. And, of course, there was always some godforsaken minority or other that these states could exclude. Such minorities had a place only in the few remaining fragmented nations where the construction of the past was itself plural and could not easily be built on a romanticized imperial memory.

The concept of the state that emerged from this experience had some distinguishing features. Among other things, the new concept assumed a closer fit between the realities of ethnicity, nation and state; it gave a more central role to the state in the society than the *ancien regime* had done; and it redefined the state as the harbinger and main instrument of social change, which in the European context meant being the trigger for and protector of the modern institutions associated with industrial capitalism. These newly assumed functions naturally made the modern nation-state suspicious of all cultural differences, not on grounds of racial or ethnic prejudice, but on the ground that such differences intervened between the 'liberated' individual and the republican state and interfered with the more professional aspects of statecraft.

Even more important, thanks to the new institutional ordering that went with the new concept of the state and the expansion of the colonial empires (which had already begun to become globally visible), within a short time the concept of nation-state not only marginalized all other concepts of the state in Europe but also began to enter the interstices of public consciousness all over Asia, South America and Africa.

This had two important pay-offs. First, under the influence of the concept of the nation-state, the state was increasingly seen as an impartial, secular arbiter among different classes, ethnicities and interests. Most states did not live up to the image but few states disowned it. Some states even negotiated this gap between principles and practice the hard way. For instance, some of them went democratic but with clear-cut structural limits on democracy. In England in the 18th and 19th centuries, a line was drawn between democracy and national freedom, and the popular as well as elite view of the state came to include the belief that freedom sometimes needed to be protected from democracy, if necessary by curbing the participation of the lower classes, including women, in politics. Likewise, some states managed to become more tolerant of ethnicity only after ghettoizing or driving out from their territories their problematic minorities. What France did to the Huguenots or, later on, Poland to the Jews, other states like the United States or Australia did less conspicuously, but just as ruthlessly, to their aboriginal and black minorities.

The second pay-off was that each nation-state began to see itself as a repository of cultural values even though, in reality, each sought to equate these values with a territorial concept of nationality that militated against the subtler meanings of the idea of culture. Occasionally, the states vied with one another to emerge as the upholder of particular culture values. England and France both spoke on behalf of European civilization, even when they went to war with each other. And Nazi Germany, while to much of the world it seemed an anti-culture, also tried hard to become a symbol of European civilization, albeit in its somewhat idiosyncratic fashion, and to at least some of the best minds of this century — from Ezra Pound to Knut Hamsun to Martin Heidegger — the claim did not seem particularly exaggerated.

Hegemony of the European Concept

At the beginning, the new concept of the state in Europe and its corresponding institutional arrangements had to contend with other surviving concepts and structures of the state that were different from and antagonistic to the new concept. These contending concepts and structures often went with culturally distinctive expectations and demands from the state. British colonialism, for instance, though it was perfectly at home with the concept of the nation-state in Britain, operated in India within the broad cultural framework of the Mughal empire which had preceded it. This it did explicitly and self-consciously during the early decades of the Raj, and more tacitly and partly unwittingly till roughly the First World War.[1] During the first 65 years of British rule, it is even doubtful if the new ruling circles in India had an operational concept of any 'civilizing mission' on their part. They certainly did not have a programme of state-directed social change and they resisted, in virtually every instance, Indian attempts to introduce major social reforms in the country. As for its secular commitment at that time, it suffices to say that the British–Indian state not merely proscribed Christian missionary activities, but even participated in running some Hindu temples and claimed a part of the donations made to the temples on that basis.

Despite these early compromises, gradually the concept of the nation-state did manage to disparage and displace all other surviving notions of the state in the Third World as so many instances of medievalism and primitivism. The process was strengthened when, in one society after another, indigenous intellectuals and political activists confronting the colonial power found in the idea of the nation-state *the* clue to the West's economic success and political dominance. The idea of a native nation-state, thus, was increasingly seen as the cure-all for every ill of the Third World. Rarely did anyone think of an indigenous modern state as a contradiction in terms. Indeed no other idea, except probably the twin notions of modern science and development, was accepted so uncritically by the elites of old continuous civilizations like China and India. Even modern science and development became, for Third World elites, the responsibility precisely of the nation-state and two new rationalizations for its predominant role. It is possible to argue that the story of the modernization of Asia that began in the 19th century is actually a story of the internalization and enculturation of the idea of the modern state by individuals as diverse as Rammohun Roy (1772–1833), Sun Yat-sen (1866–1925) and Kemal Ataturk (1881–1938).

As a result today, in most of the world, when one talks of a state, one usually has in mind the modern nation-state. All political arrangements and all state systems are now judged by the extent to which they serve the needs of — or conform to — the idea of the nation-state. Even the various modes of defiance of the state are usually informed by this standardized concept of the state. Karl Marx (1818–1883), while he spoke of the state withering away, had in mind a nation-state which would have to be first captured by a dedicated vanguard fully versed in the intricacies of a modern — read 'Western' — polity. And when the likes of Piotr Kropotkin (1842–1921) talked of the ills of the state, they invariably had in mind the Western nation-state. The anarchists were as ignorant as the Marxists were contemptuous of the very different kinds of state that lesser mortals in the Third World had lived or experimented with.

It is only now, 45 years after the Second World War, that some social analysts have again begun to take seriously the growing inability of the nation-state to serve the needs of civil society in large parts of the world. As I have already pointed out, there had been critics of the state in Europe as early as the 19th century. Some like Marx expected the state to wither away after playing its role in history, some like Leo Tolstoy (1828–1910) found it a moral abomination which had to be kept in strict check, and some like George Sorel (1847–1922) and Piotr Kropotkin thought the state could be done away with straightaway — but all these critics, almost without exception, were severely Eurocentric. They showed little knowledge of, or respect for, the diverse traditions of conceptualizing the state in other parts of the world. What little concept of diversity they had, consisted primarily of a vague idea of the non-Western state which was later to be formalized by scholars like Karl Wittfogel as Oriental despotism and by Max Weber as the pre-modern state.

Predictably, this mythical pre-modern state propagated by the better known European scholars looked remarkably like a primitive Afro-Asian version of the *ancien regime*. It was mythical because it analytically steamrolled the diverse pasts of the non-West, collapsing them into a single ideal type which, as in the case of Weber, instead of increasing the understanding of these societies, diminished it. It was, primarily, simply an effort to make manageable the world's diverse non-Western pasts by incorporating them into a more familiar Western past. Later, this process of incorporation was to be scientifically sanctioned and institutionalized through Weberian political sociology, particularly its post World War II Parsonian variant which dominated the behavioural persuasion in Western political science till the 1970s.[2]

Not that everyone during the last three centuries has dutifully jumped on the bandwagon of the modern state. But those who have not are the exceptions. And these exceptions have been systematically neutralized by the dominant culture of knowledge. Given the overall spirit of post-Enlightenment Europe, it has been easy to reread intellectuals such as William Blake (1757–1827), David Thoreau (1817–1862) and John Ruskin (1819–1900) either as incurable romantic visionaries or as grand eccentrics. They are respected as poets, critics and moral persons, but not as thinkers who have something to say about public life and the fate of civil society the world over. It goes against these intellectuals that they sensed the growing links between the state, organized nationalism, mega-science and the growth of an urban–industrial society and, especially, the way the combination has marginalized some of the older, less totalist conceptions of the state. Particularly industrialism and scientism have been, since the late 18th century, the ruling ideologies in Europe and anyone even slightly critical of the urban–industrial or technocratic future of humankind is seen as outside the bounds of normality and sanity.

This hegemony of the idea of the modern nation-state has created a clear political paradox in the debates on the state today. The new critics find the concept of the modern state looking more and more tired, out of line with realities, and unable to cope with the new problems and threats to human survival. Yet, in the meanwhile, the concept has acquired immense institutional power and a wide base in the global mass culture. It has become an axiomatic part of conventional wisdom or commonsense. This paradox has ensured that organized political power cannot easily be mobilized, even in the Southern world, to resist the pathologies of the modern state. Either the resistance has to come from the fringes of the polity or it has to legitimize itself in the language of the mainstream. The vested interests which have grown up around the idea of the modern state define, thus, not merely the mainstream but also most of the popular concepts of dissent.

The results are plain. In society after society, in the name of protecting or helping the state, rulers have begun to extract new kinds of economic and political surplus from the ruled and have unleashed on the citizens who resist this project new forms of oppression. Simultaneously, in society after society, for the sake of the state, a growing proportion of the citizens is willing to tolerate that oppression as a sacrifice they must make as patriotic citizens for the future generations of their compatriots. Even as the idea of the nation-state loses a part of its gloss, as in West Europe in the 1980s, it strengthens its hold on the imagination of many in the Third World who see in it one of the few instruments available to ensure progress and equality within the global system. That the state is also a means of ensuring First World standards of living for those having control or access to the state in the Third World is, of course, seen as an unfortunate and incidental by-product of the inexorable laws of history.

Development as *Raison d'état*

What explains this anomalous relationship between the state and society in large parts of the world? The answer differs from society to society but there are some common threads.

First, the idea of the nation-state entered most Southern societies through the colonial connection, riding piggyback on the concept of the white man's burden. That experience was internalized. When, after decolonization, the indigenous elites acquired control over the state apparatus, they quickly learnt to seek legitimacy in a native version of the civilizing mission and sought to establish a similar colonial relationship between state and society.[3]

They found excellent justification for this in the various theories of modernization and guarantors of national security. Instead, now they were no that had once been made to colonial regimes for their civilizing mission were now demanded by those controlling the indigenous states as agents of modernization and guarantors of national security. Instead now they were no longer called payments. Now they were called sacrifices for the future of one's country, and they invariably came more from those who had less access to — or facility in — handling modern institutions. Even authoritarian regimes in the Third World have systematically justified themselves thus. From Ferdinand Marcos to Lee Kuan Yew, from Ayub Khan during the second period of military rule in Pakistan to Mrs Indira Gandhi during the Emergency in India, it has been the same story. None of these worthies has ever bothered to justify him or herself as a guardian of civil rights or democracy, though all of them were indirect beneficiaries of democratic movements for self-rule in the colonial period. At most, they have justified themselves as removing the roadblocks to some future democracy which the citizens in their societies could one day come to deserve if they, the citizens, got themselves properly educated in the meanwhile in the intricacies of modern social and economic institutions.

A second common thread in the relationship between state and society are the direct links which the modern state has established with mega-technology on the one hand, and doctrines of national security and development on the other. These links have become more and more conspicuous to the victims of state violence, thanks to the consistent attacks by many states in the Third World on their citizens in the name of development and national security, and the systematic export of violence and authoritarianism by some Western states, both liberal capitalist and socialist, during the past 150 years.

These elements in the ideology of the state have also come under criticism because, apart from becoming the justification for new kinds of violence, they have become conceptually hollow in terms of real life. Let me give one or two examples. The changing nature of modern technology has ensured that the state can provide security primarily only to itself, not to its citizens.[4] If there were to be a nuclear war between the United States and Soviet Russia for example, and Switzerland maintained its traditional neutrality, that neutrality could no longer guarantee the personal security of a single Swiss citizen. For good or ill, our hypothetical average Swiss citizen must look for security elsewhere. The modern state can always ask the citizen to make sacrifices in the name of security; but it cannot always deliver that security.

Likewise, even spectacular state-controlled development processes in a society are no guarantor of the development of the society, however paradoxical this may sound. There are a number of states in the world where development means only the development of the state itself or, at most, the state sector. In fact, in a number of cases, the development of the state has been the best predictor of the underdevelopment of society. (There is a closely associated category of such states — Herb Feith calls them repressive-developmentalist regimes — which we are not considering here; in them, the state's role as the ultimate development agency legitimizes its authoritarian nature and repressive policies.) Some scholars have, consequently, defined development as the process in the name of which the state mobilizes resources internally and externally and, then, eats them up itself, instead of allowing them to reach the bottom and the peripheries of the society.[5]

National security and development are only two of the major themes in the ideology of the modern state. A third is the state as representing the principle of scientific rationality (which rationalizes, in Freud's sense of the term, all actions of the state which in turn seeks to rationalize, this time in Max Weber's sense of the term, the society it lands over). And a fourth is the state as a means of secularizing the society.

The concepts of the state as the epitome of scientific rationality and the chief secularizing agent have also come under attack in recent times. The modern state has established such a close relationship with modern science and technology that it has now become the major source of attack on all non-modern systems of knowledge. In the politics of knowledge today, nobody can imagine one without the other. About 95 per cent of all scientific research in the world is now applied research and, out of this 95 per cent, roughly 65 per cent is military research sponsored by the state. Nearly the entire coercive power of the modern state now comes from mega-science and mega-technology and developing the state today means primarily equipping it with greater coercive might as a result of the help of modern science and technology. Once again, the brunt of this attack on the plurality of knowledge is felt more in the (former) Second and Third Worlds. There are institutional checks in the First World against the use of certain kinds of force against the citizens. These checks hardly existed in the Second World before its collapse and are often subverted with the help of the First World in the Third World.

As for that other major ideological pillar of the modern state, secularism, instead of leading to greater tolerance of ethnic diversity, state-sponsored secularism has often only managed to secularize ethnic conflicts and bring them within the purview of the state. In the process, politics organized around the state has worsened the relationship between communities and ensured, in the name of progress, the destruction of hundreds of lifestyles and the life-support systems which traditionally sustained cultural diversity in different parts of the world.[6]

The various kinds of traditional state systems that in times past used to be spread all over the world were often violent and authoritarian. But one thing they did not — or could not — do. They did not try to enter all areas of human life and they did not set up total systems for social and political engineering, based on a theory of inexorable historical laws. Such states neither had the technological wherewithal nor, in most cases, the philosophical hubris to mount any such ambitious effort. As a result, the citizens, even when victims of state violence, had a few escape routes open. The state, too, knowing that its writ did not run beyond a point, had to learn to live with human diversity, if not on ideological grounds, at least on grounds of *realpolitik* and pragmatic considerations.

Under the dispensation of the modern nation state, similar escape routes can be kept open only when the polity is fully democratic. Otherwise, the state's control over a citizen's rights and freedoms is much more total. With the help of modern technology, management systems and information control, such a state can successfully plug the escape routes that used to be available to the citizen of pre-modern or non-modern societies.[7]

Towards a Lighter State

It is easy to identify many of the problems associated with the prevalent idea of the state. It is less easy, when dealing with a social entity as fundamental as the state, to foretell the future or guess what forms may ultimately emerge in place of the modern state. Some scattered non- or post-modern concepts of state have, however, begun to emerge in response to the crisis of the nation state in our times. For while it is an open question what forms the post-modern state will take, there is little doubt that the dominant concept of the state will have to be drastically altered. If not in response to intellectual doubts and criticisms, at least in response to the larger processes of democratization going on all over the world. For the crisis of the modern state springs primarily from the contradiction that has arisen between it and the demands for democratization of the world of knowledge and restoration of the dignity of peoples peripheralized during the last 200 years.

First, there has emerged the concept of multi-national and multi-ethnic states as correctives to the standard idea of the unitary nation-state. In the past the bureaucratic socialist states like the USSR or Yugoslavia (before its break-up) preferred the first approach; Western liberal societies like the United States and Britain the latter. Neither has been an unmixed blessing and the strains have begun to show in both systems. The concept of the multi-national state has not helped China or the Soviet Union to avoid ethnic politics and strife; that of the multi-ethnic state has not helped Britain or France to live in peace with their non-European minorities.

Second, some people, noticing how the concept of the nation state seeks to pummel major civilizations into shape, have tried to redefine the state. At least one scholar has pleaded for the use of the concept of a civilizational state in case of large countries such as India.[8] Prima facie the concept seems to presume an overlap of geographical and state boundaries which may be impossible to obtain in reality. In the case of India, it does not seem to account adequately for the political status of independent Hindu monarchical states like Nepal. Nor does the concept adequately explain the cultural status of states such as Pakistan and Sri Lanka, separated from India not by civilizational but by state boundaries.

Third, there have been others to whom the concept of a moderate or civil state promises some respite, if not a remedy.[9] It is possible, they feel, to recover the liberal, pace-setting role of the state through detailed monitoring of the state by those politically active outside the state sector, in areas such as environment, peace, human rights, feminism, alternative sciences and technologies. The enrichment of civil society and reform of the state through such monitoring, they feel, will automatically bring about a redefinition of the scope of the modern state. Though this is the way resistance against state-initiated oppression has gone in many societies, one wonders if the liberal state has retained enough flexibility to allow for such monitoring. Specially so, given the wide consensus most modern states have now built against the idea of diversity and in favour of professional expertise. Both these kinds of consensus allow the nation state democratically to marginalize grassroots initiatives of all kinds, especially if they happen to be non party political.

Finally, there has been a re-emergence of anarchism of various hues. In the West, this response is usually anaemic and defensive, and survives camouflaged in some forms of environmentalism and in alternative science movements. When directly political, such anarchism somehow conveys the impression of being a form of eccentricity or esoterica. In the Third World, it occasionally has some political clout, thanks to the fact that the anti-imperialist movements, *in practice*, often had to operate from outside the state sector. Probably the best instance is the 'anarchism' associated with the name of Mohandas Karamchand Gandhi.[10] Many Indian Gandhians are still trying to live down that heritage and convert Gandhism into a non-threatening, official voluntarism acting as an adjunct to the Indian state. But Gandhi, 40 years after his death, has obviously retained some nuisance value and at least some young Gandhians have come closer to those for whom a return to a revised and updated idea of a culturally rooted, less monolithic, 'softer', pre-modern minimal state holds the most promise.

*   *   *

None of these dissenting new approaches, however, pose as yet much of a threat to the dominant culture of the state, despite the widespread awareness that everything is not well with the state of the state. None of the alternatives mentioned here has captured the imagination of the public, except perhaps for short stretches of time. On the other hand, given the mounting problems with the dominant model of the state, these fringe dissenters do not look as insane as they once did. It is possible that in the future they may begin to look more formidable enemies of public order and political rationality. In the meanwhile, the dissenters can perhaps, as a consolation, remind themselves that no system becomes morally acceptable merely because human imagination has failed to produce an alternative to it at a given point in time.

References

1. See, for instance, Bernard S. Cohn, 'The Command of Language and the Language of Command', in Ranajit Guha (ed.), *Subaltern Studies*, New Delhi: Oxford University Press, 1985, Vol. 4, pp. 276–329; and 'Representing Authority in Victorian England', in Eric Hobsbawm and Terence Ranger, *The Invention of Tradition*, Cambridge: Cambridge University Press, 1983, pp. 165–209.

2. Satish Arora, 'Pre-Empted Future? Notes on Theories of Political Development', in Rajni Kothari (ed.), *State and Nation Building*, New Delhi: Allied Publishers, 1976, pp. 23–66. For a more recent attempt to locate such critiques in the overall culture of the globally dominant knowledge system, see Tariq Banuri, 'Modernization and Its Discontents: A Cultural Perspective on Theories of Development', in Frederique Apffel Marglin and Stephen Marglin (eds), *Dominating Knowledge: Development, Culture and Resistance*, Oxford: Clarendon Press, 1990, pp. 73–101; and Chai-Anan Samudavanija, 'The Three-Dimensional State', paper presented at the International Conference on Political Institutions in the Third World in the process of Adjustment and Modernization, Berlin, July 4–7, 1989, mimeo.

3. Ashis Nandy, 'Culture, State and the Rediscovery of Indian Politics', *Interculture*, Spring/April 1988, 21(2), pp. 2–17.

4. For instance Giri Deshingkar, 'People's Security Versus National Security', *Seminar*, December 1982, (280), pp. 28–30.

5. Herb Feith's comprehensive and superbly insightful 'Repressive-Developmentalist Regimes in Asia: Old Strengths, New Vulnerabilities', paper presented at the conference of the World Order Models Project, New York, June 1979, and published in *International Affairs*; Christian Conference of Asia, *Escape From Domination: A Consultation Report on Patterns of Domination and People's Movements in Asia*, Tokyo: April 1980; and Richard Falk, 'A World Order Perspective on Authoritarianism', New York: World Order Models Project, 1978, mimeo.

6. Vandana Shiva, *The Violence of Green Revolution*, Penang: Third World Network and London: Zed Books, 1991; Ashis Nandy, 'The Politics of Secularism and the Rediscovery of Religious Tolerance', *Alternatives*, 1988, 13(3), pp. 177–94. See also Veena Das, 'Community, Riots, Survival', in Veena Das (ed.), *Mirrors of Violence: Community, Riots, Survival*, New Delhi: Oxford University Press, in press; and Tariq Banuri and Durre Sameen Ahmed, 'Official Nationalism, Ethnic Politics, and Collective Violence: Karachi in the 1980s', presented at the UN University–WIDER Conference on Ethnicity, Karachi, January 14–18 1989, mimeo.

7. Rabindranath Tagore, *Nationalism*, Madras: Macmillan, 1985. This is a collection of lectures delivered in 1930s. Often maudlin and unreadably purple, it remains the first, and an impressive, critique of the modern state on the ground of its totalism. Predictably, the lectures were not particularly popular in Japan and India.

8. Ravinder Kumar, 'Nation-State or Civilizational State?', New Delhi: Nehru Memorial Museum and Library, 1989, Occasional Papers, mimeo.

9. Rajni Kothari, 'Crisis of the Moderate State and Decline of Democracy', in Peter Lyon and James Manor (eds), *Transfer and Transformation: Political Institutions in the New Commonwealth: Essays in Honour of W. H. Morris-Jones*, Leicester: Leicester University Press, 1983; and D. L. Sheth, Grassroots Stirrings and the Future of Politics', *Alternatives*, March 1983, 9(1), pp. 1–24.

10. For example, M. K. Gandhi, 'Hind Swaraj', in *Collected Works of Mahatma Gandhi*, Delhi: Publications Division, Government of India, 1963, Vol. 4, pp. 81–208.

Bibliography

The standard historical, philosophical and social scientific scholarship on the state offers little scope to those savages in the Southern world who want to see the modern, post-17th century concept of the state as less than perennial. Nevertheless, studies exploring the historical (and therefore possibly transient) character of the state are helpful, like J. Strayer, *Les origines de l'état moderne*, Paris: Payot, 1980, or E. Morgan, *Inventing the People: The Rise of Popular Sovereignty in England and America*, New York: Norton, 1988. On the level of intellectual history, the emergence of the state as a key concept of modernity is traced in O. Brunner et al., *Geschichtliche Grundbegriffe*, Vol. 6, Stuttgart: Klett, 1990.

Despite their anti-state rhetoric, the anarchist and Marxist traditions have nothing but their touching faith in the European concept of the state to offer to non-Europeans. In fact, reading Marx, one gets the impression that the prophet would be very angry if European-style states are not first established in the Southern world, before they are made to wither away as a consequence of revolutionary activism. For elements of a fundamental critique of the idea of the state, therefore, one is sometimes better off studying rather conservative thinkers like M. Oakeshott, 'The Character of a Modern European State', in his *On Human Conduct*, Oxford: Clarendon, 1975, or the young radical of his time, W. von Humboldt, *Limits to State Action*, Cambridge: Cambridge University Press, 1969, (first written in 1792). For my part, I have drawn more insight from non-academic intellectuals like D. Thoreau, *The Selected Works of Thoreau*, Boston: Houghton Mifflin, 1975, or M. Gandhi, 'Hind Swaraj', in *Collected Works of Mahatma Gandhi*, Delhi: Government of India, 1963, Vol. 4, pp. 81–103.

In the Southern countries the main *raison d'etre* of the state has been development. For a critique of development as a process and an ideology, I have learnt from G. Esteva, 'Regenerating People's Space', in *Alternatives*, 12, 1987, pp. 125–52, and on the fate of the development idea from A. Escobar, *Power and Visibility: The Invention and Management of Development in the Third World*, unpublished Ph.D. dissertation, University of California, Berkeley, 1987, and T. Banuri, 'Development and the Politics of Knowledge: A Critical Interpretation of the Social Role of Modernization Theories in Development', in S. Marglin & F. Apffel-Marglin, *Dominating Knowledge*, Oxford: Clarendon, 1990, pp. 29–72. On the intimate connection between the state and the coercive might of science, see S. Visvanathan, 'From the Annals of the Laboratory State', in A. Nandy (ed.), *Science, Hegemony and Violence: A Requiem for Modernity*, New Delhi: Oxford University Press, 1988, pp. 257–88, and C. Alvares, *Science, Development and Violence*, New Delhi: Oxford University Press, forthcoming.

My occasional association with human rights activism has convinced me that the nation-state, when transplanted into Third World situations, can out-perform any old-style oriental despotism in authoritarianism and organized violence. A. Eghbal, 'L'état contre l'ethnicité', *IFDA Dossier*, July–August 1983, pp. 17–29, has highlighted the exclusion of ethnicities, and V. Das (ed.), *Mirrors of Violence: Community, Riots, Survival*, New Delhi: Oxford University Press, 1990, the instrumentalization of communal tension under the pretence of secularism. B. Anderson, *Imagined Communities: Reflections on the Origin and Spread of Nationalism*, London: Verso, 1983, describes nation/nationalism as products of social imagination. I have explored the contradictions of secularism in A. Nandy, 'The Politics of Secularism and the Rediscovery of Religious Tolerance', *Alternatives*, 13, 1988, pp. 177–94, and reflected on the issue of the state in the context of present-day India in A. Nandy, 'The Political Culture of the Indian State', *Daedalus*, 118, Fall 1989, pp. 1–26.

Technology

Otto Ullrich

Harry S. Truman's famous statement of January 20, 1949, can be regarded as the official proclamation of the end of the colonial age. He announced a plan for economic growth and prosperity for the entire world, explicitly including the 'underdeveloped areas'.

> We must embark on a bold new program for making the benefits of our scientific advances and industrial progress available for the improvement and growth of underdeveloped areas. . . . The old imperialism — exploitation for foreign profit — has no place in our plans. . . . Greater production is the key to prosperity and peace. And the key to greater production is a wider and more vigorous application of modern scientific and technical knowledge.[1]

Greater prosperity calls for increased production, and more production requires scientific technology — this message has been proclaimed ever since in countless statements by the political elites of both West and East. John F. Kennedy, for example, emphatically challenged Congress on March 14, 1961, to be conscious of its historical task and authorize the financial means necessary for the Alliance for Progress:

> Throughout Latin America millions of people are struggling to free themselves from the bonds of poverty and hunger and ignorance. To the North and East they see the abundance which modern science can bring. They know the tools of progress are within their reach.[2]

With the age of development, science and technology took over the leading role altogether. They were regarded as the reason for the superiority of the North and the guarantee of the promise of development. As the 'key to prosperity' they were to open up the realm of material surplus and, as the 'tools of progress', to lead the countries of the world toward the sunny uplands of the future. No wonder that for decades numerous conferences all over the world and particularly in the United Nations, focused, in a spirit of near religious hopefulness, on the 'mighty forces of science and technology'.

Such a message of worldwide assistance seemed finally to leave the bloody traces of colonialism behind. Had not the earlier conquerors turned into generous helpers willing to share the instruments of their wealth with the poor? It seemed that the times were past when white people had marched in to force pagans on to the path of Christian salvation, savages into civilization, and natives into labour discipline. No more subordination. Instead 'partners in progress' working together under the banner of development to take advantage of scientific and technological progress for the global rise to prosperity.

And these hopes for the future blessings of progress were shared by nearly all in the so-called Third World in a position to express themselves. Despite occasional critical voices, among them Mahatma Gandhi as one of the most weighty, the faith in a prosperity-creating scientific and technological progress spread like a universal new religion over the entire globe. Despite occasional relapses and insecurities, the religion of progress has installed itself so firmly in most people's minds that, even today, a critique of it is more likely to be regarded as incorrigible heresy than as a voice warning of a false path.

But a number of fundamental questions have now arisen. Did the new orientation, in which the 'other' cultures of the world were declared to be 'developing countries' and given assistance to foster their forces of production, really introduce the end of colonialism? Or is our present era to be regarded as a new, less immediately recognizable, and therefore more effective, stage in Western imperialism? If that is the case, then how is it that the 'developing countries' accepted so readily the imperial message of the blessings of science and technology? And are they in fact finding the promises of material prosperity through the import of modern technologies being fulfilled? Or are they simply bringing into their countries the destruction of culture, the destruction of nature and a modernized form of poverty? Is the fundamental assumption in regard to the industrial countries themselves even valid, that material surplus in the Western metropoles was created by modern scientific technology? Or was it fed from other sources altogether? For, if the belief in the redemptive effects of technological progress is already becoming a myth in the industrial countries, it could hardly be suitable as the basis of a 'development concept' in other cultures.

Before one begins speaking about the effects of Western technology in the Third World, one should therefore try to gain the most realistic estimation possible of the achievements of modern scientific technology in the industrial countries themselves.

Delivering the Goods?

Shortly after the First World War, the mathematician and philosopher, Bertrand Russell, attempted in his book, *The Prospects of Industrial Civilization*, to determine the position of industrial culture. At the centre of his considerations were the effects of science and technology. He arrived at the following conclusion: the application of science has been 'in the main immeasurably harmful',[3] and it would only cease to be so 'when men have a less strenuous outlook on life'. Russell also asserted:

> Science, hitherto, has been used for three purposes: to increase the total production of commodities; to make wars more destructive; and to substitute trivial amusements for those that had some artistic or hygienic value. Increase in total production, though it had its importance a hundred years ago, has now become far less important than increase of leisure and the wise direction of production.[4]

Russell was a widely travelled and sagacious observer of his times, and it is reasonable to assume that this conclusion was already valid at that date, at least in the eyes of an informed and reasonable friend of humanity. So when one reads these same lines today, the immediate conclusion can only be that people in the industrial countries have lost all sense of proportion. In retrospect, the harmful effects of science Russell commmplained about — increase in the total production of commodities, increase in the destructive potential of the war machine, and the mechanization and trivialization of cultural activities — have all gathered momentum in an explosive fashion since the Second World War.

The most outstanding achievement of scientized technology has undoubtedly been the increase in the destructive power of the war machine. Here the results are gigantic. Life on earth can be extinguished almost instantaneously many times over, and yet scientific endeavours continue to be concentrated in the main (in money and personnel) on increasing the war machine's productivity in killing. This is no accident. Nor are the scientists forced to do such work. For the perfecting of these 'objects' awakens the greatest interest in the brain of a normally educated natural scientist by virtue of a certain inner logic.

A rocket which flies 'relentlessly', that is, without any disturbances through space, which can be guided with great precision to a predetermined target to release forces of cosmic proportions upon arrival there — such a mighty technological system belongs at the very top of the list of products possessed of an ideal correspondence with the logic of the experimental, mathematical natural sciences. That is why it is no accident that nearly all the state of the art achievements of contemporary technology are concentrated, for example, in a cruise missile — computer technology; radio, radar and video technology; rocket propulsion and nuclear technology; metallurgy; aerodynamics; logistics and information technology; etc.

Many countries in the Third World became acquainted, above all else, with these accomplishments of Western technology. By way of the military bases of the larger powers, of their own military regimes, or their governments' megalomania, substantial portions of their limited financial resources were, and are, consumed by the import of military technologies. In addition, abundant instruments of war arrive through 'military development aid'. I suspect, and this must be more thoroughly investigated sometime, that till now the largest part of Western technological assistance has comprised these destructive weapons. The effect of all this highly modern technology in these lands can be described unambiguously — it increases hunger and misery, it hinders independent development, and it secures corrupt regimes against popular revolutions.

Secret Path to Paradise

The forces of production — based on modern science and technology — that are required for the production of ever larger mountains of 'essential goods' have assumed gigantic proportions in the industrial countries in the 70 years since Russell's analysis. Nearly all the energies of industrial peoples focus ever more intensively on the production, marketing, use and disposal of 'essential goods' of all sorts. Industrial society thereby acts in accordance with its central myth as to the meaning of life. For modern European society has been obsessed by one idea above all — that through the production of material goods, the necessary conditions for the good life were supposed to have been created; through work, science and technology, the 'secret path to paradise' was supposed to have been forged, as Francis Bacon, one of the theoretical founders of modernity, formulated it some 300 years ago.

The central myth of European modernity is also a plan for salvation to be applied worldwide. Its starting point is the assumption that unremitting diligence, constant progress in the production of material goods, the unbroken conquest of nature, the restructuring of the world into predictable, technologically and organizationally manipulable processes will automatically and simultaneously produce the conditions of human happiness, emancipation and redemption from all evils.

This assumption 'bewitched the self-conception of modernity' — in Jürgen Habermas's brilliant phrase. Today it is recognizable as 'the great illusion of the epoch'. Scientistic technology was a dream of happiness without sacrifice. Technology fulfils this dream 'by repressing the sacrifice and making the happiness hollow' (Günther Ortmann). Through the evolution of scientistic forces of production a higher development of humanity was supposed to ensue. The established industrial countries first applied this idea of development to themselves. One can therefore speak with justice of an internal colonization of European culture through industrialism.

The view among the more critical and far-sighted observers of our time is that peoples in the West, too, must liberate themselves from this internal colonization. For the central hypothesis of industrialism, that the unremitting development of the forces of production will create the conditions for the good life, has proven to be false. The attempt to satisfy the full spectrum of human needs through the production and consumption of goods has failed. Those dimensions of life that are important to people — whether West or East, North or South — such as ties of affection with other people and a sense of esteem in society, cannot be replaced effectively by material consumption. Especially children and older people, the sick and the handicapped, get a sense of the social coldness resulting from the 'busy-ness' of industrial society.

What is more, the boundless dynamic of production in industrialism is so structured that material needs are created faster than the conditions for their gratification. There arises, therefore, the phenomenon of permanently frustrated people caught in an endless spiral of needs. Since the conditions of existence in the industrial system have been reduced to the persistent and overwhelming compulsion of having to sell one's labour power in competition with other sellers, there arises a frantic race of all against all.

Alongside the endless spiral of needs, *homo industriae* has also been made subject to an accelerating time stress, which leaves little space for his feelings, soul and thoughts to catch up with the busy doings of the world of work.

Ultimately, this futile attempt to create the conditions for the good life principally through the development of the forces of production has to take place on the basis of a higher, ever increasing flow of materials, energy and information, which is plundering and destroying the planet. For these and still other reasons, a search has begun to get under way in the industrial countries for a new orientation toward the good life, one that goes beyond productionism and consumerism.

So much for a few catchwords in the critique of the industrial myth of production, which cannot be developed further here, but without which an understanding of modern technology is not to be had. I want now to illumine, in somewhat more detail, a few of the characteristics of industrial technology and, first of all, to pursue the question of its alleged high productivity, long admired and, indeed, one of the reasons for its great attractiveness in the Third World.

Wealth through Transferring the Costs

Marx and Engels, who were likewise 'bewitched' by the thought of redemption through the development of the forces of production, nearly swooned in admiration at what was, in fact, their class enemy in the *Communist Manifesto*:

> The bourgeoisie, during its rule of scarce one hundred years, has created more massive and more colossal productive forces than have all the preceding generations together. Subjection of Nature's forces to man, machinery, application of chemistry to industry and agriculture, steam-navigation, railways, electric telegraphs, clearing of whole continents for cultivation, canalisation of rivers, whole populations conjured out of the ground — what earlier century had even a presentiment that such productive forces slumbered in the lap of social labour?

For this mighty and violent transformation of society and nature, an energy source had to be exploited which, until then, had been little used because it smoked and stank — coal. Industrial capitalism may have begun on the basis of wood as its source of energy, but without the possibility of using a more highly concentrated and abundantly available source like coal, the productive avalanche so admired by Marx and Engles would not have gotten under way. Without sources of fossil fuel, European society would have remained 'wooden' despite all its production myths. Or, at the very least, its production mania would not have been able to become so violent and imperial. The expansion dynamic of industrial capitalism would have run up against a natural barrier.

But fossil fuels were available and, combined with the production myth, an 'economic mode' began that would be characteristic of the industrial system from then on. The economy was no longer driven by replenishable resources and the constant supply of energy from the sun, but became based instead on the consumption of the earth's accumulated energy reserves, which had not been created by those who now used them, while these same users ignored the consequences. Already at the beginning of the 19th century, there was so much coal burned in England that the entire surface of England and Wales would have had to have been forested if energy consumption were to have been met by replenishable wood.

Currently, there is as much fossil fuel burnt every year as has been stored up in a period of nearly a million years. The lion's share, approximately 80 per cent, is used up in the industrial countries, where only about 25 per cent of the world's people live. This voracious appetite for resources is demonstrated yet more clearly in the example of the United States: less than 6 per cent of the world's population consume there about 40 per cent of the world's natural resources. If one were to extend this industrial mode of production and lifestyle to all the people of the earth, five or six further planets like the earth would be required for resource plundering and waste disposal.

The historian, Rolf Peter Sieferle, writes on this question:

> Juxtaposed to the 10,000 year duration of the agrarian system, the industrial system appears as a brief, one-time paroxysm of intoxication in which the resources gathered over many millions of years are used up in a couple of hundred. This applies to fossil energy sources, but also to the concentrations of minerals which are exploited and depleted with the help of the former. There is much to suggest that this paroxysm will be followed by a bad hangover.[5]

The consumption of fossil energy reserves threatens life on earth in a number of ways. The air pollutants released damage plants and destroy the equilibrium of the earth's protective atmosphere. The 'energy-centred view of life' (Bertrand Russell) can declare everything to be raw material and transform it into 'essential goods' only with the help of fossil fuel. In the process the earth's resources are transformed at an ever greater tempo into usually poisonous waste. The production mania of the petrochemical industry, in particular, which delivers all the world's plastic products we cannot do without, produces gigantic amounts of non-biodegradable pollution in the form of synthetic hydrocarbon compounds that pose a sustained threat to life over the entire earth. It is already possible to determine from the flesh of a South Pole penguin what substances are being used in the northern half of the globe to create economic growth.

This is the still not properly acknowledged background to the much praised efficiency of the industrial system and the allegedly high productivity of industrial technology. These come about only through the plundering of the pre-existing accomplishments of nature for which they bear no credit (internalization of the so-called free goods of the earth) and through the massive transfer of costs on to nature, on to the Third World, and on to future generations (externalization of costs in the form of pollutants, waste problems, and so on). The allegedly highly productive industrial system is, in reality, a parasite on the earth, the likes of which have never before been seen in the history of humanity. It has the towering productivity of a bank robber who resorts to quick, violent attacks in an attempt to create for himself a life of prosperity at the cost of others.

This state of affairs and its implications, is still being repressed from their consciousness by the majority of people in the industrial societies. It can be characterized as the essential lie of the industrial system, the pretence that the material prosperity won through plundering and the transfer of costs was 'created' by industrial production, by science and technology, by the tools of prosperity themselves. On the basis of this lie, the additional belief arises that the problems of the ever more apparent destruction of nature can be eliminated without a sacrifice of prosperity *solely by technological means*, and that the export of these 'productive' technologies will also allow the Third World to have a share in the much delayed promise of its material prosperity.

Techniques of Plunder

But if one takes a look at one after the other of the technologies and technologically created 'essential goods' that appear so alluring, it becomes clear that they overwhelmingly take the form of techniques that plunder the earth's resources and externalize their costs. This is true of the massive fossil fuel and nuclear power plants, airplanes and automobiles, washing machines and dishwashers, factories for the production of plastics and the countless plastic products, industrialized and chemicalized agriculture, the industry for the 'improvement' of foodstuffs, the packaging industry, buildings made of concrete, steel and chemicals, paper production, etc., etc. None of these brilliant accomplishments of industrial technology function without the massive consumption of 'free' natural resources and without the expulsion of waste, poisons, noise and stench.

It requires a lengthy search to find anywhere in this gigantic mountain of industrial processes and products examples that are not part of the system of externalizing techniques of plunder and which might be recommended without reservation to the Third World. It is for this reason that there has been not only a debate over appropriate technologies for the Third World, but for years now, also a discussion of 'other' technologies for the industrial countries themselves. The critical technology debate in the industrial countries has led to the conclusion that the only future for a series of once celebrated triumphs of scientific–technological progress lies in renunciation. The need to renounce the use of atomic energy, the chlorine industry, most aspects of synthesizing chemistry, reliance on the automobile, and industrialized and chemicalized agriculture has become self-evident to ecologically conscious people.

The majority of industrial technological products are not generalizable. As desired luxury items for the few, they lose their use value upon mass distribution and their sheer numbers usually make them responsible at the same time for environmental problems. For instance, when there are only a few cars on the street, they can be comfortable (and prestige-giving) vehicles for their drivers. But already in the industrial countries the automobile is not generalizable. Although only a fraction of the people in cities use it as their everyday means of conveyance, many cities are already suffocating in poisonous gases, noise and stench. If, to take an example, the proportion of motorcars in China were equal to that in the industrial countries, then in a short time oil supplies would run out and the earth's atmosphere be ruined.

Something similar applies to nearly all the other prosperity and comfort producing industrial techniques. The push-button comforts people in the West have grown accustomed to and the unquestioned consumer expectations like running hot water at one's fingertips, continually heated or cooled rooms, motorized conveyance, foodstuffs from all over the world wrapped in plastic and frozen and always available, mountains of goods people feel they can never do without and which the accelerated pace of fashion turns ever more quickly into mountains of garbage — all this American way of life, as it is often called, is composed of countless little plunderings of nature and transferred costs. It is precisely this that makes up the envied prosperity of the industrial powers, and precisely this prosperity that is not generalizable globally. It can be had by only a few generations in a few countries before the earth will have been plundered to death and rendered no longer habitable.

The message of Truman, Kennedy and many others to the 'peoples of the world', that they could achieve the material prosperity of the West by taking over Western scientized technology, therefore, turns out to be empirically untenable. The available industrial technologies for the West are nearly all designed for plunder and the transfer of costs. Even in the best of scenarios, these technologies could only allow the first 'developing countries', those that are able to develop most rapidly and ahead of the others, to achieve prosperity on Western lines. For the peoples of the entire earth, it is impossible.

The illusion that Western prosperity was created by science and technology — an illusion promoted with tremendous naivety by Truman and Kennedy, but which is no longer seriously supportable — has recently been resurrected again by a few people with exceptional faith in new generations of technology allegedly able to 'handle' the environmental problems that have resulted. Although the massive assaults by existing technologies on nature have had to be admitted, these optimists, or charlatans, now profess to believe that solutions can be found without a sacrifice of prosperity, as a result of an 'ecological modernization' of industry.

New technologies, yet to be created, are supposed to make possible a continuation of precisely the same prosperity facilitated by the old technologies, but now in 'ecologically tolerable' form. Through the miraculous but unspecified powers of technology — an ingenious new formula, a new principle, a technological 'breakthrough' — all the things that were previously possible only by way of plunder and the transfer of costs are now supposed to be conjured up as efficiently, as economically, and, above all, as abundantly as before.

The energy debate alone shows the extent to which this is all wishful thinking. The beginnings of solar power which, because of the materials used, is still very far from being truly generalizable and tolerable to nature, are shoved scornfully by the energy bosses into the realm of mere 'add-ons', merely complementary energy producing technologies, because solar power cannot compete with their grand technologies in terms of economy and deliverable amounts of energy. They are right. The amounts of energy consumed currently are not to be had at a realistic cost on a solar basis. And as long as no institutions exist that can present users with the bill for the transfer costs their activities cause, solar power technologies will not be able to compete with traditional ones. Whoever believes that material prosperity can be created in a way tolerable to nature as 'efficiently' and 'cheaply' as has been possible through externalizing techniques of plunder, is like someone expecting a workable perpetual motion machine to be about to be invented.

The scientific civilization of the West has scarcely any technologies on offer truly suited to the future — that is, humane and appropriate over the long term to nature. That is why the hopes of some in the West came to be focused on a solution from quite another direction. After it became clear in the 1970s, with the collapse of the initial euphoria over technology transfer, that the import of Western technologies into Third World countries resulted primarily in monocultures, large-scale slums, devastation of nature, the destruction of cultures and human ruination, there were, especially in India, initiatives to pursue an independent technological development more intensively. Robert Jungk was still hopeful when he wrote in 1973:

> We are still at the beginning of the development of specifically Asian, African and Latin American variations in technology. What they have in common, despite the great geographical distances, is their desire to conform more closely to life and nature. The cause of this is not hard to recognize. They all arose in protest against the mechanical, insensitive, standardizing occidental technology geared predominantly to speed and maximum output. It is completely conceivable that, before the end of the millennium, yellow, brown and black development advisers will be called to the summits of industry in our half of the globe to show their former teachers how vital necessities can be produced without waste and without harm to people and the environment, without haste and without alienation.[6]

Myopia Makes for Fascination

This hope is currently finding few proponents. The attraction of 'high-performance' Western techniques has once again become too overwhelming. The current resurgence of the attractiveness of Western technology is presumably closely associated with its two main features: its ability to transfer costs and its characteristic of plunder.

The capacity to transfer costs makes it possible for modern technology to appear in a mystified form. It tricks the senses as to its performance capacities and seduces reason with an understanding based on short-term calculations. The costs are usually transferred and scattered over very considerable times and spaces. The spatial and temporal horizon of our perception is, however, significantly nearer. What we know of measured pollution levels, and of costs in the future or in distant areas, remains abstract to us and too far removed from currently perceived realities. It touches none, or very few, of the feelings and thoughts that determine behaviour here and now. Who can imagine a 300,000-year, radioactive half-life in concrete form? How much does the knowledge of a hole in the ozone layer count for against the utility advantage, impressed upon our senses right now, of instantly available cool drinks from the fridge or the comfortable transportation offered by a high-performance private automobile? The temporal, spatial and personal separation of utilities and costs — the separation of an act committed now from the suffering that ensues, or the non-intersection between advantages that are privately consumable and disadvantages that have to be borne collectively — is an exceedingly seductive characteristic of modern scientistic technologies.

When, moreover, this individually attractive characteristic of Western technologies is coupled with the modern attitude of 'consume and enjoy now, pay later,' and when 'later' means 'later generations', then any alternative, non-mystifying technology, which makes all of its costs and disadvantages immediately palpable to the user, seems very unattractive, even 'primitive'. As long as there is no procedure whereby the transferred costs deriving from the use of a technology or product are charged in the present, then any alternative technology that is humane and appropriate to nature will have no chance against the great attractiveness of externalizing techniques.

For similar reasons, the aspect of plunder in Western technologies contributes to their considerable attractiveness. Schooled in Western ways of thinking and pervaded by the thought of the historically unavoidable 'modernization' of their country, many in the Third World do not understand why they should leave the advantages of plundering natural resources to the industrial countries. They want to participate in instant prosperity, and therefore demand nuclear power plants and the 'efficient' technologies of petroleum exploitation. And they regard the offer of technology appropriate to the Third World, an intermediate or gentle technology, as a sophisticated attempt to keep them in the stage of 'underdevelopment'. The partners in progress want to become partners in plunder. At one international conference on the protection of the earth's atmosphere, when plans for the large-scale production of CFCs for Chinese refrigerators were regarded as problematic, the Chinese modernizers saw the matter completely differently. For them it was self-evident that the Chinese should also drink their Coca-Cola ice-cold, and that it should come from refrigerators produced cost-effectively with CFC technology. *Après nous, le deluge* is a phrase that can be expressed equally well in the languages of China, India, or Africa.

If the industrial countries do not immediately set in motion an intensified, exemplary impulse towards industrial, technological and economic 'disarmament', a deceleration of material production processes, alternative and attractive models for a low-performance society, for changes in the cultural paradigm so as to supercede modernity's myth of production, then the transformation of our blue planet into a moonscape is certain.

Friendly Imperialism

Aside from its environmental and physical costs, the social and cultural costs of the introduction of Western technologies also remained largely hidden during the technological enthusiasm of the 1950s and '60s. Even 'clean' technologies force their laws upon society in such a way that cultural self-definition and autonomy cannot be maintained for long. That the import of Western industrial technologies combines a creeping cultural imperialism with the destruction of native culture is related to a little noted characteristic of these technologies. This characteristic is another dimension of their mystification, with its separation of phenomenal form and reality, immediate impact and later effects. The alleged tools of progress are not tools at all, but technical systems that worm their way into every aspect of life and tolerate no alternatives.

In their exterior aspect industrial machines and products are isolated objects that can be freely and everywhere employed like tools, according to the decision of the user. With them, however, there typically comes an infrastructural network of technical, social and psychological conditions, without which the machines and products do not work. For an automobile to be truly used, one needs a technological infrastructure composed of networks of streets with petrol stations, refineries, oil wells, workshops, insurance, police and ambulance services, lawyers, automobile factories, warehouses for spare parts, and much more besides. And, on the psycho-social side, one needs people who will conform to all the installations and facilities and institutions and who can function within them. And so one needs driving lessons, training for children in crossing streets, conscientious petrol station and garage repair owners, and in general, the expert and diligent industrial worker, which in turn means schooling, disciplining, and yet more schooling. Every industrial product like this brings with it its corresponding requirements and they can only function with their associated infrastructure and the psycho-social preparation of people.

The introduction of factory labour and industrialization in Europe meant a similar 'great transformation' of the entire society, culture and psychological constitution of the people. Industrialization made its way on to the historical stage only with much violence, degradation, misery and humiliation. The expansion of scientistic technology was, as Bertrand Russell claimed, 'immeasurably damaging' to European culture because cultural activity was mechanized and trivialized. Nevertheless, it must not be forgotten that industrialization arose in and through European culture and is therefore not essentially alien to it.

For the cultures of other countries, the requisite psycho-social preparation of people and the cultural transformation looks much more traumatic because it confronts them with an essentially alien culture. Through technological 'development aid' more euphemistically called technical assistance, from the industrialized countries, they receive 'trojan machines' (to use Robert Jungk's phrase), which conquer their culture and society from within. They are forced gradually to absorb an alien industrial work ethic, to subordinate themselves completely to unaccustomed time rhythms, to value objective relations higher than human relations, to experience increasing stress and to regard it as normal, and to accept jobs without regard to motivation or meaning. Wage labour and commodity fetishism expand, and they define the competitive struggle of all against all as the social synthesis. It becomes self-evident that everyone is to be a mechanical cog in a great production apparatus dominated by the world market. As Johan Galtung described the process:

> The total picture . . . is one of transfer of technology as structural and cultural invasion, an invasion, possibly more insidious than colonialism and neo-colonialism, because such an invasion is not always accompanied by a physical Western presence.[7]

The age of Western imperialism is therefore not over by a long shot, particularly as long as there exists, primarily on the part of the United States, a direct and open technological imperialism against the countries of the Third World. Examples abound. They include the mighty arsenal of electronic superiority in the form of communication satellites for 'remote sensing' of local weather and harvest conditions in the countries of the Third World (for purposes of ascertaining in advance of these countries themselves the market value of their coming harvests); computer banks for the technical information monopoly; media corporations for the direct cultural propaganda that floods all local broadcasters; and so on. 'In truth the threat of the new electronics to independence could be greater in the late 20th century than even colonialism was.'[8]

References

1. H. Truman, Inaugural Address, Washington DC, 20 January 1949.
2. J. F. Kennedy, Special Message to the Congress, Washington DC, 14 March 1961.
3. B. Russell, *The Prospects of Industrial Civilization*, New York: The Century Company, 1923, p. 186.
4. Ibid., p. 187.
5. R. P. Sieferle, *Der unterirdische Wald: Energiekrise und industrielle Revolution*, München: Beck, 1982, p. 64.
6. R. Jungk, *Der Jahrtausendmensch: Berichte aus den Werkstätten der neuen Gesellschaft*, Munich: Econ, 1973, pp. 69–70.
7. J. Galtung, 'Towards a New International Technological Order', *Alternatives*, Vol. 4, January 1979, p. 288. Quoted in V. Rittberger (ed.), *Science and Technology in a Changing International Order: The United Nations Conference on Science and Technology for Development*, Boulder: Westview Press, 1982.
8. A. Smith, *Geopolitics of Information*, New York: 1980, p. 176. Quoted in H. Schiller, *Who Knows: Information in the Age of the Fortune 500*, Norwood, N.J.: 1981.

Bibliography

The towering figures in thinking about modern technology are L. Mumford, *The Myth of the Machine*, 2 vols., New York: Harcourt Brace Jovanovich, 1964, and J. Ellul, *The Technological Society*, New York: Knopf, 1964. For exploring the human condition in the age of technology, I found G. Anders, *Die Antiquiertheit des Menschen*, 2 vols., München: Beck, 1980, very illuminating in his aphoristic style. L. Winner contributed a thorough study on the modern experience of 'technology out of countrol', *Autonomous Technology*, Cambridge: MIT Press, 1977, as well as a collection of fine essays, *The Whale and the Reactor: A Search for Limits in the Age of High Technology*, Chicago: Chicago University Press, 1985.

I. Illich, *Tools for Conviviality*, London: Boyars, 1973, called attention to the specific counter-productivity of modern tools, a line of argument which has been expanded upon by A. Gorz, *Ecology as Politics*, London: Pluto, 1983. Along similar lines, I criticized the socialist belief in productive forces, *Weltniveau: In der Sackgasse des Industriesystems*, Berlin: Rotbuch, 1980, after having tried to elucidate the relationship between domination and technology in *Technik und Herrschaft*, Frankfurt: Suhrkamp, 1977. A landmark for ethical reflection on the rapacious nature of technology is H. Jonas, *Imperative of Responsibility: In Search of an Ethic for the Technological Age*, Chicago: University of Chicago Press, 1984.

How standards of technical performance have governed European perceptions of non-Western peoples, is abundantly illustrated by M. Adas, *Machines as the Measure of Man*,

Ithaca: Cornell University Press, 1989. L. Kohr, *The Overdeveloped Nations*, New York: Simon & Schuster, 1978, and F. Schumacher, *Small Is Beautiful*, London: Blond & Briggs, 1973, have tried to make a virtue out of 'underperformance'. They have led the way to the discussion on 'appropriate technologies', on which J. Galtung, Towards A New International Technological Order', in *Alternatives*, Vol. 4, January 1979, p. 288, provided a systematic perspective; F. Stewart, *Technology and Underdevelopment*, London: Macmillan, 1978, a penetrating analysis; N. Jequier (ed.) *Appropriate Technologies: Problems and Promises*, Paris: OECD, 1976, an inventory; and J. Müller, *Liquidation or Consolidation of Indigenous Technology: A Study of the Changing Conditions of Production of Village Blacksmiths in Tanzania*, Aalborg: Aalborg University Press, 1980, a telling case study.

How particular technologies have shaped minds and lifestyles can be studied through W. Schivelbusch, *The Railway Journey*, Oxford: Blackwells, 1980; S. Strasser, *Never Done: A History of American Housework*, New York: Random House, 1982; or W. Sachs, *For Love of the Automobile: Looking Back into the History of Our Desires*, Berkeley: University of California Press, forthcoming. How, in turn, technologies themselves are products of power and interest, can be learnt from W. Bijker et al., *The Social Construction of Technological Systems*, Cambridge: Cambridge University Press, 1987. A classic remains S. Giedion, *Mechanization Takes Command*, New York: Norton, 1969, while R. Romanyshyn, *Technology as Symptom and Dream*, London: Routledge, 1989, recounts fascinatingly the cultural dream at the roots of the rise of technology.

Contributors

Claude Alvares is a free-lance writer and investigative journalist in India. His numerous reports on development blunders, from the building of dams to the seed business, have gained him a wide reputation. He deeply mistrusts the modern knowledge industry, in particular its liaison with the state. Recently, he published *Science, Development and Violence*, New Delhi: Oxford University Press, 1991 and *Decolonizing History: Technology and Culture in India, China and the West*, New York: Apex Press and London: Zed Books, 1991. He lives in Goa.

Gérald Berthoud has focused his research on the history and anthropology of the market as an institution and an idea. He is a professor at the Institute of Anthropology and Sociology at the University of Lausanne and co-edits *La Revue du MAUSS*, a quarterly in Paris, which is dedicated to the critique of economic ideology.

Harry Cleaver teaches in the Department of Economics at the University of Texas in Austin. Since the 1960s he has been studying popular resistance to capitalism as well as deciphering the tactical and strategic content of economic theory and policies. He is one of the few economists in the US who critique both capitalism and socialism while finding alternatives within the creative self-constitution of popular struggles.

Barbara Duden is concerned about the cultural power of modern medicine. To highlight how medicine has transformed the image of women, she is engaged in historical research to uncover the experience of pregnant women and the image of the unborn in early modern times. Her book, *History Beneath the Skin*, Cambridge, Mass: Harvard University Press, 1991, has just been published in English. She is a fellow at the Institute for Cultural Studies in Essen, Germany.

Arturo Escobar is Colombian and teaches Anthropology at Smith College in Massachusetts. He has written a large study on the history of the development discourse, in which he analyses, inspired by Foucault, development as a domain of knowledge and a set of specific practices. To recognize the power of this form of knowledge is, in his view, crucial for social movements in the South.

Gustavo Esteva calls himself a deprofessionalized intellectual. In the seventies, he served in the Mexican ministry of planning and published several books on economics. He left this career and later became chairman of ANADEGES and other networks of grassroots initiatives in Mexico. Searching intellectually and practically for ways to 'marginalize the economy', he now lives near Oaxaca.

Marianne Gronemeyer is a German university teacher and author. Experiences in the peace and Third World movements have stimulated her inquiries into the hidden basis of consensus. She is impressed by the 'elegance of power' which roots itself in popular needs. As a social philosopher, she has written a theory of needs as a theory of power, and is presently working on an essay on security needs as the correlate to the acceleration of industrial growth.

Ivan Illich is an itinerant philosopher. Born in Vienna, he has lived most of his life in the US and Mexico, where he directed CIDOC, a meeting ground of dissident intellectuals in the seventies and early eighties. In his work, he has called attention to the counter-productivity of modern institutions. More recently, he uses the tools of an historian to put the certainties of the modern mind into perspective. His numerous books have inspired social movements and concerned scholars worldwide.

Serge Latouche examines the epistemological foundations of economics and social science. He belongs to MAUSS (Mouvement anti-utilitariste dans les sciences sociales) which animates research and debate on the economistic bias in modern thinking. His books *Faut-il refuser le developpment?*, Paris: Presses Universitaires de France, 1985, and *L'occidentalisation du monde*, Paris: La Decouverte, 1989, have denounced development as the rise of the economic worldview to global hegemony. He is a university professor in Lille and Paris.

C. Douglas Lummis, an American, lives in Japan and teaches political theory at Tsuda College, Tokyo. His recent research aims at revitalizing the tradition of radical democracy as a principle of opposition rather than as a legitimation of rule. He is on the editorial staff of *AMPO*, a journal close to the social movements in the Far East. He is presently completing a book tentatively entitled *The Art of the Possible: Toward a Philosophy of Radical Democracy*.

Ashis Nandy is a senior researcher at the Centre for the Study of Developing Societies, Delhi, and chairman of the Committee for Cultural Choices and Global Futures. His work aims at creatively assessing Western systems of knowledge as well as traditional visions of knowledge in order to find an Indian response to the crisis of modernity. He exposed the hidden myths of colonial culture in his *The Intimate Enemy: Loss and Recovery of Self under Colonialism*, Delhi: Oxford University Press, 1983, and science as a model of domination in the recent volume, edited by him, *Science, Hegemony, and Violence*, Delhi: Oxford University Press, 1988.

Majid Rahnema was a minister in the Iranian government in the late sixties. Later, he left Iran and joined UNDP, among other assignments, as representative in Mali. At present, he is an author and guest professor at the University of California, Berkeley. Having worked on the inside, he is in a good position to critically examine development practices. His attention focuses on the blind spots of the developmental mind and the recovery of a spiritual dimension in the search for regeneration. He is currently preparing *The Alternative Development Reader*, London: Zed Books, forthcoming. He lives in France.

Jean Robert is Swiss, but has lived in Mexico for the last 20 years. Though trained as an architect, he devotes most of his time to researching and writing on the history of modern consciousness. Immersing himself in the cultural history of the 19th century, he investigates the social construction of the concept of energy and its impact on the perception of time and space. Apart from his research, he is involved in designing and constructing flush-less toilets.

Wolfgang Sachs, who has been with the German and Italian green movement, is concerned with how ecology has changed from a knowledge of opposition to a knowledge of domination. He has been co-editor of the journal *Development* and guest professor of science, technology and society at Penn State University in the US. His book *For Love of the Automobile: Looking Back into the History of Our Desires*, Berkeley: University of California Press, 1992, is about to be published in English. He is presently a fellow at the Institute for Cultural Studies in Essen, Germany.

José María Sbert was an editor of CIDOC Informa in Cuernavaca during the early sixties. He acted later in the Mexican government's dealings with the World Bank and as a head of the National Film Library, manager of a subway trains factory and Under Secretary of Planning. At present, he runs an advertising business in Mexico City. He has translated books by Marcel Schwob and Ivan Illich and is currently working on a book about faith.

Vandana Shiva lives in Dehradun, India, at the foot of the Himalayas. As an activist and a scholar, she has been shaped by the Chipko movement which grew in the seventies in defence of the forests. The clash between the economy of the market on the one side and the economy of nature and the economy of subsistence on the other is at the centre of her attention. Having been trained as a physicist, she has critically reviewed the praxis of forestry, agricultural science and biotechnology in India. Her book *Staying Alive. Women, Ecology, and Development*, London: Zed, 1989, has been translated into several languages. She has recently published *The Violence of the Green Revolution: Agriculture, Ecology and Politics*, Penang: Third World Network and London: Zed Books, 1991.

Otto Ullrich is an engineer and sociologist. His work centres on the counterproductiveness of modern technology and design criteria for democratic and environmentally sound technologies. He has published widely on the history and philosophy of technology and has animated the public debate on energy, transportation and artificial intelligence in Germany. On behalf of the Green Party, he served as a member of the study commission of the German Bundestag on technology assessment. He lives in Berlin.

Index

Zed Books Ltd

is a publisher whose international and Third World lists span:

- **Women's Studies**
- **Development**
- **Environment**
- **Current Affairs**
- **International Relations**
- **Children's Studies**
- **Labour Studies**
- **Cultural Studies**
- **Human Rights**
- **Indigenous Peoples**
- **Health**

We also specialize in Area Studies where we have extensive lists in African Studies, Asian Studies, Caribbean and Latin American Studies, Middle East Studies, and Pacific Studies.

For further information about books available from Zed Books, please write to: Catalogue Enquiries, Zed Books Ltd, 57 Caledonian Road, London N1 9BU. Our books are available from distributors in many countries (for full details, see our catalogues), including:

In the USA
Humanities Press International, Inc., 165 First Avenue, Atlantic Highlands, New Jersey 07716.
Tel: (201) 872 1441;
Fax: (201) 872 0717.

In Canada
DEC, 229 College Street, Toronto, Ontario M5T 1R4.
Tel: (416) 971 7051.

In Australia
Wild and Woolley Ltd, 16 Darghan Street, Glebe, NSW 2037.

In India
Bibliomania, C-236 Defence Colony, New Delhi 110 024.

In Southern Africa
David Philip Publisher (Pty) Ltd, PO Box 408, Claremont 7735, South Africa.

NEW FROM ZED BOOKS

Edited by Wolfgang Sachs
GLOBAL ECOLOGY
Conflicts and Contradictions

Behind the public's hopes for effective action by governments on the environmental issues, lie a complex terrain of conceptual confusion, conflicts of interest and philosophical dispute. This is why some of the world's leading environmental thinkers have come together in this volume to probe critically the new language being developed by the environmental professionals.

Hb 1 85649 163 3 £36.95 $59.95   Pb 1 85649 164 1 £14.95 $25.00

Serge Latouche
PARADIGMS LOST
An Exploration of Post-Development

'Serge Latouche's realistic study is neither an attack nor a vindication of Western civilisation. It is a sober sociological account of the unviability of our present system without ideological *a priori*s. It has the power to convince those who are not of his opinion. It is sociology at its best.' — Professor R. Panikkar, Professor Emeritus, UCLA

Hb 1 86549 171 4 £32.95 $55.00   Pb 1 85649 172 2 £12.95 $19.95

Vandana Shiva
MONOCULTURES OF THE MIND
Biodiversity, Biotechnology and 'Scientific' Agriculture

This book brings together Vandana Shiva's thinking on the protection of biodiversity, the implications of biotechnology, and the consequences for agriculture of the global pre-eminence of Western-style scientific knowledge.

Hb 1 85649 217 6 £29.95 $49.95   Pb 1 85649 218 4 £9.95 $15.00

ALSO BY VANDANA SHIVA

'One of the world's most prominent radical scientists' — *Guardian*
'A Green International Star' — *The Observer*

STAYING ALIVE
Women, Ecology and Development

'It is a polemical plea for the rediscovery of the "feminine principle"
in human interaction with the natural world.' — *Guardian*

Hb 0 86232 822 5 £29.95 $49.95   Pb 0 86232 823 3 £8.95 $15.00

THE VIOLENCE OF THE GREEN REVOLUTION
Third World Agriculture, Ecology and Politics

'A case study book, but one of the best, in which the single grain
of sand can truly reflect . . . the desert'. — *Food Magazine*

Hb 0 86232 964 7 £29.95 $49.95   Pb 0 86232 965 5 £10.95 $17.50

BIODIVERSITY
Social and Ecological Perspectives

'A stimulating compilation of five essays by members of the World
Rainforest Movement' — *World Birdwatch*

'Shiva joins with other leading environmental thinkers in a radical
challenge to current thinking on the protection of diversity' —
Chronica Horticulturae

Hb 1 85649 053 X £29.95 $49.95   Pb 1 85649 054 8 £9.95 $15.00